Oprah Winfrey

Oprah Winfrey
The Real Story

GEORGE MAIR

A Birch Lane Press Book
Published by Carol Publishing Group

A Birch Lane Press Book
Published by Carol Publishing Group
Birch Lane Press is a registered trademark of Carol Communications, Inc.
Editorial Offices: 600 Madison Avenue, New York, N.Y. 10022
Sales and Distribution Offices: 120 Enterprise Avenue,
Secaucus, N.J. 07094
In Canada: Canadian Manda Group, P.O. Box 920, Station, U,
Toronto, Ontario M8Z 5P9
Queries regarding rights and permissions should be addressed to
Carol Publishing Group, 600 Madison Avenue, New York, N.Y. 10022

Carol Publishing Group books are available at special discounts for
bulk purchases, sales promotion, fund-raising, or educational
purposes. Special editions can be created to specifications.
For details, contact: Special Sales Department, Carol Publishing
Group, 120 Enterprise Avenue, Secaucus, N.J. 07094

Book design by Mher Raffi Nercessian

Manufactured in the United States of America
10 9 8 7 6 5 4 3 2 1

Library of Congress Cataloging-in-Publication Data
Mair, George, 1929–
Oprah Winfrey : the real story / by George Mair.
p.   cm.
"A Birch Lane Press book."
ISBN 1-55972-250-9
1. Winfrey, Oprah.   2. Television personalities—United States—
Biography.   3. Motion picture actors and actresses—United States—
Biography.   I. Title.
PN1992.4.W56M35   1994
791.45'028'092—dc20
[B]   94-18112
CIP

I dedicate this book to my mother,
Josephine Briechle Mair,
who was also a writer, suffragette, peace activist, and
decent person who made this a better world for her
granddaughters and great granddaughters.
And for me, my son, and grandson, too.

THANKS TO...

The beautiful and talented Natasha Kern,
my literary agent,
for making it happen.

The dedicated and competent Hillel Black,
my editor,
for helping me put it together.

CONTENTS

PART

I

From Birth To Baltimore

1

Reading Bible Stories
to Pigs

It had been a romantic interlude, and nine months later, on January 29, 1954, a girl baby arrived. Years later that girl baby would describe the occasion of her conception as a "one-day fling under an oak tree." Vernon Winfrey found out about it soon after, when a newspaper clipping arrived in the mail at his army camp and announced the birth of Oprah Gail Winfrey. Enclosed was a cryptic note that said, simply: "Send clothes."

It came as a surprise to the twenty-year-old soldier Vernon Winfrey, and it was not an easy thing for the mother, Vernita Lee. Winfrey had returned to Fort Rucker not knowing he had left behind a pregnant young woman. Given what we learned about him later, he was not the kind of man who would have walked out on his own child had he known then. He would prove a caring and responsible father, much to little Oprah's benefit.

Children get named after all sorts of people: relatives, rich uncles and aunts, movie stars, sports figures, and the most common literary source, the Bible. Oprah's name was supposed to be biblical, after the sister-in-law of Ruth, who is mentioned briefly in the Old Testament's Book of Ruth. She was the sister-in-law who stayed behind in the land of Moab when she was widowed, while her sister-in-law Ruth and mother-in-law Naomi, returned to Naomi's homeland of Bethlehem. She was never heard of again in the Bible, which is ironic now, given how well known Oprah is today.

The biblical character Vernita Lee's sister had in mind from the Book of Ruth was Orpah. As often happens in life, somebody—the midwife or the birth records clerk—got the name scrambled, and it went down on the official birth directory for Kosciusko, Mississippi, as Oprah. And so she is known to this day.

Like any young woman looking to her future, Vernita Lee wanted to escape the poverty and prejudice of Mississippi, particularly after the local cotton mill shut down and there were no more jobs. Friends had told her there was a better life up north, where she would find less racial prejudice and could earn money. As life grew harder for her, she decided to get on a Greyhound bus and head for Milwaukee. It would be too difficult to bring her baby with her—the most she could hope for was a job as a cleaning lady for fifty dollars a week. Oprah's grandmother was willing to care for the child, and so Vernita left Mississippi in 1954 and headed for Milwaukee, leaving behind her illegitimate daughter to live on a Mississippi pig farm with her grandmother, Hattie Mae, and her terrifying husband, Earless Lee.

The farm stood alongside a meandering, unpaved Mississippi road in the East Gulf Coastal Plain between the Big Black and the Pearl rivers. It was surrounded by rolling hills covered with the arrow-straight pine trees common to Mississippi, along with the magnolia, whose blossoms scented the hot, humid air.

Somebody once said of the place where Oprah grew up during those years, "Mississippi is strong on weather." They cautioned that you could be sweating your soul out in the summer months and then experience a sudden freeze in October that would chill your bones. The seasons tended to be warm, with temperatures usually in the eighties and often rising into the nineties during the long summers and short winters. The offshore winds drove the rain-laden clouds from the Gulf to Hattie Mae's farm and dropped their rain nine or ten days of every month year-round.

As uncomfortable as the humid and hot days could be, there was the beauty of azaleas everywhere in the spring and fall, along with black-eyed Susans, camellias, crape myrtle, dogwood, and both pink and white Cherokee roses punctuating the countryside.

The nearby town of Kosciusko served as part of one of the most important and infamous frontier routes in American history. It was the 449-mile interstate "highway" of two hundred years ago that led from Natchez—once the wealthiest city in America—on the Mississippi River, diagonally north to Nashville, where Oprah would spend some of her most important teen years with her father and stepmother.

In the days before the famous side- and stern-wheelers made the passage against the current up the Mississippi, the hardworking, hard-drinking frontier flatboatmen traveled differently. Upriver at Memphis and northward, they would build great flat rafts and load them with flour, pork, tobacco, hemp, and iron and float them down the Mississippi River to Natchez or New Orleans. Then, rather than endure the struggle of pushing the rafts back upstream with long poles, they would break the rafts apart and sell the logs.

From there, after an interlude of tasting the wine and women of New Orleans and Natchez, these rugged frontiersmen would trek back north to Tennessee or Kentucky through Jackson, Kosciusko, and Tupelo. The wilderness road they used ran from Natchez to Nashville and became known officially as "the Natchez Trace" and informally as "the Devil's Backbone."

Dotted along the Trace were resting places ranging from dirt-floored tepees to crude huts and taverns sporting such names as She-Boss, Buzzard Roost, French Camp, and Red Bluff. It was said that along the Trace, the only thing cheaper than the body of a woman was the life of a man.

Typical rules for overnight guests in the early 1800s at places such as Connelley's Tavern included: "Four pence a night for bed, six pence with supper. No more than five to sleep in one bed. No boots to be worn in bed. Organ grinders to sleep in the wash house. No dogs allowed upstairs. No beer allowed in the kitchen."

Slavery was the reality of America in both the North and South in the first half of the 1800s. Absalom Winfrey and his wife, Sarah Lucinda, lived in the area of the Bluff Hills region of the Natchez Trace with their two slaves, Constantine and Violet. They had moved there from Georgia, settling on a modest farm with a three-bedroom house near the community of Poplar Creek in 1850. Dr. Winthrop Jordan, professor of African-American studies at the University of Mississippi, believes that Constantine and Violet, who were married in 1860 when he was twenty-four and she was twenty-one, probably lived in one of the three bedrooms of the house.

When the Civil War began in 1861, Absalom joined the Confederate army, while Constantine and Violet, along with Sarah Lucinda, remained on the Winfrey place and took care of the farm. Four years later, the war over, Absalom came home, and Constantine and Violet—Oprah's great-great-grand-parents—were freed. They took Absalom's last name and moved to a place of their own about half a mile away. A warm and friendly relationship apparently existed between Absalom and Sarah Lucinda and their former slaves, Constantine and Violet, as both families struggled to survive the poverty that ravaged Mississippi after the war. According to Dr. Jordan, "It was uncommon for slaves to settle so close to their former masters. They more often wanted to get away." Then Absalom's two sons, William and James, were accused of burning down a black family's house in a fire that killed a woman and two small children. Rather than face trial, William and James left the area and headed for Temple, Texas, where they settled down and where some of their ancestors still live today.

In time, Constantine had saved enough money working and tenant farming to buy eighty acres of land and farm for himself, which he needed to do in order to feed his family of nine children.

One of Constantine's sons, Neinous, became a teacher in an all-black school; when not teaching, he farmed. Basil Palmertree's family has lived near the black Winfreys for over

100 years, and the two families know each other well. Palmertree relates the story of trouble Neinous got into at school: "In the mid-1880s, one of his fourteen-year-old pupils became pregnant, and Neinous was responsible. She was the daughter of a local blacksmith, John Bennett, and the disgrace started a feud." The feuding between the two families became so antagonistic that Andrew, Neinous's brother, burned down the Bennetts' house and killed Mrs. Bennett and the Bennetts' two daughters. John escaped because he was away from home when the arson occurred, and Andrew immediately left Mississippi and moved to Chicago. He would return in 1940 a broken man, having lost his own wife and children in tragic accidents.

In spite of all this feuding and tragedy, Neinous continued to teach and farm until 1931, when calamity struck his family: One of his two sons, Vendee, killed his own brother, Buddy. After Vendee was caught and convicted, Neinous made an impassioned plea to the judge. "I've already lost one son. Please don't take another one from me," Neinous begged the judge. Instead of sentencing him to hang, the judge sent Vendee to the state prison for several years. When he was released, everybody in the community was fearful of him, according to Laura Winfrey Henson, seventy-one, Oprah's second cousin, who still lives on the original land that Constantine and Violet had purchased and which is now owned by the state. "I was still a little girl when he was released and came back. For the rest of Vendee's life, people were afraid of him." A number of Winfreys continue to live in the area of Mississippi where Constantine and Violet had their farm, which was taken over in recent years by the state of Mississippi and is now only available for lease. The original house stood until 1974, when it was so damaged by a tornado that it had to be destroyed.

And so the Winfrey family grew in Mississippi from the slaves who had survived the voyage from Africa and worked their way west until that May day in 1953 when Vernon and Vernita clung together for a time under that tree in Kosciusko to spawn Oprah.

Oprah would spend her time mostly barefoot on her grandmother's farm, hard by the Natchez Trace, tending to the pigs, chickens, and cows. Looking back on those six years with her grandmother, Oprah never remembers having a mother around, just Grandmother and big Earless.

Oprah's life centered around the farm and the Faith United Mississippi Baptist Church and, later, school. Determined that Oprah should get the best possible education, Hattie Mae tutored the little girl so that she could do arithmetic, read, and write by the time she was three. There was no television in Hattie Mae's home, and reading became a pleasure for Oprah that would always remain with her.

At church Oprah made Hattie Mae feel proud. She had a natural talent for recitation and performing, and she soon became the little darling of the adult congregation with her readings and acting in church plays. Years later, Oprah would recall those times to Jane Pauley: "I started out speaking there, and it was a way of getting love. And you know, the sisters sitting in the front row would fan themselves and nod to my grandmother, Hattie Mae. And they'd say, 'Hattie Mae, this child is gifted.' And somehow, with no education, my grandmother instilled in me a belief that I could aspire to do great things in my life."

Oprah would later remember: "At a Sunday school performance—all weekend, they'd say, 'And little Mistress Winfrey is here to do the recitation...,' and I'd have these little, little patent leather shoes. Oh, very proper."

In one of her first recitations before the entire congregation, three-year-old Oprah told the story of Jesus' resurrection on Easter. "Jesus rose on Easter Day. Halelu, halelu, all the angels did proclaim!" She impressed the adults, who praised both Oprah and her grandmother.

Of course, the kids in the congregation thought she was a little show-off, and they soon nicknamed her "the Preacher" and "Miss Jesus." It meant a lonely life for Oprah; she was for the most part accepted and appreciated by adults but not by her schoolmates, some of whom would literally spit at her.

When she was an adult, she remembered those days in Mississippi and later in Milwaukee: "All the kids hated me, all through school. Kids have always hated me, but the teachers loved me. [When] I memorized "Invictus" by William Ernest Henley [for example]. 'Out of the night that covers me, / black as a pit from pole to pole, / I thank whatever gods there be for my unconquerable soul. . . . I am the master of my fate. / I'm the captain of my soul.'"

Oprah followed the same pattern when she first went to kindergarten, and the teacher quickly decided that she was too advanced and moved her to the first grade. Again, the adults admired her, and her contemporaries were irritated, but Oprah survived and continued to find sanctuary in the world of books and her friends, the farm animals.

Just as Hattie Mae knew that the key to survival for a black female was education, she also understood that careful behavior, self-discipline, and God were important. Critical to surviving in the segregationist Deep South was courtesy and good manners. Those are traits of the southern culture in any case, but they were particularly important to blacks in avoiding unpleasant confrontations. So Grandmother would not tolerate any foolishness. She hadn't the strength or the temperament.

In those first six years, Oprah could count on a whipping whenever she disobeyed her imperious grandmother, and that was almost daily for the precocious Oprah. At times, she felt she was being whipped just so her grandmother could keep in practice. Hattie Mae would send Oprah into the piney woods where they lived to find and bring back a switch. It had to be a sturdy, lithe switch or she would be sent back again. First there was the whipping, and then there was the insulting justification that she was being whipped for her own good. Oprah never thought so.

One of the reasons that Oprah envied white girls her own age was that they didn't seem to get whipped all the time. From what she saw on TV occasionally at other people's houses, white girls all looked like Shirley Temple and had lots of store-bought clothes, a pretty room with toys, and a mother who was always nice to them.

Besides there being no TV at Hattie Mae's house, Oprah wore clothes Hattie Mae made, and she didn't have a room of her own. Much of what they ate they raised themselves, and

Hattie Mae would make some money by selling pigs and eggs. She also instilled Oprah with a reverence for God to be venerated through a ritual of daily prayer. She later remembered, "As long as you have the power to bow your head and bend your knees, you do it and God will hear you better. I have not been able to get that out of my brain."

The little girl slept with her grandmother under a big quilt, while Grandfather Earless—described as a "dark presence" who Oprah feared would slip into bed during the darkness and strangle her—slept in another room. No one in the family, including Oprah, has said a lot about Earless other than that he was a menacing shadow to the little girl and was not allowed to sleep in the same bed with his wife.

Oprah describes a time when she was four and Earless came into the bedroom she shared with her grandmother. "She couldn't get him back in his room. There was an old blind man who lived down the road, and I remember my grandma going out on the porch and screaming, 'Henry! Henry!' And when I saw his light going on, I knew that we were going to be saved."

The outhouse was too far and too scary for anyone to trek to during the night, so a slop jar was kept in the bedroom. Every morning, it was Oprah's job to empty it and to draw water for use in the house during that day. Her life during her first six years was a solitary routine filled with daily farm chores— drawing water, feeding pigs, and tending cows—without playmates, television, or toys except for a corncob doll. Oprah used to amuse herself riding one of the pigs bareback and reading Bible stories out loud to the other animals on the farm.

The years Oprah lived with her grandmother were a bittersweet mixture of country life, with all its natural but lonely pleasures; the fun and acceptance of performance at school and church; and the nighttime terror of Earless and the daytime terror of Hattie Mae's stinging switch on the buttocks. The rural world would soon be replaced by life in a big northern city.

CHAPTER

2

The Years With Mother

When Oprah's mother, Vernita, came to Milwaukee in 1954, she must have felt like Dorothy arriving in the Land of Oz. Vernita was part of the migration of blacks who had first swarmed north to the factories in World War II and continued to move to the big cities during the 1950s and 1960s. It was colder, but the jobs were better, the life was more exciting, and racial segregation was a little more subtle. There were no signs designating separate black and white drinking fountains, restrooms, and sections in such public places as theaters and park swimming pools. Yet there was serious segregation, and blacks knew that there were places where they should not eat, live, work, or play. Desegregation of public places had not yet become the law, and proprietors could refuse service to whomever they pleased. Still, Milwaukee wasn't blatant in its racism, and there wasn't the violence that could make life in Mississippi so terrifying.

In 1954, the year Oprah was born, after hearing the arguments of Thurgood Marshall, the lawyer from the National Association for the Advancement of Colored People (NAACP), the U.S. Supreme Court ruled that the compulsory segregation of public schools was unconstitutional. This landmark event would mark the beginning of more civil rights activism, which was focused on hard-core segregationist places like Mississippi. The next year, a black woman became the new

11

symbol of the fight for racial equality when Rosa Parks refused to give up her seat on a Montgomery, Alabama, bus and launched the national career of a charismatic minister as the spokesman for civil rights in America, Martin Luther King Jr. Two years later, President Eisenhower sent U.S. troops into Little Rock, Arkansas, to force the desegregation of Central High School and start the integration of schools all over the country, including East Nashville High, where Oprah would attend several years later.

In 1960, when Oprah had turned six, four black college students staged a sit-in at a Woolworth's lunch counter in Greensboro, North Carolina, when they were refused service. This was the year Oprah left Mississippi and moved north to live with her mother. Back in 1960, Vernita was doing better financially, with a job as a maid and a new boyfriend who promised to marry her and move them all into a house. Now she wanted her child back. She asked Hattie Mae to send six-year-old Oprah to live with her in Milwaukee, which Oprah would do for almost a decade except for a break in 1962.

It wasn't a perfect arrangement; Vernita had given birth to another love child, Patricia, but hoped to marry the father. Vernita and her two children were jammed into one room in a rooming house on Ninth Street, and Oprah didn't have the freedom and space she enjoyed on her grandmother's farm. Vernita's love affairs seemed constantly to be a triumph of hope over reality. The rooming house was in the heart of the downtown ghetto of Milwaukee—noisy, dirty, with streets filled with traffic and mostly black people. The majority of blacks living in the Milwaukee ghetto worked some distance away and had to get up early to catch buses for the long trip to their jobs. Vernita worked as a maid in homes in the distant suburbs. That meant leaving very early, returning home very late, and making several changes of buses in the process.

As constraining as the new living arrangement seemed to the children, Oprah and her younger half sister, Patricia, Vernita was happy with it. She was pulling her family together, she had a pretty good job, and she dressed well. Dressing well was an obsession with Vernita.

Early on, sibling rivalry with her younger half sister made

life uncomfortable for Oprah. Patricia seemed to be prettier; six-year-old Oprah, smarter. Oprah was starting in a new school and did well because of her love of books and her knack of pleasing older people.

Again, the child found amusement where she could, and in that close, stuffy apartment, she said, it was playing with two cockroaches, whom she had named Melinda and Sandy. Patricia says that Oprah made up this story, but it has now become part of the standard Oprah biography.

By 1962, Vernita found out things weren't going to work out as she had hoped. The boyfriend was reneging on marriage, and she and her two daughters were crammed into that one room with not enough space or enough patience for everyone to get along. Patricia was easier to take care of because she was younger, and Oprah was nine and not as easy to control for a single mother. Grandmother wasn't too enthusiastic about taking Oprah back; she was getting old, and Oprah was also becoming more of a responsibility.

So Vernita checked with Vernon and his wife, Zelma, to see if Oprah could stay with them in Nashville, where Vernon had settled after getting out of the army. Vernon and Zelma had tried to have children, but Zelma miscarried and was told another pregnancy would be dangerous. Thus, bringing Oprah south to live with them also filled a void in their lives. At the time, Vernon held two menial jobs—one cleaning floors at Vanderbilt University and the other cleaning kitchen pots for seventy-five cents an hour. They weren't rich, but they thought they could manage with Oprah and were glad to have her live with them. So it was back on the bus again for Oprah, but this time she wasn't returning to stern Hattie Mae, but to live with her father, Vernon Winfrey, and his new wife, Zelma.

The beginning of the third grade arrived with Oprah now in Nashville, facing her stepmother, Zelma, who was even more strict than her grandmother. Under the new regime Oprah had to read a book a week and write a report on it at the same time that she also practiced adding new words to her vocabulary. It was during this time that she received her first reward for studying so hard. She was paid $500 for a speech to a church group. For a young girl of seven that was a lot of money and a harbinger of what her poise and ability to engage an audience would mean twenty years later.

It had been a busy year, and she was happy to get a summer break to visit her mother back in Milwaukee, but that visit did not turn out as planned. Vernita wanted her back permanently and wouldn't let her return to Nashville and her father and stepmother. Hurt and depressed by this development, Vernon said, "We had brought her out of that atmosphere, out of a house into a home, so I knew it was not good for her, being in that environment again."

Vernita was determined to keep the girl; besides, once again she thought her latest man was going to marry her and give them a better home. Instead, another child arrived, a boy, Jeffrey, and when the boyfriend decided he didn't want to get married, they all moved in together in a crowded two-bedroom apartment.

Oprah missed being with her father and Zelma; their house was more like a family home than the apartment her mother had. Besides, in Vernon and Zelma's house, Oprah was the only child, the center of attention, and she liked that feeling, as every child does. In Milwaukee, there was the new two-bedroom apartment with lots of people—friends and family—staying there, including her mother, two younger siblings, her mother's boyfriend, and assorted relatives who drifted in and out.

Oprah at twelve and thirteen was not the center of attention for those who lived in the apartment except for her fourteen-year-old male cousin, who slept in the same bed with Oprah. Before long, he began to fondle her small breasts and run his hands around her body, and finally, he raped her. It was a painful and confusing experience, compounded by her cousin's warnings to keep silent about what he—or rather, they—had done.

She later said, "I didn't tell anybody about it because I thought I would be blamed for it. I remember blaming myself for it, thinking something must be wrong with me."

In exchange for her silence, her cousin took her to the zoo the next day and bought her an ice-cream cone. She was confused; she thought she had done something wrong because of the clandestine and guilty way her cousin behaved. Yet, as she would admit later, the sex felt good. In her mixture of feelings and sensations about pleasure and guilt, Oprah became more rebellious and began to have sex with a variety of men and boys, some of whom were relatives.

Years later, in a 1988 *People* magazine interview, she said that the sexual attention from these boys and men was pleasing and she liked it. "When that article came out, the response I got was, how dare you say that you liked it? Which wasn't what I was saying at all. If someone is stroking your little breasts, you get a sexy, physical feeling. It can be a good feeling, and it's confusing, because you then blame yourself for feeling good, not knowing that you had nothing to do with that kind of arousal. A child is never to blame."

She said that she desperately wanted love from her mother, but she was too busy working and tending to her own life, and the bonding never took place. She recalled, "Not getting much attention from my mother made me seek it in other places, the wrong places."

In the years that followed, Oprah became more and more of a sex toy to male family members and their friends. Another cousin's boyfriend seemed friendly to her and soon was fondling her in the car and at home. "Over a period of time," she said, "I became his pet. People would try to put him with me even though I began to try to be scarce. I began to wonder: Don't they know this is happening?"

As it had back in Kosciusko, all of thirteen-year-old Oprah's reading and learning made her unpopular with her peers at Lincoln School in Milwaukee, and that hurt because Oprah was searching for acceptance and love. On several occasions, classmates cornered her and threatened to beat her up. She talked her way out of the confrontations, but it left her fearful of the next time, when maybe she might not get away. Her salvation would be a teacher, Gene Abrams, who noticed that Oprah was withdrawn and buried in her books while other students were playing around. He made it a point to get to know her better and decided to get her out of the rough environment of Lincoln School.

Later, Oprah would say, "[Mr. Abrams was] one of those

great teachers who had the ability to make you believe in yourself."

The chance came in 1968, when Oprah had turned fourteen. Abrams recommended her for a special scholarship program called Upward Bound that was designed to bring minorities, mostly blacks, into private all-white high schools. The payoff came with a full scholarship to Nicolet High School, an all-white school in the expensive Milwaukee suburb called Fox Lake. Nicolet's students came from upper-middle-class homes with educated parents, every economic advantage, and an atmosphere dedicated to learning, college attendance, and professional careers. It was twenty miles and three bus transfers from the crowded, mostly black inner-city neighborhood where Oprah lived with her mother and her live-in boyfriend, as well as Oprah's half sister and half brother. Besides getting a good education, she also became a curiosity as the only black child at the school. More would follow and become known as "the bus kids."

Twenty-five years later, a white British exchange student, Irene Hoe, who is now an editor of the *Straits Times* in Singapore, reflected on the experience she and Oprah shared from two different viewpoints. Oprah brought to Mrs. Hoe's mind "an image of a short girl who shared my own passion for the textured panty hose so much in fashion at that time.

"Fancy panty hose apart, Oprah stood out for another reason. She did not live in the predominantly affluent, mostly white suburban neighborhoods of Milwaukee which fed their children to our high school. Back in those politically incorrect days, in the aftermath of civil rights upheaval that led to race riots in the city itself, it might have been said that she did not belong.

"Oprah was part of a late sixties experiment, if I remember correctly, to desegregate schools by ferrying children from mostly black neighborhoods to mostly white suburban schools. My American history class had discussed the civil rights issue, but it was a discussion about something that happened to other people. Once or twice, I felt like asking one of the 'bus kids' what their neighborhoods were like and how they felt about the issue. But worried they might think me rude, I never did.

"Some of my classmates said that Oprah had once spoken publicly [in later years] about being at school in Wisconsin. They could not recall if she recounted any good memories. It could not have been a wonderful year for her.

"As a freshman, she would have been about fourteen then, the age at which news reports say she gave birth to a premature baby, who died. By the time she was fourteen, she had been raped by a teenage cousin, sexually abused by an uncle, and had run away from home. Her life, or what has been revealed of it in recent years, had been lived on a different planet from most of our schoolmates.

"Nineteen sixty-eight was the year which saw the black civil rights leader Martin Luther King murdered and Robert Kennedy assassinated in a presidential campaign which would lead to the election of Richard Nixon. I wonder if those tumultuous events also influenced Oprah in her choice of a career, a career which has brought her an estimated income of $98 million over the last two years and made her the first woman to top *Forbes*'s annual list [of the highest paid performers].

"Her homes include an elegant white-on-white apartment with a view of Chicago's Lake Michigan and a farm in Indiana. Mine is a no-fuss flat with no marble flooring, no chandeliers, and no designer kitchen. Oprah and I still live on different planets."

Beyond being a curiosity, she was a prized guest at her classmates' homes, where the only blacks were housemaids like Oprah's mother. It was intoxicating for a little black girl who lived on the wrong side of town, jammed into a two-bedroom apartment and forced to change buses to get to school.

She recalled, "I was feeling a sense of anguish, because living with my mother in Milwaukee, I was in a situation where I was the only black kid, and I mean the only one, in a school of two thousand upper-middle-class suburban Jewish kids. I would take the bus in the morning to school with the maids who worked in their homes.

"The life that I saw those children lead was so totally different from what I went home to, from what I saw when I took the bus home with the maids in the evening. I wanted my mother to be like their mothers. I wanted my mother to have cookies ready for me when I came home and to say, 'How was your day?' But she was one of those maids. And she was tired. And she was just trying to survive. Her way of showing love to me was getting out and going to work every day, putting clothes on my back, and having food on the table. At that time, I didn't understand it."

Oprah couldn't afford to keep pace with her classmates from affluent white homes, so she stole from her mother, faked home robberies to account for missing articles she had taken, and became a thief in her search for money and peer acceptance. She was looking to be accepted and trying to rebel against parent and home. She began running away, hanging out with the crowd, chasing after anything male, and giving the boys what they wanted—sex—in exchange for what she wanted but never got from them, love and belonging.

One of the men who wanted sex wasn't a boy from someplace else; it was her favorite uncle, her father's brother, whom she admired. She said that one day when she was fourteen and the two of them were alone and they began to talk about the boys in her life, he asked her if she had ever kissed a boy. Suddenly, Oprah said that Trenton had stripped her panties off before she knew what was happening. He fondled her and penetrated her with his fingers, and it was the beginning of an incestuous affair that would last for some time. Trenton claims this is a lie.

Her half sister, Patricia, didn't understand what was going on, but later, when she did, she wasn't above talking about it. By the time Oprah was thirteen and fourteen, she was inviting nineteen- and twenty-year-old young men over to the apartment so they could do "the Horse," which was her name for sexual intercourse. When the young men arrived, Oprah got rid of seven-year-old Patricia by giving her an ice cream or candy treat and sending her outside to play for a couple of hours.

Oprah's wildness wasn't confined to home. She started staying out late, claiming she was visiting a girlfriend's house and then remaining away for the entire night. Finally, when she was fourteen, Oprah ran away from home for a week, during which she claimed she met Aretha Franklin, who gave her $100. The running away had actually been planned, with Oprah set to spend the week at a girlfriend's house. Their signals got crossed, and when Oprah showed up at the girlfriend's house, the family had gone on vacation. So, uncertain what to do, Oprah says she wandered the streets of downtown Milwaukee, and that's when she met Aretha Franklin and got enough money to stay in a motel for a few days. Eventually, Oprah ran out of money and called the family minister, asking him to help placate her mother when she, Oprah, returned home. The minister helped her get home, but there was no placating Vernita. Worried and angry, Vernita became fed up with Oprah. Vernita had enough problems in her life, and she didn't need another full-time one living under her roof.

Vernita was not a moral beacon, but she knew she had a problem she couldn't handle, so she tried to commit Oprah to a home for troubled teens. As Oprah would later tell an audience of lawyers at the Chicago Bar Association in 1991, her mother was on welfare, really didn't know much about raising kids, and was trying to create a life for herself.

The two of them went to be interviewed to get Oprah committed to this Milwaukee home for wayward girls. "I remember going to the interview process, where they treat you like you're already a known convict, and thinking to myself, How in the world is this happening to me? I was fourteen, and I knew that I was a smart person. I knew I wasn't a bad person, and I remember thinking: How did this happen? How did I get here?"

By sheer chance the home for wayward girls had no room, and Vernita was told to come back in two weeks. Vernita, who had had enough with the troublesome, promiscuous teenager, called Vernon in Nashville—the man she wouldn't let have Oprah eight years before—and told him that Oprah was more than Vernita could handle. Vernon called Zelma, who loved Oprah, and she agreed that they should welcome her back. Vernon drove to Milwaukee to get Oprah and headed back to Nashville.

After they had been home for a few weeks, Zelma discovered to her surprise that Oprah was pregnant and had been hiding her condition from everyone until she couldn't anymore. She miscarried a male fetus. Zelma told Vernon and Vernita, who came to Nashville immediately to be with them and discuss what had happened. It was then that Oprah began naming all the males she had been with sexually, including Trent, her uncle and Vernon's brother. That was a bombshell, but as Oprah said fifteen years later, "Everybody in the family sort of shoved it under a rock."

When he was confronted with Oprah's accusation, Uncle Trent protested. "I knew she was pregnant as a young girl. We all knew, but it wasn't me. I know who the real father is, but I ain't telling. He's a powerful man from Milwaukee."

Here the brothers agreed initially that Trent was *not* the father of the child. Trent was bewildered why his niece would make up the story about him and said that the Winfrey family was supportive of him because they know the real truth. None of the rest of the family, Trent claimed, thought he raped Oprah or fathered her child, and that included his brother, Vernon. For his part, Vernon originally agreed with Trenton and thought the real father was one of two men he knew but refused to name publicly. He has tried to contact them both, but one dropped out of sight, and he wasn't able to find the other one.

However, some years later, Oprah and Vernon changed their stories. Now Vernon apparently believes that Trent did father the baby boy that Oprah had miscarried. He said that Trent was his closest brother and that the shock of what Trent had done was too much to handle. The whole family was torn up about it. Some healing took place when Stedman Graham, Oprah's boyfriend, made a secret trip to Nashville to meet with his future father-in-law and they talked about the things that troubled Oprah's life.

Oprah now says that Trent was *not* the father of her baby. Oprah said she just named everybody she could think of who might have been the father and that Trent may have been the one. For Oprah this experience would be her greatest, haunting shame, and she would keep the guilt buried deep inside her until years later, when her own half sister, Patricia, would humiliate her by revealing it to a tabloid newspaper after Oprah had become the famous daytime-TV talk-show host.

That revelation, years later, would be a sisterly betrayal that would so stun Oprah that she would take to her bed sick, believing all the world would hate her for what she had done. It would be two years before she would ever speak to her half sister again. Then she told herself she was a hypocrite for preaching forgiveness to her audiences and not practicing it herself. In 1992 she gathered her mother, with whom she has long had a tangled and troubled relationship; her half sister, Patricia; Patricia's seventeen-year-old daughter, Chrishaunda; and her favorite cousin, Alice, at the 160-acre Indiana farm she had bought for weekend getaways.

The women thrashed out their emotional hang-ups and confronted the reality that Oprah had followed the same pattern as her mother, who said she had carried Oprah in shame.

"Fourteen years later," she declared, "I did the exact same thing my mother had done. I hid my pregnancy until the day the child was born. And I named all of the people who could have possibly been responsible. My mom did the same thing."

Given the trauma of her pregnancy, it is ironic that twenty-five years later she would humiliate two Florida teenagers in the exact same situation. Tammy Bakker and Susanna Perez, both fifteen, were flown from their Dade City, Florida, homes to Chicago to be on the Oprah show about teenagers who wanted to get pregnant. After they arrived, Susanna did not appear on the show because her pregnancy was an accident and she and the father had gotten married.

Tammy and three other girls were interviewed on tape with Oprah because they admitted they had wanted to get pregnant. What they didn't know was that their taped interview would then be shown to a hostile live audience among whom they would be seated. The segment with the live audience and Oprah speaking disapprovingly of the four girls turned into an enormous and unexpected humiliation for the girls. Tammy said, "It was more like she was trying to embarrass me and the other three [girls who did the private interview]. She was being negative and not helpful at all."

Both Tammy and Susanna said they were upset by something they overheard. One of the other three girls to be interviewed told one of Oprah's aides before the private taped interview that she didn't deliberately try to get pregnant and that it had been an accident. Oprah's assistant then cynically asked her, "How bad do you want to be on the *Oprah* show?"

Susanna's assessment of Oprah at that point was devastating to anyone who would believe she went through hell as a pregnant teenager. "In my opinion," she said, "Oprah has let the money get to her head and has forgotten all about the experience of being eleven through fourteen and is plainly rude."

In a way, Oprah had started down the same path her mother had trod. She, too, might have ended up an unwed mother on welfare, but her mother realized in time that Milwaukee was not the place for Oprah. Vernita sent Oprah back to the man who she apparently believed was her father—there was no way of knowing for sure. It was the best decision of Oprah's teenage years.

CHAPTER

3

Life With Father

Oprah's years from age fourteen to twenty-two were spent living with her father in Nashville, the center of the country music business, with the Grand Ole Opry and Opryland and religious publishing, as well as the home of eight universities, including Vanderbilt and Fisk. A medium-sized city about as large as Milwaukee, it is both a government center and diversified manufacturing hub for Tennessee in addition to being the home of Presidents James Polk and Andrew Jackson. Situated on the Cumberland River, it is dotted with a number of buildings patterned after the Greek Revival style of architecture, which lends to its reputation as the southern Athens.

Its weather is hot and humid in the southern style, more like Kosciusko than Milwaukee, with summers in the nineties and mild winters. The neighborhood where Vernon and Zelma lived was fairly typical lower middle class, predominantly black and with a lot of street traffic and a feeling of connection about it. While not everybody is everyone's close friend, a good many people who see each other on the street and in the stores know each other on sight. The Faith United Church, which is central in the Winfreys' life and where Vernon serves as one of the deacons, is part of the neighborhood.

Zelma and Vernon found a different Oprah when she returned to them in 1968 at the age of fourteen than the girl

23

who had left as a nine-year-old in 1963. They were determined to tone down this smart-aleck, overpainted, underdressed young lady. Halter tops, short, tight skirts, and heavy makeup were banned, and serious studying, along with extracurricular reading, became the priority. This time, chaste behavior and high grades were demanded by her father, while her step-mother increased the book-reading quota to five books, with reports every two weeks.

The discipline was strict, and it worked. Vernon, who opened his own barbershop in 1964, expressed his attitude toward teen rebellion with a sign he hung on the wall:

"Attention Teenagers: If You Are Tired of Being Hassled by Unreasonable Parents, Now Is the Time for Action! Leave Home and Pay Your Own Way While You Still Know Everything."

That was the policy at the shop and at home. Oprah, as usual, was a quick study and got the message. By her own assessment, if she hadn't moved back with her father and stepmother, today she would be a poor, unwed mother, just another failed statistic on the urban landscape.

"My dad really held me in with a tight rein," she said. "Without his direction, I'd have wound up pregnant and another statistic. I was definitely headed for a career as a juvenile delinquent."

Oprah's eight years with her father were marked by Vernon's strong hand and Zelma's equally strong support. They instilled discipline and the value of hard work. They also gave her a real home.

She recalled: "I got sent to live with my father so that my father could straighten me out, and that he did. When I got sent, this [house] was where I got sent to...and actually it's a very small house, but when I arrived at this house, I thought it was a mansion. I thought, My God, I've never lived in a full brick house." The only thing that she didn't like was the plastic slipcovers on the couch, because in the hot and humid Nashville summers, her bare legs would stick to the plastic.

No daughter of Vernon Winfrey was going to be cheap and slutty. Oprah would become a lady, and she would announce that fact to the world by dressing, talking, and acting like one.

That was the social part, and an ex-boyfriend from those days would later reminisce about an Oprah that none of the boys in Milwaukee who had done the Horse with Oprah would recognize. Oprah shifted to wearing conservative high-school-girl clothes, like knee-length plaid pinafores with white long-sleeved blouses buttoned at the neck, traditional low-heel schoolgirl shoes, and hair done in the Marlo Thomas *That Girl* flip, as was the fashion.

Anthony Otey became Oprah's boyfriend during their high school years. He met her at a community center where both would come with friends. He was another of the few blacks attending East Nashville High, which immediately gave them common grounds to get to know each other. They began dating in their senior year. Then Anthony asked Gail, as she was known in high school, if she would go steady, and she replied in a long note dated September 22, 1970, putting him off temporarily.

She wrote Tony, regretting that she didn't participate in the Junior Miss pageant, and answered his proposal that they go steady coyly. "Regarding your question—if the offer still stands—I refuse to answer right now simply because this atmosphere is so blah."

Part of the reason for the delay was that Oprah had to get her father's permission to go steady, and it was a big thing in the Winfrey household when Vernon finally agreed.

Then they began to see each other frequently, going to Burger King and Pizza Hut, Jackson 5 concerts, Ali McGraw movies, listening to "their song," which was "Bridge Over Troubled Water," and yet they never—never—had sex. Tony said that he and Oprah made a pact when they started dating not to have sex until they got married. In his eyes it was part of their religious belief and their determination to amount to something worthwhile when they were grown up.

Anthony is now married and living with his wife, Barbara, and their two sons in Chattanooga, Tennessee. He directs Students Taking A Right Stand, which sponsors drug prevention programs in schools around the country, and a second program, An Hour of Minority Enrichment, which produces cultural material for single black parents.

There was a lot about Oprah's background that Anthony didn't know about and that he only discovered years later, after she became a TV talk-show host in Chicago. She almost never talked about her mother, Vernita. Anthony said she never mentioned having a half sister and a half brother. To him, she was just the new girl in town with a bubbly personality whom he met at a community dance and who always seemed very much in control of herself. He remembered the first time he saw her. "She came to a dance at the community center that I was working in. And she came in and sat in the corner. And she had these pigtails on and this guy and I were working the door at the Fred Douglass Community Center. She watched all these kids dancing and the guys kept saying, 'Who's that girl?' I said, 'I have no earthly idea.' Then she came to our school."

Their idea of a fun date would be to go to Shelby Park after school and just hang out with eight or ten of their friends, feeding the ducks or flipping Frisbees. Their dating was innocent and circumscribed by the rigid rules set by Vernon and Zelma. Whenever they went out after dark, either Anthony came to the Winfrey house to pick up Oprah, or she would go over to his house. In either case, the parents were always there, and the opportunity for fooling around or playing the Horse didn't exist even if they had wanted to, and Anthony firmly believed that Oprah didn't want to do anything like that. If it was an evening date for a movie or a concert, Oprah had to be home by eleven o'clock. To Anthony, that meant that at 11:01 Vernon would be on the street looking for them.

In terms of her education and school, the rules Vernon and Zelma spelled out were equally demanding. They were not enforced by physical abuse or spankings but by Vernon's stern lectures, to the point that Oprah would sometimes wish her father would whip her instead of preaching to her. Vernon was stern and made it clear that his word was law and nonnegotiable. Zelma and Vernon insisted on the extracurricular reading that would have a long-term effect on Oprah. It would broaden her knowledge, but it would also introduce her to her black heritage through authors like Margaret Walker and *Jubilee* and, her favorite, Maya Angelou's *I Know Why the Caged Bird Sings*.

There was an electric connection between teenage Oprah and Angelou's autobiography. The book is Angelou's own story of being buffeted between parents, with a mother in Texas and a father in California. She tells the tale of a young girl who is raped and so traumatized by the experience that she loses the power to speak for many years, a story to which Oprah could relate. In later years they would become such close friends that they viewed each other as surrogate mother and daughter.

Oprah would give Angelou the most spectacular sixty-fifth birthday party, lasting three days and attended by distinguished guests from around the world. Angelou would dedicate her latest book of poetry to Oprah in 1993, and they would act together in the movies.

In addition to her assigned reading, Oprah had to learn twenty new words every week. Only school grades of A's would be acceptable, which came as a shock to Oprah, who had been getting C's in Milwaukee; in fact, she brought home a couple of C's on her first report card from East Nashville High.

This report card was received with bad grace by Vernon and Zelma. Oprah was a smart girl, they emphasized, and she could earn A's. Therefore, she must. Again, this rule was not to be discussed—just followed. Beyond that, it was 1968, and Oprah and Anthony were among the first blacks admitted to East Nashville, and they had a duty to demonstrate how accomplished they were.

East Nashville High was one of the first Nashville schools to integrate after the Supreme Court decision mandating integrated schools. It is no longer open, having shut down about ten years ago, but it was a clean, well-administered place, as opposed to the all-black schools in which there were never enough supplies and books. Its middle-class student body produced a more comfortable environment for Oprah than upscale Nicolet High School in Milwaukee. Oprah blossomed at East Nashville. Active in drama classes and in student politics, she became the student council president by running on a platform of better food in the cafeteria and a live band at the school prom.

In addition, at seventeen she was invited to a White House Conference on Youth in Colorado and represented East

Nashville in a national speaking competition as a result of her articulate presentation of Margaret Walker's *Jubilee*, the story of a slave family during the Civil War and immediately afterward. *Jubilee* was first published in 1965, and Oprah came upon it soon afterward. Taken by it, she memorized it as part of her repertoire of recitations, along with Sojourner Truth's "Ain't I a Woman?," which she used on appropriate occasions for the rest of her life. Oprah would stand before the congregation or audience and thunder out the words on behalf of women's equality that Sojourner Truth spoke at the Woman's Rights Convention in Akron, Ohio, in 1851.

"That man over there says that women need to be helped into carriages and lifted over ditches and to have the best place everywhere. Nobody ever helps me into carriages or over mud puddles or gives me any best place and ain't I a woman? Look at me! Look at my arm! I have plowed and planted and gathered into barns and no man could head me—and ain't I a woman? I could work as much and eat as much as a man (when I could get it) and bear the lash as well—and ain't I a woman?"

Oprah was adept at such recitations; ever since she had been with her grandmother, she had enjoyed performing for church groups. Now, in Nashville, her popularity spread, and she was asked to perform before church and civil groups several times a month.

As for boys, Vernon told his daughter that young fellows would not respect her if she didn't respect herself. She did, and they did. When she began dating Anthony Otey in her senior year, she wrote him impassioned love letters almost every day. For example, one of them read, "On today, June 22nd, 1971, I've decided to voice my thoughts on paper to prevent my brain from becoming disrupted." Then she noted that she and Tony had been dating for nine months and she really loved him. Even though her father didn't understand about love, wrote Oprah, she was sure God did.

Surprisingly for a young man, Anthony answered in kind, with artistic flourishes of drawings, clouds, faces, and so on. In a card he wrote to Oprah, even though she was called Gail then, Tony said, "Hi. I got a feeling this day's going to be great. And do you know why? Go on, guess. Well, that's long enough. This day is going to be beautiful and great because I'm in love with you. Has anybody ever told you that a day without you is like a day without sunshine. Smile!"

Anthony said that they each wrote their love notes at night before going to bed and would then slip them to each other at school the next day. Otey claims he still has hundreds of those letters. During their courtship they had little love codes so they could communicate secretly. For example, instead of saying, "I love you," they would tell each other when others were nearby, "The green grass is growing all around."

Oprah has saved all of Tony's cards to her. "One of the reasons, if you're wondering why I'm saving them, he had these books that everybody had to buy. So you really have all your senior memories and favorite songs and all that stuff."

Besides the great boyfriend, Oprah was doing well in school and was excited by her theater arts and speech classes. She continued to give dramatic readings from *Jubilee* and hone her skills as a public speaker. She was elected "Most Popular Girl" in her senior year, and Tony was elected "Most Popular Boy."

Rejoicing in her black ancestry and delving into the heroes and heroines—particularly the heroines—of American blacks' struggle for freedom, she learned all she could about her people's experiences in slavery. She was particularly taken by the writings of Sojourner Truth, Margaret Walker, and Harriet Tubman, and a few years later one of Alice Walker's novels, *The Color Purple*, would move Oprah and play a very important role in her career. She first read *The Color Purple* when she was working in Baltimore, but its major impact would not be felt until Oprah had moved to Chicago.

To Oprah, Sojourner Truth and Harriet Tubman were inspirational both as blacks fighting slavery and as women achievers. Sojourner Truth was born into slavery in New York State as Isabella Baumfree in 1797. She ran away from her master and became a preacher, abolitionist, and feminist, adopting a name to symbolize her new life and mission to free the slaves and women from the oppression they suffered.

Harriet Tubman was born a generation later in Maryland and at twenty-eight escaped to freedom by hiding during the day and following the North Star at night. Then, astonishingly, she returned to the South to help with the underground railroad, a chain of safe houses stretching from the South northward into free territory and, in some cases, all the way to Canada. At great danger to herself, Tubman made repeated trips back into slave territory to rescue other slaves—including her own parents—and lead them to freedom. At times, she brandished a loaded pistol at her exhausted or panicky charges to force them to keep moving. During the Civil War she served in the Union army as a spy, and when she finally died just before the outbreak of World War I, she was buried with full military honors.

These were the ex-slave black women who were Oprah's forebears and whom she wanted to emulate. Her articulate and passionate speeches about them as a teenager began winning her recognition and prizes.

She and Tony Otey talked about marrying and having a family, and each spoke as if they would be together forever, but Tony felt in his heart that Oprah was destined for a more glamorous and exciting life than he would ever be able to provide. He didn't say so at the time, but he sensed that she was slipping away from him.

Years later, when he learned about her life in Milwaukee, the promiscuous path she followed playing the Horse with so many boys and, of course, the stillborn pregnancy, he was startled beyond anything he could have imagined. The chances are that he would have found out about the lurid past of his teenage sweetheart, and as a result marriage might not have come easy.

In 1970, when she was 16, Oprah got a chance to travel to Los Angeles to give one of her recitations to a church congregation. While there, she took the Hollywood tour and came home vowing to her father that her handprints would someday be in the concrete courtyard of Grauman's Chinese Theatre along with all the other great stars. We don't know what Vernon's reaction was to this prediction, but he probably recognized by this time, as did many others around Oprah, that this was no ordinary young woman. She possessed a driving ambition and a determination to be somebody.

In 1971, radio station WVOL sponsored seventeen-year-old Oprah in the Miss Fire Prevention contest. She became the first black woman to win in Nashville. She won it in a way that millions today recognize as pure, unadulterated Oprah. When the contest had come down to three finalists, each was asked what she would do if she had a million dollars. The first contestant said she would buy some much-needed things for her mother and father. The second said she would give all the money to the poor. When Oprah stood in front of the microphone, she answered, with her effervescent smile, "If I had a million dollars...I'd be a spending fool!" It brought the house down and won her the crown as Miss Fire Prevention.

She did the same with other beauty and popularity contests, although Vernon was not enthusiastic about them; he wanted her to concentrate on academic achievement. But he was pleased when she won an Elks Club beauty contest which had a four-year scholarship to Tennessee State as the prize.

Oprah's life became busier and busier. She spoke, acted in plays, studied, entered contests, and got elected student council president with the slogan Vote for the Grand Ole Oprah. On Valentine's Day of her senior year in high school, she took Tony aside. "We gotta talk," she told him.

Tony remembers that conversation to this day "I knew right then that I was going to lose the girl I loved. She told me she was breaking up with me because she didn't have the time for a relationship. We both sat there and cried. It broke my heart."

Tony had anticipated that this parting would occur, although he had hoped it would not. He would recall twenty years later: "One thing I remember most about Gail [Oprah] is that she knew what she wanted very early in life. She said she wanted to be a movie star. She wanted to be an actress. And I praise God that she's done that. She was willing to put aside a lot of other things. Back in the seventies, drugs had started entering the schools, and that kind of thing. We were involved in integration and those fights in those years. We were actively involved in that, but she knew what she wanted to do. She worked hard at it, and when her ship started to sail, she got aboard."

One of the reasons that Oprah thought she didn't have time

for a romantic relationship was that she was beginning an exciting new love affair. It was a romance that would last the rest of her life. She fell in love with broadcasting, and broadcasting fell in love with her. Her voice, her quick wit, and her personality made her a natural from the moment she first spoke into a microphone.

Oprah landed her first job in 1970 working days and the weekend shift in her father's small grocery store that he had opened adjacent to the barbershop, and she despised it. Vernon underscores that point by saying that Oprah hated working in that store with a passion. She would arrive in her 1963 Mercury from school, park, and go inside to spend the next eight to ten hours selling items like pickles and other kinds of groceries. At one counter she sold penny candy, and she complained that one had to sell 100 pieces of that candy just to make a dollar.

"Back then everybody used to buy something called Now or Laters," she recalled. "Some kind of candy, [but] I never ate because I was crazy from selling them all the time. The only thing that got me out of the store was the fact that I got myself a job in radio broadcasting. Thank goodness."

Oprah had volunteered to be in a March of Dimes walkathon. The scheme was to get some business to pay for every mile a volunteer walked. Oprah, now a high school senior, went to radio station WVOL on a whim to ask one of the disc jockeys, John Heidelberg, to sponsor her in the walkathon.

He agreed but when she came to collect the money he had forgotten about it; he paid her anyhow. Then he talked her into doing a demonstration tape, for she had a resonant voice he thought would play well on the air. "I admired her voice," he said. "She was articulate."

He gave her some news copy off the teletype wire and asked her to read from it into the microphone. After he and the engineer heard her and agreed that she not only read well but communicated the kind of intimacy and warmth that are essential in radio, they called Clarence Kilcrese, the station manager. "Come listen to this girl read," they said.

Kilcrese walked into the studio and liked her sound. "I needed part-timers at that time," he recalled. "I had two girls in mind, and I walked in and Oprah never stumbled one time.

I said, 'This is the lady right here.'" Kilcrese hired Oprah to do news reports on weekends and after school. She was paid $100 a week, which was big money in that day to a seventeen-year-old black girl for sitting down and talking into a microphone.

Heidelberg took her under his wing and taught her all the technical things she had to know; her personality carried her along the rest of the way. The job would last through high school and into her first year of college.

Admittedly, Oprah was a "twofer," which was very important in those days, when racial groups were exerting pressure on broadcasters, who had to renew their licenses every three years. She was both black and female; thus, the station got credit for two minorities for the price of one. That didn't bother Oprah. She was getting what she wanted out of the deal: show business experience.

She graduated from East Nashville and entered all-black Tennessee State University (TSU) as a speech and drama major. She was taught by Dr. Thomas E. Poag, Dr. William Cox, and Dr. Jamie Williams, all of whom recognized her unusual talents and considered her a wonderful student. Still, she hated college. She did not want to become part of the black militancy that dominated the student mood in those years. She was content to be working at WVOL. Beyond that she appeared in school plays and performed poetry and dramatic readings at various local churches most Sundays, sometimes alone and sometimes with musical accompaniment.

Seventeen-year-old Oprah's first intense, to-die-for love affair occurred several months after she had broken up with Anthony Otey, in 1971. She fell in love with William "Bubba" Taylor, whom she met at school. They started dating, and she helped him get a job at WVOL, which didn't last long. Neither did his love for Oprah, because he became nervous or bored or both and wanted out of any serious commitment. Oprah was crushed that the first man she loved romantically could leave her. Still a teenager, she wanted to marry William Taylor and did everything to keep him, including literally begging him on her knees to stay with her. She said later, "Lord, I wanted him! Oh, I wanted him."

Brokenhearted, she went on with her broadcasting career,

while Bill Taylor studied to become a mortician. They remained friends, but later Oprah said, "[If he'd stayed,] I'd be married to a mortician and probably be teaching Sunday school in Nashville someplace. To this day, I thank God he left!"

Oprah entered beauty contests whenever she could, and on March 10, 1972, at the downtown Elks Lodge in Nashville, she became one of twenty-two young black women in the final competition for the Miss Black Nashville contest. The director of the contest was a man named Gordon El-Greco Brown, who had just been given the Nashville franchise from the Miss Black America contest organization. Although at this time in her life Oprah was a size 11 with a 36-25-37 figure that was quite appealing, many in the audience were surprised that she won. The audience favorite was a stunning Maude Mobley, who most people predicted would be the winner.

In the physical segments of the contest, swimsuit and evening dress, Oprah received average scores from the judges, but in the talent segment, Brown said, "when Oprah's talent turn came, she did a dramatic reading and sang—and she knocked the audience off their feet. She was so good, it moved her into the top five."

Still, Brown felt that Maude Mobley was equally qualified in the talent segment and far outshone Oprah in swimsuit and evening gown. He sensed something was wrong when the master of ceremonies announced Mobley as fourth runner-up, and he knew there was a problem when the master of ceremonies finally told the waiting audience, "The winner and new Miss Black Nashville is Oprah Gail Winfrey!" His own anxiety was made worse when a number of people came up to him in the hall afterward to charge that the contest had been rigged.

Afterward, Brown checked the ballots again and discovered a scoring error. According to Brown, Oprah didn't actually win the Miss Black Nashville contest. It really should have gone to Maude Mobley, with Oprah coming in fifth! Brown went to see Oprah the following day and explained what had happened, but Oprah refused to surrender the title.

Faced with a possible scandal in his new beauty contest franchise, Gordon El-Greco Brown backed off and entered

Oprah in the Miss Black Tennessee contest, which she also won. She struck out at the national Miss Black America contest but proved she could win beauty pageants. She also had shown that she was not somebody to tangle with if you tried to take away something that she thought was hers.

Brown kept quiet about what happened for many years until he was no longer in the beauty contest business and finally got angry with Oprah for claiming she had won the Miss Black Nashville contest, which helped her career.

Brown recalled, "At the time, Oprah was a college student who worked part-time at a local black radio station, and that contest was a stepping-stone for the big career she so desperately wanted. She's kept this story a secret all these years. But I'm telling it now because I'm angry after reading interviews in which she takes credit for winning the pageant."

Today Oprah's representatives at Harpo Productions, Oprah's production company in Chicago, contend they are not aware of Brown's claims. Maude Mobley now lives and works in Detroit and doesn't want to talk about it, either. Apparently, she feels that Oprah is rich and powerful and could cause her a lot of trouble if she were to speak out.

Broadcasting and Oprah worked well together from the beginning. She had started part-time at radio station WVOL in her senior year of high school in 1971. Her relaxed, down-home quality connected with the listeners so well that by 1973, when station WTVF-TV—Channel 5, the CBS affiliate in Nashville— was looking for minority employees, Oprah was offered a job.

She was uncertain about taking the WTVF-TV job, for it meant quitting Tennessee State University, which she secretly didn't like, but she feared that her father would disapprove of her dropping out of college. Help came from her drama coach, Dr. William Cox, who told her and her father that the reason for getting a college degree was to pave the way to a good job. She was already being offered the kind of position that the college was supposed to help her find. He said she should seize the opportunity and take the job. "Don't you know that's why people go to college?" Dr. Cox asked. "So that CBS can call them." That she had been Miss Black Nashville and Miss Black Tennessee didn't hurt, either. She was nineteen years old and earning $15,000 a year as the first female—and the first black—newscaster in Nashville.

While her peers were mounting campus demonstrations, Oprah was winning beauty contests and learning where to look when the red light appeared on the camera. "The other kids were all into black power. I wasn't a dashiki kind of woman," she remarked.

She deeply believed in her heritage and always felt she was a direct descendant of Harriet Tubman and Sojourner Truth, but she followed the philosophy of Jesse Jackson, who said you worked hard and achieved. Instead of getting involved in demonstrations, she was finding out quickly what it took to succeed at the real work of life and devoted full time to what she was becoming: a polished broadcaster. "Sure I was a token," she said, "but honey, I was one happy token."

Coincidentally, there was a white young man at another Nashville television station, WSM-TV, whose television career would cross Oprah's and become connected in the years to come. He was a small, cute fellow and the local weatherman at WSM-TV. One day in 1977, Bob Eaton, then news director at NBC's owned and operated TV station in Los Angeles, KNBC, was passing through Nashville, spending time in his hotel room flipping the television channels so he could check out the local TV talent. He spotted this young weatherman, called him at station WSM-TV, and offered him a big raise to come to L.A. Once in L.A., the weatherman got a better job as the host of what would turn out to be the most popular TV game show in America, *Wheel of Fortune*. The young Nashville weatherman was Pat Sajak, whose successful *Wheel of Fortune* gave King World television syndicators the money they needed to sign up the *Oprah Winfrey Show* in 1985 for national syndication and make Oprah the richest black woman in the world.

Neither Zelma, Vernon, nor Oprah knew it, but the years of living with her father were coming to a close. She had been with Vernon from 1968 until 1976, and those eight years changed her life. Her father and stepmother had been strict and demanding of Oprah, and the upbringing she received turned out well because the raw materials of determination, ambition, and talent were there.

Certainly those genes were in Vernon, who had been honorably discharged from the army. He began as a dishwasher and janitor and became a city councilman from the Fifth District in Nashville and a deacon in the Faith United Baptist Church. He owned a barbershop—and, later, a small grocery store adjacent to the barbershop—while nurturing his daughter, who, in turn, became one of the most phenomenal successes of this generation.

Vernon Winfrey was a special man in many ways, and that included his acceptance of Oprah as his daughter from the moment he received the printed birth announcement in the mail while at Fort Rucker. Curiously, this created an ambivalent feeling in Oprah.

"Emotionally, I still feel disconnected," she says. "I feel like these [Vernon and Zelma] were some nice people who took me in. Because my mother named several people [men who might have gotten her pregnant with Oprah] and my father was one of them. He took responsibility because I could have been his. To this day there has never been an official test. And over the years people have said, 'Well, I don't know if he really is your dad.' But he is the only father that I know. He took responsibility for me when he didn't have to. So my father saved my life at a time when I needed to be saved. But we're not, like, bonded."

This comment gives a glimpse of part of Oprah that very few people understand—that she is a much more private person than she appears to be. Her out-front, brassy, smiling personality that engulfs people, and her buzzwords about intimacy, love, and secrets appear to be revealing her innermost self. In fact, there is much about her that she does not share, and there are recurring contradictions in what she claims is true about herself.

If you have read about or learned her life story as told until recently, there is no mention of her half brother, who has since died of AIDS, or her half sister. The details of her promiscuity and the stillborn child were never discussed until the last few years, and even now the details are blurred.

In her profile on Oprah for the *New York Times Magazine*, author Barbara Grizzuti Harrison sensed the same thing. "This is the story [of her, Oprah's, life] as she has crafted it and as she tells it. Her half-sister and her half-brother have no place in this story. Her candor is more apparent than real." In fairness, it must be noted again that Ms. Harrison doesn't really like Oprah and writes about her as if she suspects she has a secret agenda she shares with no one. However, Ms. Harrison is an experienced interviewer and brings a certain insight to Oprah's persona.

It seemed like a curious attitude on Oprah's part when she openly acknowledged that what Vernon—and Zelma—did for her made all the difference in her life. "My father turned my life around by insisting I be more than I was and by believing I could be more. His love of learning showed me the way."

But now the years with her father were winding down. Oprah was a restless young lady who loved her father and stepmother but was not happy that her daddy still insisted on strict behavior. She was a TV anchorwoman and her father's rule was: "Be home by midnight or, by God, sleep on the porch!"

Oprah was about to take a big leap forward that would temporarily turn into a huge personal disaster.

4

Almost Dead in Baltimore

After spending three years at WTVF-TV in Nashville working for news director Chris Clark, Oprah, then twenty-two, moved on in the summer of 1976 to WJZ-TV in Baltimore and the hardest seven years of her TV career.

Baltimore, a rough blue-collar town, is one of the biggest manufacturing cities and ports on the Atlantic Coast. Sixty percent of the population is black; the remaining 40 percent is white. The whites live in tight little insular ethnic neighborhoods that are predominantly Polish, Greek, Italian, and Jewish. Baltimore has always maintained a pervasively southern culture. The official dividing line between the North and the South is the northern boundary of Maryland known as the Mason-Dixon Line, and during the Civil War, northern and southern sympathizers often rioted there. While Baltimore and Maryland remained in the Union during the Civil War, Baltimore had to be kept under martial law throughout the war, and it was in Baltimore that the first failed attempt was made to assassinate President Lincoln.

It was also the home of several great American literary figures, including H. L. Mencken, the irascible "Bard of

Baltimore," regarded as the most important social critic of the first half of the twentieth century, author of many books, and notorious for acerbic observations of common Americans, whom he called the Booboisie and who read his columns in the *Baltimore Sun*. Oprah would have loved to interview him for his pithy observations, including his comment that "puritanism is the haunting fear that someone, somewhere, may be happy"; or his observation that "conscience is the inner voice which warns us that someone may be looking"; and, "It is now quite lawful for a Catholic woman to avoid pregnancy by a resort to mathematics, though she is still forbidden to resort to physics and chemistry." He died in 1956, two years after Oprah was born, but his legacy was still viewed with pride in Baltimore.

Baltimore was also the sometimes home of the poet and creator of the detective story and psychological thriller, Edgar Allan Poe. A man who knew hardship, rejection, drunkenness, and poverty, Poe died on his way to pick up his aunt to take her to his wedding. He never arrived at either his aunt's home or at the church, but was found in the street mysteriously stricken. He was buried in Baltimore, and every year to the present time, on October 7, the anniversary of his death, a mysterious woman, shrouded in black, visits his grave to leave a single rose and a bottle of brandy.

Baltimore is also the final resting place of Dorothy Parker, one of America's great women of letters. A brilliant writer and an alcoholic, she was the only regular woman member of the historic Algonquin Roundtable which met regularly at the Manhattan hotel of that name on Forty-Fourth Street to exchange barbs, critiques, and witty conversation about the nature of humankind.

Oprah, who was pregnant the year Parker died, would have related to her terrible experiences with men when she wrote, "It serves me right for putting all my eggs in one bastard." She, like Oprah, would consider suicide over an unhappy love affair but would also decide against it. When Parker died, she was cremated, but then no one knew where to bury her. So the urn containing her ashes remained in a file-cabinet drawer of her attorney's office for many years. She was finally buried in the cemetery of the National Association for the Advancement of Colored People (NAACP) in Baltimore. Her self-chosen epitaph—EXCUSE MY DUST.

Also affiliated with the NAACP in Baltimore was the late black Supreme Court justice Thurgood Marshall, who attended Lincoln University in Baltimore and graduated first in his law class from Howard University in nearby Washington, D.C. He became the chief lawyer for the NAACP in 1940, arguing and winning twenty-nine of thirty-two civil rights cases brought before the Supreme Court by the NAACP. Marshall's most famous case was *Brown vs. Board of Education of Topeka, Kansas*, which ended segregation in the public schools in 1954, the year Oprah was born. When Marshall was appointed to the Supreme Court by President Lyndon Johnson in 1967, Oprah was thirteen and attending Nicolet High School, which had been desegregated, along with thousands of other schools, as a result of Marshall's victory in *Brown*.

Baltimore is a lively city, with arts and theater groups and an array of ethnic restaurants unmatched outside of San Francisco and New York. Anchored by the classic Little Italy and Fells Point districts on the north and the Orioles' beautiful baseball stadium, Camden Yards, on the south, the once-decrepit Inner Harbor was completely rejuvenated when Oprah arrived in 1976. The Inner Harbor became a major tourist attraction of shops and restaurants, the Morris Mechanic theater, the Baltimore Symphony and the Baltimore Opera, the original Revolutionary War man-o-war and oldest U.S. warship afloat, the USF *Constellation*. Chesapeake Bay is the largest estuary in the world, which makes Baltimore distinctive for its seafood, including its traditional crab cakes.

The city is also home to the world-famous Johns Hopkins University, with one of the finest medical schools anywhere, and historic Fort McHenry, whose defense in 1814 inspired Francis Scott Key to write "The Star-Spangled Banner."

In her three years at WTVF-TV in Nashville under Chris Clark, who was both anchorman and news director, Oprah moved from weekend news coanchor to weeknight coanchor, which is covering a lot of ground for a young woman. Clark was always impressed by how Oprah came across as genuine and warm, a talent hard to find in a television reporter. Now, in early 1976, she was approached by WJZ-TV in Baltimore about being a coanchor on an expanded evening news show there. The job appealed to her because it took her out of town and on her own, without her father, Vernon, and stepmother, Zelma, chaperoning her. It was step up in her career. To WJZ-TV, Oprah was appealing because of a dramatic change in the nature of television news.

In the 1960s, the top executives in television made a discovery that surprised them: News can be profitable. Before then, they put on a news segment every day because the Federal Communications Commission (FCC) required it as proof that they were using the public airwaves to serve the general population.

When the networks realized that news shows could make a profit and were cheaper to produce than entertainment programs, they expanded their news coverage. Television technology contributed to expansion of the news through the development of videotape, which made it possible to shoot a story, rush it to the studio, and show it immediately instead of waiting for two hours to develop film. More immediate and dramatic footage made for more exciting newscasts, which attracted bigger audiences.

Local news was expanding from a half hour to an hour around the country, and Baltimore followed that pattern. Since producers didn't think one anchorperson could carry an entire hour, they introduced a coanchor who was usually of a different gender and ethnic background. This approach satisfied the same FCC pressure to desegregate that had helped Oprah obtain her first job in TV at WTVF-TV in Nashville. It also broadened the appeal of television, so that these programs reached a wider audience.

WJZ-TV, a Westinghouse-owned ABC affiliate, had a very popular news anchor for its half-hour evening news, but the station manager thought they needed another anchorperson besides Jerry Turner when they expanded the news to a full hour. The idea of a black anchor made sense in a city with a predominantly African-American population. Moreover, the idea of hiring a woman for this assignment became increasingly popular, since ABC hired Barbara Walters to coanchor the evening news for the unprecedented salary of $5 million for five years. Because she was popular in Nashville coanchoring with Harry Chapman, a white man, with an audience somewhat like that in Baltimore, Oprah seemed like a natural for WJZ-TV, and, again, being both female and black, she was a two-for-one hire.

Not everybody at WJZ agreed with the news director, Gary Elion, that Oprah was a good choice. Some thought the coanchor spot should be given to Al Sanders, who was the station's star number-two man and had the highest-rated Sunday news show in Baltimore. Some asked, why bring a black woman no one knew and who, in turn, knew nothing about Baltimore? Nevertheless, Oprah was the best black woman Gary Elion could find and represented the gender-ethnic mix the station wanted.

She convinced her parents that it was the right thing for her career, but inside her head and heart, she felt it was the right thing to do for her life, too. It was time she got out on her own and didn't have curfews and dating restrictions.

The break with her parents was accompanied by another emotional separation from Bill "Bubba" Taylor, whom she loved so much. "We really did care for each other," Oprah recalled. "We shared a deep love. A love I will never forget." To comfort himself and her family, Bubba helped her pack and drove with her in her car to Baltimore in June 1976. There was a tearful good-bye at Baltimore's Friendship Airport, off the Washington-Baltimore Parkway.

Symbolic of her new freedom, twenty-two-year-old Oprah went to a staff WJZ-TV party on the very first day she hit town and kept going until dawn to prove she had become a grown-up. But Oprah faced a lot of problems that just being a grown-up and staying out late wouldn't solve.

A big promotion campaign trumpeted Oprah's arrival. "What's an Oprah?" demanded the billboards around the city. Oprah hated the slogan. It sounded too precious, and she thought it would turn a lot of people off even before they saw and heard her on the air. "It was *calculated* on their part," she said. "I think it hindered me. It's best if you get to the city first, if people like you on your own merits, by word of mouth."

The station had trouble coordinating the equipment, staff, and talent necessary to expand its news to a full hour, but finally, on August 16, 1976, WJZ-TV debuted the show, starring a cool, relaxed Jerry Turner and a somewhat stiff Oprah. Baltimore soon found the answer to "What's an Oprah?" on the six o'clock news. Oprah was a black woman newscaster who quickly became an embarrassment to her news colleagues, who had been schooled in the nonpartisan tradition of Edward R. Morrow. That tradition meant unemotional reporting and telling what happened to whom, when, and where but did not include the reporter's involving him- or herself in the story. Oprah couldn't report the murders, rapes, and mayhem without compassion. Her feelings for the victims of disasters and crime came across television clearly, and she was moved by tragic stories. She soon transformed from a budding new star to a problem for WJZ-TV.

A classic example of the conflict between Oprah's emotional reaction to people's stories was the account of a fatal house fire. Oprah arrived at the scene of this disastrous house fire, and what she discovered was too grotesque to report. So she called in to the station and explained that they really shouldn't do the story and if they wanted it done, she couldn't do it. She was surprised when the news desk at the station told her it was a great story and that she should cover it and come back with the details on film. Determined to do her job, Oprah went back to talk to the woman who owned the house and who had survived the fire that burned it to the ground. The poor woman was traumatized with grief; all *seven* of her children had died in the fire.

Oprah returned to the station, protesting that the film was too terrible to air, but her superiors broadcast the tape with commentary from Oprah, who apologized to her audience afterward on air for her inability to handle the tragedy dispassionately. The apology struck many of her colleagues as unprofessional, and they told her so.

She recalled: "It was not good for a news reporter to be out covering a fire and crying with a woman who has lost her home.... It was very hard for me to all of a sudden become 'Ms. Broadcast Journalist' and not feel things. How do you *not* worry about a woman who has lost all seven children and everything she's owned in a fire? How do you not cry about that?"

In addition, Oprah was not as well trained technically as others who worked at WJZ-TV. A more relaxed atmosphere prevailed at the Nashville news operation under Chris Clark. At WJZ-TV, Oprah's coworkers discovered, to their surprise, that she didn't read the news copy as it was written. Back in Nashville she would see what was on the TelePrompTer and then ad-lib in her own style. Chris Clark said, "If she was reading a sentence and it was just instinctively better to use different words, she would use them. It wasn't planned that way. She made them sound more conversational. It would sound great." Nashville loved it, but Baltimore did not.

While Oprah had empathy with most people, she didn't feel the same way about her coanchor on the WJZ-TV news, Jerry Turner, and that feeling became obvious on the air. Moreover, Turner didn't like working with Oprah. Beyond that, Oprah was having trouble with pronunciation—she goofed on "Canada" three times in one newscast. It soon became clear that Oprah was a performer and not a reporter.

On April Fools' Day, 1977, nine months after she went on the air in Baltimore, news director Gary Elion pulled her off the news anchor's desk, and Al Sanders took her place. She later told the *Baltimore News American* that she shouldn't have been assigned immediately to appear with the star of local TV news, Jerry Turner. She needed a chance to grow and become seasoned in the job.

"I was twenty-two years old," she recalled. "I had no business anchoring the news in a major market. Sitting down with the god of local anchormen intimidated me."

A lot of knowing heads nodded that her failure was inevitable; after all, she was a chubby black female trying to crack into a world dominated by older, svelte white males.

So, having hired Oprah to come to the big city to be Oprah, the management at WJZ-TV realized they had made a mistake; Oprah wasn't turning out as they hoped. Gary Elion had left WJZ-TV, and the new management decided to make Oprah into somebody else who would succeed. She told Mike Wallace of *60*

Minutes, when he interviewed her years later, that the assistant news director told her that her eyes were too wide apart, her nose was too flat and broad, her chin was too big, and her hair was too thick and a complete mess. It made Oprah wonder what they had seen in her in the first place.

The station sent her to a famous dressmaker to change the way she dressed, and then she went to what she called a "chichi, pooh-pooh" French beauty salon in New York City for the complete makeover. The makeover was certainly as dramatic as anyone could have imagined, and Oprah endured a cosmetic heaven transformed into hell.

They did something to her hair that made her scalp feel as if it were on fire. A week later, she looked like a female Montel Williams—black and bald as an eight ball.

"I had a French perm, and it all fell out," she said. "Every little strand. I was left with three little squiggles in the front."

It is hard to envision a more humiliating thing happening to a woman whose career depended on how she looked on television. Worse, nobody could locate a wig big enough to fit Oprah's head. "There's no wig made to fit my head," she recalled. "I had to walk around wearing scarves. All my self-esteem was gone. My whole self-image. I cried constantly."

Having messed up her looks, the station management then sent her to a voice coach to complete the job of changing the Oprah who had so enchanted them when she was in Nashville. The voice coach told her that her problem was *not* her voice. The voice coach said the problem was psychological. *Oprah was too nice for television!* The voice teacher lectured her like a football coach with a team that was two touchdowns behind at halftime. Stop being nice! Be tough. Be demanding. *Make* people do what you want them to do, the coach told her. Unfortunately, that advice didn't fit Oprah any better than those wigs. Oprah was nice, polite, and caring. That's the way her grandmother, Hattie Mae, and her parents, Vernon and Zelma, had raised her.

Even today Oprah is a woman who sings when she is walking around the TV studio. She hugs people joyously at the slightest provocation. She bubbles. She fizzes. She emits vibrations of energy and happiness. Oprah went back to the station even more depressed than when she left.

The WJZ-TV approach differed from how Chris Clark at WTVF-TV had handled her. "You had to let Oprah be Oprah," he said. "I don't think we made the first suggestion as to how she should wear her hair or what she should dress in. We just let Oprah do her thing. That's the only way it ever really works out. You can't change people. In television what you see is what you get. We saw that with Oprah."

Oprah's hair gradually grew back, but not her ego and self-esteem. She knew that the bosses thought of her as a total loser and were sorry they couldn't get her out of the station—she had a six-year contract. They had to find some way to make use of her. It is amazing that Oprah could function at all with all her handicaps—disliked by station management, low personal self-esteem, being totally bald, and ousted from the prestigious coanchor news spot at night.

Some people came to her side and tried to bolster her crumbling ego. One reporter, Lloyd Kramer, would not only help keep her spirits up but wedged in a little romance. "Lloyd was just the best," Oprah remembers. "That man loved me even when I was bald! He was wonderful. He stuck with me through the whole demoralizing experience. That man was the most fun romance I ever had."

Things began to change with the arrival of Bill Carter, the new station manager at WJZ-TV, in the spring of 1977. He quickly made two decisions about Oprah. First, Carter decided to try a local morning talk-interview show, focused on Baltimore people, opposite Donahue, who was on a competing station, and second, Oprah would become a cohost with Richard Sher, another on-air talent. Sher had experience on both sides of the camera and, as a native of Baltimore, knew the town. It took time to implement these decisions, but two years after she came to Baltimore, Oprah was back on the air full-time with Richard Sher and a new show: *People Are Talking*.

Realistically, the show faced tough competition from Donahue, even though the program had a good lead-in show ahead of it, *Good Morning America*. Donahue then enjoyed the highest ratings of any TV talk show on the air in the country. Some people at WJZ-TV privately thought *People Are Talking* was doomed to fail, but something happened. The cohosts clicked, and Oprah blossomed because the show's format allowed her to freewheel with guests and the studio audience. There was a synergy and spontaneity between her and her cohost that made for the best of live television.

"I said to myself, This is what I should be doing," she recalled. "It's like breathing." It certainly was a different on-camera relationship than Oprah had experienced with Jerry Turner when she first started at the station.

The one major difference between Oprah and Richard Sher related to how they listened to their guests. Commonly, broadcast interviewers ask questions and do not listen to the answers; They are either distracted by something else or thinking about the next question. Richard interviewed that way, but Oprah listened closely to the guest and used the previous answer to delve deeper into the topic. That is her style to this day, and it works very well, for she communicates to the audience and the guest that she cares about what is going on in their lives. What the executives of WJZ-TV listened to was that Oprah and Richard were beating Donahue in Baltimore. Their little local morning show outrated the biggest name in daytime talk television!

Sherry Burns, the producer of the show, knew from the start that Oprah was a natural for this format: "She's the universal woman. She gets right past the black thing. She's a totally approachable, real, warm person."

Sherry quickly learned that keeping Oprah unscripted would be the key to making her a smash. Left to do whatever came into her mind at that instant—along with her uncanny talent for asking the questions viewers wanted answered—Oprah could be golden. Debra DiMaio, an assistant producer on the show, said she never saw anyone work so hard. "Her stamina was boggling."

In her personal life, Oprah ran into man trouble again: Her boyfriend, Lloyd Kramer, moved to NBC in New York. Oprah fought off the disappointment and loneliness with a knife and fork. This need to overeat would continue as the enigma of

Oprah's life—the one thing she couldn't figure out and the one thing she couldn't handle herself for a long time. She just wanted love and acceptance and got part of that from her work, but she also needed it in her private life. This yearning intuitively communicated with the millions of women in her audience from those first days in Baltimore to her success in Chicago. It is a bond between her and her viewers.

Sherry Burns summarized how Oprah's special energy connected to her audience in Baltimore. "She is a wonderful, wonderful person. Who she is on camera is exactly what she is off camera. That is one of her main charms. She was and is *the* communicator." Oprah's electric personality became the talk of Baltimore, and the show, *People Are Talking*, had people talking about her and her guests every day.

After Lloyd Kramer moved on to New York, Oprah became drawn to another man whom her friends had warned her was a disaster she should avoid. She has continued to keep his identity secret while talking freely about the relationship.

"I'd had a relationship with a man for four years. I wasn't living with him—I'd never lived with anyone—and I thought I was worthless without him. The more he rejected me, the more I wanted him. I felt depleted, powerless. At the end, I was down on the floor on my knees groveling and pleading with him."

The major problem with this intense love affair arose from her lover's being married, with no plans to divorce his wife. Patricia Lee, in Milwaukee, knew about the romance. "After Oprah went to Baltimore, she met a married man and fell for him," Patricia recalled. "He was her first real love. He wouldn't leave his wife, so Oprah broke off their romance, even though she loved him."

At this nadir in her life Oprah, twenty-seven, decided that living no longer seemed worthwhile, and she considered suicide. In her organized way, on September 8, 1981, she sat down and wrote a careful note to her best friend, Gayle King Bumpas, whom she met while working in the WJZ-TV news-room in 1976. Their friendship continues to the present, and they talk and share everything that happens to them several times every day on the phone.

In her note, she gave Gayle all the details necessary to handle all the arrangements after her death, including instructions to water her plants. As Oprah later told it to *Ms.* magazine's Joan Barthel—who would later become the ghostwriter of Oprah's ill-fated autobiography—she never intended to commit suicide. "I don't think I was really serious about suicide. That suicide note has been much overplayed. I couldn't kill myself. I would be afraid the minute I did it; something really good would happen, and I'd miss it."

She had become so depressed that she did not know what to do, but with time the depression passed. One of Oprah's earlier biographers, Margaret Beaton, wisely wrote, "Oprah is not the first person who felt [depressed] over an unhappy love affair. She says that she was never serious about suicide. For one thing, she says, she would have been too curious to see what would happen tomorrow. Optimists don't commit suicide and apparently neither do curious people. Oprah is both."

The experience with this rejected love affair tempered Oprah's determination. "I had given this man the power over my life. And I will never, never—as long as I'm black—I will never give up my power to another person."

She wondered why she seemed to become involved in abusive relationships. There had been Bill, Lloyd, and now this married man. Moreover, she realized that her weight and her relationships were related. When she wanted to please a man, she slimmed down, and when she was robbed of the emotional and sexual gratification, she sought out oral fulfillment through food.

She said, "The reason I gained all that weight in the first place and the reason I had such a sorry history of abusive relationships with men was I just needed approval so much. I needed everyone to like me, because I didn't like myself much. So I'd wind up getting involved with these cruel, self-absorbed guys who'd tell me how selfish I was, and I'd say, 'Oh, thank you, you're so right,' and be grateful to them. Because I had no sense that I deserved anything else. Which is also why I gained so much weight later on. It was a perfect way of cushioning myself against the world's disapproval."

Meanwhile, she spent those seven years in Baltimore

perfecting her style and learning, always learning, how to do her talk show better and better. In the end, she had literally reinvented herself into a successful talk-show host with poise. *People Are Talking* continued for six years with Oprah. Reruns were aired at night, and Group W, which owned WJZ-TV, syndicated the program to stations in twelve other cities. This attempt to go national did not work because *People Are Talking* was too much of a Baltimore show. After a few months, Group W stopped syndicating the show to those other cities but kept it in Baltimore opposite Donahue, where it consistently beat him in the ratings.

Oprah became aware of the synergy she experienced with a live audience. She needed the energy and emotion that she drew from being with people that recharged her psyche and radiated back to those around her. She also discovered that while she enjoyed working with Richard Sher and knew they made a good team, she really preferred to work alone. What happened to Oprah in her seven years in Baltimore was essentially the same thing that happened to her during the years in Nashville.

All of Vernon and Zelma's strict discipline and the stable home they provided kept Oprah out of trouble and prepared her to take advantage of opportunities. Oprah believed luck happened when preparation and opportunity met. If Oprah had not been determined and ambitious on her own, much of that preparation would have been lost. Oprah kept pushing and developing herself into the best of what she wanted to be: a talk-show host relating to people in front of a TV camera. In Baltimore, she gained the opportunity to work in a big television market and to have a talk show, but none of that would have mattered if she hadn't had the innate talent to excite and bond with her viewers.

She related to the women in her audience in a way that the *Washington Post* would later describe: "She's Fat City. Dr. Ruth, Mr. Rogers and Mrs. Olson all rolled into one. She's big. Really big. If she gets any bigger, she'll have to go to wide-screen TV. She's Oprah Winfrey, zaftig gab queen, soaking up the bubble bathos of life and threatening to send poor, yakked out Phil Donahue into video menopause. She's every woman's friend.

The kind of brassy neighbor who barges into your house and immediately goes to the refrigerator for a little Cheez Whiz and bacon dip. And you love her for it. Because when you tell her your husband is bisexual, she understands. When you tell her you were molested by your doctor or you haven't spoken to your mother in a year, she understands. When you tell her you went on a diet, lost 40 pounds, then gained it back, she really understands."

The difference between the questions she asks guests and the questions other talk-show hosts ask guests mark just how well she does understand. When Donahue interviews a hooker who services twenty men a night, he wants to know how much money she makes. Oprah wants to know if she's sore. When Donahue interviews Dudley Moore, he asks about his next movie. Oprah wants to know how such a short man can make love to all the very tall girlfriends Moore has had. When Donahue interviews a satanist, he wants to know where devil worshipers go when they die. Oprah wants to know if her guest has personally made human sacrifices of small children on the altar of Satan. It was Oprah who asked Sally Field if Burt Reynolds wore his toupee while they made love and Michael Jackson if he was still a virgin. Who else would have the nerve but Oprah?

Oprah is audacious and senses what the people in her audience secretly want to ask of the guest. Then she asks it. Curiously, most guests are so entranced by Oprah that they reveal their innermost secrets. When Oprah had couples onstage, husbands along with both their wives and mistresses, one of the husbands blurted out the news to his wife on national television that his mistress was pregnant. Robin Acardian, a media-wise journalist from the *Los Angeles Times* and an experienced interviewer herself, appeared on *Oprah* and afterward admitted she would have told her anything—anything—she wanted to know, including the intimate details of her sex life. Dick Maurice, with the *Las Vegas Sun*, who also has been interviewed by Oprah, experienced her special quality. "There was this way she had of looking at you and you felt that the only person she was thinking about was you. It was a look in her eyes. You could see a soul there."

Oprah found her niche in the world of television and had the time and space to hone her skills and make mistakes in those seven years in Baltimore. After she felt good about the way *People Are Talking* had developed and her bosses were pleased with her success, at the ratings and at the advertising revenue it brought in, Oprah began to seek ways of varying the show.

It was one thing to have the local preacher or candlestick maker appear, or somebody from Johns Hopkins School of Medicine, but she thought she could edge into a little more controversy and try to make the shows more stimulating—for herself as well as the audience. She found a mother lode of audience interest in personal subjects, intimate subjects, and relationship subjects—love, romance, betrayal, adultery, sex, obesity, divorce, suicide, incest, and family finances. Introducing these subjects made ratings jump higher, and Oprah began to get restless for even greater opportunities in even larger marketplaces.

In some occupations, longevity in one company marks success, but in television moving on to bigger and better marketplaces signifies success. The ultimate TV success consists of a national TV show in prime time, and to get there you have to keep changing jobs upward. As some women put it, they want to marry the prince but know they have to kiss a lot of frogs until they find him. Both the producer of *People Are Talking*, Sherry Burns, and the associate producer, Debra DiMaio, were determined to move up. Sherry went on to WPLG-TV in Miami, and Debra was shopping for positions with stations in New York, Chicago, and Los Angeles. Oprah had thought about it but couldn't decide where she wanted to land next. She didn't like New York, there were too many women and too few men in Washington, and Los Angeles seemed like a Hispanic town to her. Still, she knew she had better move on when she could. She said, "When you have finished growing in one place or time, you know. Your soul tells you when it's time to move on."

Meanwhile, the way talk shows were being presented had shifted nationally in the same fashion that Oprah's show had changed locally. Programs were becoming provocative. Moreover, talk-show hosts were descending from their stages and moving in among the studio audience, which Oprah was doing, too. She continued to search for more interesting guests whose experience and attitudes she could probe for the audience. She was having a wonderful time, getting paid for it, and quietly thinking of bigger television stations in other, bigger cities.

Oprah's local rival, the national *Donahue* show, followed the same pattern. An outgrowth of a small local talk show called *Conversation Piece*, the *Donahue* show had come into existence after Phil Donahue had been in and out of broadcasting several times. In 1963, Phil Donahue was well known around Dayton, Ohio, as the news coanchorman on the CBS affiliate WHIO-TV in addition to a popular interview program he did called *Conversation Piece*. Don Dahlman was the general manager of the competing ABC affiliate, WLWD, one of the stations in the small AVCO group of television stations in Ohio, and he liked what Donahue was doing and wanted to hire him away; but he couldn't do it for four years. Then Dahlman hired George Resing, a new program director. Resing wanted to imitate a program format developed by three Westinghouse Broadcasting Group stations. The program was called *Contact*. Unlike many of the feature programs of the day, such as Dinah Shore and Mike Douglas, *Contact* didn't have a band or a singer or a bunch of guests or a live audience. It just had a host with a guest being interviewed one-on-one and callers phoning in to ask questions. Bare-bones simple and inexpensive. It was a radio talk show on television.

Resing called Donahue, and the two men met. Resing recalls: "It was Good Friday, and we met in a bar, two Irish Catholics who should have been in church." They had lunch, and Resing explained he wanted to do a show like *Contact* and wanted Donahue to be the host as soon as they could work out a time slot for it. Donahue thought that was interesting, but he had just quit WHIO. He had tried to move on to bigger jobs at bigger stations in bigger markets and had been repeatedly turned down. Plus the broadcasting life, with its long and irregular hours, was hurting his marriage. So, although he loved broadcasting, he decided he would take another job that was less stressful and more stable. He signed on with the E. F. McDonald Company selling sales incentive programs to companies. So Donahue declined Resing's offer of a job and went on to selling sales incentives.

A month later, Johnny Gilbert, a WLWD personality who hosted the station's morning news-and-entertainment show, quit to go to New York for a better job. Ironically, that better job did not work out, and Gilbert has ended up today as the off-camera voice on *Jeopardy*. Meanwhile, Resing and Dahlman decided that they needed the *Contact* format, with Donahue as the host to replace Johnny Gilbert. Resing called Donahue again. They had another lunch, but this time Resing had an agreement in his pocket for Donahue to sign if he wanted it. Resing offered Donahue a firm contract, something he had never had before, at $24,000 a year, which was more than he had ever earned. Even so, Donahue was cautious, as a man with a family of five children tends to be, and he didn't accept for several weeks, until he had checked everything and everyone out.

Once he accepted, Resing and Donahue met in Donahue's basement. On a blackboard they worked out the programs for the first six weeks. They realized the programs had to focus on topics women liked because they were the audience, but they didn't have in mind cooking tips and how to put on mascara. Donahue went on the air on November 6, 1967, from 10:30 to 11:30 in the morning, and started out with serious topics that stunned the first few audiences that had obtained tickets months in advance for the Johnny Gilbert show and were now sitting in a studio listening to Madalyn Murray O'Hair preach atheism or, on subsequent shows, a panel of men talking about what they liked in women, an undertaker, a gynecologist, and on the fifth day, something that almost shut down the Dayton telephone system.

Donahue brought an anatomically correct male doll into the studio, undressed it, and held it up for all to see in the studio and at home. Then he asked the viewers at home to call in and register their opinions. Minutes later, the president of Ohio Bell was on the phone to General Manager Don Dahlman, screaming that calls to the *Donahue* show had swamped the phone system. He demanded that the telephone poll be suspended immediately or Ohio Bell would have to cut off WLWD's lines to allow emergency calls to get through to the police and fire departments. The public-opinion power of Donahue's kind of talk show had been established in the first week he was on the air.

The ratings for November certified Donahue as a giant hit, with a 15-point rating and 50 percent share, meaning that half of all the television sets on in Dayton at that time period were tuned to him. The closest competition was the very popular game show *Concentration*, with a 7-point rating and a 23 percent share.

Six weeks into the show, Donahue did something that would later be regarded as a talk-show milestone: He got out of his interviewer's chair and took his microphone into the studio audience to involve the people there actively in the program. It had an electric effect on the audience in the studio, on the viewers at home, and on Donahue himself, because it energized him even more.

At first, the studio audience didn't quite know what to do, but after a few days, people in the audience began to feed questions to Donahue during the commercial breaks to ask the guest. Finally, weeks later, Donahue had on the striking Swedish model Gunilla Knudsen, who did television commercials and was now touting her book on Swedish exercise. During a commercial one of the women in the audience wanted to know why Knudsen never appeared in her television commercials with her hair in braids. Knudsen said she had never learned how to do braids, and the woman offered to show her how. Donahue picked up on the opportunity and, as the show resumed, had the woman come up onstage and teach Knudsen how to braid her hair. From that point on, Donahue involved the audience in the topics and with the guests. The show's popularity grew, and it began being carried on other AVCO group stations in Ohio.

That was all happening in 1967, when Oprah was still living with her mother in Milwaukee, and in 1969, after Oprah had moved to Nashville to spend the rest of her teen years with her father and stepmother. The *Donahue* show prospered, went into syndication, and was seen in thirty-eight cities, but then it stopped growing and had to go to a bigger city, where it could attract more important guests. Donahue said his goal had always been to live in a city with two airports, and in 1974, while Oprah was still at WTVF-TV in Nashville, AVCO found a Chicago station with which it could make a mutually satisfactory deal for the *Donahue* show. Donahue moved to Chicago's biggest independent station, WGN-TV, and the show's syndication began to grow again.

Oprah followed this same traditional pattern: starting at WVOL radio, then to WTVF-TV and WJZ-TV in Baltimore. After seven years, the time to move once more had arrived.

CHAPTER

5

Birth of Talk and Why We Love It

Oprah, Donahue, and their colleagues on radio and television talk shows have an astonishing impact on our lives, which helps to put talk shows in the context of our culture and of broadcasting during the last seventy-five years of its existence. Where did talk radio and talk television come from, and why do we love it so much?

Just as many of today's talk-show hosts on radio and TV started out being something else, so did talk shows start out as an amalgam of celebrity promotion, entertainment, advocacy, news, and information, along with a kind of group therapy.

Of today's most successful talk-show hosts, one is a compulsive gambler and womanizer who almost went to jail; another is a former coupon salesman; one was an advice-to-the lovelorn counselor who was fired eighteen times; another is a candidate for governor of New York who talks to thousands of strangers about having sex with his wife; one is an ex-hippie doctor who dispenses serious medical advice; another is an ex-reporter who changed his name and ethnic background; one is a 270-pound, baby-face adolescent who failed at his five previous jobs and two previous marriages; and there is Oprah, an illegitimate black girl who almost became an unwed welfare mother.

They are part of the cadre of talk-show hosts that have inundated us from Malibu to Manhattan with a rainbow of opinion, prattle, vitriol, controversy, sophomoric philosophy, psychobabble, and caring concern. *Newsweek* published a cover story on talk shows in February 1993 in which it said: "Talk-show democracy changed politics in the presidential race last year, bringing candidates phone-to-phone with voters. Having tasted power, voter-callers want more; having risen through talk, Clinton is being rattled by it. But, it also raises the specter of government by feverish plebiscite—an entertaining, manipulable and trivializing process that could eat away at the essence of representative democracy. It's probably inevitable."

It used to be Hedda, Louella, Walter, and *Confidential* magazine. Now it's Oprah, Donahue, Sally Jessy, Larry, Rush, Howard, Ted, Geraldo, Montel, *Newsweek*, and *Time*. What used to be whispered behind closed doors has become serious news on America's talk circuit. Today's talk was spawned on radio and moved to television and can be heard on 10 percent of the radio stations across the country. In short, the big news about talk radio and television today is that it has become part of mainstream America.

The *Economist* (London) provided an insightful assessment of the impact of talk broadcasting on our quadrennial minuet of selecting a president. "In their different ways, radio [and television] talk show hosts have stolen the media coverage of the election campaign from under the noses of their more conventional colleagues in newspapers and broadcasting. History is on their side. Since 1970, America's population has risen by more than 22%, while newspaper circulation has been just about static. The network television news shows, meanwhile, seem to have lost their point. But, call-in radio and television are in their heyday."

The power of talk radio and television is mind-boggling. Audiences range from 138,000 for David Gold in Dallas to Rush Limbaugh's 15 million and Oprah Winfrey's 16 million viewers daily. Collectively, the talk show hosts are heard by more people than regularly hear the president, the pope, or Mother Teresa. More people listen to the views of talk hosts in one day than heard the messages of the great prophets of every religion in the first one thousand years of recorded history.

Geoffrey Morris, executive editor of *National Review*, believes that if nineteenth-century French historian Alexis de Tocqueville were to visit America today, he would tune in to talk shows, since that's where the lively exchange of ideas he so admired about American life can be found. Morris assessed talk radio like this: "In contrast to most forms of mass media, talk radio [and television] is not contrived. The listener is most of the show. Nor is it any longer a phenomenon attracting mainly kooks, the disfranchised, and the unemployed. Talk radio [and television] today has become attractive to the mainstream citizen espousing mainstream conservative or liberal opinions. Indeed, the cellular phone has enabled high-powered commuters to join in on the fun."

While Oprah has been involved in talk television for most of her career, her roots and the origin of talk television are talk radio, which has been around since after World War II, when Barry Gray sat down in a booth at Chandler's Restaurant in Manhattan with a live microphone and telephone to chat with callers and restaurant guests who dropped by between salad and coffee. And as with any new media outlet, his show soon became the place for celebrities, those with star aspirations, and their press agents, who sought to manipulate the opportunity for free self-promotion.

This was fine with Barry and his sponsors; they understood that the media and celebrities are symbiotic. They thrive only when they can feed on each other. It is a relationship clearly understood by Oprah, Donahue, Rush Limbaugh, and Larry King as they entertain guests who come on their shows to promote an idea, a book, a movie, or a product.

Commercial broadcasting was invented by Lee De Forest, a man of questionable ethics who almost went to jail for fraud when he claimed radio could send and receive voices out of thin air. Proof that De Forest was right appeared on November 2, 1920, in a small shack on top of a six-story building in East Pittsburgh, Pennsylvania, when KDKA first went on the air with the results of the Warren Harding–James Cox race for President. When broadcasting began in the early 1920s, all the pundits were busy predicting its doom, and even Thomas

Edison said in 1922, "The radio craze will die out in time."

Within a year after KDKA's first broadcast, there were several hundred stations on the air, and by 1930 it was a $2 billion industry employing 325,000 people and serving 15 million American homes. Much of early radio was entertainment, and both radio and television today offer somewhat similar fare. Even programs such as *Oprah*, *Donahue*, and their competitors have a strong entertainment component in their format and presentation.

By the 1930s, the most popular radio program featured two men pretending to be black broadcasting from Chicago, just as today the most popular daytime television program features a black woman broadcasting from Chicago. The old radio program was *Sam 'n' Henry* and originated out of WLBH. *Sam 'n' Henry* commanded the largest audience share of any program in the history of broadcasting up to today, with 40 million listeners. It was lured to another station, WMAQ, but the management insisted on a new name for the show. In the elevator on the way up to work the first day, Sam and Henry— two white men playing "Negroes"—decided on the spur of the moment to change their characters' names to Amos 'n' Andy.

Beyond entertainment, early talk-show hosts began promoting self-improvement, self-help though religion or politics, with Billy Sunday and Aimee Semple McPherson airing their services, Jiddu Krishnamurti proclaiming himself the new messiah, and Dr. John Brinkly, over KFKB out of Milford, Kansas, providing faith healing on the radio. "Put your right hand on the radio and repeat after me...." The earliest political figure to capitalize on the new medium was President Franklin D. Roosevelt, whose fireside chats became enormous levers of political power, projecting his personality and ideas directly into every home everywhere instead of having the press or the Congress filter the relationship between the president and the public. Presidents who followed Roosevelt soon followed him into the world of radio and, beginning with Eisenhower, television.

World War I was the newspapers' war. World War II was radio's war, and Vietnam would be television's war. Radio reports from war fronts all over the world, interwoven with rallying speeches by political leaders, propelled the American industrial machine to outproduce and overwhelm the Germans and the Japanese. After World War II, radio returned to being primarily an entertainment medium for mainstream America.

Back in 1884 the first patent relating to television was filed with the German patent office, and by 1928, Englishman John Baird had perfected the technology and invented a way of sending *pictures* over the air, but he had trouble getting anybody interested in the process. He was ejected from the offices of the *Times* (London) by an editor who was convinced that Baird was a certifiable crazy and probably armed with a knife. Even so, technicians began to experiment with Baird's toy, and by the beginning of World War II there were ten thousand experimental TV sets with 2-inch screens around the United States. After the war, TV exploded. In 1949 there were less than 100,000 TV sets in America; two years later, there were 20 *million*. Radio went into an eclipse in the public consciousness, even though everybody still had a radio and still listened. All the great stars of radio moved to television. It became the most persuasive and pervasive medium in the history of the world.

In addition to Barry Gray over station WMCA in the early 1950s there was another talk-show host, Jack Eigan. Eigan started at WHN, New York, as the show business reporter, until one night in 1947, Monte Proser, an owner of the Copacabana, complained that business was dying. Off the cuff, Eigen suggested he do a radio show from the lounge, and several weeks later, the program began with Milton Berle and Red Buttons as the first guests.

Many couples emerged during this era as forerunners of such morning TV shows as *Today* and *Good Morning America*, with chatty formats to ease us into the day. These shows included Tex McCrary and Jinx Falkenburg, Ed and Pegeen Fitzgerald, Dorothy Kilgallen and Richard Kolmar, Faye Emerson and Skitch Henderson out of New York, and Mike and Buff in Chicago. Mike and Buff were a young radio reporter named Mike Wallace, and Buff Cobb, the actress-daughter of wit Irvin S. Cobb. They wanted to get married, but decided their marriage wouldn't work if he was stuck in Chicago and she was traveling with stage plays.

The couple had heard that Jack Eigan broadcast from the Copacabana, where he interviewed celebrity guests. So they went to New York to spend an evening watching Eigan do his show from a nearby booth. They returned to Chicago and started their own version from the Chez Paree. Their show lasted longer than their marriage.

In Los Angeles, Ben Hunter started a late-night program over KFI called the *Night Owl Show* in April 1949 that took calls from listeners without a tape delay. A tape delay is a device that tape-records the program as the calls come in and then sends it out over the air a few seconds later. To listeners, it sounds as if the program is live, but they are actually hearing something recorded seven to ten seconds earlier.

After one caller phoned Ben and blurted out, "Last night I fucked my neighbor's wife twice," and another caller insisted on repeatedly calling her daughter, "a cute little fart," management wanted a tape delay, but Ben liked the spontaneity of his program and wouldn't let them do it. Oprah's show and other television talk programs are almost always taped to avoid that problem today and to make sure that the host looks and sounds good.

The first television talk show, in 1952, was a combination of talk, news, and celebrity interviews created by a redheaded iconoclast named Pat Weaver. An NBC programming executive who did not fit the staid dark suit–white shirt mold, he made fun of other NBC executives—particularly his boss, General Sarnoff, the president of NBC. Weaver came up with unconventional ideas for the popular new medium of television. Even more famous was Pat's madcap brother, "Doodles Weaver," a zany musician with the Spike Jones band.

Since he was used to a zany brother, Pat was intrigued by a show that started in November 1950 over Philadelphia station WPTZ featuring a former radio disc jockey by the name of Ernie Kovacs. The program ran from 7:00 until 9:00 A.M. weekdays and was called *Three to Get Ready*, during which Kovacs gave some news and some weather, played some music, and did insane routines for which he would later be famous, such as spending several minutes picking his teeth or inter-viewing a flock of sheep.

The program drew high ratings, and Weaver, following the axiom of the late comedian Fred Allen, who said, "Imitation is the sincerest form of television," stole the idea. Pat's idea consisted of an early-morning show called *Rise and Shine*, which was fortunately changed to *Today* before it went on the air, and while the network was willing to try it, Pat had trouble getting *Today* launched. Just days before it was due to begin, the host died and had to be replaced by a broadcast personality from Chicago by the name of Dave Garroway, whose whimsi-cal, academic manner was enhanced by his cohost, J. Fred Muggs, a chimpanzee. Two years after starting the *Today* show, Weaver got NBC to launch a late-night version called *Tonight*, starring Steve Allen. That was in 1954, the same year Oprah Winfrey was born in Kosciusko, Mississippi.

The radio and television talk-show host is just part of the equation; the audience at home is the other part. It is the synergy between the talk jock and the home audience that determines the talk-show host's success in attracting adver-tisers willing to pay for commercials. Prof. Joseph Turow of Purdue and Robert K. Avery of the University of Utah have studied listeners who call in. Turow concluded that most of them phoned in questions because they had a need for inter-personal contact rather than because of a burning fervor over some issue being discussed. In simple terms, they were lonely and needed some human contact. They were literally reaching out and touch-toning somebody.

Professor Avery concluded: "People consider talk [shows] an information source and an outlet for their need to express themselves. The host serves not only as a source of information but as a responsive human being who can confirm or discon-firm a caller's self-concept. It is a medium for interpersonal communication and callers use it as a window on the world." This is true of the audience for the *Oprah Winfrey Show* today.

There are basically two kinds of talk programs: advocacy and therapy. The advocacy talk program is attempting to sell a viewpoint, a religious belief, a political doctrine, an invest-ment, a case of snake oil, or a miracle elixir. The advocacy talk jock is promoting something. In 1992, the big subject was promotion of politics. To illustrate, the *New Yorker* contended that morning talk-show host Don Imus in New York helped sell Bill Clinton to his millions of listeners, and that's why Clinton carried the state in the primaries.

Mike Hoyt wrote in the *Columbia Journalism Review*: "Talk radio is growing, in terms of political influence as well as in listeners, and the big topic on talk radio in 1992 has been politics. Politicians pay attention to talk radio because the people do." While political advocacy—particularly by such talk-show hosts as Rush Limbaugh—took the spotlight in 1992, talk-radio advocacy programs span the range of every issue and interest in America, from financial-investment promotions—many of which turn out to be scams, such as those of Brian Sheen broadcasting out of Boca Raton—to ecology promotion pitches, such as "Good Dirt," with Bill Gilbert and Dave Morine. And, of course, there have been the religious advocates since the beginning of talk radio.

As *Newsweek* observed, "Dial-in democracy is attracting the same forces of manipulation that prey on the other levers of power; interest groups on the right and left have the technology and determination to patch themselves into the national conversation."

The Rush Limbaugh advocacy is currently the hot topic for people interested in the power of talk radio and television. Again, as with Larry King and many other hosts, he is a man with little education who had an unsuccessful personal and professional life until he was plucked from a small Sacramento, California, station and packaged by promoter Ed McLaughlin, who transformed Rush into a celebrity on both radio and television. Through successive firings and failed marriages, the one thing he persisted in was talk radio. It is a love he contracted as a teenager growing up in Cape Girardeau, Missouri, with his conservative lawyer-father and brothers. His mother, Millie, said he didn't start talking until he was two and he hasn't shut up since.

The point about Limbaugh, who has become a cottage industry with a top-rated talk show, two bestselling books, and a $25,000-per-appearance fee, is that none of his past inadequacies or failures amount to a pile of legumes. Even people who regard his politics as pre-Neanderthal find him *entertaining*! Often to their surprise.

His attacks on feminazis, eco-wackos, and the whole litany of left-wing evils, is done in a way that is engaging and amusing. Norman Lear, the ultimate Hollywood liberal, listens to Limbaugh because "in the land of the sitting and reading dead, Limbaugh's got passion." Harry Shearer, with the *Simpsons* show, concluded, "This country runs on personality, not on ideas. I think if Rush were spouting diametrically opposed ideas, he'd be just as popular." Fifteen million Americans agree every day.

The great attraction of the second kind of show, the therapy talk show, such as the *Oprah Winfrey Show*, is that the host is going to save you, make you well, make you happy, make the hurt go away, do things for you that you can't do for yourself. Americans are obsessed with self-improvement, self-help, self-everything. It is a national fixation. No nation in the world has so many improvement courses, videocassettes, audiotapes, consultants, counselors, books, seminars, and regimes.

Longtime television-talk-show host Maury Povich has an explanation for the people who call in asking for help with a personal problem. He says the reason they unburden their most intimate secrets on the air is: "Catharsis. I've had dozens tell me afterward they felt so relieved to unburden themselves." This is why we love talk shows so much.

A central aspect of talk shows is what psychologists call *supportive psychotherapy*. This is a form of group psychotherapy that concentrates on creating communication among people of like emotional and mental conditions and is the essence of talk programs. The objective of this kind of group therapy is to be supportive, reassuring, and reinforcing so as to make each person in the group have a feeling of self-esteem and self-worth.

When depressed people listen to the woes and experiences of others on therapy shows hosted by Oprah, Donahue, Sally Jessy, or Dr. Dean Edell, there are indications that their depression lessens. They hear that they are not alone in their feelings and that there is a solution.

Henry Dreher defines the popularity of such group therapy in contemporary psychology circles: "Group therapy has become a seeming panacea for many of the 1990s problems: alcoholism, drug and sex addictions, workaholism, unemployment, gambling, codependency, and just plain loneliness. Now we can add physical diseases, including cancer and AIDS, to the list of illnesses that may respond to the healing power of group therapy."

Remarkably, researchers are finding evidence that group therapy can help people physically as well as emotionally and can prolong the lives of cancer and AIDS patients and of the elderly. Dr. David Spiegel, Stanford University psychiatrist, has shown in a landmark study that advanced-breast-cancer patients in group therapy survived twice as long as those who were isolated from group contact.

Drs. David Capuzzi, Douglas Gross, and Susan Eileen Friel report: "Individuals today must exist in a society of increasing complexity in which their personal sense of value may be undermined by the hectic, achievement-oriented pace of our modern culture. Withdrawal, isolation, and loneliness may be their response and may lead to depression and loss of self-esteem. Professional research indicates that group contact can have a counteracting positive effect by increasing personal interactions and decreasing loneliness and withdrawal."

Loneliness is more widespread than many of us admit. It is the most pervasive secret emotion a lot of us harbor. We are too often, as Emerson observed, living lives of quiet desperation. Listening to talk radio and television is for numbers of people one of the best, least threatening ways of connecting with other humans in the world.

Fearful of rejection and failure, we move through the world seeking connection and sustenance from others. Dr. James L. Spira calls it supportive-expressive therapy, which is the unique, interactive style of groups in which sharing support and expression of the most private emotions—both painful and positive—takes place. The essence of broadcast-talk group therapy is that we need reassurance that we are not alone, not crazy, not the only ones who feel, fear, and fret.

Barbara Harrison, who did a milestone interview of Oprah

for the *New York Times* in 1989, assessed the role of the talk show in America today for *Mademoiselle* and concluded that people watch and listen to learn how others live, to feel superior, and to be a part of society. "Talk shows," she said, "have taken the place of exorcisms and public hangings in 1990s society."

That is how the talk show evolved in broadcasting. It is this societal and cultural context that allows and explains in part why so many people love the *Oprah Winfrey Show*.

Alive and Hot in Chicago

CHAPTER

6

Definitely Alive in Chicago

Debra DiMaio helped produce *People Are Talking* and admired Oprah for her on-air poise and skill as well as for the hard work she did off the air. As Debra looked for another station in a bigger market with more stature and more money, she narrowed her search to a position producing *A.M. Chicago* at WLS-TV in Chicago. TV people create videotapes of their work as their form of resumé, and Debra sent her demonstration tape of *People Are Talking* to illustrate her talent as a producer. It worked, and she was hired to start in January 1984.

A.M. Chicago was the outgrowth of another trend in the evolving world of television programming. Television programmers try to design shows that appeal to different audiences throughout the day. Always searching for new ways to attract and hold new audiences, they keep fiddling with the matrix of programs. In 1954 television programming became national with the completion of the first transcontinental coaxial cable, which allowed stations across the country to receive and air the same program on the same day. Before then, tapes were made of programs in New York and Los Angeles and flown around the country for delayed showing. As we

have seen, NBC employed one of the most imaginative programming executives in the country, Pat Weaver, who sired
both the *Today* and *Tonight* shows. He would later be better
known for having sired the popular movie actress Sigourney
Weaver.

ABC-TV started a bicoastal show to compete with *Today*
called *A.M. America* in 1974. It had a West Coast host, Ralph
Story, and an East Coast host who moved to New York from
WLS-TV in Chicago, Bob Kennedy. To report the news segments on *A.M. America* they had a Canadian newscaster who
had immigrated to New York, Peter Jennings. The plan called
for local ABC stations to capitalize on the guests and programming coming from *A.M. America* by following the national
program with a local version called *A.M. New York, A.M. Los
Angeles, A.M. Chicago*, and so on. The *A.M. America* show in
Chicago replaced an early-morning talk show on WLS-TV
called *Kennedy and Company*, hosted by Bob Kennedy. Trag-
ically, Kennedy never did get to host *A.M. America* from New
York. He found out he had terminal cancer and left the show
before it premiered on November 3, 1975, and was replaced at
the last minute by Bill Beutel.

At WLS-TV, a likable emcee named Steve Edwards hosted
A.M. Chicago, with *A.M. America* as a lead-in, but did only fair
in the ratings. Then *A.M. America* was canceled before it was a
year old. The switching back and forth between East and West
coasts confused viewers, and they tuned out. Still, *A.M.
Chicago* was kept on the air, and when Edwards decided to
leave after three years to search for greater success in Hollywood, he was replaced by Robb Weller. Soon after, in 1980, a
competing local station, WGN-TV, brought in Donahue, and
that meant a ratings disaster for *A.M. Chicago*.

Debra DiMaio had signed on to produce the third-ranking
local morning show in Chicago. To make matters worse, Robb
Weller suddenly quit to go to New York. Debra thought, Great.
Here I've just walked away from a successful TV talk show in
Baltimore to produce a third-rate one that now doesn't have a
permanent host! Debra immediately thought of Oprah and
suggested her to Dennis Swanson.

Swanson had just arrived at WLS-TV in 1983 to run the

station from the ABC network station in Los Angeles, KABC-TV, and in his first week had his number-one news anchor, Fahey Flynn, drop dead and the host of his morning show quit. Desperately needing someone, Swanson looked at the audition tape Debra had of the WJZ show *People Are Talking*.

"I didn't much care about the man," he recalled, "but that young woman was sensational. I brought in all my program people, and they agreed. So I called her. When you've looked at as many audition tapes as I have, hers just jumped out of the stack."

Swanson and DiMaio arranged for Oprah to fly to Chicago over Labor Day weekend. Meanwhile, Swanson checked the ratings of shows in Baltimore and found that the show Oprah cohosted was beating Donahue in that market regularly. Swanson thought that if Oprah could best Donahue in Baltimore, maybe she could do the same thing in Chicago.

Swanson's call bothered Oprah in a way. She wanted to leave Baltimore for personal and professional reasons. Personally, she needed to get out of the town, away from her married lover. Professionally, her WJZ-TV contact expired at the end of 1983, and she knew she should move on, but she wasn't sure where. In the end, only two people favored her going to Chicago if she could get the job: Debra DiMaio, who knew she would do well and who needed somebody for the show she was producing, and her closest friend, Gayle King Bumpas, who was enthusiastic about her making the move and also had faith that she would succeed.

"Everybody, with the exception of my best friend, told me it wouldn't work," Oprah recalled. "They said I was black, female, and overweight. They said Chicago is a racist city and the talk-show formula was on its way out."

Filled with apprehension and self-doubt, she flew to Chicago for an audition and interview. Oprah recalled: "I'll tell you this, my first day in Chicago, September fourth, 1983, I set foot in this city, and just walking down the street, it was like roots, like the motherland. I knew I belonged here."

By this time *A.M. Chicago* had a string of guest hosts because Weller had left for New York, and Oprah watched one of the shows before going to the station for her audition and interview. "I thought, Listen! Not good! Too frivolous!" And she knew what the show needed. It needed her as well as subjects that riveted people to the set.

On Saturday of Labor Day weekend, 1983, Oprah did a mock *A.M. Chicago* show as a way of auditioning for the job as host. Swanson's reaction told it all: "Sitting in my office, watching this audition, I said, Holy smokes. This is something. I had looked at tapes for years, but never had I seen anything like Oprah. She is a unique personality. So up. So effervescent. So television. So spontaneous and unrehearsed. She was not like anyone else on the tube."

In the meeting with Dennis Swanson that followed her audition, Oprah raised the issue that she was black in a racist town. How would that fact affect her success? Swanson refused to discuss the subject. "I don't care what color you are. You can be green. All we want to do is win. I am in the business of winning, and I want you to go for it. I'm only worried about one thing."

"I'll lose weight," Oprah responded, assuming that's what he meant.

"No," Swanson replied. "Stay as you are. I'm only worried how you'll handle being famous."

"You really think it will go that well?"

"I would bet on it."

That settled it. Swanson wanted her, and Oprah, now twenty-nine, wanted the job. She signed a four-year deal with WLS-TV for $200,000 a year. Debra was delighted, particularly because of the nerve it took for Swanson to hire Oprah. She said, "It was a bold move to hire a black female to host a talk show in a city so racially polarized."

DiMaio had helped herself by getting a winning show host; Oprah, by elevating her career to a new plateau. Oprah said that she had never been more frightened than when she became the host of *A.M. Chicago* in that very cold January, 1984.

Cities are created for various reasons. Sometimes they are political cities whose principal function is housing the government, such as Albany, New York, or Washington, D.C. Or they may become cities created to tap a natural resource, such as minerals or agriculture. One of the most common reasons for creating a city is to have it serve as a transportation hub, such as a great seaport or railhead, and that was the original reason for Chicago. From the eighteenth century on it had been the main portage point linking the Great Lakes with the Mississippi River and a center of operations for traders when the settlement of Fort Dearborn was founded in 1803. In the middle of the 1800s, it became the rail-hub connection between the East Coast and points west. People joked that a hog in a freight train could go across country nonstop but people going from New York to San Francisco had to change trains in Chicago. What was true of rail passengers yesterday is true of airline passengers today, with millions of travelers changing planes in the major airline hub of the country, O'Hare Airport.

This central location and transportation hub made it a natural place to concentrate economic conversion plants where raw materials would be transformed into manufactured goods. For example, it was a focal point for livestock from all over the Midwest to be processed into prepared meats. With the founding of Gary, Indiana just to the east of Chicago, the area became a major steel-manufacturing center, combining iron ore from the Mesaba Range along the Great Lakes to the north, limestone from Indiana, and coal from West Virginia to the south. This was all part of the heavily industrialized, blue-collar nature of the greater Chicago area which the locals refer to as Chicagoland.

Much of the city was destroyed by the famous Chicago Fire on October 8–9, 1871 but was rebuilt largely with stone buildings. At the end of the nineteenth century a surge of European immigrants came to the city, and the labor movement worked hard to organize them into unions, which led to serious violence in the Haymarket Riot (1886) and the Pullman Strike (1894). Unions ultimately prevailed, and a strong Democratic political machine based on old ward politics soon controlled the city. The most notable leader in recent times was the late mayor Richard Daley, who oversaw Chicago and northern Illinois with the iron hand of a magnanimous tyrant from his election in 1955 until his death in 1976. He was the last of the old-fashioned big-city bosses.

Daley died but the system of local political control lived on. When Oprah came to Chicago, it was still a blue-collar, racist, machine-run city. She felt a little better about racism, because after electing its first woman mayor, Jane Byrne, to succeed the late Richard Daley, Chicago had elected its first black mayor, Harold Washington, in April 1983, five months before Oprah signed her new contract with WLS-TV. A black mayor made Oprah believe that racial conditions were somewhat improved in the Windy City, an issue that mattered to her because of her involvement with her race and the proud tradition of her heritage.

Back in Baltimore there were a lot of people who thought she wouldn't succeed in Chicago, but one who had confidence in her was Bill Carter, her old station manager at Baltimore's WJZ-TV. He tried to keep her there with a salary increase, but he couldn't match the $200,000 WLS-TV had offered and had to let her go with his blessing.

"When she went to Chicago, I did think she had a chance to succeed," he said, "but a lot of people didn't. There was an undercurrent of feeling here that this woman was not all that special. . . . Oprah is a very black looking black woman. Personally, I think she's very attractive, but it was that element. I knew that was baloney, because I had seen so many other people connecting with her."

The move to Chicago was also Oprah's final emancipation as an adult woman. She was now twenty-nine years old, on the verge of turning thirty, free of all family and of her married lover, with a good job in a new town and entirely on her own. She connected with a lawyer of her own, Jeffrey Jacobs, who would advise her on business affairs and negotiate contracts. This was an affiliation that would be very important for both Oprah and Jacobs, who had been a trial lawyer originally and then increasingly moved into counseling business clients. The business relationship between Oprah and Jacobs began in 1984, soon after she decided to move to WLS-TV, and it blossomed into a very fruitful arrangement.

"As her career progressed," Jacobs recalled, "I was handling more and more of her matters. It got to where I was spending sixty or seventy percent of my time working with her, so I shut down my practice and came in-house in 1987."

The move made Oprah feel wonderful, but it was a little scary, too. She had progressively swum into bigger and bigger ponds since her radio adolescence in Tennessee. Now she faced the most popular talk-show host in the business, and even on the local level, the challenge would prove daunting. She said, "Everybody kept telling me that it was going to be impossible to succeed because I was going into Phil Donahue's hometown. So you know, I'd eat and eat. I'd eat out of the nervousness of it all."

During her first Christmas in Chicago she was alone and lonely, but New Year's Eve proved a little better. The station asked her to attend the State Street party held every New Year's in Chicago, and that's how they introduced her to the city. She went on the air on January 2, 1984, and put on twenty pounds in the next six months.

Oprah did well, and that was evident from the first show. She boned up on each guest the day before, read what they had written, understood their point of view, and let herself roll when the camera light flashed on. The woman who escaped being a mortician's wife in Nashville now consorted with Stevie Wonder, Shirley MacLaine, Tom Selleck, Christie Brinkley, Dudley Moore, Candice Bergen, Billy Dee Williams, Paul McCartney, Goldie Hawn, Barbara Walters, and Maya Angelou. These last two guests were the most difficult interviews of her early months in Chicago, for both were her idols, and for once Oprah had trouble talking.

Before she went on the air with her first program, Oprah prepared. She studied the town, and most of all, she read the clippings about previous hosts of *A.M. Chicago*. In the past, Chicago television reviewers assumed that competing programs were losers once Donahue rode into town in 1974. With *A.M. Chicago*, it seemed to Oprah, the format consisted of a mixture of lighthearted talk, some fashion notes, a cooking bit, a little homemaking, and, if possible, a guest personality.

Well, that wouldn't work with Oprah, who saw the audience as the basic white middle-class housewife. Oprah was not a white middle-class housewife and did little housework or little cooking. But she held in common with them "a belief system we all share in. I'm really no different from all of those women who are watching, because I wanted the same things for my life that they want. I want to be happy, a sense of fulfillment, children who love me, respect from my husband."

The concept worked, and Oprah quickly connected to her audience and dazzled the professionals in the studio who had seen performers come and go but nothing like Oprah. Tim Bennett, the program director for the station, said, "She has an incredible entertainment range. She cuts right through the screen."

Chicago television critics echoed the growing admiration for her presence and poise. Jon Anderson wrote in the *Chicago Tribune*: "On and off-screen, her presence is undeniable, despite her short Chicago track record. She is greeted by strangers on the street, recognized in restaurants and once was driven to work by a Chicago policeman when she was late and couldn't get a cab."

Her style reached out and connected with what every woman was thinking because she asked the questions and said the things that they understood. Sometimes Oprah would flip off her high heels in the middle of a show and simply announce, "My feet hurt," and every woman would relate to it. Or say that she hated Calvin Klein jeans commercials because all of his models had such tiny little butts in those ads.

And, of course, the one rejoinder that everyone loves to quote is her classic Oprahism during a serious discussion with a female scientist about penis size and female satisfaction. She blurted out, "If you had your choice, you'd like to have a big one if you could! Right? Bring a big one home to Mama."

When he hired her, Dennis Swanson predicted Oprah would be a success, and now he watched in amazement as his prediction came true. "What a sensation [she] turned out to be! Oprah hit Chicago like a bucket of cold water. It was amazing. There was no gradual build. We went from last in the time period to number one in about four weeks. She just took over the town."

Within twelve weeks, the sixteen-year reign of the king of Chicago talk television, Donahue, was over when he lost in the local ratings to Oprah—265,000 Oprah watchers to 147,230

Donahue watchers. The thirty-year-old Oprah Winfrey had come a long way from slopping pigs on Hattie Mae's farm.

In December 1984, *Newsweek* pronounced Oprah the hottest press star in Chicago, just waiting to be launched onto the national scene. In January 1985, Donahue pulled out of Chicago almost without notice to anyone and moved to New York. People affiliated with Donahue claim he did so because Marlo Thomas, Donahue's wife, was appearing in a Broadway play and the couple wanted to be together. Some thought that Oprah had driven him out of town. Oprah thinks it was Marlo. Another Chicago broadcaster left town for New York in 1985, Dennis Swanson, the man who hired Oprah. The ABC network promoted him to become head of its television station division. Eventually, he would be in charge of ABC Sports and children's programming, and working directly with Oprah again.

The Big Year of 1985

$\mathbf{W}$ithout much promotion, Oprah began broadcasting in Chicago, and what happened in the next six months has become embedded in television history. People began flipping to her channel. Station manager Dennis Swanson said, "There aren't a lot of black people in Chicago media...it was like you could hear TVs clicking on [to Oprah] all over the city." And the ratings for *A.M. Chicago* reflected her exploding audience. Within the first month, Oprah had pulled in the highest ratings *A.M. Chicago* had ever had since it went on the air nine years before.

Swanson's choice of Oprah turned out to be a big success, as did two other programming changes he made in late 1984 that made things look so bright in 1985 for WLS-TV. He redid his evening news show, hiring Floyd Kalber as anchorman and the core of a new on-air news team and format that boosted WLS-TV's evening news to number one in the market. He also made a deal with two hard-driving, ambitious brothers, Roger and Michael King, and their company, King World, to bring in a new, popular syndicated game show, *Wheel of Fortune*. Quickly *Wheel* became number one in its time slot, too, and would feature Pat Sajak, who had worked at WSM-TV in Nashville at the same time as Oprah. As previously noted, the money King World was making around the country from *Wheel* and their other hit, *Jeopardy*, ultimately made it possible for them to cast about for more shows to syndicate.

Audiences related to Oprah because she was one of them and always came up with surprising questions or revelations. She startled everybody on her staff and in her audience by sympathizing with a child-abuse victim and revealing for the first time on the air that she had also been abused as a child. The reaction was electric. Hundreds of phone calls swamped the switchboard from viewers grateful she had the courage to discuss the controversial subject and to share her own experiences.

Seven months from the time she debuted in Chicago, the show expanded to one hour and beat Donahue in the Chicago market regularly. The advertising dollars rolled in. Several years later, *Time* magazine would review the wonder of those first six months in 1984 and what happened in the world of daytime television.

"Few would have bet on Oprah Winfrey's swift rise to host of the most popular talk show on TV. In a field dominated by white males, she is a black woman of ample bulk. As interviewers go, she is no match for, say, Phil Donahue. . . . What she lacks in journalistic toughness, however, she makes up in plainspoken curiosity, robust humor and, above all, empathy. Guests with sad stories to tell are apt to rouse a tear in Oprah's eye. . . . They, in turn, often find themselves revealing things they would not imagine telling anyone, much less a national TV audience. It is the talk show as group-therapy session."

Oprah says she succeeded in Chicago because she did her show solo. "Up until now," she said, "I've always been paired with somebody else. The thing about working with a coanchor or a cohost is that it can be stifling, like a bad marriage. Somebody always has to surrender to the other person. And usually the person doing the surrendering was me. . . . I feel good about where I am right now. I feel I've earned the right to be here."

Before she took over *A.M. Chicago*, the program spent a lot of time interviewing soap-opera actors, and Oprah changed that format to real-life interviews that made soap operas seem mild by comparison. It was riveting television talk about sex, incest, child abuse, self-mutilation of genitalia, fat, hated bosses, how a woman can find a husband, children born of incest, children who kill, or men who pay for sex.

During January 1984 and the early days of *A.M. Chicago* with Oprah, the production staff at WLS-TV tried to script interviews with guests carefully, as other shows did. They gave Oprah questions like "What is your favorite color?" "What is the first thing you do in the morning when you wake up?" "What's in your refrigerator?" With her first guest interview, Tom Selleck, Oprah discarded all those banal queries. She opened by telling Tom he had very unusual eyes, a crystal-blue sea color, and the audience loved it. They didn't care what was in his refrigerator; they fantasized about being in his arms, and Oprah understood that, but the staff didn't. From then on, the staff simply gave Oprah background material on each of her guests for her to study before the show, and Oprah winged it with questions that just popped into her head and seemed natural to her. Her success is partly due to the fact that those questions seem natural to her audience, too.

Oprah had an impact on Chicago. *Chicago* magazine proudly concluded that she made over the way America looked: "The Oprah Winfrey Show has been one of the true astonishments of television. Single-handedly, she and it have revolutionized talk shows and rendered the notion of Midwestern reticence quaint and obsolete. No one else on television has been as open as Oprah. Within months of coming to Chicago she'd told viewers about her troubles with men, [her weight problems] and the terrifying history of her childhood sexual abuse. She told them they could take control of their life energies...[and] she gave them the practical means of doing so."

By the time the Oprah show had been on a year at the beginning of 1985, the operation had Oprah's stamp all over it. She hosted the show and decided who the guests would be, what topics would be discussed, and who would do what and with whom and when. It became her show in more than name alone. This is most unusual in television, and it reveals a special facet of Oprah's personality: her obsession with control.

8

Lucky Color Purple

After the December 1984 story in *Newsweek* proclaiming her a hit came the call from the *Tonight* show with Johnny Carson, inviting her to appear, except it would be on a night that Joan Rivers would be substituting for Carson, but none of that mattered. Being on the premier late-night national TV show gave recognition to her rising status. The appearance was slated for January 29, 1985, and came with a promise that she would be invited back to join Carson himself at a later date. The timing was good, since Oprah had to tape a special edition of *A.M. Chicago* to promote the ABC-TV miniseries based on the Jackie Collins book *Hollywood Wives*. So Oprah and a crew from WLS-TV would fly to Los Angeles at the same time as her *Tonight* appearance, which, coincidentally, marked her thirty-first birthday.

It was her first national television exposure, and Oprah was very agitated and nervous as she arrived at the NBC studios at Alameda and Olive in Burbank. Her appearance meant a lot, and she didn't want anything to go wrong. She feared she might make a mistake or that the razor-tongued Joan Rivers might embarrass her about her weight or that something crazy might happen to humiliate her.

Minutes before her introduction, Oprah slipped into the bathroom and prayed that it would all be all right. A few moments later, standing behind the curtain, she heard Joan Rivers say, "I'm so anxious to meet her. They talk about her as streetwise, brassy, and soulful. Please help me welcome Miss Oprah Winfrey!" And Oprah stepped out onto the stage flashing a big smile. The interview went well between these two energetic, extroverted women and ended with Joan challenging Oprah to a dieting contest—to which Oprah agreed.

To top the glamorous evening of her birthday, she rode in the *Tonight* show limousine to Wolfgang Puck's restaurant, Spago's, on the hillside above the Sunset Strip where Quincy Jones and ten other friends sang Happy Birthday to her. That night marked a very special day for the girl from Mississippi.

One year later, Quincy Jones was in Chicago to testify on behalf of Michael Jackson in a 1984 lawsuit over the authorship of the song "The Girl Is Mine" and hating it. Jones was a four-time Academy Award winner and star maker in the music business, and he grudgingly came to Chicago because it took him away from his work in Los Angeles, where he was engrossed in a very special project. He was coproducing a movie based on Alice Walker's third novel, *The Color Purple*, with Kathleen Kennedy and Frank Marshall and Steven Spielberg as director, with Jones writing the musical score. The Walker novel is about the life of Celie, a black southern woman played by Whoopi Goldberg, and how she was abused and exploited by black men. They were now in the midst of casting the film.

Quincy Jones moved around his hotel room that morning, shaving, showering, and getting dressed, and then the room-service waiter tapped on the door and delivered his toast and coffee. As he sat down to have breakfast, he flipped on the television set and surfed from channel to channel, finally settling on a talk show. The credit line on the screen read "Oprah Winfrey," but that's not what Jones saw as he became transfixed by one character on the program. The name "Sofia" flashed in his brain, not "Oprah." Quincy Jones was the only one who knew it at that moment, but the role of Sofia in the movie version of *The Color Purple* had just been cast. She was the brassy, strong Sofia of the book who is Celie's stepdaughter, and that's what he told Reuben Cannon and Associates. They were doing the casting of the movie in Los Angeles.

Even though Oprah gave five speeches a week around Chicago and was consumed with her show, the book-reading discipline was strongly instilled in her. Back in Baltimore, Oprah read a review of *The Color Purple*, Alice Walker's Pulitzer Prize novel. It stirred her so much that she bought a copy as soon as she could. The novel had such an impact on her that it became her favorite contemporary work of fiction. She bought dozens of copies and gave them away to everyone she knew. Oprah became enraptured with the character of Sofia, a strong woman abused by her insensitive husband and mistreated by prison guards without losing her spirit or dignity.

When the phone rang in Oprah's office a week later, the Reuben Cannon office wanted to know if she would be willing to come to Hollywood to test for the role of Sofia. Oprah wasn't sure she understood correctly. One reason was that the original title of the project was *Moonsong* and not *The Color Purple*. When that brief confusion was sorted out, Oprah was delighted at the prospect of playing a character she loved. In Hollywood, she met Steven Spielberg, who was wearing a Mickey Mouse T-shirt and sneakers; he made sure she understood that other, more experienced actresses were trying out for the role of Sofia. Later, Spielberg would tell friends that her audition for the part just blew him away. Oprah thought it was a good sign, when she auditioned with the actor Willard Pugh, who would play Sofia's husband in the film, that his name in the movie would be Harpo—Oprah spelled backward.

For Spielberg, *The Color Purple* was a breakthrough movie, for it dealt with a serious subject. Spielberg, the wunderkind of Hollywood, seemed to materialize out of nowhere one day, just like some of his movie characters. He was a bewildering prodigy to many because he kept making enormous movies that seemed to explode beyond the screen, engulf audiences, and gorge the box office. He directed movies like *E.T.*, *Jaws*, *Raiders of the Lost Ark*, and *Close Encounters of the Third Kind*, which critics claimed had a comic-book quality about them, reflecting Spielberg's immaturity. They admired, envied, hated, and loved him, but many in Hollywood believed he was incapable of making a "serious" movie, even though four of Spielberg's movies were in the top ten among all-time money-makers. Hollywood would repeatedly deny him an Oscar for directing.

Now he had a movie involving such serious issues as race and gender relations, and he wanted it done in a tasteful and dramatic way to demonstrate that he could direct an important film, although Hollywood wags quietly referred to the movie as *Close Encounters of the Third World*. Spielberg said, "I listened to the criticism. It gets to you."

Thus, the casting was critically important. Finally, Spielberg chose Oprah to do Sofia. When she heard the news, she called it "the single happiest day in my life" and Quincy Jones her most favorite person in the universe. "Quincy is the first person I have unconditionally loved in my whole life," she said. "He walks in the light. If something were to happen to Quincy Jones, I would weep for the rest of my life."

One of the things the casting people immediately told her to do was stop dieting. They didn't want a svelte, slender Sofia.

Oprah's excitement gave way to concern over appearing in Chicago for her show while dividing time between Hollywood and South Carolina for the film.

An important change involving control of her financial future took root in 1986, after Oprah was given the chance to play Sofia in *The Color Purple*, back in 1985. As much as she wanted to do the film, a scheduling problem surfaced imme-diately. She wanted so much to play the Sofia role that she told her attorney–business manager, Jeffrey Jacobs, that she would do the part for nothing if necessary. A logistics problem grew out of the fact that she hosted a successful show in Chicago that she loved and which constituted the main element of her career. To play Sofia, she would have to spend time in Holly-wood and South Carolina, where the film was being shot. She thought she could do it if WLS-TV would just give her a week off, but, in fact, she learned she would have to spend eight weeks shooting in California and in South Carolina, and the Chicago station did not feel it could spare her for two months.

WLS-TV did not wish to jeopardize the hold they had on

Oprah's audience and all the advertising money that it meant to the station, but Dennis Swanson understood that Oprah wanted to grow in her career and that her becoming a movie star might even enhance her show in the long run. Oprah was caught between the present and the future. She needed to keep the show rolling in Chicago because that was the basis of her present career, but she wanted to appear in the movie because it promised great possibilities in the future. Beyond that, appearing in *Purple* meant so much to Oprah emotionally that she had secretly decided that if she couldn't work out a temporary release from the WLS-TV contract, she would quit so she could play Sofia. Both sides recognized that each had a lot at stake, and a compromise was worked out, with Oprah taking off six weeks—it would turn out to be almost twice that long—to film *Purple* while the talk show continued with guest hosts and reruns.

That took care of the short-term problem, but Jeffrey Jacobs wisely saw that this problem would come up again and that the long-term issue involved a matter of control. Whoever has control in business makes the decisions. He told Oprah that as long as her program was controlled by WLS-TV, the station would make the significant decisions. Admittedly, WLS-TV had to use that control with tact so as not to anger its star and destroy the program, but the fact remained that the ultimate control of the show rested on the desk of the man who replaced Dennis Swanson at WLS-TV in 1985, Joe Ahern. To be in charge, Oprah had to gain control of her own program and then rent it to WLS-TV and any other station that might want it. In Jeffrey's view syndication was the path for Oprah to take.

But why would WLS-TV, the ABC-owned-and-operated station in Chicago, agree to give up control of the show for syndication? It might do so if the station became part of the syndication deal and would make a lot more money from the *Oprah* show when it was rented to other stations. At the time, the King brothers, Roger and Michael, who operated as King World syndicators, were successfully syndicating two shows produced by Merv Griffin, *Wheel of Fortune* and *Jeopardy*. They were casting about for another show to add to their stable of offerings.

In September 1985, Stuart Hersch, the chief operating officer of King World, met with Jeffrey Jacobs and worked out a deal to syndicate Oprah. The money question remained unsettled at the beginning because Oprah's compensation would be 24 percent of the gross income from syndication. The exact dollar amount couldn't be settled until the package had been sold. The obvious first step was to change the name of the show from *A.M. Chicago* to *The Oprah Winfrey Show*. WLS-TV agreed to make that change immediately. A deal was struck to spend the next twelve months selling the show with a target date of September 8, 1986, to begin broadcasting nationally. Release of *The Color Purple* in December 1985 helped because of the national publicity it gave Oprah.

On the movie set of *The Color Purple* Oprah discovered the difference between live television and making movies. With television, you usually have to play it the way it happens, while with film you can fluff a line several times and keep reshooting the scene until you get it the way the director wants it. At the same time, you have to remember your lines, your body positions and movements, and most difficult of all, emote on cue regardless of how you actually feel at the moment. Oprah didn't do any of these things letter-perfect, but she kept trying and learning. In one scene, Sofia had to cry, and when Spielberg called for Oprah to do so, she couldn't. She tried pulling hair out of her eyebrows surreptitiously and putting them in her contact lenses to force the tears, but even that didn't work. The crying had to wait until another day.

An exchange of letters tells the story of Sofia and how she meets and marries Harpo, who becomes agitated with her independence and strong will. Another female character, Celie, played by Whoopi Goldberg, advises Harpo to give Sofia a good beating to put her in her place. Betrayed, a battered Sofia confronts Celie: "You told Harpo to beat me! All my life I had to fight. I had to fight my daddy, I had to fight my uncles, I had to fight my brothers. A child ain't safe in a family of mens."

Later in the story, Sofia gives a smart-aleck answer to the white mayor's wife, who wants her to come work as a maid, and the white men of the town set upon her and beat her up. She is then arrested and put in prison, gaining her release years later on the condition that she become the mayor's maid.

At the end, everybody agreed that Oprah's interpretation of the role of Sofia was stunning. That may be because Oprah, the person, believed in the doctrine of self-faith and optimism just as strongly as does Sofia, the character in *The Color Purple*. The idea of self-faith is that no matter how whipped and defeated a person feels, he or she can still recover, still bounce back, still become a winner. Self-faith transforms victims into winners and empowers people to take charge of their lives and their destiny.

Oprah's most important scene takes place at the end of the movie. As Sofia she appears at the family dinner table after her release from prison, finally speaking out against injustice. She only had one line, but when the time came, an impassioned Oprah poured out what she had inside her of Sofia. Oprah says she drew upon the memories in her heart as she waited for three days of shooting to do her last scene.

"Mine was the last angle to be shot," she recalled. "I had been sitting there watching everybody else. I had a lot of time to think about the years Sofia spent in jail and how thousands of men and women, all the people who marched in Selma, were thrown in jail and what those years must have been like. Sofia finally speaking was a victory for all of us and for me."

Realizing that she was ad-libbing, the cast and crew were caught by surprise, but the cameras kept rolling. Everyone became transfixed by Oprah's speech, in which she poured out the centuries of pain of black women in the character of Sofia:

"She represents a legacy of black women and the bridges that I've crossed over to get where I am. She's a combination to me of Sojourner Truth and Harriet Tubman and Fannie Lou Hamer and grandmothers and aunts of mine and other black women who have gone unnamed but who represent a significant part of our history."

It was a magic moment in the film and remained in the final release. When Oprah's college professor, Dr. Jamie Williams, saw the ending, he recalled the fervor with which Oprah had delivered readings from *Jubilee* while she was his student. The intensity of how she remembered her black heritage came blazing through then and in the film.

When the film opened in December 1985, the critics had a variety of reactions. Generally, they viewed it as moving in parts and a bit overblown and uneven in others. Oprah and Margaret Avery were the two actors who were praised, but other roles in the film, as well as script, direction, and focus, all received mixed reviews.

Something totally unexpected surfaced after the film was shown. It had never happened before to Oprah but would now occur again and again. It dismayed her and many other people who knew her. A backlash erupted from black men, many of whom regarded *The Color Purple* as black male bashing and Oprah as the central villain.

The roots of this deep-seated response have been hidden from much of the white community for the last three hundred years. American slavery forced two institutions upon black Americans that are part of their heritage today. The first was the church, which was the only organization that the plantation owners tolerated among their slaves, and so the black church became a universal institution with spiritual and civil authority.

Matriarchy became the second institution. Slave masters would routinely sell off adult male slaves and separate them from their families, but they kept the slave women and their children together so that mothers could care for their children. This automatically created a black slave matriarchy, with the adult woman as the central figure in the family and the adult male expendable and unreliable.

Typically, the government, while trying to help poor black families, did it in such a way as to emasculate black males by refusing to give welfare to families with an able-bodied male present. Thus, in modern-day America the black man constantly tries to prove he is a man of dignity and stature. During the era of civil rights violence, this fact became central to the rhetoric of the Black Muslims and Jesse Jackson and other civil rights leaders.

The Color Purple shows black men mistreating women and

generally acting out the stereotypes black males have struggled to erase. The theme of the movie connected to black women, and that made the backlash even worse. *Washington Post* columnist Courtland Milloy went to see the movie in a theater, prepared to trash it for its male bashing, but he came out into the open air afterward in confusion. He wrote, "By the time Sofia was released from prison and came home all swollen and beaten with that dead eye, I was emotionally drained. Not because of the pain on the screen, but because of that which had been revealed around me." In that dark Washington, D.C., theater he heard scores of sobbing black women who understood and related to the lives of the black women portrayed in that scene.

In Beverly Hills, Willis Edward, an NAACP chapter president, condemned the film for denigrating black men, and when it opened on December 18, 1985, in Los Angeles, black men picketed the theater. In Oprah's home base of Chicago, a thousand black men and women filled the Progressive Community Church to argue and yell at each other; *Ebony* magazine lashed out at the film and Steven Spielberg and, by inference, Oprah; the *Chicago Sun-Times* concluded that it was part of a right-wing plot to bring back slavery; and respected black journalist Earl Caldwell drove a dagger into *Purple* with his personal view; "'The Color Purple' can make you see red. That's especially true if you are a man and you happen to be black. There is not much in the movie you want to see."

The reaction surprised Oprah for one of the few times in her life, and she responded by pointing out that it wasn't a movie about black men but about black women. "I was surprised to see the way people reacted to *The Color Purple*," she said. "I believe people see what they want to see in a work of art. When you see joy and beauty in something, it's because it's part of you. When you see negative anger and fear in something, it's because it is a part of you." Beyond that, she countered her black male critics with "I'm tired of hearing about what it's doing to the black men. Let's talk about the issues of wife abuse, violence against women, sexual abuse of children in the home."

For Hollywood, the dispute benefited the movie because it

boosted the box-office receipts to almost $40 million in the first two months of the film's run and focused the Hollywood community's attention on *Purple* as a controversial movie—which means "important" in Hollywood. For Oprah, who loved the idea of being a movie actress, it also meant that her first major movie role was in a significant drama instead of some marginal film.

The Color Purple also brought Oprah a totally unexpected dividend. With the help of her attorney–business adviser, *The Color Purple* enhanced Oprah's value because it gave her national exposure and boosted her ratings in Chicago. Jeffrey Jacobs began negotiating for more money for Oprah. At the end of the year, WLS-TV decided not to give her seven key staff members a bonus. Oprah dipped into her own pocket and gave each one $10,000!

9

1986—If Oprah Had Been Fine Wine

Oprah's career and her life were about to take off in ways she could have only dreamed about. For 1986, when she became thirty-two, turned out to be a phenomenal year, with enough glory to fill the lifetime of an ordinary person.

In February 1986, *The Color Purple* received eleven Academy Award nominations, with one for Oprah as Best Supporting Actress. Academy Awards night, March 24, was an experience in itself; Oprah had ordered a special dress for the occasion. She had gained some weight, but designer Tony Chase came to the Beverly Wilshire Hotel and fitted the gold-and-ivory-beaded creation to her new figure. He then took it away for some final modifications and delivered it back to Oprah the next day. Just before it was time for Oprah, her boyfriend, Stedman Graham, and friends to leave for the Music Center in downtown Los Angeles, she discovered to her horror that she couldn't get into the dress! Finally, by lying on the floor and with the help of friends she wiggled into the gown. Her friends then helped her up and brought her downstairs to the limousine. Everybody was afraid she would literally split the dress seams if she sat upright, and so she lay on the floor of the limousine for the entire trip.

At the Dorothy Chandler Pavilion she was helped out of the limousine, into her $10,000 fox coat, dyed purple for the occasion, and walked gingerly to her seat. Once in the theater, Oprah was afraid of winning. She was sure the dress would split open as she walked up the steps to the stage to accept the Oscar.

Neither the picture nor Oprah won anything. It was a bittersweet night for Oprah, who felt she had never experienced elation to match that of playing Sofia. She would later confide to Lyn Tornabene of *Woman's Day*, "I could not go through the night pretending that it was okay that 'Color Purple' did not win an Oscar. I was pissed and I was stunned."

Even if the Academy Awards ceremony was not to her liking, she and Stedman did appear at several other awards events during the year, including the Daytime Emmys, the NAACP Image Awards, and the Golden Apple Awards.

It was also a year that opened newer horizons for Oprah, who announced that she wanted to do more movies and still continue with her TV talk show. "I intend to do and have it all," she said. "I want to have a movie career, a television career, a talk-show career. I will continue to be fulfilled doing all of these things, because no one can tell me how to live my life. I believe in my own possibilities, and I feel I can do it all." After what had happened the previous two years, marked by her move to Chicago, no one could argue with her.

Although 1986 began with the disappointment of the Academy Awards, the year was filled with many wonderful days, such as the day after the Academy Awards, when Oprah started shooting her second motion picture in Chicago, *Native Son*, based on the book by Richard Wright about an angry young black man who strikes back at the racism oppressing him by murdering a rich white girl. Oprah had been disappointed by Oscar night in Hollywood, and the role of the thirty-six-year-old mother of the angry young black man suited her mood at the time. "It was good," she said, "because the character I play was a weary woman—tired, honey. It was good to have that, so I didn't have to stretch to play the character."

That same month, she jetted to Hyannis, Massachusetts, to attend the April 25 wedding of Arnold Schwarzenegger and Maria Shriver at the St. Francis Xavier Roman Catholic Church before 450 invited guests and thousands of spectators. The affair was a gathering of the Kennedy clan led by Bob's widow, Ethel, and Jack's widow, Jackie O., wearing a navy blue suit. The mob of well-wishers, curious onlookers, the press, and security personnel created a crush of people and endless confusion. The Federal Aviation Administration invoked a rule created to please the wealthy and famous in America—the Celebrity Event Rule—and sealed off the airspace above the Kennedy compound where the champagne lunch reception was scheduled. On the ground, eighty-five local policemen checked each person approaching for the small gold button that marked them as invitees.

During the three days of festivities, the guests tasted food from two different worlds, with New England clam chowder at the Friday luncheon; guests received souvenir chowder mugs inscribed with the wedding date. At the rehearsal dinner that night (with Arnold wearing Tyrolean garb) the groom's mother, Mrs. Aurelia Schwarzenegger Jadrny, hosted a dinner of Wiener schnitzel, lobster, and Sacher torte.

The ceremony lasted an hour and a quarter, with ten bridesmaids in moiré silk—in blues, pinks, and violets. The bride appeared radiant in a pearl-trimmed gown of white satin, with an eleven-foot train designed by Christian Dior's Marc Bohan. It was a traditional Catholic nuptial mass, with some variations, and both the bride and groom appeared superbly calm and poised, even though Maria had two broken toes from stumbling in her New York apartment a few days before. As part of the service, Oprah, who had been Maria Shriver's friend since they had worked together at WJZ-TV in Baltimore, recited Elizabeth Barrett Browning's "How Do I Love Thee?" After the ceremony the star-studded group of guests adjourned to the reception in heated tents featuring oysters, cold lobster, and chicken breasts with champagne sauce; a 425-pound, seven-foot-high cake; and music provided by Peter Duchin's seven-piece band.

Back in Chicago, Oprah, with the guidance of her now

ever-present business manager, Jeffrey Jacobs, formed Harpo Productions as a vehicle for her future television and motion picture work. Her television show now dominated its time slot in Chicago, attracting twice as many viewers as Donahue. Her success was due in significant part to the titillating subjects and her insistence on having lots of "ordinary" people as guests instead of "experts." Diet was a major staple of Oprah's shows over the years, and she would rather interview a half-dozen ordinary women desperately trying to slim down than have one expert pontificating to her audience.

Some critics were troubled by the marginally tasteful subjects on some of her shows, particularly those with sexual themes, such as when she explored men's sexual ability to satisfy women and made her classic remark about Mama wanting a big one. She also interviewed a group of naked nudists who were photographed from the waist up only as well as porno film stars who talked about what is called in the porno industry "the money shot," which is the mandatory scene in porno movies graphically showing actual intercourse or oral sex.

The television critic for the temporarily defunct magazine *Spy* commented, "Capaciously built, black and extremely noisy, Oprah Winfrey is an aberration among talk show doyennes and her press materials bleat as much. She is awash in adjectival suds: *earthy, spontaneous, genuine, brassy, down-home.* A hyperkinetic amalgam of Mae West, Reverend Ike, Richard Simmons and Hulk Hogan is more to the point." Probably a mean but accurate description of Oprah. She is still number one on daytime talk television, and *Spy* magazine went out of business in the spring of 1994 but was revived several months later.

Having been poor, the thirty-two-year-old Oprah now began to enjoy being rich; her first major extravagance was a luxury high-rise condo overlooking Lake Michigan. It had all the symbolism of conspicuous consumption, with four bathrooms, gold dolphin spigots, wine cellar, and crystal chandelier in the closet. The first time she came home to this palatial residence she told herself, "Girl! Look at you! You're not on the farm in Mississippi feeding those chickens no more!"

That was in the summer of 1986, while the King brothers were syndicating the *Oprah Winfrey Show* to stations around the country and the media drumbeat of the impending showdown between Oprah and Donahue nationally was growing louder. TV columnist Howard Rosenberg said, "She's a roundhouse, a full-course meal, big, brassy, loud, aggressive, hyper, laughable, lovable, soulful, tender, low-down, earthy and hungry. And she may know the way to Phil Donahue's jugular."

Oprah's Academy Award nomination had heightened her national visibility, and the King brothers added an extensive advertising campaign in the media trade publications for station executives. The brothers proved clever at how they marketed Oprah in that they took a major risk while avoiding a major confrontation at the same time. The major risk was to sell Oprah retail instead of wholesale. Thus, instead of making the easy sale by going to companies owning several TV stations and selling them Oprah for all of their stations, the King brothers sold one station at a time. If their plan succeeded, it would mean more money. The group station owners wanted to pay a wholesale price for their entire group, but individual stations had to pay a higher retail price.

Moreover, the King brothers refused to promote a confrontation between Oprah and Donahue, even though the media saw it that way. The media always needed controversy and conflict to bring drama to their stories. Instead, the King brothers focused on Oprah as an exciting new talent without bringing Donahue into the discussion. The plan worked well, but not perfectly, and by the targeted air date of September 8, the *Oprah Winfrey Show* was slated to begin on 180 stations around the country. Ironically, in Baltimore she would not be on her old station, WJZ-TV. The King brothers had a good relationship with WJZ's competition, WMAR-TV, which bought *Wheel of Fortune* and *Jeopardy* from them, and it got preference over WJZ-TV for the *Oprah Winfrey Show*.

With all the fanfare, Oprah was under a great deal of pressure to perform well against Donahue. In that critical first week, she did and, predictably, outdrew Donahue in audience ratings. Donahue edged Oprah the first day of their confrontation with a 26 percent share of the viewing audience over Oprah's 23 percent share. The next day she got 30 percent to his 18; the following day, 29 percent to 22 percent. "Predictably" because a lot of people tuned in to the new show and the star they had heard so much about just to see what she was like during the first week. The real test would be if she could endure and continue to draw high ratings after the first month and the first quarter and the first year. Even so, beating Donahue in the ratings that first week ensured that she would have a long-term chance at permanently besting him.

For her first national show Oprah undertook the issue of how to catch a man, while Donahue had as his guest the Mayflower Madam, who talked about how to get a man to pay for sex. The following day, Oprah went with fighting families, including two white sisters feuding because one squealed to their mother that her sister had a black boyfriend and a mother who refused to attend her daughter's wedding confronting the son-in-law she hated. Donahue came on with Baby Jesse, who was refused a heart transplant because his parents weren't married. On the third day, Oprah brought on neo-Nazis to tell about how much they hated Jews, while Donahue had divorced couples confronting each other. Next, Oprah had women who had been raped by their doctors, and Donahue had a show on designer drugs.

At the end of the week, the critics feasted on the contest and agreed that Oprah had come out ahead. Steve Daley of the *Chicago Tribune* said that Oprah was only an inch deep but irresistible; *Newsday's* Les Payne said, "Oprah Winfrey is sharper than Donahue, wittier, more genuine and far better attuned to her audience, if not the world"; and Martha Bayles of the *Wall Street Journal* wrote, "It's a relief to see a gabmonger with a fond, but realistic assessment of her own cultural and religious roots."

Why did any of this matter that much? It's a reasonable question, and the answer is money. Daytime television programming from the beginning of television going national in 1954 had been largely the domain of the three television networks, whose programming came from what took place on radio for decades, soap operas. Nonnetwork stations or independent stations struggled to find programs that could command some audience and make a little money in the daytime, and that's why Donahue, operating initially out of WLWD in Dayton, Ohio, became attractive. He had a ready-made package that was relatively cheap and drew audiences away from the soap operas, game shows, and reruns of movies and sitcoms. The advertising income from daytime shows was usually only about 25 percent of nighttime programs, and so the former tended to be inexpensive.

In contrast to other shows, Donahue not only attracted audiences that had watched competing programs, he also brought in new viewers who had not previously paid attention to daytime television. Overall daytime advertising income was rising, so that by 1986, when Oprah went national, the gross income of daytime television was $2.5 billion, compared to $800 million ten years earlier, when Oprah moved to WJZ-TV in Baltimore. Daytime television revenue was growing at the rate of 30 percent a year, and that's why the competition between Donahue and Oprah seemed so important in the broadcasting world.

By Thanksgiving, 1986, Oprah was exhausted from all the work in launching her national show and sustaining it at a high level of energy and interest. She decided to visit her father on a trip of renewal back to Nashville, with a side visit farther south to Kosciusko, on the Natchez Trace. In Nashville she would spend time relaxing and talking and getting to know her father and stepmother all over again. Then she and her father went to Kosciusko to visit family and familiar places, including the old Baptist church where Oprah gave her first public performance as a little girl.

Then she returned to cold Chicago and her show and continued to captivate America. She and Stedman also flew to New York for the opening of *Native Son* at the Apollo Theatre in Harlem. It was just one year since *The Color Purple* had opened, and there wasn't the same controversy this time. Or the box-office appeal. *Native Son* quickly disappeared, even though Oprah was praised by the critics for her performance, particularly in the scene where she begged the mother of her son's victim to help spare his life. Then came the call from *60 Minutes*; Mike Wallace wanted her on the program on December 14. Introducing her, Wallace called Oprah colorful, controversial, and a soaring, sudden success.

Oprah explained her success to Wallace. "The reason I communicate with all these people is because I think I'm every woman and I've had every malady and I've been on every diet and I've had men who have done me wrong, honey. So I related to all of that. And I'm not afraid or ashamed to say it. So whatever is happening, if I can relate to it personally, I always do."

Talking about her attitude toward success with Mike Wallace, she set the stage for the final and wonderful ending note for her marvelous 1986. "It's going to do well [her show]. If it doesn't, I will still do well. I will do well because I am not defined by a show. I think we are defined by the way we treat ourselves and the way we treat other people." She was right; the show proved very successful. At the end of December, the figures were in on the syndication income, and everybody, including the King brothers, was amazed and happy.

Even though Oprah had been on the air since the beginning of September, it took time to develop a meaningful estimate of the gross income. Television stations evaluate a program and calculate what they can charge for the commercials in the program. This is only an estimate initially, for the advertising world usually works on the basis of "cost-per-thousand," which means the advertiser and the advertising agency will only pay so many dollars per thousand people reached by the program. Since everybody has to wait for the ratings until *after* the program has aired, nobody is exactly sure how much advertising income it will generate. When everybody knows how many thousands of people watched the show, then the exact dollar amount for the commercial can be determined. Out of the gross income generated by selling commercials, the stations keep a percentage, and the syndicator gets a percentage. In this case, King World's percentage had to be divided among the production costs of the show, ABC's cut, the Kings' percentage, and finally, Oprah's percentage.

What made everybody so happy at the end of December 1986 was that the figures were in and deals were made for the following 1987–88 season based on those figures. The *Oprah Winfrey Show* would gross $125 million, which was far more than anybody expected, and Oprah's cut would come to $30 million for that one year—a ballistic increase over the $200,000 that she was paid when she signed on with Dennis Swanson only two years before.

CHAPTER

10

Talk Turned Into Gold

The multi-million-dollar business that would make Oprah Winfrey wealthy is called "syndication" and simply involves renting programs to television stations to show on the air.

The syndicator is basically a middleman who has the exclusive right to rent certain programs he has under contract to the more than seven hundred television stations in the country. Like most agents, he is paid a percentage of the income for the shows he places. Many of the syndicated programs are reruns of movies, sitcoms, game shows, and dramas scheduled for broadcast during the day. The fees the stations pay for the programs vary with the size of the viewing audience, and the syndicator usually gets one-third of the gross.

Syndication of programs to television stations has been around since the 1950s, when stations were anxious to obtain programs to fill all their airtime and when, initially, the motion picture industry was hostile to television for fear it would keep people from seeing movies. The motion picture industry has resisted every technological advance in visual entertainment. Hollywood has always felt that any innovation would doom the movie industry. Therefore, it resisted talkies, color, television, cable TV, and videotapes. In the end, however, the movie studios made huge profits from all of these technological advances. At one point, several studios joined together to sue the Sony Company to prohibit it from selling videocassette players in the United States on the grounds that it would destroy the movie industry. In a classic anomaly, by the time that case reached the U.S. Supreme Court, rental of movies on videocassette was the biggest single source of revenue for the movie studios!

Still, in time, movie libraries were being rented or syndicated to television stations around the world and that included such short movies as *The Little Rascals*, which a man named Charlie King used to launch his small syndication company King World. It would make Oprah rich a few years later.

The arithmetic of syndication is not that hard to understand. Somebody owns a television show and rents it to stations that sell commercials in the show. If it's a dramatic show or comedy like *Hill Street Blues* or *Cheers* or the *Cosby Show* or *I Love Lucy*, it is largely timeless and may run forever. The only caveat is that you need enough original shows in your library or, as they say in the business, enough shows "in the can" to go into syndication, because while the show was originally shown once a week, in syndication such shows are usually shown on independent stations every weekday in the same time slot. So producers of such shows need to be on the air for about four years, during which they will produce something on the order of 35-40 shows a year and end up with 140–160 ready for syndication. If the syndicator had 140 shows in the can, they could be shown daily on weekdays for twenty-eight weeks before any reruns would surface, which is important, because too many reruns drive away the audience.

Syndicating Oprah is simpler because she does five shows a week. However, she cannot sell all of those shows in foreign markets. There are some shows that cannot be run in Japan, or in England, either, because the subject matter is too offensive to that culture or because it doesn't mean anything to the audience.

For years, since television networks became national in the early 1950s, the time period from 7:00 P.M. to 11:00 P.M. every evening was considered "prime time." Networks are groupings of TV stations around the country, most of which are owned by private parties or private groups. For years, for example, the three networks were only permitted to own seven VHF television stations, and these were the core of their network and were stations usually located in the ten most populous market areas in the country. This meant that the seven stations owned by ABC, CBS, and NBC were usually in New York, Chicago, Los Angeles, Philadelphia, Detroit, Boston, Pittsburgh, and San Francisco. The networks had the best, that is, the most popular, programs. They paid big salaries to performers and asked stations around the country to sign contracts with them to air these popular programs during prime time. The stations agreed, in turn, to broadcast all the programs the networks supplied them during prime-time hours.

So Procter & Gamble, R. J. Reynolds, and the Ford Motor Company, for example, could ask their advertising agencies to create and place their commercials for them on TV stations around the country. Since the networks controlled the prime-time hours, the advertising agency arranged with the network to place the commercials of its clients on particular programs. The cost of those commercials depended on how many people were watching, the size of the audience measured by the rating services. Advertising agencies generally have a formula of paying just so much per thousand people watching the program. For example, $7 per thousand people would mean it would pay $70,000 for every million people watching. There are variables in such deals, because some products specifically want to be associated with certain types of programs and will pay a premium to be on them because they provide prestige (like the Super Bowl) or because the program has special appeal to the customers they are trying to reach. Commercials for feminine products, for example, would not be suitable for professional-football television programs no matter what the price per thousand.

This continued until a key executive in the Group W organization, Don Gannon, began a crusade to cut down on prime time controlled by the networks. That same Group W sold *People Are Talking*, Oprah's Baltimore show, to stations outside of that city for a time until it wasn't working in syndication.

For years Don Gannon campaigned to make the networks release their stranglehold—those four hours when most people watch television in the evening. Finally, in 1975, the Federal Communications Commission (FCC) passed a rule that said the networks could no longer control the prime-time hour of 7:00 P.M. to 8:00 P.M. so that individual station owners could select the programs they wanted. The concept that Don had pushed and the FCC had agreed to is that freeing this hour of prime time would give access to many wonderful, classical, creative new programs that would blossom all over the country. It was dubbed "the prime time access rule," or PTAR.

Well, something happened on the way to the noble goal of the PTAR: Station owners found out they could put cheap programming into the prime access hour and make lots of money. That hour instantly became home to all sorts of inexpensively produced game shows.

Some stations pooled their efforts to create Operation Prime Time in the latter part of the 1970s, and some individual stations began developing programs on their own. Oprah was twenty-two and working at WJZ-TV in Baltimore when the PTAR was passed. It prompted King World to find inexpensive programs they could sell to stations and groups of stations to put into that hour. That's when they made a deal with Merv Griffin, who had developed and owned several television shows, particularly *Wheel of Fortune* and *Jeopardy*. The King brothers, Roger and Michael, are the spark plugs of King World and succeeded in renting episodes of *Wheel* and *Jeopardy* for daily viewing around the country. They did so with two-year contracts.

Here is the simple arithmetic of syndicating Oprah. Oprah will appear on approximately two hundred stations each week, which will pay King World between $100,000 and $200,000 per week for five shows. The figure varies with the size of the audience in each market. The $200,000 figure is quite high, and that is the amount the ABC station in Los Angeles, KABC-TV, has agreed to pay under the new contract, due to run through the 1994–95 season. It was forced to pay that amount in the face of a strong counterbid from the rival CBS station. Similar competition occurred in other markets where CBS faced ABC because the *Oprah Winfrey Show* served as a lead for two hours of local news. As noted elsewhere, this programming sequence helps build local news ratings.

If you use the lower figure of $100,000 and multiply it by the approximately two hundred U.S. stations buying Oprah, you see how King World grosses $20 million a week on the *Oprah Winfrey Show*, against which the production cost of the show runs about $200,000 a week. Thus, low-cost shows sold to hundreds of stations can make a fortune for the participants and the star. Even if the program is not as highly rated as the *Oprah Winfrey Show*, it can make a lot of money, which is why everyone wants to get into the syndicated talk-show business.

CHAPTER

11

The Selling of Ms. Oprah

Two middle-aged white men, Roger and Michael King of King World Productions, Inc., turned Oprah into the richest black woman in the world, and because they have a great deal to do with her, we need to know them and King World Productions for the insight they provide about Oprah.

King World began as the brainchild of Charlie King, the six-foot-three, 350-pound super–media salesman who always wore a fresh flower in his lapel. In the 1940s he earned $80,000 a week selling radio shows, with two outsized talents: the ability to make an enormous amount of money and the inability to hold on to any of it. But radio and Charlie were overwhelmed by the coming of television, which engulfed America in the 1950s. Charlie's fortunes plummeted as he tried to sell refrigerator-freezers, personalized "Santa-Grams," and "Jackpot Golf," which consisted of signing up a string of golf driving ranges around the country to run hole-in-one contests, with anyone making a hole in one of over 220 yards winning a new Cadillac. The idea failed, and Charlie returned to broadcasting.

Because nobody wanted to hire an old radio retread,

Charlie started his own television syndication business, King World. It got off to a shaky start in 1964 when he bought the syndication rights to *The Little Rascals*—movie shorts featuring an integrated cast of stereotypical roles made by Hal Roach in the 1930s—from Official Films for $300,000 or $250,000, depending on whom you talk to about the deal. Whatever the price, everybody agreed that Charlie didn't have the money, and the people at Official Films went apoplectic when they found out that Charlie couldn't pay them. However, salesman that he was, he convinced the executives at Official to wait a week, and in that week Charlie sold the *Rascals* to one station for $50,000. That sale kept the executives at Official happy until Charlie raised the rest of the money.

Suddenly, the money poured in, and life was good again for the King family. Unexpectedly, the civil rights movement struck TV in the early 1970s, and a kids' comedy with a black stereotype named Alfalfa became politically incorrect. Soon afterward, Charlie died in his San Antonio hotel room on a sales trip. There was a fresh flower in his lapel.

When Charlie King passed away, he left behind a floundering business, almost no money, and six kids who worshiped his memory. They all became involved in Charlie's syndication business, but it ultimately shook out to mostly Michael and Roger. Following literally in Charlie's footsteps, the brothers sold second-rate features like *The Little Rascals* and *Tic Tac Dough*. The two traveled from Sunday to Friday, covering eight cities a week for forty-eight weeks out of the year. They sold hard, played hard, and followed their father's basic sales rule: "Make a deal that both parties walk away from smiling. Then give them a little extra." By 1982—ten years after Charlie died—King World was grossing $60 million a year.

The brothers pored through several years of rating books. They wanted to expand into the game-show end of the business because a new FCC ruling had opened up an extra hour of evening time to syndicators. It was the same approach that would ultimately connect them with Oprah several years later. They zeroed in on a seven-year-old game show called *Wheel of Fortune*, produced by an ex-talk-show host and band singer whose main claim to fame had been singing "I've Got A

Loverly Bunch of Coconuts" several times a night for the Freddy Martin band at the Coconut Grove in the Ambassador Hotel in Los Angeles. *Wheel* never made top ratings, but it beat every show that preceded it in any given time slot. In other words, more people would tune in to *Wheel* than had been watching whatever appeared on the screen before it. That signified an audience loyalty unusual for a daytime game show.

So the King brothers called Merv Griffin about syndicating a nighttime version of *Wheel*, but Griffin never called them back because he didn't know who they were. As Griffin would later say, "The entire world had not heard of King World." A few nights later, Roger and Michael's brother, Bob, ran into Griffin in the bar of a New York hotel, introduced himself, and did some fast selling. After a few days of negotiating and a payment of $50,000, King World had the syndication rights to a nighttime *Wheel*, and Griffin thought he had outwitted the Kings. He knew that the big-time syndicators like Viacom, Metromedia, and Fox had been unable to sell the daytime version in the major markets on which syndicators depend to make their shows a success: New York, Chicago, and Los Angeles.

With their new nighttime form of *Wheel*, the brothers decided on a back-door strategy: sell it in smaller markets and let it grow into the big ones. As part of this strategy Roger called one day on the general manager of San Francisco's KRON-TV. He sat, ignored, all day in the lobby of the station while other salesmen went in and out. He couldn't get in to see the general manager. Finally, the security guard asked him to leave, which he did, but he came back again and again and finally sold the station on *Wheel of Fortune*.

By the time the nighttime *Wheel* began in September 1983, it appeared on fifty-nine stations around the country, which was a very weak beginning in the TV syndication business. However, at KRON-TV, *Wheel* suddenly turned the station's ratings around, to the surprise of everybody, and that happened in station after station. Then the King brothers, whose name was now recognized by Griffin when they called, convinced Merv to let them syndicate a nighttime version of another program, *Jeopardy*. This time they had 120 stations signed up before they called Griffin, and the show blasted off like a rocket.

Roger is the more flamboyant of the two brothers and enjoys high living, which has been both his trademark and his downfall. His wardrobe has a slept-in look, which may be due to his being on the road 80 percent of the time. He lives in the company jet, flying 500,000 miles a year on business. His younger but grayer brother, Michael, is not so flamboyant. He lives a more conventional entertainment-world life in a Mediterranean house between the Malibu homes of George C. Scott and Charles Bronson.

Michael smokes too much, eats too much, and like his brother, sometimes drinks too much in between rather credible Ronald Reagan impressions. After working out every morning in his private gym in the beachfront house, he drives along the Pacific Coast Highway between the towering adobe palisades and the Pacific surf, up the California Incline road to his penthouse office, with its unbelievable view of the Pacific and of Los Angeles. While Roger is on the road constantly selling, Michael listens to twenty or thirty pitches every week from producers' agents trying to sell King World on another show to syndicate. Both are nervous about their heavy dependence on the *Oprah Winfrey Show*, which is one reason they are syndicating everywhere in the world that they can, with *La Roue de la Fortune* now in France and other versions in Italy, Germany, and Scotland.

Roger and Michael are wheeler-dealers in every way, but they also do their homework. Always looking for ways to expand and get new program products to sell, they studied the rating books over and over again, just as they had done for *Wheel of Fortune*. When they learned that a new talk show in Chicago had been doing better than Donahue, in his own hometown, they were on the phone. That was the spring of 1985, and they weren't the only syndicators who wanted Oprah at that point. Still, they convinced Oprah and Jeffrey Jacobs that they were the right men for her. They *didn't* want to rush her program into syndication immediately.

Oprah and Jacobs were impressed when Roger and Michael said they intended to prepare the way first instead of going for the quick sale. They told Oprah and Jacobs that they would promote the show heavily in advance and that they would research topics that would play best so as to attract the largest national audience immediately. They knew that for the viewing audience to be sold on a big, bubbly black woman host with a funny name, they had to be hooked on the first shows. If the audience didn't like Oprah immediately, it would prove very difficult to build an audience later.

They also understood something else, since they grew up in the syndication business and knew most of the station and program managers on a first-name basis. The spring was a bad time to sell a new syndicated program. During the spring months, stations were halfway through their old budgets and didn't have money to gamble. In the winter, there would be new budget money coming up, and managers had more leeway to take a chance. Oprah and Jeffrey Jacobs were quick to grasp that these two flashy syndicators, Michael and Roger, were very savvy, and that's what Oprah and Jeffrey wanted. They went with the King brothers.

Roger and Michael went on the road with tapes of Oprah's show and a sales pitch about why the *Oprah Winfrey Show* would bring bigger ratings than Donahue, which was then the most successful show in daytime TV. They contrasted Donahue as a cerebral male who touched people's minds, with Oprah as an empathetic female who touched people's hearts. David Sams, formerly an executive with King World, described how Michael and Roger sold the *Oprah Winfrey Show*:

"When they went in and sold Oprah, they very seldom would go in and pitch a general manager without bringing in his secretary or another woman or two into the meeting. They knew it was very difficult for a lot of male, fifty-plus general managers to really look at an Oprah who went against every stereotypical personality on television and say, 'Yeah, she's a hit.'"

The *Oprah Winfrey Show* went national on September 8, 1986, on 138 stations with a projected annual gross income of $125 million, of which Oprah would eventually receive $30 million. Though everyone connected with the syndication felt hopeful, they still were apprehensive as to how she would do against Donahue and the other talk-show icons on the national stage. The reviews were almost universally ebullient, and her coverage quickly grew to 198 stations and a daily audience of over 10 million. Two years later, the King World–Oprah relationship was so solid and Oprah was so rich, and becoming richer by the moment, that she agreed to renew her syndication contract with the King brothers for five years—unusually long for any program on TV. They turned around and also sold renewals of her syndication contracts with ABC-owned stations around the country for an unprecedented five-year term.

The King brothers, Roger and Michael, have built King World Productions into the country's number-one seller of game and talk shows. In the process, they have made themselves and their kinfolk the richest family in television. Today King World Productions is growing, even though it has made some missteps. In 1993, it showed a 7.4 percent jump in profits and had *Wheel of Fortune, Jeopardy,* and the *Oprah Winfrey Show* in syndication and was also producing *Inside Edition* and *American Journal.* Among these programs, the *Oprah Winfrey Show* was the main moneymaker, accounting for 40 percent of King World's 1993 income of $474.3 million and a net profit of $101.9 million.

And, indeed, the King brothers have searched hard for their next Oprah success, preferably a morning show. Roger King said they wanted someone to dominate the morning television schedule the way Oprah dominates the competition in the afternoon. Roger phrased it as doing away with the four J's : Joan Rivers, Jenny Jones, Jane Whitney, and Jerry Springer.

One problem is that while King World is the best syndicator, it hasn't had a lot of success as a producer of shows. Many of its productions have failed, including its 1991 revival of *Candid Camera,* starring Dom DeLuise; *Headline Chasers*; *Nitetime,* with Dick Clark; *Nightlife,* with David Brenner; *Rock 'n' Roll News*; a new version of *Hollywood Squares*; and *Monopoly.* This last program prompted Roger to comment, "*Monopoly* was like communism. It looked great on paper, but it didn't work in real life."

Paul Marsh, investment analyst for Kemper Securities, contends that the management of King World is iffy but touts it as a good stock buy for those who like its cash flow. He is disturbed by the King brothers' inability to produce regular winners and the deep problems they got into with the purchase of a TV station in Buffalo and a badly timed investment in the Financial News Network in 1990 that lost $3 million. And, of course, Roger King's run-ins with the law relating to his excessive drinking, drug use, and inclination toward beating people have not inspired confidence in King World's management.

Everybody agrees that Roger is a dazzling salesman who knows station managers all over the country and spends most of his life traveling. "I travel," he says. "I'm out there in the trenches, with dirt all over me." Of course, knowing everybody doesn't mean being loved by everybody, although Jim Coopersmith, president of WCVB-TV in Boston and a major King World customer, has a lot of respect for the Kings.

"I like street people," Coopersmith says. "They have a reverse chic style. They are not Grant Tinker, with the two-thousand-dollar suit, the thirty-two-inch waist, and the Gucci loafers. They are big, healthy guys who look more like wrestlers. They're not like studio guys who come in with their Armani shirts and have nicer tushes than their wives. I hope I never get into a barroom fight, but if I do, I hope it's with the King brothers on my side."

Both friends and enemies of Roger's agree that he goes overboard celebrating his successes and that it has gotten him into trouble. He is notorious for whooping it up after closing a big deal by treating everybody on his sales team to $1,000-a-bottle wine and gambling sprees. In October 1991 he became involved in a drunken brawl in Las Vegas, was arrested, and spent time in an alcohol-abuse treatment program. In 1987 the police arrested him for car theft, possession of cocaine, and robbery because he had a fight with a cabdriver whom he refused to pay. A little embarrassed and defensive, Roger says, "I function very well for King World. It has not affected my work. We have personal problems, all of us."

These are the two men who have negotiated contracts on behalf of Oprah that have earned her over $100 million—maybe over $200 million—since she became nationally syndicated in 1986, after picking Roger and Michael to represent her. If Oprah had not become involved with the King brothers and continued at the same salary of $200,000 that she received under her initial WLS-TV contract, it would have taken her a thousand years to earn what the King brothers have helped her earn in the last eight.

Consolidating Success

CHAPTER

12

The "S" Man Cometh

It was in May of that same landmark year, 1986, that her private longing was fulfilled when she and a handsome ex–basketball player, Stedman Graham Jr., began dating. A six-foot-five-inch man with a master's degree in education from Ball State University, Graham ran a drug-counseling program called Athletes Against Drugs. He had tried to get a date with Oprah for a long time after having met her at various social events around Chicago while with his then girlfriend, Channel 2 newsanchor Robin Robinson.

Stedman had come to Chicago in pursuit of the romance he had started with Robinson when she was a television personality in Denver, but the romance cooled, and in January 1986, Robinson announced her engagement to NBC-TV spot salesman Terrence Brantley, who was based in New York but was going to move to Chicago to be with her.

That's when Stedman began seeking dates with Oprah, but she kept putting him off because this poised, attractive, successful television star was afraid. She didn't think she was pretty enough to hold this male-model-handsome man, and besides, the thirty-something women with whom she surrounded herself on her staff were very protective of her and defensive against predatory males who might exploit *their* Oprah for her money or stardom.

Oprah recalled: "At first, I wasn't really that interested because, for one, I still had doubts about myself. He's a very attractive man. And I was thinking that kind of man usually goes for cupcakes—one of those women with long hair who has had her nose done. Actually, he called three times over a period of time. The first time, I stood him up. The second time, I made excuses. Finally, the third time, he said, 'I'm not going to ask you anymore.' So I went out with him."

Oprah's production colleague, Mary Kay Clinton, said, "She was overweight, and he was so attractive, and we wanted to know: What's he after? What's he coming here for? Where did he come from?" That wonderment continues even now, to the point that Oprah occasionally feels she must openly disclaim on the air that Stedman is not interested in her money.

Stedman was charming and polite, and on the way to the theater he bought her flowers, which no man had done in a long time. She found, to her surprise, that she had a good time and, to nobody's surprise, decided it would be nice to have more good times. So she went out with Graham a second time and found he was what she had always said she wanted in a man: He was confident and not intimidated by her success; he had his own money and was not trying to get hers; and, most important, he was taller than she.

Later, she told interviewers that she had recently written in her daily journal, "I'm not married. I'm *never* going to be.... Lord, could you do something about this man situation in my life?... Lord, could he be smart? And if you don't mind, could he be tall?"

She shared her anxieties with her audience, as she seemed to share all of her personal problems with the millions who watch her by complaining about the sexual abstinence she was enduring and not liking it. She used to quip, "Mr. Right is coming, only he must be in Africa, and he's walking."

When her friend Whoopi Goldberg got married in 1986, Oprah sent her a telegram asking for her black book listing all the men she had dated, and publicly indulged in her sexual fantasy about actor Robert De Niro: "If he ever wants me, he can have me. No questions asked."

Clearly, Stedman, cool and quietly firm, was the one in

charge at the beginning of the relationship. Oprah was not the national TV icon in his presence, simply a woman in love reaching out for the sanctuary of a loving, trusting relationship that she had yearned for all of her adult years. One of six children born to Stedman Sr. and Mary Graham, Stedman Jr. grew up in Whitesboro, New Jersey, where his father was a construction worker and his mother worked nights in a school for the handicapped. Stedman Jr. married Glenda Brown, a woman he had met at Hardin-Simmons University, had a daughter, Wendy, and divorced a few years later. The Grahams later moved to North Carolina, while Stedman played professional basketball in Europe and Glenda and Wendy moved to Dallas, Texas.

Stedman had trouble with his relationship with Oprah because he was a proud man who loved a wealthy celebrity and that was not easy. He endured the gossip coming from strangers, family, and Oprah's close colleagues that he was only a fortune hunter. The innuendo and gossip hurt him so much that he and Oprah would repeatedly fight over a prenuptial agreement. He insists on one to prove that he is not after her money, and she hates the idea of his-and-hers bank accounts, as she calls them.

Beyond that conflict, Stedman is sensitive to the attitude of the "spending fool" Oprah told the audience she would become when she was running for Miss Fire Prevention in Nashville and they asked what she would do with a million dollars. Oprah quickly slipped into the role of the rich woman who could order up limousines, fancy meals, and chartered jets at the snap of her fingers. Stedman insists that he is a *man* and will be treated that way in the relationship and that even if she can order others around, she can't do the same with him.

After living in Chicago for a time, Stedman moved back to High Point, North Carolina, where his public relations business had its headquarters. The romance became a commuter affair, with Stedman flying to Chicago on weekends to be with Oprah or Oprah traveling south to visit him. Oprah didn't like it that way and said so. "I just hate it. It's going to last another year. He says he's going to move back to Chicago."

Once, in 1989, when they were agitated about their relationship, they got into a limousine, locked the doors, and ordered the driver to just drive around while they talked without the interruptions of telephones, fans, or staff. That's when Stedman made it clear to Oprah that he wanted to have a real relationship with her on a permanent basis but that she had to understand she wasn't adopting him or renting him and that her money did not give her power over him. It may have been the toughest five-hour ride either one ever took, but it helped settle both of them.

Oprah understood intellectually what she needed from the relationship and had to affirm it to herself emotionally. "I was trying to get from my relationships the same kind of response I was trying to get from my mother and from my uncles and aunts. I wanted someone to affirm me, to show me that they really, really, loved me."

Stedman is director of Athletes Against Drugs and president of a public relations firm called the Graham Williams Group. He is vague about what the company does, saying only that "it helps people become all they can be." The Williams part of the Graham Williams Group is the more interesting and controversial side of the partnership. Stedman's business partner is thirty-five-year-old Armstrong Williams. A rarity among well-to-do, upper-middle-class blacks, he is a conservative with a talk show that reaches a predominantly black audience. He hosts *The Right Side*, which airs Wednesdays and Fridays from 7:00 P.M. to 9:00 P.M. on Washington, D.C., radio station WOL-AM. One observer compared his animated style on the air to a bee in a jar, bouncing in and out of his chair, reeling forward and back, shouting into the microphone, and chopping the air with his right hand.

Armstrong Williams is called preacher, pundit, and PR man rolled into one. He asks his audience to rethink its politics and admit it belongs in the Republican party, which is one of his and Stedman's PR clients. He slams the civil rights movement and labels welfare as slavery and black civil rights leaders as high priests of blackness and wanna-bes. A former assistant to Sen. Strom Thurmond and then to Clarence Thomas when the two of them and Anita Hill were all at the Equal Employ-

A slimmed-down Oprah in a dazzling ivory Gianfranco Ferree evening suit at the White House dinner honoring the Emperor and Empress of Japan, June 13, 1994, without long-time boyfriend, Stedman Graham. Her escort for the evening was close friend Quincy Jones. (Photo Steve Jaffe/Reuter/Bettman)

Oprah often ties her show topics to events of the day. Here in a November 1987 show she hosts surviving relatives of the space shuttle *Challenger* crew. Left to right: Marcia Jarvis, widow of Gregory Jarvis; Lorna Onizuka, widow of Ellison Onizuka; Grace Corrigan, mother of Christa McAuliffe; Oprah; June Scobee, widow of Francis "Dick" Scobee; Cheryl McNair, widow of Ronald McNair; Dr. Charles Resnick, brother of Judy Resnick; and, Jane Smith, widow of Michael Smith. (Photo by Cliff Owen/UPI/Bettman)

Woman activist Gloria Steinem presents Oprah with one of *MS.* Magazine's Woman of the Year Awards in January 1989. Steinem lauded Oprah for being a role model showing women they can achieve whatever they dream of achieving. (Photo/UPI/Ezio/ Bettman)

Oprah receiving 1993 Daytime Emmy Award in New York City. (Photo by John Barrett/Globe Photos, 1993)

Oprah presiding over her daily show. (Globe Photos)

Oprah in the role of Sofia in *The Color Purple*. (Globe Photos)

Oprah at the opening of her restaurant, THE ECCENTRIC, in Chicago. (Globe Photos)

Michael Jackson taking Oprah on a tour of his Neverland estate during historic interview. (Globe Photos)

Oprah testifies before Congress about "her" bill to require registration of child molesters. (Photo by *National Enquirer*)

Oprah's Colorado ski lodge. (Photo by *National Enquirer*)

Oprah's ready to try out the ski slopes accompanied by two friends. (Photo by *National Enquirer*)

Slimmed down Oprah out doing what she does regularly now—jogging eight to ten miles a day. (Photo by *National Enquirer*)

Oprah tests the waters as she and boyfriend, Stedman Graham, prepare for romantic cruise. (Photo by *National Enquirer*)

Oprah with her friend actress Goldie Hawn. (Photo by *The Star* Magazine)

Oprah and boyfriend, Stedman Graham, at her fortieth birthday party at L'Orangerie Restaurant in Los Angeles. (Photo by *National Enquirer*)

ment Opportunity Commission, he is still close to Thomas and rarely misses a chance to skewer Anita Hill on his program. Occasionally, Stedman's partner also writes columns for *USA Today*, the *Wall Street Journal*, and *Newsday*.

As one of the rare black conservatives who is trying to transform Malcolm X into a black conservative, he joins with writers such as Jeff Morsenburg, who proclaims, "Afrocentrists are dead wrong when they claim that young black people can develop a sense of pride and self-worth only from exposure to historical figures or through the glory of some great, ancient pan-African society created out of whole cloth. [The answer for young blacks] is education, individual accomplishment, moral behavior, and positive social values and a yearning to grab a piece of the American dream."

Williams attacked movie producer Spike Lee for his movie *Malcolm X* because it promotes racial confrontation and conflict when blacks need to become part of contemporary America instead of clinging to roots. "Why do we have to go back to Africa to understand my roots?" he asks. "My roots are here! This is my home." Which, of course, is in direct conflict with Oprah's repeated devotion to her roots and her black heritage.

Recently, Williams became the creative consultant to the new Norman Lear sitcom *704 Hauser* on CBS. It is a twist on the Archie Bunker family comedy casting John Amos as Ernie Cumberbatch, a liberal black father, and T. E. Russell as Thurgood Marshall "Goodie" Cumberbatch, his conservative son who thinks blacks are too promiscuous, into victimization while feeling sorry for themselves, and too ready to blame their problems on white strangers.

The *Los Angeles Times* says Williams is "one of the show's key behind-the-scenes" players and model for the son, Goodie. "Black people need to be made mad," Williams said. "Truth always hurts. Black people need to be uncomfortable. This show never forgets it's a comedy, but it also looks at how black people complain about their problems. There's too much focus on victimization and 'blame whitey' and not enough focus on helping ourselves and self-motivation."

Williams hopes black parents will point to Goodie Cumberbatch as a new role model, even though he has a little trouble with the Goodie character's white girlfriend and shaved bald head.

Given the liberal positions espoused by Oprah, her fiancé's connections with Williams appear to be surprising. However, Oprah's connection with Stedman is love. "Yes, I am definitely in love, and it's a wonderful feeling," she says. "The success of my show is great, losing weight is great, but nothing compares with being in love. Zippity-doo-dah, I'm in love!"

13

Gaining National Recognition

On January 23, 1987, just six days before her thirty-third birthday, Oprah appeared at another of the numerous benefits she does when she helped WLS-TV and the *Chicago Sun-Times* launch a yearlong campaign against drugs, *Say No*, on the air by interviewing reformed drug abusers and superstar athletes who had never used drugs. This was the program her boyfriend, Stedman Graham Jr., headed as director of Athletes Against Drugs. A reviewer for *Variety* came away saying that Oprah had created a tent-meeting-revival atmosphere on the program, pulling from each of the ex-addicts expressions of pain that turned into a feeling of resurrection.

Oprah's impact on everything she does is dynamic, as has been her effect on sales of books she endorses on her show. That was clear before she went national with the diet–health book *Callanetics* by Callan Pinckney. The first 12,500 copies of *Callanetics* did not sell in spite of Pinckney's efforts to promote the work. Pinckney had become almost crippled from a haphazard lifestyle of backpacking around Europe and returned home to devise her own variations of her adolescent ballet lessons. She developed a system of deep stretching and contraction exercises that tightened the stomach and lifted the rear, but she still couldn't get many buyers when she described her system in a book.

Finally, she talked her way onto Oprah Winfrey's local show, and soon the sales of the book began to skyrocket, which brought her to the *Donahue* and *Sally Jessy Raphael* shows. Within months, her book sales topped 300,000. This phenomenon would be repeated many times after Oprah went national.

When she recommended Marianne Williamson's book, *A Return to Love*, in February 1992 it immediately sold 70,000 copies and ultimately went on to sell 750,000 in hardcover and 500,000 in paperback. Her endorsement of Robert James Waller's novel, *The Bridges of Madison County*, including doing one of her shows from Winterset, Iowa, and one of those bridges, gave the novel stunning staying power on the best seller list where it stayed for 102 weeks! That same impact on book sales would later be seen in the booming sales for Dr. Deepak Chopra's *Ageless Body, Timeless Mind*, John Gray's *Men Are From Mars, Women Are From Venus*, Richard and Linda Eyre's *Teaching Your Children Values* and the cookbook that become a publishing record-breaker, *In the Kitchen with Rosie*, for which Oprah wrote the introduction.

Oprah's syndicated show began making more and more money. She had a 25 percent share of the program, which brought her $7.5 million in 1986, with a big jump in 1987 as stations paid quadruple their 1986 fees for the *Oprah Winfrey Show*. On her birthday, January 29, 1987, Oprah said, "I'm doing exactly what I wanted to be doing at age thirty-three. I feel I'm ripening, coming into my own." That happiness was symbolized by her new, luxurious lifestyle, which included an $800,000 condo on the Fifty-seventh floor of a lakefront luxury building and a chauffeur-driven Mercedes limousine.

In March she returned to Hollywood and another Academy Awards ceremony as a presenter of the Oscar for Documentary Feature. There were two first-place winners, a documentary on Artie Shaw and another entitled *Down and Out in America*, about the homeless. She again wore a gown by Tony Chase, but this time she could breathe while she presented the Oscars, even though her weight was hovering around 180 pounds. Determined to slim down again, she hired Phil Damen, nutritionist, cook, and trainer, to help her lose weight. June was a triumphant month. She swept the Daytime Emmy Awards and shut out Donahue by winning Outstanding Talk/Service Show, Outstanding Talk/Service Show host, and Outstanding Direction of a Talk/Service Show, which she shared with executive producer Debra DiMaio and producers Mary Kay Clinton, Christine Tardio, Dianne Hudson, and Ellen Rakietan. The ceremony took place at the Sheraton Centre in New York City. It was aired by ABC and seen by 36 percent of the daytime audience. Afterward, Oprah and Stedman danced until dawn at Stringfellows nightclub. By July she had lost twenty pounds and bought a $25,000 new wardrobe in size 14.

Early in the year, Oprah seized the opportunity to make a statement about her heritage and her people by taking her show on the road to Forsyth County, Georgia, from which blacks had been banned since 1912. It had become the focus of news attention—and therefore something for the *Oprah Winfrey Show* to capitalize on—when twenty thousand people marched in celebration of Martin Luther King's birthday three weeks before in January. The Ku Klux Klan threatened the demonstrators, but they marched anyway, and Oprah saw this occasion as an opportunity to do a show on racism.

The all-white control of Forsyth County began with the wrenching violence that white-black relations often did in turn-of-the-century America when a white teenage girl was supposedly raped by three black men. The year was 1912, and the outcome was certain even before there was a trial. Technically, they were hanged after a trial, but the three black men were dead as soon as the accusation was made.

Immediately thereafter, every black person in Forsyth County was warned to move elsewhere or they would be lynched. The blacks moved out, and they have been barred from living in this county of Georgia ever since.

Ironically, Oprah barred blacks from the audience, and this enraged such black activists as civil rights leader Rev. Hosea L. Williams, who picketed the show outside. He was arrested, and that alienated even more blacks. Oprah explained that she only wanted people from Forsyth County in the audience of 125, which meant no blacks; besides, allowing militant blacks to attend would have been disruptive.

During the program there were sharp exchanges between Oprah and many members of the audience as she challenged their viewpoints. When one woman continued to refer to "them," meaning blacks, Oprah wondered out loud if she thought that blacks came from a different planet. In another exchange with a longtime male resident who claimed that Forsyth was a pleasant place in which to live and raise a family, Oprah added, "For whites." Another member of the audience lectured Oprah on the difference between "blacks" and "niggers." A nigger, he explained, is a black person who makes trouble. Another said it was unfair to call Forsyth County "all white" because two people of Chinese extraction lived there, too.

Oprah believed that she had reached her objective of getting whites of Forsyth to rethink their racial attitudes and to talk about them. She also quickly cut off several more liberal members of the audience because she feared they might bring retribution down on themselves with their pro-black comments. She said, "We came here today not to argue whether black people have a right to be here—the Civil Rights Act guaranteed them that right. We are here to try to understand the attitudes and motivations of those who threw rocks at the recent demonstrators."

The Forsyth County show demonstrated something about television talk shows more openly than is usual and something that the public often doesn't understand. Talk-show hosts use their audiences as an active part of the show, which is a departure from the traditionally passive role audiences have played—their participation used to be limited to applauding and laughing on cue.

Oprah, whose key talent is operating extemporaneously, ironically insists on working in a controlled environment. Everything about her show is carefully scripted and controlled *except* Oprah, but she doesn't always want the audience to know this. People who are allowed to sit in the audience do not just wander in off the street. They are deliberately screened, a number of them are purposely planted, and all the incoming telephone calls are sifted to fit what Oprah wants on the program.

Some of this control may be dismissed as essential to coherent programming, but much of it is intended to hype the program and to avoid bringing up subjects that Oprah doesn't want to handle on the air. Sometimes an element of the viewing audience is manipulated through the selected and controlled composition of the studio and phone-in audience. In the Forsyth County program, that control was open, and while contentious, everybody knew that the studio audience was limited to Forsyth County whites.

For some African-Americans who do not like to criticize prominent blacks in public, Oprah's Forsyth County program demonstrated again that Oprah was not the liberal civil rights crusader she would like some people to believe. To them, Oprah's exclusion of blacks from this program and her demeanor in general were consistent with the Sofia role she played in *The Color Purple* and with her newly acquired wealth. Oprah is not the black person that a lot of whites think she is, and more and more black community leaders know that. She is rich and thinks rich. She is not into black militancy and never has been. She is into feminine militancy and its issues, such as domestic violence and child and spousal abuse. She identifies with the white power structure, with whom she shares the same socioeconomic class, as does a virtually invisible class of successful, wealthy blacks. She socializes with black creative artists, not black politicians and black civil rights advocates.

In the fall of 1987, Oprah took care of some family business when she retired Vernita from her job as hospital dietitian, bought her a condo in Milwaukee, and began sending her $5,000 a month for the rest of her life. Vernon asked for nothing but a ticket to the Tyson–Tyrell Biggs fight, new tires for his truck, and a better TV set for his barbershop on which he could watch Oprah. She got him the tires and the TV set and flew with him to Vegas to watch the fight.

In May 1987, she gave the commencement address at Tennessee State University (TSU) and finally received her diploma so that she could say, "See, Daddy, I amounted to something." She underscored that proud sentiment by endowing ten scholarships, for a total of $770,000, at TSU in Vernon's name. These scholarships pay for tuition, room and board, books, and spending money for the students who receive them.

In early September, Oprah threw a giant party in Chicago for one thousand guests—staff, friends, show guests, stars— to celebrate how far she had come. Oprah, in black, with a sleeveless top, rhinestone buttons, plunging neckline, and short, straight skirt and emerald-green jacket, and with Stedman on her arm, mingled with the guests, who were munching on beef tenderloin, barbecued ribs, baked Brie, and skewered vegetables and pastry desserts. Each table had two dozen long-stemmed roses and *Oprah Winfrey Show* T-shirts. When it came time for the program, Oprah thanked everyone who had helped along the way, including her father Vernon, a small man who blew her a kiss from his seat.

"He's a skinny little man," she said. "I didn't take those genes from him."

She thanked King World for making her rich, Jeffrey Jacobs for keeping track of the money, and Stedman because "he's the balance, pleasure, and delight in my life." She added one little note: "This is the last party I'm having until I get married." On that cue, Stedman led her out to the dance floor.

In September she appeared at another charity function and spoke at an AIDS fund-raiser in Chicago. There she revealed with sadness that a dear friend of hers had AIDS, her aide Billy Rizzo. It is one of the many speeches she gives year-round at churches, YMCAs, charitable fund-raisers, and public events. She and Stedman do not do much socializing, and Oprah still spends time reading, especially the Bible, biographies, black history, and black women's books.

Capitalizing on the enormous popularity of Oprah's daytime show, King World announced on December 14 that it would make the *Oprah Winfrey Show* available for late-night broadcast in the fall of 1988. Steven Palley, senior vice president and chief operating officer of King World, said that King World research revealed a big potential market for Oprah's show among people who couldn't watch during the day because they worked. Just two days later, Palley and King World had to backtrack because of contract problems with WLS-TV, which still produced the show, and with the 198 stations that aired the daytime show. Joe Ahern, the president and general manager of WLS-TV, said that the station's production contract prohibited syndication of Oprah in the late-night market. He didn't go into detail, but some things could be assumed by professionals in the broadcasting industry.

Releasing Oprah for late-night rebroadcast could cut down the number of daytime viewers and the income from the daytime show for WLS-TV and ABC-TV. The 198 stations that carried Oprah in the daytime slot had first rights to the night run of the program, but because of other late-night commitments, many couldn't take a late-night Oprah. Some fifty-eight of them were NBC affiliates and were committed to the *Tonight* show. Of the remainder, seventy-five were ABC affiliates that were already committed to carrying *Night Court, Bob Newhart, Cheers, Family Ties,* or *Nightline,* which are less expensive than Oprah and draw reasonably good ratings. Stations already committed to these other shows would have to turn down late-night Oprah. That would leave King World free to sell Oprah to competing stations in the same market, to the detriment of the stations that carried her show during the day. The bottom line, whatever else the *Oprah Winfrey Show* may be, is that it is a business and everybody connected with it wants to make money from it.

What King World had in mind for the late-night show paralleled what they did with the daytime show. In the broadcasting industry this arrangement is called a "cash and barter" deal. The local station pays some cash, usually enough to cover their pro-rata share of basic production cost. Then the rest is bartered in the form of commercial minutes in the show. Assuming twelve minutes of commercials in the show, the local station keeps, say, ten minutes for itself to sell to local sponsors and gives King World two minutes for it to sell. This means that King World has two minutes of commercial time on 198 stations, with 16 million viewers, around the country. In turn, King World can sell this time to national advertisers who want to get into the Oprah audience and can't do it any other way. This arrangement works well for the stations, in that they are not locked into a completely fixed, flat price for the show, because the rates charged for the commercials reflect the popularity of the program and can thus fluctuate.

The making of the show required a loyal staff, and Oprah continued to reward key staffers in her unique way. Just before Christmas, Oprah took three of her producers and her publicist to New York, and after they had all settled into their rooms, they found a note slipped under their doors: "Bergdorf's or Bloomingdale's—you have 10 minutes to decide." Christine Tardio, one of the producers and deeply devoted to Oprah, said they picked Bergdorf's. Then they all piled into the limousine and cruised off to the store. As they went in, Oprah handed each of them an envelope with a slip of paper on which was written an outrageous sum of money. They were then told that this was their spending allowance in the store, and off they rushed to buy everything they could.

The fairy-tale experience continued the next morning with another note under the door: "You have five minutes to decide where you want to buy boots and shoes—Walter Steiger or Maud Frizon."

Later, they were driving around in the limousine drinking champagne, and Oprah insisted they all put on blindfolds. Dutifully, they did, the limousine stopped, and they were led into a building. The blindfolds were whisked off, and they were all standing in the middle of a furrier's.

Oprah's instructions: "You can have anything in the store you want except sable." They got three minks and one fox. A generous Oprah could afford such largesse. By the end of 1987, she reached 9 million homes and was among the top five in syndication.

CHAPTER

14

1988—A Year of Important Moves

At the beginning of 1988, Oprah was still trying to take off weight, jogging seven miles a day, and working on her next film project, a four-hour ABC-TV miniseries, *The Women of Brewster Place*.

On February 1, 1988, the *New York Times* printed a story that exposed the myth that she was beating Donahue in the ratings all over America. In the nine cities where the two of them went head-to-head, Oprah generally got the bigger ratings, but they were opposite each other only in those nine cities out of a total of approximately 190 stations. Donahue appeared in the mornings in 149 cities, as opposed to Oprah on only 24. The balance flipped in the afternoon, with Oprah appearing in 168 cities and Donahue in 38. So Donahue was king of the morning, and Oprah was queen of the afternoon, with neither fading or slipping. In fact, while Oprah achieved high ratings around the country, Donahue did better than ever, with 31 percent share of the audience as compared with 27 percent three years before. Oprah reached 30 percent of the viewing audience, which has been her share since she went national in 1986.

As for personal animosity, that really didn't exist, and in 1987, when Oprah received the Emmy Award for the Best Talk

Show, she thanked Donahue for blazing the trail for their kind of provocative show and preparing the audience for her.

"One of the biggest moments of my life came right then," Oprah said later. "After I thanked him, he came up to my table, and he kissed me, and that's when I knew that it was all media-contrived and he didn't hate me at all! 'You deserve it, you deserve it, you deserve it!' he told me."

Donahue reiterated his feeling while admitting that Oprah's appearance on the television-talk-show scene did bruise the Donahue ego a little bit: "The biggest emotional adjustment has been to our ego," he said. "After all these years of enjoying this premier place all by ourselves, we looked up to see somebody doing what we do and getting light-years more publicity. Her success certainly was newsworthy, and it has energized everybody in the studio."

In order to do more film roles, Oprah needed to control her show completely in order to solve her scheduling problems. So Jeffrey Jacobs and Oprah began talking to King World and Cap Cities/ABC about dropping the show when her contract ended in 1991, even though she received 25 percent of what King World grossed, which gave her $2 million in 1986, $12 million in 1987, and probably $25 million in 1988. Both Cap Cities/ABC and King World had to be part of the deal because Cap Cities/ABC and the other TV networks were forbidden by law from syndicating shows that they own. Therefore, an independent syndicator was necessary.

Jacobs said, "We began to discuss that subject with King World, then Cap Cities/ABC management, and through a long, protracted negotiation, Oprah agreed to do the show through August 1993." Jacobs had wanted a better deal, and on July 14, 1988, he got it. Harpo Productions, owned by Oprah, obtained ownership and control of the *Oprah Winfrey Show* and a guarantee that stations owned and operated by ABC would carry it for five years. King World would distribute the show until August 1993.

This new arrangement allowed Oprah to buy two important pieces of real estate for herself that year: the square-block production facility in Chicago, which she renamed Harpo Studios, for $10 million, and the 160-acre farm in Indiana where she and Stedman and family and friends often go for weekends. The farm in the community of Rolling Prairie is designed to look like an English country estate. Built of stone, it has twelve bedrooms, a screening room, and a library, along with grounds punctuated by the trappings of the very rich: tennis courts, riding-horse stables, double garage, swimming pool, and of course, satellite dishes. The only thing lacking to complete the picture is scarlet-jacketed huntsmen and a pack of hounds, although Stedman and Oprah do have five golden retrievers, and she does jog in a red sweat suit.

Oprah invested an additional $10 million remodeling Harpo Studios to make it into a first-rate film and television production facility, the best in the Midwest. The new plant at 1058 West Washington Street, half a mile from downtown Chicago, had previously belonged to Studio Network, Inc. It consisted of the three large studios, office, workshops for carpentry and painting, screening rooms, darkroom, kitchen, and inside parking.

The purchase of the 88,000-square-foot production complex was announced in mid-September of 1988, just two days after Oprah took over control of her show. The purchase involved money from King World as part of the deal to keep its main moneymaker happy and would serve as the home of the *Oprah Winfrey Show*, then being shot at WLS-TV. The facility would have two additional studios besides the one built for the *Oprah* show. Oprah hoped to attract other productions, including movies that she herself owned. She would appear in such TV films as *The Women of Brewster Place*, which would become the first television series produced in the newly named Harpo Studios.

The studio purchase came after making the new deal with King World and Cap Cities/ABC-TV, for the two are inter-related. She said, "Had I not taken ownership of the show, I would not have pursued the whole idea of having my own studio. One thing would not have worked out without the other. I did this to really expand into the areas I wanted to and take over the show to create more time for me to do features and TV specials."

Oprah is the first black to own a major studio facility and

the third woman, after Mary Pickford and Lucille Ball. "Words can't really express how this feels," she added. "I was jogging yesterday when it finally hit me. I never think about how far I've come, but there are moments when I think, This really is something. I think this is the 'big time' I've heard so much about."

She wanted to produce works that added to the reputation of black people but that are not limited to a racial straitjacket; she regards such projects as too restrictive and, in fact, unfair to blacks as creative artists. For example, she made a pilot for an ABC-TV sitcom for Brandon Stoddard based on her own experience as a talk-show host, with the usual concept of fictionalizing true life that already went beyond fiction, but the pilot disappointed her.

"It is dead," she said. "I saw the pilot, called Brandon Stoddard, flew to New York, and asked him not to put it on because I thought it was C-grade material, and he agreed that it certainly could have been better." Instead, Oprah wants to see her facility used to create better pilots for other artists.

With control of the production of her own show, Oprah became free to tape more of her programs so that she could take on other projects. For her this freedom meant greater flexibility as well as greater responsibility, since she had become not only the star but the boss who signed everybody's paychecks. In contrast Donahue's show is owned, produced, and distributed by Multimedia Entertainment, in which Donahue is a major stockholder.

The range of topics on Oprah's shows indicates where her focus, or at least the focus of millions of American women on a given afternoon, is. Subject matter quite normally has to do with sex and relationships; religion, cults, and the New Age movement; fat and personal appearance. The emphasis is on psychology and sociology and rarely on the economy, foreign affairs, politics, or what might be called male subjects. In this format Oprah follows the pattern set by Donahue.

The February 17, 1988, *Oprah* show concentrated on the worship of the devil and satanic religions, with guests Dr. Michael Aquino, a high priest in the satanic Temple of Set, and Lilith Aquino, his wife and assistant; Lauren Stratford, author of the work *Satan's Underground*; Johanna Michaelsen, author of *The Beautiful Side of Evil*; and Det. Larry Jones, an investigator of satanism. The show began with Oprah saying that authorities in every state were investigating satanic activities, including witches' covens in Ohio that practiced human sacrifices; day-care centers teaching children satanic rituals; and infants being killed as offerings to Satan.

Then she introduced Dr. Michael Aquino and his wife, Lilith, who have been high priest and high priestess of the Temple of Set for twenty years. Dr. Aquino claimed that satanic worship is not evil, just different from conventional religion: "Satanism is a recognition that humanity, unique among life-forms, is something that can perceive itself as an actor against the rest of the material universe, that we can reach out and we can change it; we can do things because we have free will, not because we're governed by instinct or by some sort of a large universal machine or mechanism. We are not servants of some God. We are our own gods; we are our own decision makers."

When Oprah brought up the question lurking in everyone's mind about human or animal sacrifice, Dr. Aquino said that such things are absolutely not sanctioned by satanic worship. He declared, "I would say that if you were to attribute that kind of perverted behavior to anyone you would have to take people who had been brought up in the system where the term 'Satan' represented something perverted, which I would lay at the doorstep of the Christian value system and say that what you have here are Christians gone wrong."

And then Oprah and Dr. Aquino connected satanism to the New Age movement in that it, too, works for the good of humankind "under the realm of Satan; under the realm of the exploration of this element of the human psyche that is responsible for its own virtue and responsible for its own ethics."

To which Oprah responded, "This is very much the way a lot of people who are into metaphysics now and New Age movement and New Age thinking, they say the very same thing." Aquino agreed and blamed acts done by others in the supposed name of Satan as depraved behavior arising out of degenerate Christian behavior. Oprah's announcement that Dr.

Aquino was also a career army officer and lt. colonel surprised many in the audience.

Then Oprah took a break and went into the audience for questions and comments; as usual, some audience members were not there by coincidence. The first speaker identified himself as a satanist church member in Chicago and former head acolyte for the satanist ceremony of *Walpurgisnacht* and claimed that at the end of the ceremony somebody was murdered. He described the conclusion of the witches' Sabbath ritual, which he said took place in Chicago in 1980 or 1981. He declared, "The high priest brought out these seven daggers, and they impaled him [the human sacrifice] in the form of a cross with the seven daggers."

This man said he quit satanism in fear, had been stalked and threatened by other satanic church members, and had a nervous breakdown. He claimed to have reported the killing to the police, who investigated, but while they found the trappings of the ritual killing, they could never find the body. The man refused to identify the killers on the air, saying that if he did, they would find out about it and come after him again.

Aquino called the man a liar, pointing out inconsistencies in his story, and then denied connections with the Nazis, as charged by another audience speaker. At that point, Oprah introduced authors Lauren Stratford and Johanna Michaelsen, who alleged that most satanic cults in America are dangerous and should be stamped out. Ms. Stratford said that as a young child in a satanic cult, she was drugged and forced to witness devil rituals and eventually, as an adult, the sacrifice of her own children.

The second new guest was Johanna Michaelsen, a member of a satanic cult that practiced mind control, and the third was Det. Larry Jones, director of the Cult Crime Impact Network of Boise, Idaho. Jones believed satanism had infiltrated day-care centers and schools at all levels. Ms. Stratford said she had been an illegitimate child given to a family involved in pornography and satanism that used her as a breeder of two 6-week-old children used in snuff films—pornographic films in which someone is tortured, sexually abused, and murdered—and a third, Joey, whom she watched being slain in a satanic ritual when he was six months old. Ms. Stratford said the satanic worshipers who controlled her were professional people: doctors, lawyers, Sunday school teachers, and fundamentalist pastors.

Throughout all of this, Dr. Aquino protested that the stories were vague, filled with errors, and that much of the perverted behavior was mistakenly being labeled satanic worship. Several other audience members spoke up, saying they were criminal investigators who dealt with cases where devil worship and human sacrifice were involved, and finally, Ms. Stratford closed the show with her own claims of persecution.

"Victims are coming out now," she declared. "I've been threatened with death; I've had pigeons on my door, blood-covered notes. I have gone to the police. It is reported. It is in the record, and victims are speaking out now. And there is a way out, through the freedom of Jesus Christ."

Other program topics during early 1988 included "Is Monogamy Possible?," "Robin Williams," "the New Age Movement," "Women Hearing the Biological Clock," "Teen Promiscuity," "Pornography Addicts," "Pregnant and Angry," "Skinheads," "Do All Men Cheat?," "Women Who Turn to Lesbianism," "the Cast of *L.A. Law*," and "Sexual Exploitation of Children."

Between taping these shows, Oprah was flying back and forth between Chicago and Hollywood to film *The Women of Brewster Place* on the back lot at Universal Studios. The shuttling tired Oprah, especially since it kept her away from Stedman, so they only saw each other occasionally. "He's in different cities all the time. I tell him, 'I'll meet you at the American Airlines counter.'"

Marriage occupied Oprah's mind a lot during this spring of 1988, according to Robin Givens, the former wife of heavyweight boxing champion Mike Tyson. "All Oprah talked about was marriage—why we chose each other, if it was good, if she should get married. Michael said to me, 'I feel like we're being interviewed.' We wanted to kid her and ask, 'Is it okay if we go on with our marriage?'" Later, Robin and Mike would divorce. Mike would go to jail for rape and Robin would do a nude spread for the September 1994 issue of *Playboy*.

While Oprah said she didn't feel any pressure to get married, she also said, "My friends tell me, 'Three years into a relationship, you have to decide.' And I'm getting that ol' biological clock pressure, too."

Back in Chicago on May 11 she put on another sex-related show. She opened with a warning to viewers that the material might not be suitable for children. It dealt with something that most of the people in her audience had never heard of before, autoerotic asphyxia, which she said killed hundreds of teenage boys every year. The teenage slang for the practice is "scarfing," or "head rushing," and it involves cutting off one's oxygen while masturbating.

This peculiar exercise is accomplished in a variety of ways, such as tightening a noose around one's neck or covering the head with a plastic bag pulled tight around the neck with a drawstring while masturbating. The deprivation of oxygen is supposed to create a physical high comparable to what happens to some undersea divers or high-altitude fliers and mountain climbers. This practice presumably heightens the sexual experience.

In fact, autoerotic asphyxia should not be thought of as limited to teenage boys. A number of grown men also do it, including a member of the cabinet of England's prime minister, John Major, who was found in early 1994 wearing women's underwear with a plastic bag over his head and sprawled over a kitchen table. He was dead as a result of a miscalculation while engaged in autoerotic asphyxia.

Oprah and her staff, particularly her producer Debra Di-Maio, argued for a long time over whether to air this show because of its provocative nature and the possibility that it might inspire some unsophisticated viewers to imitate the behavior described on the program. Debra apparently checked with some experts on the subject of autoerotic asphyxia, particularly Dr. Park Dietz, who at that time was on the faculty of the University of Virginia School of Medicine. Today Dr. Dietz is in private psychiatric practice as a consultant to police and security services. He frequently appears as an expert forensic witness in bizarre and unusual criminal cases. Based in Newport Beach, California, Dr. Dietz spends most of his waking hours studying the dark side of the human mind, as an explorer into the hidden recesses we would prefer not to admit exist inside all of us. At forty-six, the doctor spends a lot of time talking with, sitting in prison cells of, and probing the mental labyrinth of people like serial killer Jeffrey Dahmer and John Hinckley Jr., who shot President Ronald Reagan and James Brady, and John Wayne Gacy, who was executed in Illinois on May 10, 1994.

Dr. Park Dietz is a little bit more frightened of daily life than most of us are. He may know too much—certainly more than we know—about the aberrant mind and how frequently it occurs in society. In his judgment, there are at least 5 million psychopaths currently loose in the country. The doctor believes that 5 percent of the national work force is "clinically depressed," human time bombs waiting for an excuse to go off.

His Cornell college roommate knew him well, he thought, but was surprised when he discovered Park's interest in deviant behavior. Now a lawyer in Manhattan, the former roommate, Greg Milmoe, says of Dr. Dietz, "He was a dyed-in-the-wool preppy conservative. He wore penny loafers, a suit and tie, and was a stuffed pompous ass, but a very smart one. He had the ability to charm people."

The big change in Dr. Dietz's life came when he browsed through Keith Simpson's book *Forensic Medicine*, which fascinated the young medical student who came from a family tradition of three generations of doctors. Dr. Dietz was intrigued by the grotesque cases he encountered in the book. One in particular seized his mind. It was a black-and-white photo of a man who had hanged himself with a display of pornography spread out under his dangling body. It was his first encounter with autoerotic asphyxia, and Dr. Dietz became fascinated and disturbed by the fact that anyone would do this to himself.

Later, Dr. Dietz published the only authoritative work on the subject of autoerotic asphyxia. His journey into exploring the crazed half of our minds began with his probing pornography, torture, sadism, masochism, ritual murder, and psychologically odd behavior. Ironically, his first major case involved testifying for the prosecution in the trial of John Hinckley Jr.

Dr. Dietz's side lost. Dr. Dietz and the prosecution claimed that Hinckley was sane and should stand trial for murder and attempted murder. The jury ruled that Hinckley was insane. Then, at the next Hinckley trial, the prosecution did a complete flip-flop and claimed that Hinckley was insane and should be incarcerated in a mental hospital.

Dr. Dietz vehemently warned Oprah's staff against broadcasting the show. He said that he wanted nothing to do with the program. To him television was not a suitable medium for discussing a subject as intimate as autoerotic asphyxia. He said, "On May 10, the day before the Oprah show was to be done, I had a heated discussion with the producer. I told her that if the show were aired, it would foreseeably result in one or more deaths."

Dr. Dietz warned that he intended to offer himself as an expert witness to anyone who sued Oprah for reckless and negligent conduct and would tell the jury that he had spoken to the producer and had warned against broadcasting the program. The producer told Dr. Dietz that they intended to air the show. Later, Oprah said she had meditated and concluded that they should broadcast the program, and they did so the next day.

Her first guests were Margot Cusimano and Denna Calandrillo, along with Marilyn and Louis Bove, all of whose sons had accidentally killed themselves during autoerotic asphyxia. Marilyn Bove said that many parents prefer to call the death of a son from autoerotic asphyxia a suicide when it is actually an accident. Mrs. Bove felt she had to speak out to warn other parents.

She told the audience, "My daughter, who's twenty-three, called the county coroner to ask what autoerotic [entered as the cause of death on the death certificate] was.... when I first heard it, I said, 'Oh, no, my son would not do this,' and I felt like taking everything in the room and just throwing it."

Oprah wanted to know if there are signs to alert parents about a boy involved in autoerotic asphyxia, and Mrs. Bove said there were none that she understood at the time, even though she knew he had ropes and pornographic tabloids in his room. Mr. Bove said that he had attended nine schools on two continents and been exposed to many different cultures and had never heard of it, but after the death of his son, he learned that the practice dated back to the fourteenth century.

Early in the show, Oprah announced that their switchboard was receiving a lot of telephone calls from viewers who didn't understand what they were talking about, so she turned back to the Boves and asked them to describe graphically what had happened. Their son Sean had a noose around his neck, with the other end of the rope secured, so that when he sat down, he was about an inch off the floor and air was cut off from his lungs. Seated in this way, he faced the pornographic material and began to masturbate. Apparently, he lost consciousness before he ejaculated or could stand up, and he choked to death. A similar accidental death occurred with Margot Cusimano's son Tim and Deanna Calandrillo's son Matthew, whom she thought at first had been murdered, even though the medical authorities listed the death as a suicide.

Mrs. Cusimano said that she tried to get their school to deal with autoerotic asphyxia in sex-education classes but that the authorities refused because they feared it would encourage other young men to experiment with the practice. Mrs. Calandrillo's surviving sixteen-year-old son asked the school to devote an assembly to it, but, again, school authorities didn't want to deal with the subject. Adam Calandrillo, Matthew's brother, discovered his body and called his mother, who came running, along with Matthew's six-year-old brother. Afterward, she learned that autoerotic asphyxia is widely known among teens. Rock groups sing songs about it, and magazines print step-by-step articles on how to do it.

Oprah next introduced Diane Herceg, the parent of another victim, who said, "When [she] found her son dead from autoerotic asphyxiation, he was leaning over a pornographic magazine, open to a page which contained the step-by-step instructions of how to perform this practice. She attempted to sue the magazine for the death of her son. The case was lost at the Supreme Court level."

Then Oprah introduced Dr. Harvey Resnick, a clinical psychiatrist and director of suicide prevention at George Washington University and an expert on autoerotic asphyxia. "Over the twenty years that I've known about the phenomenon [autoerotic asphyxia], there has been no information really available to survivors. Just as with other problems we have in mental health, we know that self-help groups and the ability to share grief and to share information is really helpful."

Dr. Resnick explained to Oprah and the audience that the constriction around the neck both cuts off circulation of blood and reduces oxygen to the brain and can compress a nerve complex in the carotid artery. That slows the heart, producing a quick blackout before the person realizes what is happening, and the victim hangs himself accidentally.

Next, Oprah moved into the audience to begin interviewing planted members and callers as part of her orchestration of the show. In this instance, Oprah explained to her viewers that it was not an "ordinary" audience. She said, "If you're asking why there are so many people in this audience who have this problem, we do an on-the-air promotion and ask for people who are relating to whatever particular subject we're doing that day, and that's how we got all of these people in this audience."

Several people in the audience had children who had died from autoerotic asphyxia, and one shopped around sex shops and found that they were selling hanging devices that were supposed to have automatic releases when the user falls unconscious. Another said that a twenty-three-year-old girl used that kind of hanging noose, but her hair tangled in the release and jammed it, so she died.

Dr. Resnick said, "As you get older, you might involve that [autoerotic asphyxia] in your sex play with a partner. . . . It's safer behavior, because if you do get altered consciousness, someone is there to rescue you."

Some in the audience were surprised by the concept of autoerotic asphyxia as a dual sex-play activity for adults and were even more surprised when another audience member rose to announce that her thirty-six-year-old husband of nine years had died of autoerotic asphyxia and that she had been unaware he had been doing it all the while they had been married.

At the end, Dr. Resnick explained that he did what he

thought all parents should do. He talked to his son and two of his son's friends. "I said to them, 'I know that you masturbate, and I think that's really normal, but if you are involved in any kind of ritual that has to do with your necks, you need to know there's a nervous reflex that can get your heart out of beat and render you unconscious and you'll die."

With that final comment Oprah closed out the show, unaware of some of the consequences that might follow.

That afternoon at four o'clock, thirty-eight-year-old John Holm watched the *Oprah* show on ABC (Channel 7) in the home he shared with his sixty-eight-year-old father, Robert, in Thousand Oaks, California. When Robert came home after attending an evening Elks meeting, he found that "the television was still set on Channel Seven, the channel he'd watched Oprah on. The garage lights were on, but the door was locked from the inside. I banged on the door, but there was no answer. I had to break in. That's when I found his body. It was horrible. When the rescue squad came, one of the workers said he knew how my son had died because he'd seen the *Oprah* show that afternoon. I blame the *Oprah* show for my boy's death. I lost my son and my best friend in the world."

Expert pathologists reviewing the case tried to figure out the cause of the death, as they do with every fatality they encounter. The first question is, how does the victim learn to do autoerotic asphyxia? It is not in general-circulation magazines or newspapers, nor is it reported on television. In this particular case, the evidence was very strong that the victim learned about it from the *Oprah* show that day and immediately tried it out, with fatal results. As previously noted, the television set was still on and was tuned to the channel Oprah had been on several hours earlier.

John Holm hired a lawyer to investigate suing Oprah. He said, "Her show led to John's death—and I will never forgive her for that." However, no suit has been filed and the *Oprah* staff rejects the thought that they have any liability. Chris Tardio, one of Oprah's many public relations spokespersons, said, "We were incredibly responsible in doing that show." Dr. Boyd Stephens, chief medical examiner for San Francisco, disputed that view. "It's like teaching people how to make explosives out of household chemicals. The *Oprah* show should be banned," he said.

Then came an incident that was almost inevitable. In September, Oprah, Geraldo, and Sally Jessy found themselves publicly embarrassed by Tani Freiwald, thirty-seven, a part-time actress who faked her way onto each of their shows, claiming to be a sexual surrogate, along with another actor friend, Wes Bailey. She then appeared on Oprah's show in November 1986, claiming to be "Barbara Hall," a married woman who hated sex and whose husband of fourteen years had started to complain about it. Barbara Hall said that she didn't mind that her husband openly sought sex with other women, and it only seemed fair, since she refused to provide it for him. That generated a lot of negative reactions from the studio audience. Colleen Raleigh, Oprah's assistant publicist, said that Barbara Hall had been a good guest. "She was articulate. She told her story very convincingly."

In July 1988, Tani Freiwald and Wes Bailey appeared on Geraldo's show as a sex therapist with her client, "George," who claimed to be a male virgin and whom Tani said she helped achieve full manhood at the age of thirty-five. The two repeated their phony performances on Raphael's show on September 1 and soon after were uncovered by reporter Jim Flanery of the *Omaha World-Herald*. Flanery followed up on an anonymous tip from someone who recognized Freiwald and Bailey from their performances in Omaha dinner and children's theater. Raphael became outraged over the incident, Geraldo threatened to sue, and Oprah issued a statement through her executive producer, Debra DiMaio: "We take every precaution to ensure a person's credibility. We trusted the referral of Chicago psychologist Dr. Dean Dauw, who specializes in sex therapy. In the sensitive area of sexuality, there is no other way to corroborate a guest's personal story."

Dr. Dauw, a physician with a doctorate in psychology and the author of seven sex-therapy self-help books, is known throughout the daytime TV talk world as an energetic promoter of his books and provider of guests with sexual problems for those shows. Ms. Freiwald's appearance on the *Oprah* show apparently came when the doctor was hard-pressed in 1986 for a guest on the subject of "Women Who Hate Sex." Dr. Dauw sent his office manager, Ms. Freiwald, to fill in as a guest on Oprah, and she brought along Mr. Bailey in what both regarded as an acting lark.

After the press uncovered the hoax, Dr. Dauw and Ms. Freiwald got in a public feud. Dr. Dauw said that he had given Ms. Freiwald some sex surrogate training but never told her to fake what she was or what she did. Ms. Freiwald contradicted everything the doctor said and claimed he directed her to play the surrogate and to bring along a phony patient.

Sally Jessy Raphael railed against the hoax and reflected in an awkward way, "We help people. Of all the things to attack, please attack the game show or soap opera. We have to feel our form of broadcasting is better than some of the pap—not that we're not pap. Maybe we're pap with redeeming public values."

Geraldo expressed himself in a more earthy tone. "I'd like to take this lying wimp and put his nose in something smelly and squishy."

Oprah's producer, Debra DiMaio, worried out loud that *Oprah* viewers in the future might begin to get "that flash in their minds telling them that what they're seeing might not be true."

Raphael decided to make the hoax itself the subject of a show on September 8, 1988, as "an improvisational challenge I [Raphael] couldn't pass up." On camera Sally Jessy confronted the hoaxers and charged them with making her and her entire audience a laughingstock. The audience supported her and turned its hostility against Tani and Wes to the point that the show was reduced to a circus. Bailey said, "The audience is screaming for our vital organs. Sally is accusing us of having harmed her personally. Mostly it was yelling and trying to humiliate and discredit us."

A professional hoaxer from New York, Alan Abel, also appeared on the same show to talk about how easy it is to deceive producers, hosts, and viewers. He had been responsible for numerous such illusions over the years. He added,

"These shows don't have the time or necessarily the concern to do in-depth research. They play fast and loose. They want the ratings."

Something that Oprah had no illusions about while this was happening was her continuing weight problem and obsession. Oprah's weight has been a problem in her life since she was a teenager, and in 1988 she decided to do something about it. She went on a physician-supervised liquid diet, hired a special cook, and worked out every day. On November 15, 1988, she wheeled a little red wagon onto the stage with sixty-seven pounds of animal fat sitting in it and announced that was how much she had taken off. She had trimmed down to 145 pounds and proclaimed, "Right now I feel about as good as you can feel and still live." Her medically supervised diet had been discussed almost daily on her show. Millions of American women went through Oprah's dieting discipline with her as she methodically shed those sixty-seven pounds on live television.

The hardest moment of that show was when her boyfriend called in and told millions of viewers (and Oprah) that the weight loss made it easier for them to walk into a crowded room. Oprah's heart sank because it signified that her physical appearance was key to his love. Later, she would tell her audience that Graham *really* meant to say that the only problem he had with Oprah's extra poundage was that it troubled her and affected her sweet disposition. Nevertheless, it was a natural high for Oprah; she felt so good about herself in her size 10 jeans. It was also a big boost for the maker of Optifast, the medically supervised liquid diet to which she subjected herself.

At the time, she said that losing that weight "was the single greatest achievement in my life." When some skeptics asked if she would be able to maintain her discipline and desire to stay slim, she heatedly responded, "Asking me if I'll keep the weight off is like asking 'Will you ever be in a relationship again where you allow yourself to be emotionally battered?' I've been there, and I don't intend to go back."

Her publicist, Christine Tardio, said it was Oprah's biggest accomplishment. Stephen W. Palley, the chief operating officer of King World, agreed, but for different reasons. The Oprah diet show of November 15, 1988, pulled in a 16.4 rating, meaning that 45 percent of viewers watched it. "These are unbelievable numbers," Palley said. "Those people who didn't see the show certainly heard about it." To achieve her weight loss, Oprah didn't eat any solid food from July 6 to October 17 and sustained herself on five liquid protein drinks totaling 400 calories. Oprah also jogged morning and night on machines for forty-five minutes and got down to size 10. It was a struggle, but pulling that red wagon onstage made it worth all the effort.

CHAPTER

15

1989—Not a Good Year

The year 1989 started out well when *Ms.* magazine declared Oprah one of its six women of the year who had one common characteristic: grit. It saluted Oprah "for showing women that we can climb as high as we want to go and inspiring us to take control of our resources and make them work for us and for a better world."

There was an essay by poet Maya Angelou: "Although she is only 34 years old, Oprah's road has been long and her path has been stony.... She was left in the care of her grandmother who believed in the laying on of hands, in all ways, in prayers, and that God answered prayers. She kneels nightly to thank God for His protection and forgiveness.... Unheralded success has not robbed her of wonder, nor have possessions made her a slave to property."

As she approached her thirty-fifth birthday, Oprah could rely on other successful black celebrities to guide her with advice based on their own experiences. Bill Cosby warned her to always sign her own checks. Angelou cautioned her against spreading herself too thin. "Baby, all you have to do is stay black and die."

When her birthday came at the end of January, Oprah celebrated in Deer Valley, Utah, with Stedman and her staff. The staff's appearance came as a surprise, but that conformed to the relationship Oprah has with the seven people—who are under thirty, single, and mostly female—who work closely with her. They are a tight-knit family that spends fifteen or more hours together every day and often eat breakfast, lunch, and dinner with one another. When Oprah is not in Chicago, which happened with greater frequency as she became more famous, they would send her CARE packages of various goodies and visit her wherever she had gone.

Cheryl Lavin of the *Chicago Tribune* says that they are all so close that when they talk about Oprah, they sound like Moonies. When Oprah learned that she had the part of Sofia in *The Color Purple*—what she called the happiest day of her life—her first call was to her staff to share her happiness with them. They are such a close-knit group that once, in 1985, when Oprah told them to each bring five new people to her New Year's Eve party, they couldn't come up with that many new people that were outside their intimate Oprah circle.

Oprah also spends time with larger groups of strangers as she travels around the country speaking. The American Woman's Economic Development (AWED) Corporation booked Oprah as keynote speaker for its February conference, and thirty-five hundred women came from all over the United States to attend. The AWED is a nonprofit organization that helps women succeed as independent businesspeople through seminars, training programs, and conferences. Oprah's speech outlined her fundamental formula for success; specifically, that each of us is responsible for ourselves, and we have the free will to do and be whatever we want. She declared, "If you are struggling and it doesn't seem to be coming together, you can't look outside of yourself for why it isn't working. You just have to stop right where you are and look right inside yourself."

This statement contradicts her oft-expressed belief in predestination and everybody being and doing what God directs. She once said, "If I can just do what Paul says in the Bible—press to the mark of the high calling of God—then I will have done what I am supposed to do."

She concluded her speech to this enthusiastic audience by listing her ten rules for a successful life—some of the homilies that the all-female audience embraced: Don't try to please others and don't let others control you. Count on yourself and surround yourself with good people. Have harmony in life, dispose of betrayers, be nice, and don't ever give up. And from the richest black woman in the world: Don't do anything for the money.

Oprah's philosophy on and off the air commonly revolves around self-actualization, self-fulfillment catchphrases such as: "You can't see love, you have to be love." "Nothing happens that's not supposed to happen." "Everything stems from loving yourself." "Life is reciprocal." And, "I ask that I be able to live my life so that it magnifies the power of God that is in me."

Oprah needed her own advice to get through the month of March, which was a tense time for her and her kinfolk, whom she had been ignoring for a long time. In most of the stories she tells of her life, her mother, half brother, and half sister are ignored, and while Oprah has taken care of her mother financially, she prefers not to talk about her in public; the same is true for her half brother and half sister. Like many celebrities, Oprah is embarrassed by the ways that some of her family occasionally try to capitalize on their blood connection, such as the time Patricia spilled the story of Oprah's pregnancy and miscarriage to the tabloids.

In March the sad story of Oprah's half brother, Jeffrey, surfaced with the announcement that he was gay, had AIDS, and felt abandoned by his rich half sister, Oprah. He said she thought it served him right that he contracted AIDS, because every gay was going to die from the disease, and when he had been in the hospital several months before, Oprah neither visited him nor sent money. Jeffrey said it particularly hurt that Oprah had responded so effusively to the news around the same time that her longtime aide, Billy Rizzo, also had AIDS. At the time she learned of Rizzo's illness, she said, "I love Billy like a brother. He's a wonderful, funny, talented guy, and it's just heartbreaking to see him so ill." She stood by him in every way she could, including checking on his condition daily.

Those people around Oprah rushed to her defense and pointed out that she was sorry her half brother had AIDS and that she had given him money but that the two had never been close since Oprah's mother sent her back to her father when she was fourteen and Jeffrey was six. More family secrets came out when Oprah claimed she gave extra money to her mother to use on herself or to help Jeffrey. Apparently, the mother used most of it on herself and gave Jeffrey's landlord a bad check for $1,400 that got Jeffrey evicted when it bounced.

Oprah felt she had to help her mother, but she frankly had received little or no support from her mother and her side of the family. She didn't feel obligated to pay back something she was never given. When she did a show on mothers and daughters, Oprah made the point that her own mother had abandoned her from infancy until Oprah was six and again from fourteen to twenty-one. When she suddenly discovered that Oprah was rich and famous, she began jetting into town regularly to borrow clothes from Oprah's closet. The family problems would continue.

In the face of that family tension, Stedman and Oprah spent part of March relaxing, with Oprah slimming down at the famous Golden Door Spa in Escondido, California, near San Diego. In addition to the few days of relaxation, Oprah would appear on the *Tonight* show with Johnny Carson on March 17, 1989. She wanted to slim down with the Golden Door's regime of strict diet, exercise, and meditation and get ready for the other projects that were lined up at Harpo, including more black-experience films like *Kaffir Boy*, the story of a South African black boy growing up; *Beloved*, about a black woman haunted by memories of slavery, based on the book by Toni Morrison; and *Their Eyes Were Watching God*, about the maturing of a black girl in America.

On June 11, 1989, writer Barbara Grizzuti Harrison sounded the theme of what was happening in daytime talk TV in her *New York Times* profile of Oprah: "Since the proliferation of trash-television programs, there has been an undertone of hysteria, an edge of danger, to daytime talk-TV; the potential for mischief is realized."

Predictably, the signal of this view was the botched May 1, 1989, program about the "Mexican Satanic Cult Murders" in which a Jewish element was inexplicably introduced by Oprah and her staff. Even though the program was about the satanic cult murders that had taken place near Matamoros on the

Mexican border and involved the killing of a preppy white male college student, a mysterious Jewish woman named "Rachel" appeared on the show. She talked about the history of her family going back to the year 1700 and how they abused children and turned them into human sacrifices. She claimed that even what seemed like nice Jewish families were engaged in secret devil worship!

Oprah repeatedly mentioned that Rachel was a Jew and displayed obvious distaste and rejection of this "secret Jewish satanic worship," implying that it was widespread among Jews. The Jewish community in the United States exploded with outrage, and the backlash swept over the *Oprah* show and the stations that carried it. The *New York Times* noted that Oprah preached that we must be responsible for what we do and that with our freedoms came the accountability for our own actions. They added that she had remained mute in the face of their rage. Finally, Oprah negotiated with leaders of the national Jewish community, and they all issued a joint statement on May 9: "The *Oprah Winfrey Show* on May 1 could have contributed to the perpetuation of historical misconceptions and canards about Jews, and we regret that any harm may have been done."

Hard on the heels of the Jewish satanic cult program, Terry Rakolta of Michigan held a news conference claiming the support of Coretta Scott King and Patrick Buchanan in the formation of "Americans for Responsible Television," whose goal was to promote efforts by advertisers and the networks to raise the standards of programming on television, such as Oprah Winfrey's show. Ms. Rakolta said that she first became aware of the need for such a movement when her daughter had watched an *Oprah Winfrey Show* dealing with sexual addictions and one of the guests talked about having sex with a dog. The Oprah production staff said that they couldn't be sure that actually happened on the show.

Everybody in Oprah's circle became involved in a different sexual story concerning Oprah and Stedman's private life when, on May 18, 1989, *Entertainment Tonight* broadcast a rumor that had been bubbling on Chicago radio talk shows and had appeared as a blind item in columnist Ann Gerber's column in the *Chicago Sun-Times*. The claim was that Oprah had discovered Stedman having sex with her hairdresser and had shot him.

The next day, Oprah denounced Gerber's column on her program. "It is a vicious, malicious lie, and no part of it, absolutely no part of it, is true," she declared. "I have chosen to speak up because this rumor has become widespread and so vulgar that I just wanted to go on record and let you know that it is not true."

Her audience became confused. While she denounced something as a lie, she never told them what it was. Stedman remained silent. Later, she would say she felt she had been raped by the rumor but that it made her stronger than ever and that her relationship with Stedman had been reinforced by the trauma of it all.

She later confessed to Laura B. Randolph of *Ebony* magazine that it was *her fault*. "I believe in my heart that had I not been an overweight woman that rumor would never have occurred. If I were lean and pretty, nobody would ever say that. What people were really saying is, why would a straight, good-looking guy be with me?"

The rumor had been making the rounds all over Chicago before it hit print in Ann Gerber's "On The Town" column in the *Chicago Sun-Times*. Then the May 23 issue of the *Sun-Times* announced that Ms. Gerber had been fired because of differences between her and the newspaper "regarding the journalistic standards used in producing her column." There was no mention of Oprah or Stedman, and Vera Johnson, an aide to the executive editor, Kenneth Towers, denied that there was any connection between the Stedman item and Ann Gerber's dismissal.

Gerber drives a blue Mercedes with a vanity license plate: CATTY. Like Oprah, she started her career as a teenager when she became a part-time summer reporter for the Lerner chain of community newspapers in the Chicago area. In 1987 she was hired by the *Sun-Times* as its new gossip columnist. Gerber's "On The Town" column soon became immensely popular, taking up three and one-half pages on Wednesdays and a page and a half on Sundays, which annoyed other writers on the staff, who also were competing for space. One irritated co-worker said that even by the sleazy standards of a Rupert Murdock newspaper like the *Sun-Times*, Gerber's work was an embarrassment. Others objected to her $77,000-a-year salary and to her dressing like a Hollywood tart and flouncing around the newsroom like some overaged starlet on the make. Many repeated the story she told about how she snared her current husband by wearing a black bikini at the Edgewater Beach Cabana Club. "There was no contest," she bragged.

Then, in early May, she was listening to a call-in talk show, *Murphy in the Morning*. She said, "Robert Murphy got a call from some woman who said, 'Is it true that Oprah Winfrey came home early from a vacation and found her boyfriend in bed with her hairdresser?' Several people also asked Ann about it, and she decided to run the story as a blind item in her column on the following Sunday, May 14. She wrote, "Can it be true that the lover of one of our richest women was found in bed with her hairdresser when she returned early from a trip abroad? The battle that ensued brought her screaming out onto Lake Shore Drive, shocking her staid neighbors."

The next day, the executive editor, Kenneth Towers, summoned Gerber to his office and demanded that she produce proof that the item was true, which, of course, Gerber could not do. Then, a few days later, *Entertainment Tonight* called Gerber. "I was so naive," she said. "They asked me, 'That item you ran, was it about Oprah?' and I said yes, because I thought everybody knew."

Then, a week later, Towers called Gerber into his office again and this time tore up her next column as she watched, told her she was fired, and demanded she sign an agreement accepting two weeks' severance pay. Instead, she got on the phone to Don Reuben, an attorney specializing in libel cases, and months of hard negotiations followed, ending with the *Sun-Times* making a substantial, but undisclosed, settlement, part of which Gerber used to buy herself a sable coat. She now writes for an upscale weekly publication, *Skyline*.

Towers still refuses to talk about the incident. He left the newspaper to join the Insurance Information Service. Gerber said that her departure seemed like a funeral to her; she received fourteen floral pieces and 120 sympathetic phone calls. She got the money, but her attorney warned her that the stigma would stay with her forever; indeed, the *Sun-Times* would never hire her again, and the *Tribune* doesn't have a gossip columnist.

Two years later, Gerber and Oprah ran into each other at a reception celebrating the opening of a new library. Gerber said that Oprah smiled at her, and so she went right over to talk to the TV star. They both said they were so sorry about the unfortunate incident that had galvanized Chicago for days in 1989 and had become the subject of endless news stories and numerous segments on talk radio.

Gerber said, "We had a good talk. Oprah's really very sweet. I felt so bad about things that had happened. And I used to think that she had something to do with the firing, but I know now that she didn't."

Other newspaper stories in 1989 were better received by Oprah's circle of friends and colleagues, for they underscored Oprah's national stature. America's newspaper of record, the *New York Times*, published three major articles on her, including an unusual in-depth profile in the June 11, 1989, *New York Times Magazine*, written by Barbara Grizzuti Harrison, an essayist and fiction writer. The profile offered insights into the actual Oprah, as well as the public Oprah we see:

"Her audiences are co-creators of the self and the persona she crafts. Her studio is a laboratory. She says hosting a talk show is as easy as breathing. Here she is, an icon, speaking. 'I just do what I do—it's amazing....Everybody's greatness is relative to what the Universe put them here to do. I always knew I was born for greatness.'"

More than any other interviewer of Oprah to date, Ms. Harrison wrote about Oprah's philosophical and metaphysical beliefs:

"She has adopted several metaphysical theories that encompass Eastern religion and Western religion and of what is called New Age. She says she has achieved peace and the serenity of total understanding. [She is thirty-five.] Knotty contradictions in the fabric of her belief have not, up to now, impeded the progress of what she calls a 'triumphal' life. Her great gift for making herself likable is married to a message smooth as silk: *Nothing is random.*"

In other words, our lives are preordained; therefore, nothing we do of our own free will can alter our destiny. Yet this is the same Oprah who preaches that you must be responsible for yourself and you can be whatever you wish, just as she, a black female, rose from an illegitimate, abandoned, poor childhood to become the most powerful black woman in the world. The contradictions are obvious, never explained, and never questioned by her 16 million loyal fans.

Ms. Harrison says that criticism of Oprah is often petty and comes from people who, for example, object to her preference for wearing green contact lenses, but it is also tangible when she is faulted for black male bashing. Another reason this *New York Times* profile seemed unusual is that Ms. Harrison really dislikes Oprah and thinks she smacks of the kind of evangelical hucksterism for which Billy Sunday and Reverend Ike became infamous. In a 1993 *Chicago* magazine article, Ms. Harrison is quoted as saying, "Her show . . . I just can't watch it. You'll forgive me, but it's white trailer trash. It debases language, it debases emotion. It provides everyone with glib psychological formulas. These people go around talking like a fortune cookie. And I think she is in very large part responsible for that."

Criticism seemed to mount in 1989 against the kind of programming Oprah provided in direct proportion to the growing popularity of her show. Other daytime talk-show hosts were mimicking her subject matter, as Geraldo Rivera, Sally Jessy Raphael, and even Donahue spiced up their topics to stay competitive. Some media observers in particular found this "tabloid" trend disturbing. It attracted big audiences and lots of advertising money, which hurt so-called legitimate news programs by making them more and more like Oprah, Rivera, Raphael, and Donahue.

MacLean's magazine wrote: "The current crop of racy, melodramatic pseudo-documentary and talk shows, packaged and sold to individual stations, is an extreme example of a trend that some TV critics say has begun to infiltrate legitimate news and public-affairs programming." The critics saw all three TV networks falling under the spell of high ratings and large profits by shifting their focus away from news content to the show-business value of the personalities presenting the programs.

News simulations and reenactments of events, including faked videotapes, exacerbated this tendency. "Mixing entertainment and information is a problem if one is concerned with credibility and the image of the news media in America," said Georgetown University media studies professor Michael Robinson. News executives defended their craft by charging that the fault lay with lurid programs that operate on the flaky edge of public-affairs programming, and they named Rivera and Oprah and their colleagues. Yet the re-creations and simulations were done on legitimate hard-news programs, such as a fake videotape used by ABC-TV in July 1989 of alleged Soviet spy Felix Bloch passing a briefcase filled with American secrets to his Soviet control agent in Paris. CBS was charged in September with using faked battle films from Afghanistan, and NBC later secretly rigged trucks with explosives to demonstrate how easily they could catch fire.

In addition, the big stars of legitimate news were given more Oprah-like programs of their own to host, with ABC launching *Prime Time*, with Diane Sawyer and Sam Donaldson, in the fall 1989 season; Barbara Walters on *20/20*; and the old perennial, *60 Minutes*, thought by some not to be that far removed from Oprah.

Matt Roush, TV critic for *USA Today*, commented, "So far, the news surrounding these shows has less to do with content than with the talent." A. M. Rosenthal, former executive editor of the *New York Times*, labeled an October 13 edition of *Hard Copy* as "deliberately sensationalized journalistic garbage."

Defense for the Oprah, Rivera, Donahue, and Raphael shows came from the distinguished journalist Robert MacNeil of the *MacNeil/Lehrer NewsHour*: "The American appetite for print journalism stretches all the way from journals like *Foreign Affairs* magazine at one end of the spectrum to papers like *Screw* on the other. Television has followed that trend by breaking out of the safe, centrist material in terms of taste, and I don't think that it is an unhealthy thing. There is a limit to the variety of human, sexual, and odd experience for these talk shows, and after they look at demonic possession and sadomasochism and fetishes, where can they go?"

Ignoring that kind of criticism, Stedman and Oprah were guests at a White House state dinner on June 27 for the prime minister of Australia, Bob Hawke. Meanwhile, family problems continued to plague Oprah as much as similar problems affected those who appeared on her show as guests. At about this time a crisis call came from Patricia Lee's daughter Chrishaunda begging her to help with her mother, Oprah's half sister, to whom Oprah was sending $1,200 a month to care for her two nieces, Chrishaunda and Alicia. Apparently, Oprah's half sister, Patricia Lee, stayed away from home days at a time, allegedly doing drugs, during which the two young girls had to fend for themselves. Chrishaunda called because she worried about her mother and because neither she nor her sister had any money or food.

Oprah exploded and cut off her half sister without any more money and arranged for the two girls to move in with their grandmother, to whom Oprah would send support money. To Oprah nothing could be done for Patricia until she recognized that she had a serious drug problem and did something about it herself. The children would be taken care of by Grandmother—a pattern reminiscent of Oprah's own early childhood.

In October, Patricia called her in tears, pleading for help to kick the drug life she had fallen into, and Oprah immediately got Patricia into a rehabilitation center. "She's still my sister," she said. "I can't abandon her. I cut off the money—not my love." In time, Patricia returned to live with Vernita, her and Oprah's mother, and the two grandchildren. That part of the family began turning around.

Not so with Jeffrey, whose condition grew worse as 1989 progressed toward Christmas. Oprah had never approved of Jeffrey's wild lifestyle of free and easy drugs and sex that brought him to his end, and she hurt from the times she tried to help him with money, only to have Jeffrey rip her off, 'cheat, and lie to her. "Now that the end is getting close," he said, "I want Oprah to know that throughout our troubles, I still loved her and was proud of her."

She forgave him and felt sorry that he was dying, but she believed gay men could never get to heaven. Then twenty-nine-year-old Jeffrey Lee passed away, just three days before Christmas at the Green Tree Health Care Center in Milwaukee, prompting a formal statement from Oprah: "For the last two years, my brother, Jeffrey Lee, had been living with AIDS. My family, like thousands of others throughout the world, grieves not just for the death of one young man, but for the many unfulfilled dreams and accomplishments that society has been denied because of AIDS."

As if Jeffrey's dying wasn't enough, Vernita Lee began to tell people that Oprah was so driven by her career that she would never have children. Vernita said that Oprah loved children but just didn't have the patience. She is constantly on the go, which is the way Oprah likes it, Vernita said, and her daughter does not have time for children and hardly enough time for her boyfriend. The last weekend Vernita spent on the Indiana farm was in July, and while Vernita really liked Stedman, she sensed that Oprah was not ready to get married in spite of rumors to the contrary.

With all these things going on in her life, Oprah's triumph over her weight problem was lessened when she admitted to her viewers that she had gained back seventeen pounds of the sixty-seven pounds she had lost. It was ironic that she opened a new restaurant, the Eccentric, at 159 West Erie Street in February, but probably the most eccentric thing to happen to Oprah occurred on August 26, when *TV Guide* published a story about her. When she refused to pose they grafted a photo of her head onto an old and obviously tinted photograph, which was ten years old, of Ann-Margret's body and showed Ann-Margret wearing a Bob Mackie gown, as Oprah often did.

The episode initially made Ann-Margret angry, thinking it a cheap stunt, and it hurt Oprah because the editor hadn't wanted to use Oprah's body, since she had gained some more weight. Later, Ann-Margret shifted her anger to *TV Guide*, realizing that Oprah had nothing to do with the phony picture.

The troubling year ended on a positive note as Oprah

continued her charitable work with a $1 million donation to Morehouse College in Atlanta, Georgia, along with her usual annual contribution of $250,000 to maintain the ten scholarships she had established at Tennessee State University in the name of her father.

16

The Women of Brewster Place

Oprah was intrigued with working on her next film project, a four-hour ABC-TV miniseries, *The Women of Brewster Place*, based on Gloria Naylor's novel about seven black women sharing the same tenement in a northern city. Oprah wanted to do another film because "people said *The Color Purple* was a fluke for me. I had my own personal doubts. I discovered I really am an actress. If you have lived as a black person in America, you know all those women [in *Brewster Place*]. They're your aunts, your mother, your cousins, your nieces."

Brewster was the first TV series for Harpo Productions, but it also turned out to be a tough sell to the older white men who run the networks. Initially, all of them turned it down. Oprah recalled, "They said it was too womanish. I said, 'Look, I know you are very wise and perceptive men and the only reason you have turned down this project is because you haven't read the book. You could not read it and turn it down. I'll be calling by Tuesday to see who's read it.' Only one wise, perceptive executive had read the book by the deadline, but he was sold."

With the concept of the *Brewster Place* film sold, Oprah, who had lost weight, regained ten pounds so she could play the role of Mattie Michael, and her company began shooting. Starting in April 1988, Oprah was practically living on the back lot at Universal Studios in Hollywood, filming *The Women of Brewster Place* after having first taped four weeks of the *Oprah Winfrey Show* in Chicago. She was back doing what she loved most, being in the movies, except this time Oprah was both the star and the boss who signed the paychecks and decided such matters as whether the grips have to pay for their own breakfast. She decided they didn't. When it came to eating, Oprah was a bit out of control herself. Food was her security blanket, and whenever there was pressure during the shooting of the film, she would descend to the corn-chip bowl and start shoveling them in her mouth.

She explained, "I have a corn-chip obsession. Chips calm me down. If I were just doing my show—you see, dieting is my hobby—I could maintain some control. But here, in the middle of a scene, I'll say, 'Corn chips!'"

Oprah thought of *The Women of Brewster Place* as a new learning experience for herself and her staff at Harpo Productions, since it was the first movie they were producing on their own. They had assembled the biggest cast of blacks since the filming of *Roots*, including Cicely Tyson, Oliva Cole, Robin Givens, Moses Gunn, Jackée, Paula Kelly, Lonette McKee, Barbara Montgomery, Phyllis Yvonne Stickney, Douglas Turner Ward, Lynn Whitfield, and Paul Winfield.

When the shooting of *Brewster Place* concluded in June 1988, Oprah threw a party outdoors on the set at Universal Studios, with 150 members of the cast and crew dancing, doing the jerk and the twist, and feasting on barbecued ribs and chicken. The mayor of Los Angeles, Tom Bradley, came to the party, and Joanne Kaufman of *People* magazine wrote a story on the film describing Oprah's first venture into the domain of producing and starring in a movie created by her own company. *People* said, "Chronicling the ghetto lives of seven black women, it's a story of broken dreams, betrayal, bitterness and survival. The themes cut close to Winfrey...she [Oprah] says, it 'makes a great statement for maintaining your dignity in a world that tries to strip you of it.'"

Oprah had seen the final edited cut of *Brewster Place* and

was pleased with it. In response to the behind-the-scenes complaints about her black male bashing by the NAACP, the images of the men in the film were softened a little, according to Oprah's publicist, Christine Tardio, but they still came across as rather rough.

On March 19, 1989, *The Women of Brewster Place* aired on national television with huge ratings—a 37 percent share—mixed reviews, more accusations of black male bashing in the story. The *New York Times* said the subtitle of the movie should be "Revenge of the Black Female," and the reviewer said the men in the story were all "vicious louts." Reviewer John Stark for *People* magazine savaged *Brewster Place*. "The unfocused, overly ambitious drama, set largely in a tenement building in an unnamed city, comes off as part 'The Color Purple,' 'A Raisin in the Sun,' O. Henry's 'Full House' and 'Torch Song Trilogy.'"

Following the usual pattern of television, a made-for-television movie or miniseries is original programming which attracts special audience attention, but it usually is also a pilot for a series. It is a form of market testing for the network TV executives, who rarely like to take unnecessary programming chances. They will find what seems to be a good program idea and do a one-shot movie or miniseries to test audience reaction to the concept and the actors. Following the good audience reaction to the miniseries *The Women of Brewster Place*, the ABC network announced it would air thirteen episodes of a spin-off as a new dramatic series for broadcasting beginning the following April.

Oprah was proud of the film miniseries, and a spin-off weekly series based on the story pleased her even more, for it gave her another opportunity to tell the story of her people, as she had been doing in every film story she had been involved with.

Oprah's first television dramatic series would premiere on May 1, 1990, at 9:30 P.M. and then settle in on Wednesday nights. The first episode dealt with poor health care, not getting respect, and having to challenge the bureaucracy. In this episode Mattie's best friend Etta Mae (Brenda Pressley) and business partner in a neighborhood restaurant has an inflamed appendix. She has pains but ignores them.

Matt Roush of *USA Today* in Chicago commented that Oprah's strict control of the shooting of *Brewster Place* was typical of her life: "...[It] symbolizes her firm grip over all aspects of her own tabloid-chronicled personal life, from fluctuating weight to her relationship with public relations executive Stedman Graham." In fact, *Brewster* is about a bigger Oprah goal, namely, to create good work for herself and others—particularly blacks—and to be able to tell stories about blacks and their lives.

She softened *Brewster's* original story. "How we can do a story about black people with no drugs or violence? The truth is most black middle-class and lower-middle-class people live like the people on *Brewster Place*. You work, have a sense of ethics, want the best for your children, and try to do what's right.

"I'm very hopeful, but if it doesn't work, I won't have the if-I'd-onlys, not at all. First, the *Oprah Winfrey Show* is still my bosom, my root, and my foundation. Without it, nothing else could happen. And I believe that when we finish our thirteen episodes, I can say I gave it everything and that will be the truth."

Brewster Place opened on May 1, 1990, and reviewers found it bland, like a black Waltons. After four episodes, the series was canceled. Naturally, it was a disappointment to Oprah and her crew. *Brewster Place* was a program they loved doing—telling real stories about life as black women in the real world, as opposed to what a lot of whites thought was the black world. The film and the weekly series was also a maiden voyage for Harpo Productions as a film and TV production company, and obviously it would have been nicer to begin with a hit. However, Oprah was sanguine about the outcome of *Brewster Place* and understood from the beginning that there was a high risk. Besides, she had the satisfaction of the TV movie–mini-series proving successful in terms of its ratings. For Oprah, the thing to do was to move on to the next of the many projects she had lined up. Later in May, ABC announced that Harpo would produce four movies, with Oprah starring in two.

CHAPTER

17

The Search for Topics, Guests, and Ratings

In September, the beginning of the 1991–92 season, Oprah grew concerned about developments in her special television world. More and more talk shows were launched to try to capture some of the market dominated by Oprah, Donahue, Geraldo, Sally Jessy, Arsenio Hall, Regis and Kathie Lee, and Joan Rivers. Many people in and out of the broadcasting industry were astonished at the number of new entrants, although those inside the industry understood that the low cost and high gross income of these shows heightened their appeal to programmers.

In September 1991, a long list of new shows announced that they would see if they could carve out a niche for themselves, with hosts that included Maury Povich, Chuck Woolery, Jenny Jones, Whoopi Goldberg, Vicki Lawrence, Dennis Miller, Jane Wallace, Christina Ferrare, and Kitty Kelley. There were additional candidates, among them, Magic Johnson, Valerie Harper, Reba McEntire, Ann Jillian, Jim Palmer, Bree Walker, Paul Rodriguez, Montel Williams, Morton Downey Jr., and a former mayor of Cincinnati, Jerry Springer. The new season would be somewhat like the first day that settlers were allowed to race into Oklahoma to homestead land—lots of people dashing forward raising a lot of dust and only a few getting the choice sites.

The October 14, 1991, issue of *Time* reviewed the growing deluge of talk shows in an article entitled: "Running Off at the Mouth: Mothers-in-law from hell and other lunacies rule the proliferating talk shows." Reporter Richard Zoglin decried the flood of talk shows. He wrote, "Self-awareness is television's big-time plague. Name the social issue, front-page crime or family trauma, and somebody is thrashing it out on a TV talk show. The glut has never been so thick."

In addition to the veteran talk-show hosts, such as Phil Donahue, Oprah Winfrey, Geraldo Rivera, and Sally Jessy Raphael, a mob of newcomers were filling the TV screen, trying to get audience acceptance in the name of human misery. "Stories of individual pain and grief are now hot-button issues," Zoglin said. "Conversation is replaced by political cant and psychological bromides. No personal story is too outlandish for nationwide consumption, no private emotion safe from public exploitation." *Time* helpfully created the "Book Your Own Talk Show" chart and invited the reader to select one from each of four columns to create a topic:

Column A	Column B	Column C	Column D
1. Overweight	Incest victims	Married to	Alcoholics
2. Battered	Couples	Raped by	Serial Killers
3. Handicapped	Prostitutes	Who murdered	Their fathers
4. Homosexual	AIDS sufferers	In love with	Organ Donors
5. Unwed	Sex addicts	Writing books	Madonna

Reporter Zoglin also rated or characterized many of the talk-show hosts for his readers: Maury Povich has a "satyrlike grin that grew in proportion to the tackiness of his story." Jenny Jones was "giggly and farm fresh"; Joan Rivers stressed Hollywood glitz; Geraldo pushed his "aggressive melodramatics more desperately than ever"; Donahue was the shrillest of all and "his hyperventilating style has reached the point of self-parody." Finally, Oprah, whose show was the highest rated of the crowd, "seems to get first call on Hollywood celebrities pushing new movies and tales of personal woe."

In an interview at the end of 1991, Marty Berman, executive producer of *Geraldo*, admitted that the glut of television talk was getting out of hand. "Yeah, I think we're at the saturation point. There's room for a couple. There's not room for everybody." Nor did Berman think there was any innovation among the horde of talk shows flooding the airwaves. "Let's face it, we're all still doing the Phil Donahue show. He's the guy who started it, and he's having his best year yet in the ratings." Of course, Donahue started in Dayton, Ohio, in 1967, when Oprah was still a teenager, and when he went national in 1970, there were only two other talk programs on the air—*Dinah*, in Hollywood, with singer Dinah Shore, and the *Mike Douglas Show*, out of Philadelphia—and they were somewhat different from *Donahue* then, and they no longer exist. If they did, they, too, would be vastly different shows.

That view was echoed by Berman's counterpart at the Sally Jessy Raphael show, Burt Dubrow. "My God, there are so many of them out there." At the 1993 NATPE convention in San Francisco, however, Dubrow's boss, Sally Jessy, commented that there was room for everybody, and she didn't think there were too many talk shows. Dubrow began in television working on the *Mike Douglas Show*, and he remembers that it was basically celebrities, cooking, and promoting new movies and new books. The sex life of a dwarf or Shinto priest was not thought of, much less mentioned. Today, instead of promoting a movie or a book, the guest comes in to hype a disease or emotional condition or to skewer somebody who has done him or her wrong. If that person is dead, fine; if not, bring them on for a confrontation onstage.

The hosts of new shows for the 1991–92 season included *Saturday Night Live* comic Dennis Miller; Academy Award winner Whoopi Goldberg; singer Kenny Rogers; Chuck Woolery, host of *The Love Connection*; and former Soviet journalist Vladimir Pozner, teamed with Donahue. Talk-show hosts that have already been given airtime and found wanting include Ron Reagan Jr., Rick Dees, Marsha Warfield, David Brenner, Jesse Jackson, Ross Schaeffer, Morton Downey Jr, and Pat Sajak, host of *Wheel of Fortune* and a star, along with Oprah, in the King World stable of talent.

The topics ranged from the dumb and hackneyed, like celebrities with books, overweight women, and terrible mothers-in-law, to the weird, such as transplant recipients who have taken on the personalities of their organ donors, women who have been repeatedly raped by the same man, and kids who regretted finding their natural parents.

Some recent topics on the leading shows in 1992 included the marriage of a cross-dressing couple in which both bride and groom wore wedding dresses; a deeply-in-love married couple where the wife is forty-four and the husband is fourteen; a woman whose breasts weigh forty pounds; a man who ruined his marriage by having sex with his brother-in-law; the man who requires pain to sleep and burns himself with lit cigarettes to doze off; the grieving widow who exposes herself to strange men; and the tattooed man who drives nails through his tongue.

Even the promoters of the shows had trouble explaining why theirs was different or better or wiser or more entertaining than any of their competitors'. Chuck Woolery of *The Love Connection* interviewed celebrities, as did Whoopi Goldberg and John Tesh of *Entertainment Tonight*. Ron Reagan, trading on his father's name and denying it at the same time, focused on deeper, more serious topics, such as gay rights and the future of the Democratic party, which may explain why his show didn't last very long. Jim Paratore, senior vice president of Telepictures, which produces the Jenny Jones show, says their show has a fun attitude rather than being newsy or confrontational. Woolery's producer, Eric Lieber, borrowing the strained syntax of computer nerds, said they make their show "guest friendly."

Dubrow defended the topics and how they are handled on talk shows, particularly, the *Sally Jessy Raphael* show. "I don't think it's what you do. I think it's how you do it. We have been told that we're a show that can do a tough topic in a soft way. We never go in saying, 'Let's do that in bad taste,' although there are some people who think we do. Sally's a lady, and we try to approach subjects in a most respectable way. We'll make an error now and then."

Maury Povich, former host of one tabloid show, *A Current Affair*, and now host of his own, thinks the criticism of talk-show topics and situations is hypocritical, that what is on television is a reflection of the real world and what is happening in America. He scoffs at the reaction to the language at the Anita Hill hearings, for example. "I kind of resented the shock on the faces of TV critics and members of that committee. I mean, where have they been? This is part of American life every day...for talk-show viewers, that's daily stuff for a long time now."

The hypocrisy of critics over the subject matter of television talk is also refuted by the audience reaction. Berman says that the *Geraldo* show doesn't have to seek bizarre subjects or guests. They are flooded with calls and mail all the time, and he thinks that is a healthy sign for the country. "With the explosion around this country of support and self-help groups, this is a society really trying to make itself well," Berman declared. "To the casual observer, it might look like this society has just gone crazy with all of these problems. I think it's just the opposite. People are talking about these things, coming out of the closet."

Which is not to say, Berman admits, that sometimes he and Geraldo may not have gotten carried away in their eagerness to build audience and ratings. "Sex sells, and so we overdid it and suffered greatly for it," said Berman ruefully. "It wasn't so much that we were doing something Oprah or Donahue weren't doing, but somehow when Geraldo did it, it was worse. Donahue went to the same brothel Geraldo went to, but Geraldo got tarred and feathered. We don't want this show to be looked at as some freak show or circus."

What Berman refers to is perceptions that are created in the public mind by the environment and which govern what the public will or won't accept. The persona of the messenger is often as important as the message itself. Professional politicians know, for example, that the Republican and Democratic parties are limited by public perception in some of the things each can do. The late Richard Nixon was able to end the long American boycott of Red China because no one could accuse

Nixon of being soft on communism. A Democratic president couldn't have done that because the liberal wing of the party is perceived to be soft on communism.

Thus, if a story about brothels that service judges and movie stars appeared in the *National Enquirer* or on *Geraldo*, it would be regarded as sleazy. If the exact same story appeared in the *New York Times* or on the Ted Koppel show, it would be regarded as a sociological study worthy of discussion. This is why, for example, many journalists who look to the *New York Times* to set the standard of what is "respectable news" were shocked when the *Times* did a front-page story on sensational biographer Kitty Kelley and printed another story on April 17, 1991, revealing the identity of the Florida woman who charged William Kennedy with rape. The *Times* not only gave the woman's name but also her academic and work record, past driving offenses, and romances. The *Times* also mentioned an out-of-wedlock daughter and provided a description of the daughter's bedroom as seen through the window, along with the observation of a friend that she was known to have "a little wild streak." The rationale given by the *Times* was that NBC had reported the name the day before, and the justification by the then president of NBC News, Michael Gartner, was that "my first real duty is to inform my viewers and that the name had already been revealed in the tabloid, *The Globe*, by editor Wendy Hewry who is today an editor at the *New York Times* and *Daily News*." It's a justification that might come in handy for Geraldo.

So when Geraldo visits a brothel, he is perceived as going to a whorehouse, and when Donahue visits a brothel, he is perceived as attending a seminar on interpersonal relationships.

The hosts come from all sorts of places. Warner Brothers Television's newest talk-show host at the beginning of 1992 was Jenny Jones, who had been a backup singer for Wayne Newton in Las Vegas, a comedy winner on Ed McMahon's *Star Search*, and a perennial game-show contestant and creator of her own controversial stand-up comedy act, "Girls' Night Out," performed at clubs around the country, during which no men— not customers, waiters, bosses, musicians—were allowed in the room. She was unveiled as a talk-show host with a big fanfare which even had her a little uneasy.

"It's scary," she said. "I didn't want this kind of hype. I didn't want people to tune in expecting to find some sort of talk-show goddess. I don't know why it sold. They must just see something that appears to be the right idea at the right time."

Les Brown became the newest host that the King brothers tried to produce and use to diversify King World's syndication offerings. Brown began his career as a Columbus, Ohio, disc jockey who turned into a motivational speaker on personal success through planning, perseverance, and hard work. His program was designed to give "people hope and motivation to achieve their personal greatness" and was set to air in January 1993. Brown's motivational speeches were successful in business seminars and videotapes, and he saw his program as totally removed from the sleaze of trash-talk TV. He said, "This show will get away from the trash that is now seen on television that focuses on people's weaknesses and whatever pain they are experiencing. Our show will give people a sense of hope and help them to see the exciting possibilities in their life. It will be thoughtful, positive, and entertaining."

His idea was to bring people on his show who, instead of whining about the bad things that have happened to them in life, would acknowledge their lives for what they are and move on to make the best of the cards that fate has dealt them. Brown's experience in doing such a television show stemmed from two successful PBS specials he hosted to raise money for public television stations. His philosophy was recently put into book form with his work *Live Your Dreams*.

The controversial and sometimes bizarre topics dealt with by talk shows is also having a serious impact on that other staple of daytime television, the soap opera. Since *The Puddle Family* and *Ma Perkins* began as daytime radio dramas in 1932, one of the best ways to sell household products, such as soap, has been with commercials on these "soap operas," so named because their original sponsors—and, indeed, their sponsors today on daytime television—were soap companies. The type of intimate feminine products advertised on them today makes one speculate what they might have been called if such products had been acceptable on the air sixty-two years ago.

In the early 1950s, soap operas followed the trend of switching to daytime television with Procter & Gamble's *Search For Tomorrow*, which touted Ivory, Tide, and Oxydol. The soap opera as an advertising medium was so popular that at one time Procter & Gamble sponsored seven of them at one time. Today it sponsors three shows, *As the World Turns*, *Another World*, and *Guiding Light*, and it will change that format because former viewers of their soap operas are switching channels to the titillating talk shows of Oprah, Donahue, Sally Jessy, Geraldo, and the rest. What Procter & Gamble has ordered the producers of its soap operas to do is to spice them up by using younger actors performing hotter sex scenes.

Sociologist Lee Harrington of Miami University in Ohio observes that while times were always desperate in the scripts of soap operas, today these are desperate times for soap operas in real life. He says, "More soaps have gone off the air in recent years than have been replaced by new ones." Market research consultant Judith Langer says, "I sense a feeling of desperation on the part of television shows in general to promote their names to get people to watch."

The *Wall Street Journal* reported that "Muriel Goldsman Cantor, a sociologist and soap-opera expert, believes soaps might someday die out altogether as viewers switch to the real-life dramas offered by the talk show." She says, "As awful as they are, the talk shows are addictive, too. They're so sensational, they move so much quicker than soaps and you feel you're getting an insight into other people's lives."

Soaps audiences are also eroded by the high percentage of women who now work outside the home and are gone when the soaps are on. Even those who have VCRs and tape their favorite soaps fast-forward through the commercials, which hurts the advertiser just as much as if those viewers didn't watch the program at all. The focus of the new soaps is on teens and, surprisingly, on a growing male audience of early retirees, unemployeds, and stay-at-home dads. There is even an expanding male audience at work, where soaps are watched during lunch or on breaks.

Even given those options, the talk show is still serious competition because of its air of reality and the pace of the format. Beyond that, the talk-show format took a leap forward with the beginning of *America's Talking* in July 1994, under the aegis of CNBC's all-cable network. Initially, *America's Talking* began with fourteen hours of live talk for the 10 million cable viewers whose cable systems have signed on to the channel. The beginning talk show was hosted by Steve Docy and Kai Kim, in addition to an hour of people's favorite gripes on *Bugged; What's New* was hosted by Mike Jerrick and review new inventions and productions; *Wellness* reports on medical problems; and *Am I Nuts*, will feature guest psychologists giving analyses of callers' problems. *America's Talking* is being guided by the controversial Roger Ailes, long known as a media consultant to Republican presidential campaigns, starting with the 1968 Nixon one, the mentor of Rush Limbaugh, and now the president of NBC's cable operation, CNBC. Right now on CNBC Ailes has talk shows featuring Donahue and Vladimir Pozner; Geraldo; Mary Matalin; Cal Thomas; MTV's Daisy Fuentes; and a sexually explicit show, *Real Personal*.

Since America is on a huge electronic group therapy binge and some of the topics on Oprah are controversial and even eccentric, the continuing justification given by the hosts is that such programs help people. The hosts and some of the experts on these shows claim that this kind of television and radio group baring of the soul performs a worthwhile function, just as the confessional does in the Catholic church, and that it leads to healing and redemption.

Some sociologists and psychologists, however, have raised serious doubts about that justification, and many people believe that these programs have little value beyond simple voyeuristic entertainment. The cynical see them as nothing more than carnival sideshows displaying the two-headed woman, the ape man of Borneo, and the amazing rubber man, designed primarily to make the promoters of these grotesque displays wealthy, as, indeed, has already happened to many of them, including Oprah.

18

Oprah on the Slave Mentality

Many blacks criticize Oprah despite her success as a role model. They call her "Aunt Jemima" for playing the lovable, happy black mammy to please whites and avoid racial controversy.

She said, "I hear this. I hear this a lot. I hear that I don't hug the black people the way I hug the white people, that I go to the white people in the audience first. First of all, there are *more* white people. There just are more! I could not survive with this show if I only catered to black people. I just could not! I couldn't be where I am if I did. That not what it's about!"

Part of the problem is Oprah's view of being black. When she was in college, she worked in broadcasting during the burgeoning civil rights movement and didn't have either time or sympathy for black militants on campus. To Oprah this was an enormous waste of time, and it still is. She thinks you have to make it on your own and be answerable for your own success or failure. But she realizes that she is resented by many of her race.

"There are still a lot of black people who are very angry and bitter," she says. "They want me to be just as angry and bitter, and I won't be. It just burns me. Some black people say I'm not black enough. I wonder, how black do you have to be? The drums of Africa still beat in my heart, and they will not rest until every black boy and every black girl has had a chance to prove their worth."

It is this philosophy that explains in part why she can tolerate her fiancé, Stedman Graham, as the business partner of the ultra-right black Armstrong Williams, whose conservative program *The Right Side* airs on WOL in Washington.

During Black History Month (February) of 1994, for example, Williams interviewed a series of guests that he felt would inform his black audience about the thoughts and concerns of white Americans and make them confront the stereotypes that blacks have of whites. One of his guests was former Klansman and candidate for governor of Louisiana, David Duke. "We frequently say that members of the white majority think about African Americans in stereotypes," Williams explains. "We may overlook that black people also stereotype white people. It works both ways." He says he wants to help blacks come to terms with their own racial attitudes.

Other conservative guests on his shows in the past included Senators Bob Dole, Phil Gramm, Alan Simpson, John Danforth, Orrin Hatch, and Strom Thurmond. The Williams show began as a once-a-week call-in program in 1992, and soon the phone calls to the station were jammed when Williams began "challenging blanket statements that blame whites for the ills of the black community."

"Some called me an Uncle Tom sellout," Williams said, "but I've also had a lot of people call and say, 'You have changed me. Before, I thought I was a liberal. I'm a conservative and never realized it!'

Williams claims his goal is to "teach forgiveness and healing; to teach kids to love themselves and each other and to judge people with their hearts, not by the color of their skin. We have to get in there and change hearts."

The show is produced by Williams's public relations firm, the Graham Williams Group. Williams began broadcasting daily in September 1993, with ultimate plans for national syndication. The *Washington Post* recently reported that Williams has signed a "near-six-figure" deal with Macmillan to write an autobiography that will offer his views about the future of race relations in America. Williams, thirty-four, also writes a column for *USA Today*.

Williams identifies himself as a third-generation Republican from one of the few black Republican families in South Carolina, where he and his nine brothers and sisters grew up on a two-hundred-acre farm owned by his family. On the farm they raised tobacco, vegetables, and livestock.

Perhaps one of his testiest confrontations occurred on November 20, 1992, after Armstrong Williams criticized Spike Lee in a *Washington Post* Op-Ed piece for the racially divisive marketing of Spike's movie *Malcolm X*. Armstrong said that the confrontation "started out like World War III," but thirty minutes later they agreed to lunch together.

Armstrong Williams, who would be Stedman's best man, reflects Oprah's views, which she expressed on the weekend of August 24–26, 1990. Oprah participated in the *Ebony-Jet* Magazines Showcase program where she listened to what she labeled the "slave mentality" and blacks' self-hatred. In her mind too many blacks criticize and ridicule other blacks in public; in doing so, they dishonor their heritage and the pantheon of black heroes whom Oprah has revered most of her life. She admitted that she had been the target of fellow blacks from the time that she was three years old, when she performed before the congregation of her grandmother Hattie Lee's church.

Ever since then she has been castigated and harassed by other blacks in school and at work. The small children who hated her for being such a good public speaker when she was small and who called her "Preacher" in derision and even spat at her were not white racists. They were black children her own age. The students in high school that tried to beat her up because she was too smart and worked too hard were blacks like Oprah. The college-age youngsters at Tennessee State who called her an Oreo—black outside and white inside—because she wouldn't join their civil rights protests and wear dashikis were fellow black students. They had ridiculed her eagerness to strive and advance in a white world.

It was not white racists who picketed her program in

Forsyth County and who publicly denounced her for *The Color Purple* and *The Women of Brewster Place*. It was other blacks. This attitude, she said, reflects a slave mentality and the hatred of blacks of their own society, their own culture, and themselves.

She declared, "I see self-hatred that makes us turn against each other and try to pull each other down. I see that, and I think that Frederick Douglass did not deserve this. He did not teach the slaves to read by candlelight to see us at our banquets and meeting halls sit and try and tear each other apart. He does not deserve this!"

One black friend who comforted her and who warned her about these kinds of attacks by blacks on other blacks, particularly those who have succeeded in the white-dominated American society, was actor Sidney Poitier. For whatever reasons, Oprah knew that her own people lashed out in envy and hatred at others of the same race who worked hard, endured prejudice, and still became famous or rich. It was not that Oprah forgot her black origins. It was just that, like all people, she is a complex personality and being black is not all-pervasive. She is also a woman, she is also a victim of abuse by blacks, and she is also rich and connected to her socioeconomic strata.

One thing that really irritated her occurred when the NAACP said it wanted to review the script of *Brewster Place* before she began to film the movie. She said, "I'm insulted. I am more conscious of my legacy as a black person than anybody."

Oprah's pride in her black heritage is reflected not only in the films and TV programs in which she becomes involved but also in her many public appearances and speeches. Oprah is the first one to say that the issue of slavery and race is foremost in her heart. In speeches she gives around the nation, but little reported upon by the media, she thunders out to the audience:

"My name is Oprah. Not Opree, nor Okree, and definitely not Okra. I consider myself one black woman, one voice. I was born in Kosciusko, Mississippi, around the corner from the Nile and down the street from Kenya. The drums of Africa still beat in my heart."

When she appeared at the 44th National Convention of the National Council of Negro Women at the Washington Hilton on December 4, 1989, she told the overflow audience:

"I come here tonight celebrating every African, every colored, black, Negro American everywhere, that ever cooked a meal, ever raised a child, ever worked in the fields, ever went to school, ever sang in a choir, ever loved a man or loved a woman, every cornrowed, every Afroed, every wig-wearing, pigtailed, weave-wearing one of us.

"I come celebrating the journey."

In her recitations of her heritage and of her history, Oprah celebrates the journey of all her people as she quotes from Carolyn Rogers's "Somiya Beauty," "Phenomenal Woman" by Maya Angelou, and the "Ain't I A Woman?" speech by Sojourner Truth. Her black audiences feel the black connection with her, and she is proud that her roots are whole and that she is part of a timeless panorama that extends from the past and into the future of blacks. She prides herself in being part of the resurrection of those blacks who went before her and who fought and died for justice and equality for their race.

She is conscious of having to proclaim herself both black and a woman, which has been part of her struggle. She lives with what the black leader and thinker W. E. B. Du Bois referred to as the "two-ness" suffered by black men. For Du Bois blackness was always present wherever he went, separating him from whites whose whiteness did not set them apart. While he became the first black man to earn a Ph.D. from Harvard and was a founder of the National Association for the Advancement of Colored People (NAACP), his achievement and his color were separate entities. There were many other Ph.D.s from Harvard whose color did not become an issue in their lives, but for Du Bois he was always Dr. Du Bois—a black man.

This is what the late novelist Ralph Ellison spoke of in his landmark bestselling 1952 novel *Invisible Man*, which is the story of a young black man becoming aware of racial discrimination and the unwillingness or inability of white Americans to see him as something apart from his race. He cries out, "I am an invisible man. I am a man of substance, of flesh and bone, fiber and liquids—and I might even be said to possess a mind. I am invisible, understand, simply because people refuse to see me."

More recently, Ellis Cose's book *The Rage of a Privileged Class* describes the frustration of those blacks who have made it economically but are still the victims of racism. They are the black professionals and executives who have succeeded and no longer fit in the ghetto economically. They remain black and are not accepted in the white world socially because they are the victims of a subtle racism deep-seated in the white world. Cose says that race does matter, and it has a grip on the American psyche that is not a phantom.

He writes, "We have trouble talking about [race] intelligently. We tend to talk in stereotypes, or in sound-bites, or from behind huge defenses we've erected. People don't see the same reality. You almost get into this caricature of a conversation. You have whites going through all kinds of contortions trying to prove that they aren't racist and then you have blacks going through the opposite sort of dance."

Cose underlines the point that members of the black middle class or upper class have worked hard to achieve their status and still find certain doors closed to them. No matter how successful they are, they remain Ellison's invisible man and live with Du Bois's two-ness.

As Du Bois, Ellison, Cose, and other blacks lived in the world of "two-ness," Oprah lives in the world of "three-ness." She must cope with her African heritage and with her gender, particularly in her work world, which is dominated by white males.

Since Oprah and other blacks like Bill Cosby are now an integral part of television and blacks seems to be everywhere on TV, it seems hard to believe that in the 1950s and 1960s blacks were almost nonexistent on television. The first regular program featuring a black performer was *Beulah*, a situation comedy about a black maid patterned after a newspaper cartoon strip and starring Ethel Waters, an extraordinarily talented dramatic actress from the movies. Later, she would be replaced by actress Louise Beavers. The only other blacks on television in the early 1960s were the characters in *Amos 'n'*

Andy, a version of the radio show, which brought complaints that it stereotyped blacks and doomed the show.

After *Amos 'n' Andy* was canceled, television finally broke the color barrier for good with the introduction of *I Spy*, starring the well-known white actor Robert Culp and a relatively unknown black comedian, Bill Cosby. In 1968 the big news in broadcasting was that a black woman, Diahann Carroll, would star in a network series playing a role that was not a black stereotype. This was regarded as an enormous step forward in the American media. That same year, Vernita Lee shipped a rebellious, pregnant Oprah to her father, Vernon Winfrey, in Nashville.

The next year, 1969, ABC brought *Room 227* to the TV screen, with several black actors in leading roles. By the 1970s, black sitcoms came to television in *Sanford and Son* (1972), *The Jeffersons* (1975), and *Good Times* (1975). In time television broadcast what became one of its most watched miniseries ever, *Roots*. Today the mark of how far blacks have come in television is that two of the richest and most powerful television performers are Bill Cosby—who was rumored to be considering buying NBC at one time—and Oprah Winfrey.

Oprah is still not, as she said in college days, a dashiki type, and she has never really related to the militant civil rights strata of black American life. She, in fact, agrees more with her boyfriend's partner, the conservative black talk-show host in Washington, D.C., Armstrong Williams, than with Hosea Williams. She does not connect with many blacks who she and Stedman and Williams believe want to play the victims of society and demand a payback and a payoff. Oprah's philosophy of being responsible for yourself and that you are what you make of yourself flies in the face of the concept of the welfare state. However, she does not want to underscore this conservative view publicly because it is bad public relations and would alienate many of her black and liberal white fans.

She is proud of her heritage as a black and rejoices in what her people have been and have done in America. She also is militant on the subject of abuse of women and children, which is an issue without color. But the politically correct black militant views are not for her, and that's why she had no patience with those who criticized her for visiting a home in an exclusive white neighborhood in Winston-Salem while spending some time with her friend Maya Angelou. The incident is illustrative of the gap between Oprah as a talented, rich black woman and those blacks who are not well off and who are caught in the vice of prejudice in their daily lives.

On April 25, 1993, Oprah paid another visit to her friend Maya Angelou, for whom she had thrown a gigantic sixty-fifth birthday part in Winston-Salem, North Carolina, and turned loose a hornet's nest with familiar antagonists: blacks against Oprah. When Oprah came to Winston-Salem to celebrate Maya Angelou's birthday with her famous party, she jogged down Arbor Road and was particularly taken by one architecturally lovely home. "I thought it was such a lovely house," she said. "I liked the dogwood trees, the front porch, I just liked everything about it. I said I would like to sit on that porch and eat muffins."

So when Oprah returned on April twenty-fifth to shoot film of Angelou's house because she wanted to include it in an Oprah program in May, Oprah impulsively decided—as is her nature—to drop by that beautiful home with a batch of muffins and shoot some film of the place. "When I told Maya that I was going there, she said, 'What are you going over there for?' I told her it was beautiful, but nothing else was said about it."

However, a lot was said about it after Oprah aired her May third program showing her visiting the white family in that house. The black community of Winston-Salem boiled over in criticism of Oprah because she was shown visiting an expensive home in an exclusive whites-only neighborhood known as Buena Vista instead of visiting a typical home in the areas where blacks, who make up a third of the Winston-Salem population, lived. The denunciation of Oprah came, as it has often in the past, from black ministers, such as the Reverend William S. Fails, pastor of the First United Baptist Church in High Point, North Carolina, and Rev. John Mendez, pastor of the Emmanuel Baptist Church, both of whom are active members of the Citizens United for Justice, a militant civil rights group in the area.

"This is another of these one-sided attempts to promote

Winston-Salem as something it is not," said Reverend Fails. "If we walked through Buena Vista late in the evening while people were jogging, we could be arrested for suspicion alone."

Reverent Mendez said, "Winston-Salem is not Buena Vista, and because Oprah says it's a nice city based on that one community implies that other people in the city are non-existent, invisible, or don't matter. It was a slap in the face and an attempt to cover up the real problems that this city faces."

Oprah was miffed by the criticism from her own people, although that has been happening to her since she was three years old. "I can't understand why people could be upset," she declared. "There was no intention on my part to insult any-body in Winston-Salem or to paint a particular picture that that was what it is like for everyone who lives in Winston-Salem. I wasn't picking the street based on the color of the people's skin. I was picking it because I happened to jog there and I thought it was very tranquil and picturesque, period. No more thought went into it than that."

Jocelyn Johnson, president of the East Winston Restoration Association, said Oprah did not exhibit the typical community in Winston-Salem. "It showed a very elitist area, but when you look at all the other things in the community...that was not the typical picture of a neighborhood in Winston-Salem."

Dr. Rembert Mallory, a black activist and retired surgeon, viewed the controversy as less a black misunderstanding than a socioeconomic difference because Oprah is rich and the people who criticized her are not. "She chooses a more or less cosmopolitan or bourgeoisie type of lifestyle. I don't think she is particularly catering to the black people. If you've been oppressed—and I think to an extent that she has been—it's hard for you not to strive to get what the world offers. You want to live like the Babylonians."

In contrast, Elvia J. Jones, a black resident of East Winston, said, "It's the middle-class people who support her. So many of us who look at her never get the chance to see her [in person], and when she came here, she went to the white neighborhood. So many of us who are in the middle class who just want to touch her garment, to just see her...they can't get near her.

The people that she embraced on [wealthy] Arbor Road, if they watch TV at all, they're going to watch Donahue or Joan Rivers before they watch her. And for her not to visit the working class, the middle class, is a disgrace."

So Oprah holds different views of race than many believe she has. That is true of many aspects of Oprah, namely, that there is another much different and more complex Oprah than meets the eye. Being black is a central theme in Oprah's life, as it is in the lives of almost all American blacks. Aside from the inequalities, there are the myths and the experiences that no white can ever understand. Oprah dwells on these.

"There are more white people than black people on welfare," she is fond of reminding her audiences.

Oprah takes on the fears and insanities of both races. She says, "A small but vocal group of black people fear me. Slavery taught us to hate ourselves. I mean, Jane Pauley doesn't have to deal with this. It all comes out of self-hatred. A black person has to ask herself, 'If Oprah Winfrey can make it, what does it say about me?' They no longer have any excuse."

Not that Oprah is clear on her attitude toward black men. She is critical of the way black men treat black women. Like most black women, she was tolerant for a time about the psychological need for black men to assert their manhood as they emerged from the centuries-old slave mentality.

Still, there are limits, and like many black women, she resents it when black men pursue white women and regard them as more desirable than black women. It relegates black women, the people who raised, loved, and supported these black men, to the lowest social level in society.

In an interview for black-oriented *Essence* magazine in August 1987, she took a swipe at black men when she was describing her new relationship with boyfriend Stedman Graham. "The greatest thing about him is his kindness," she said. "And, he knows who he is. I am thrilled that I have discovered this in a Black man."

Probably the most disturbing part of her acting career has been the negative reaction she gets from black men over the roles she has played. When *The Color Purple* premiered in December 1985, there were black pickets outside the theater in

Los Angeles. In Chicago, a furious argument broke out among black people talking about the film at a church meeting. Black reporters and reviewers slammed the film for portraying negative images of black life and of black men.

Leroy Clark, a law professor at Catholic University in Washington, D.C., attacked what he saw in the film. "The men are raping, committing incest, speaking harshly, separating people from their families, or they are incompetent; they can't fix a house or cook a simple meal. This is a lie to history. It reinforces the notion of black men as beasts."

Oprah's reaction was characteristically to the point. "The movie was not for or against men. It's egotistical and macho for men to even think it's about them. *The Color Purple* is a novel about women. If this film is going to raise some issues, I'm tired of hearing about what it's doing to the black men. Let's talk about the issues of wife abuse, violence against women, and sexual abuse of children in the home."

Typical Oprah.

Oprah with Danny Glover in *The Color Purple*. (Photo by Shooting Star)

Director Steven Spielberg arrives bearing gifts for Oprah's fortieth birthday party. (Photo by *National Enquirer*)

Michael (left) and Roger King of King World—the two men who made Oprah into a multimillionaire. (Photo by Bill Bernstein, 1991)

Street scene with Oprah from *The Women of Brewster Place* television miniseries based on Gloria Naylor's novel. (Photo by Wide World Photos)

Comedian Robin Williams reaches out to direct Oprah during taping of "Comic Relief '87" at the Improv Comedy Club in Los Angeles. Looking on are Billy Crystal, Dudley Moore, and John Larroquette. (Photo by Wide World Photos)

Oprah interviews Michael Jackson for one of the highest rated programs in television history seen worldwide by millions. (Photo by Wide World Photos)

Oprah with Vanna White, co-host of "Wheel of Fortune," at the National Association of Television Program Executives convention in Houston, Texas. (Photo by Pam MacDonald/Wide World Photos)

Oprah and Faye Dunaway at New York opening night of the play, *From the Mississippi Delta*, by Dr. Endesha Ida Mae Holland, chronicling her life from prostitute to Ph.D. Oprah was one of the play's producers in her first New York theater venture. (Photo by Mark Lennihan/Wide World Photos)

Oprah and James Earl Jones posing together backstage after a performance of *Fences* at New York's 46th Street Theatre. (Photo by Mario
Suriana/Wide World Photos)

Oprah sings along with novelist Robert James Waller during her show
from one of the covered bridges featured in Mr. Waller's novel, *The
Bridges of Madison County*, in Winterset, Iowa. (Photo by Wide World)

Nose to nose with Jesse Jackson at a political fundraiser in Atlanta. (Photo by Wide World Photos)

Oprah as a ghetto mother trying to salvage the lives of her two young sons played by Mark Lane (left) and Norman Gokien II (right) in ABC-TV movie *There Are No Children Here*. Based on Alex Kotlowitz's best-seller, the film was shot in a Chicago low-income project near Oprah's Harpo studios. Oprah used her earnings from the movie to create a scholarship fund for the children of that project. (Photo Gregory Heisler/Reuter)

The pain in Oprah's heart shows as she testifies before the U.S. Senate on behalf of the child abuse bill she initiated in memory of Angelica, the raped and murdered Chicago five-year-old Oprah promised to avenge. The bill failed on this first try. (Photo Cliff Owen/UPI/ Bettman)

Final success in memory of Angelica. President Bill Clinton gives the TV talk host the pen with which he signed into law the Child Protection Act of 1993, popularly called "Oprah's Law." Oprah hired former Illinois Governor Jim Thompson (center) to shepherd the bill through Congress. It creates a national registry to track child molesters such as the one who murdered little Angelica. (Photo Gary Cameron/Reuter/Bettman)

Exterior view of Oprah's headquarters, from where her daily TV show normally is broadcast, Harpo Studios in Chicago. (Photo by David Carter, Dayton Beach, Florida)

Oprah on the set of her show inside Harpo Studios in Chicago (Photo by David Carter, Dayton Beach, Florida)

Oprah together with long-time boyfriend, Stedman Graham. (Photo by Wide World Photos)

Oprah Into
the World

19

1990—A Year of New Places

Oprah closed out a bad 1989 with her wrenching November 15 show about her weight problem, which has been a long saga for her and her fans. Trying to get her weight under control had been a continuous, frustrating struggle, and on the November 15 show she said she was through talking about her weight and would never bring it up to her audience again—ever. A year before, she had slimmed down to her lowest weight in her adult life—120 pounds. She had paraded the sixty-seven pounds of fat she had lost around the stage in a little red wagon. Now, one year later, she had regained seventeen of those lost pounds, and it made her angry with herself and the problem.

For Oprah it had been a tough year, with tabloids harping on her Sisyphus-like contest with excess weight, her half brother's death from AIDS, her half sister's drug problem, and the hot-and-cold relationship with Stedman.

However, not everything about 1989 was bad. At the end of November, securities analyst Dennis McAlpine of Oppenheimer and Company reported that the *Oprah Winfrey Show*, grossing $55.6 million that year, was very close to passing *Wheel of Fortune* as the top syndicated show handled by

King World. Oprah had used some of her share of the previous year's income to buy interests in WIVB-TV, Buffalo, New York; WEEK-TV in Peoria, Illinois; and KBJR-TV in Duluth, Minnesota. Oprah owns her interest in the Buffalo station in partnership with the King brothers.

"I don't know anything about oil or gold," she said. "I've been doing television since I was nineteen, and TV is what I know and understand."

The year 1989 also had been a tough one for the King brothers, the key people in making Oprah a multimillionaire. They sell the *Oprah Winfrey Show* around the world in countries like Japan, New Zealand, Canada, the United Kingdom, Bermuda, Thailand, Netherlands, and Saudi Arabia. If anything damages the public image or financial health of King World, it also hurts Oprah Winfrey financially, because a substantial part of Oprah's wealth is in shares of stock in King World. That's why the continued antics of Roger King, chairman of the board of King World, proved disturbing.

In July, Roger, forty-five, finally settled a lawsuit with the estate of a Fort Lauderdale, Florida, cabdriver, Juan Solorzano, who charged Roger with beating him up and stealing his taxi. Roger insisted he had done nothing wrong in settling the civil lawsuit against him by Solorzano. Both sides agreed not to reveal the terms of the settlement, but it was thought to be quite substantial.

Roger pled no contest to criminal charges of strong-arm robbery, grand theft, and possession of cocaine. The police found him sitting behind the wheel of Solorzano's cab, with the motor running, back in February 1987.

Pleading no contest is regarded as pleading guilty by the court, and when the defendant does so, he accepts the judge entering a guilty verdict and sentencing him accordingly, but the defendant does not admit to doing wrong. This legal double talk is designed to protect the defendant from having a guilty admission used against him in a civil lawsuit while settling the criminal case quickly for the prosecutor.

As the result of this plea, King was sentenced to two years' probation. He also had to enter a drug-and-alcohol-abuse treatment program. Solorzano died in November 1988 from an accidental drug overdose, and the civil suit against King was continued by Solorzano's brother. This is the kind of publicity that makes Wall Street nervous and could affect the value of Oprah's more than 1 million shares of King World. If Roger, the supersalesman of King World, went to jail, it could hurt the income of King World and cause a drop in the value of Oprah's million shares.

The three main shows that were the central money engine for King World and guaranteed the value of Oprah's shares in the syndicator were *Wheel of Fortune, Jeopardy*, and the *Oprah Winfrey Show*. Back in 1983, only seven years before, King World had syndication rights to *The Little Rascals* and grossed $8 million. By 1989, King World was grossing $112 million mostly because of *Wheel, Jeopardy*, and *Oprah*. The King brothers, Roger and his younger brother, Michael, are King World. They are helped by some hired executives and Richie and Diana King, their brother and sister. (Another brother and sister, Bob and Karen, are not in the company and have sold off their stock). King World has a reputation in the syndication business for being rough and tough and are known for doing whatever is necessary to make a deal—schmooze, flatter, threaten, muscle.

Wheel of Fortune and *Jeopardy* are strong shows but different from *Oprah*. *Wheel* and *Jeopardy* are successful evening shows for the prime-time access hour from 7:00 to 8:00 P.M., but Oprah is what hooks the audience at 3:00 P.M., and viewers will often remain with that station through the next two hours of local news, which is a big profit center for individual stations. Roger understands the value of his star property and uses the *Oprah Winfrey Show* as a lever to bludgeon stations into paying more money for *Wheel* and *Jeopardy* by block selling. Oprah may not know about this, but this kind of marketing enhances the value of her stock and her stock options in King World.

Block booking, or requiring a station to take a program it doesn't want or pay a higher than normal price for a show in order to get one it does want, is technically illegal but not always easy to prove. Outlet Communications once filed a $10 million suit against King World for using the *Oprah Winfrey*

Show in a block-booking tactic with a station Outlet owned. As the *New York Times* commented in 1989:

"Outlet lost its case, but the complaint was not an isolated one. 'All I'm going to tell you,' grumbles one general manager, 'is that when it came time for this television station to look at the renewal potential for Oprah is when the King brothers came and said, 'Before we talk Oprah, we want to talk renewals on Wheel and Jeopardy even though they're not up for another year.'" The line separating hard-nosed salesmanship from block-booking is a blurry one; insiders acknowledge it is crossed every day in closed-door negotiations. However, the vision of some broadcasters may also be clouded by recent shifts in the industry's balance of power; syndicators never used to have that much clout. 'They think we come in and leverage,' snorts Michael King. 'We come in and sell.'"

That the King brothers are tough salesmen is exemplified by their appearance at the annual convention of the National Association of Television Programming Executives (NATPE), which was held in New Orleans in 1990. That is where syndicators and programmers try to sell new shows and expand the coverage they have of old shows, such as the *Oprah Winfrey Show*. The King brothers were particularly anxious to generate new shows to syndicate because 83 percent of the gross income of their company in 1990 depended on *Wheel*, *Jeopardy*, and *Oprah*. They knew that one day those shows could lose popular appeal, or the hosts would quit or become too expensive to produce. At the NATPE, the King brothers are legendary for their flamboyant lifestyle. As Merv Griffin, whom the King brothers also made rich by syndicating his formerly dying shows *Wheel* and *Jeopardy*, described the King brothers, "They are wild men. They never slide into a room quietly. They are the room."

At the 1990 convention of the NATPE, the King brothers were trying to promote new shows, such as the tabloid program *Inside Edition*; *New Candid Camera*, with Dom DeLuise; the nostalgia magazine show *Only Yesterday*; and a new game show based on the old board game *Monopoly*. *Inside Edition* was the only one to survive very long, with Monopoly, involving a midget in a funny suit, turning into an enormous bomb.

In New Orleans the Kings gave one of their celebrated parties, wining, dining and entertaining eight hundred station executives on the *Creole Queen* riverboat as it floated down the Mississippi River. A number of station executives partook of the Kings' hospitality but still complained afterward about their coercive sales tactics.

Glenn Wright, general manager of KIRO-TV in Seattle, said, "I don't know anyone who loves them. They have no loyalty. I wouldn't do business with them on a handshake." Wright went on to tell how he was the first to buy *Oprah* in Seattle and had promoted it heavily and even moved the program from the morning time slot it originally held to the afternoon, where the *Oprah Winfrey Show* would not have to face *Donahue*. Then, when Oprah's show came up for renewal at KIRO-TV, the Kings demonstrated their gratitude by jacking up the price 400 percent and when Wright wouldn't or couldn't pay it, they sold *Oprah* to a competing station.

"Other syndicators understand long-term relationships and don't come at you with double barrels and hold you up," Wright said. His complaint was echoed by Robert Hyland, formerly of KCBS in Los Angeles, who exclaimed he was stunned when King World wanted a renewal through 1994 for the two game shows just nine months into the first year of the contract. Hyland balked because both shows were losing audience, and "who knows what numbers they'll be doing two years from now?" So, King World dumped KCBS and sold the game shows to a competing station, KABC. This is how the King brothers made themselves and Oprah multimillionaires in the three years between when she went national in 1986 and 1989.

The King brothers' success in selling the *Oprah Winfrey Show* made the celebration of Oprah's thirty-sixth birthday on January 29 a sweet occasion. She said, "I wouldn't trade places with anybody. I'm growing up. And I think that I'm getting better because of it." Stedman gave her a restored 1957 black Mercedes coupe. She took up skiing and improved enough so that she could navigate the intermediate runs, while Stedman skied on the slopes reserved for experts. Their romance continued to build, and he was getting ready to move into Oprah's

Water Tower Place condo and open an office of his public relations company in Chicago. Half sister Patricia thought the match with Stedman perfect and said Oprah was crazy about him; they were the opposites who attracted each other. She added that he was neat and she was messy.

Early March came with the first anniversary of the restaurant Oprah owns with Richard Melman, the Eccentric, described as an American brasserie emphasizing moderately priced French, English, Italian, and American food in a comfortable atmosphere. It was the fourth restaurant in which Melman and his Lettuce Entertain You Enterprises (LEYE) had an interest—all in the same area of urban Chicago, the River North district. It is also the twenty-eighth restaurant in the LEYE business group, which owns other restaurants in Illinois, Arizona, California, and Japan.

To create the Eccentric, Melman took over an old warehouse and created different serving levels and areas, including the bar and dance floor, which is separated by a wall from the main dining area, which seats 250 people. The various dining areas are divided into a fine, intimate French restaurant seating sixty-five, some of them outside; an English-estate library-club restaurant seating thirty-five off the main bar; a modern Italian art-gallery restaurant for forty; and a lively American bar and disco seating sixty-five and featuring the usual drinks plus a juice bar with fresh apple and carrot juices.

In the center of the complex a giant mural displays maps of Florence, London, and Chicago, all interconnected by highways. Art overflows the walls in all of the areas, with the words "art," "life," "literature," and "liberté" on the outside awning and recorded readings of literature played in the rest rooms. The menu is a mixture of the foods of Italy, France, England, and America and is heavy on appetizers. The kitchen can be found behind a large glass wall covered by a dark velvet drape occasionally drawn so that the diners can see the cooks preparing food. Slogans are displayed on signs and banners around the restaurant urging patrons to Speak the Truth, No Rules—Stay Real, Never Dull, and Speak Your Mind.

Dinner entrées, initially inspired by chef Michael Kornick, start at ten dollars and include fire-grilled chicken with chili and parsnips; grilled pot-au-feu of beef with Oprah's potatoes; and capellini pasta with seafood and tomato broth. The dishes tend to avoid salt and butter and feature some lighter foods, such as braised leeks with potato vinaigrette; whole roasted mushrooms with rosemary and shallots; and salmon paillard with stone-ground mustard. Catering to meat-and-potato midwestern taste, the chef makes sure there are lots of steaks and fish cooked on his wood-burning grill. He is proud that much of what comes out of his kitchen is made fresh every day, such as stocks, soups, custards, puff dough, and ice cream.

Oprah wanted to get into the food business for a long time because it is such a central part of her life, both good and bad. She had been talking to Melman for three years about it before they opened. "I wanted a place where I could have fun and dance," she said. Oprah also contributed her potatoes, which Kornick calls "the signature dish from the outside." They sell best to people who are visiting for the first time. They are lumpy mashed potatoes flavored with horseradish. The recipe calls for putting washed and halved potatoes, still in their skins, into boiling water and cooking at a simmer for twenty-five minutes. They are then drained, keeping the skins on; butter is added, and they are mashed by hand, adding horseradish sauce, cream, salt, and pepper until creamy but slightly lumpy, and are garnished with parsley.

Equally as pleasing as the success of the Eccentric was Oprah's opening on January 15 of her luxuriously remodeled production facilities, Harpo Studios, for the production of the *Oprah Winfrey Show*. In March she ran a VIP tour for thirty-one newspaper and magazine reporters from around the country. Exercising control has been the Oprah concept in everything she has done since she has become a wealthy celebrity, and this tour proved no different.

"I think that I have managed to handle this all very well because I have insisted on having control," she said. "Yes, I do have people to help organize my life, but nobody organizes it without me knowing what I'm doing."

Fred Goodman, writing a Madonna-Oprah profile for *Working Woman* in 1991, saw that statement as a key to Oprah's way of operating. "Control, both physical and fiscal, is the mantra at Harpo. 'We've got more economic control because we own the show and no one is going to raise our rent,' said Jeffrey Jacobs. 'The question is one of quality, and the bottom line is the product. Anybody can have a good idea. Then you have to execute it. Because of our operation, we can.'"

Reporters could come into her palatial production facility, but there would be no photographs permitted and no separate interviews. You came, you bowed to the queen, and you went away to report what she wanted reported. Oprah's staff was there to guide the reporters to the important points that should be mentioned in their stories. Michael Shetter, a senior vice president of Harpo, happily emphasized that the imprint of Oprah's meticulous attention to the remodeling was everywhere: the upholstery, the wallpaper, carpeting, furniture, decorations—everything personally and carefully selected by Oprah herself.

The docile reporters followed Shetter wherever he led them, taking notes on the wall-to-wall electronic gadgetry in the control rooms, the rust-colored marble staircase with the green railings, and the tan speckle paint used to convey a feeling of a spacious warehouse motif. A must stop for the tour was the in-house fitness center, with the neat rows of stationary bicycles, stair simulators, treadmills, and weight-lifting equipment that was used by anybody who wanted to exercise, including Oprah. They were told that Oprah normally arrived at 6:30 A.M. for her daily workout and shower.

Then came the inner-sanctum visit to Oprah's private and uncharacteristically neat office. Oprah was notorious for appearing as the female version of the messy Jack Klugman character Oscar Madison in the *Odd Couple*, but on press-tour day her office was a vision of neatness, surrounded by walls papered in a fruit-basket pattern. Some publicist had strategically placed a copy of Zora Neale Hurston's *Their Eyes Were Watching God* on Oprah's desk as if she had been reading that inspirational work just before the tour group arrived.

Additional mood ornaments in the office included an autographed photo of Quincy Jones, who got her the dramatic role of Sofia in her first major motion picture, *The Color Purple*, and the ever-present bouquet of fresh-cut flowers. Then it was off to one of the smaller studios and buffet lunch, where a matronly-looking woman in a green housedress and light blue apron appeared with her gray-streaked hair in a bun. It was Oprah, dressed for shooting her role in the new ABC-TV weekly series *The Women of Brewster Place*, which was a spin-off from the made-for-TV movie of the same name. She skimmed through the group, exchanging a few pleasantries, and then disappeared out the door, en route to the *Brewster Place* set.

The *Brewster Place* weekly TV series began shooting at the newly redone Harpo Studios, also in March, and it made Oprah's schedule so tight that she would have trouble getting over to the Eccentric as often as she liked. On Monday and Tuesday mornings Oprah taped two TV talk shows each, and on Wednesday morning she did the fifth. Monday afternoon was reserved for homework for upcoming talk shows; Tuesday afternoon, for corporate business. From Wednesday afternoon until Friday afternoon, and sometimes on Saturday, she taped *Brewster*. It took five days to do an episode, and they had an order for thirteen episodes of the *Brewster Place* weekly TV series.

"The talk show is the foundation from which all of this is built," Oprah said. "I do not intend in any way to let any part of that slide or relinquish any control of that, either." To strengthen her production team on the talk show, Oprah hired Ray Nunn to fill the newly created position of senior producer working with executive producer Debra DiMiao. The forty-one-year-old Nunn came to Oprah with impressive credentials, including thirteen years with ABC News, where he had been the senior producer of documentaries and had been in discussions with Quincy Jones about producing Jesse Jackson's talk show, slated to air in the fall.

Sundays were reserved for Stedman. But seeing him didn't always work out, for Oprah often had to get ready for the upcoming week. The combination of no time for a relationship and the busy schedule meant less exercise and more junk food, which added pounds to Oprah and hurt the romance between her and Stedman. Within a few more weeks the relationship would face a crisis.

There were little controversies along the way, such as the

one over the Velez El Rey Seafood Market, rented by José Velez. The market occupied a small part of the same block dominated by Harpo Studios. Oprah wanted to buy or lease the El Rey Seafood Market property so that she could create more parking, but she didn't figure on a stubborn José Velez, who had been there for years and said he had worked hard all his life to create his business and wasn't about to vacate it for a parking lot. His pride was shared by the landlord, who had been renting to José for many years and didn't think the gigantic Harpo Studios should drive a little man out of a business that supported his family.

So the owner said he would not evict José and sell to Oprah. Instead, he would keep things the way they were and even at the same rent, even though Oprah had offered $500 more a month.

In addition to the fish-market flap, there has been an ongoing uneasiness about nonunion help in some of the Harpo productions. Trade unions, such as the National Association of Broadcast Employees and Technicians (NABET) and the International Alliance of Theatrical Stage Employees (IATSE) had a problem with Harpo Studios and Harpo Productions. They knew that they were using nonunion crews on the talk show, and perhaps on *Brewster Place*, but the unions were reluctant to confront someone as powerful as Oprah. In the first instance, she swung a lot of weight in the industry and could cause problems for the unions in other places; unions do not like to take on opponents they do not believe they can beat.

In the second instance, most of those unions are predominantly all white and male. Oprah was providing jobs for many blacks, women, and other minorities that wouldn't exist if all her work were strictly union. To challenge her could prove bad for the union's public relations. So, all in all, the unions were tiptoeing around the issue; as long as Oprah used some union crews, they didn't make too big a fuss about the nonunion workers.

Meanwhile, Jeffrey Jacobs, Oprah's majordomo and all-around man in charge of everything, offered the excuse that Harpo Studios was just a building, adding that they leased it to whoever wanted to use it without inquiring as to whether they were using union crews. Of course, the major user of the "building" was a company run by Jacobs and Oprah, and they knew very well whether their own operation was union or not.

As Oprah noted, the talk show was central to her media empire and a perfect example of the control on which she insisted. The press tour of Harpo Studios illustrated that control in action, and so did Carole A. Potter's experience as a guest on the show when it was still being produced at the WLS-TV studios some months earlier. Potter is a New York–based writer and public relations person selected by the *Oprah* show's talent coordinator, Mary Kay Clinton, to appear on a program about women aging and the problems they encounter after forty. Within twenty-four hours of agreeing to appear, Potter was flown to Chicago, put into a hotel, and was picked up the next morning by a limousine with five other women of "that certain age."

She described the others as thirty-eight-year-old knockout Pam, who thought the program would be about her fading beauty; Rosie, a thirty-four-year-old bombshell blonde who already had been through plastic surgery; an older woman introduced as "Granny June—the Aerobics Granny," who wanted to plug her book about aerobics for the elderly; and another quiet woman who, when faced with her coguests, rebelled. She declared that she had been deceived by the show's staff as to the topic of the program, which she thought would portray older women in a positive light. She said she would not go onstage, which startled the other women in the limousine, who felt it was a sacred obligation to do whatever Oprah wanted.

The women guests were guided into the green room at the studio, where a makeup man quickly dusted their faces. A few minutes before airtime, Oprah appeared, whereupon the complaining guest protested that she couldn't do the show because she had been misled. Oprah exploded. "I don't want to hear that this morning. I don't want to hear it." She turned and walked out of the green room.

Carole Potter later described her reaction. "A sense of

uneasiness began to set in. Was this the gracious woman who would stroke and gently guide us through the hazards of live TV?"

Potter was discovering that contrary to what her boosters claimed, the Oprah off the air can be much different from Oprah on the air. She recalled: "Someone hastily ushered the malcontent [guest] out to the audience, then returned with an astonished woman who had just been plucked from the jaws of obscurity. She and I were to share the second ten-minute slot. It was then that I learned that the segment would be called 'Terrified of Aging.'"

At that moment, Carole Potter was ready to revolt, too, and bolt for the audience, just as the other guest had done, but it was too late. They were on the air, and Oprah was introducing Ms. Potter and the instant new guest who was with her onstage.

"My next guests feel they're getting older and that age has taken their self-confidence and identity. They don't know who they are sometimes because youth is fading. Carole Potter is in her late forties and has lost her direction in life...."

At that instant, Carole Potter said she would have gladly socked Oprah, who was totally misrepresenting how she felt about herself and her life. She declared: "After the show we all gathered in the green room and, like children, expected the star to tell us how good we were and what a great show we had provided, and yes, we expected a simple thank you. Oprah blew into the room, consented to be photographed, and disappeared. We felt cheated. Never had the divine Oprah offered us a compliment. We exposed our souls so she could have a Friday show. You'd think she'd be on our side. But she wasn't.

"I hate to nitpick, but shouldn't a host do her homework? Oprah accused the attractive Rose, who had spent so much time and money on plastic surgery, of never dating. Rosie wanted to throw the water pitcher at her. Obviously, Oprah was attributing the statement to the wrong guest. Did she graciously joke about the error? No, she clung to it, insisting she had been told the woman didn't date. 'Just what my ex-boyfriend wants to hear,' Rosie muttered to Pam, unaware that her mike was on. After it was all over, all I could think was, if appearing on Oprah's show qualified as my fifteen minutes of fame, she blew it for me."

During that same time as Carole Potter appeared on the *Oprah Winfrey Show*, Oprah did meet her on-the-air match in Harvey McKay, author of *How To Swim With the Sharks*, a manual of corporate survival. First, Oprah had on four people who were victims of corporate backstabbing and vicious office politics. Each told a moving story of betrayal and unfair treatment at the hands of reprehensible bosses and coworkers. Then Oprah brought out Harvey McKay and challenged him to defend these malevolent practices, as if McKay were personally responsible for what had happened to these four victims.

What McKay did instead offered an insight into Oprah more than an insight into either McKay or corporate practices. Clearly, he had done his homework and studied the situation; more importantly, he had studied Oprah's personal history. McKay listened patiently to each of the four victims' stories and sympathetically offered them constructive advice about being patient, honing their skills, and building a network of allies inside the company.

Then he subtly shifted to Oprah, ostensibly using her as an example of a corporate boss but actually flattering her and defanging her before she could strike at him. He said that if she were his boss, he would take a burning interest in learning about her and what was important to her. Such as the time, he said, when she was three and gave the story of the resurrection of Jesus at her grandmother's church. With that, McKay had hooked her. "It seems to me that you are a perfectionist and a tough, fair boss." Beaming with pleasure at the flattery, Oprah addressed a rhetorical question to her offstage staff. "I'm very fair, aren't I, girls?"

Later, McKay said that once he was on the show, he realized that he had been misinformed about what was planned and that clearly Oprah had in mind skewering him as a representative of heartless, cruel corporate America in front of her audience and offering him up as the sacrificial lamb to compensate for the four ill-prepared dolts who appeared to be brutalized by men such as McKay. Instead, he turned it around and made himself look sympathetic and concerned about the four victims while showing they didn't understand how to function in their jobs and by winning over Oprah with praise.

"Something happened when I started reciting Oprah's life," he said. "She was getting a smile. If I had known exactly what they [Oprah and her staff] were going to do, I might not have done the show. She can really chew you up."

Soon after that show a magazine article appeared that disturbed Oprah. It became the one time when Jeffrey Jacobs, the omnipresent majordomo, lost his grip on Oprah since he closed out his law practice and went to work for her full-time. Jeffrey's wife had the job of dressing Oprah and tended to jam her into supertight miniskirted outfits that made Oprah look like a Polish sausage trying to escape. This look was emphasized with splashes of very bright colors that called even more attention to Oprah's increasing poundage. Finally, when Mr. Blackwell issued his 1990 "Worst Dressed" list in the October 26 issue of *TV Guide* prominently displaying Oprah, the Jennifer Jacobs era came to an end.

Oprah quietly announced at the end of November that she had decided to begin dressing herself, but soon she had hired another dresser to take Jennifer's place. This was a difficult move for Oprah because of the role that Jeffrey Jacobs played in her life. While most celebrities surround themselves with an entourage of people with vague and overlapping titles, such as manager, personal manager, financial manager, publicist, public relations, press liaison, business manager, agent, lawyer, agent-lawyer, lawyer-agent, and media manager and pay them a cut of the celebrity's income, Oprah just has Jeffrey, who is a forty-four-year-old ex-entertainment lawyer. That is why *Forbes* magazine noted in its October 1 issue that Madonna was the year's highest-grossing female entertainer but Oprah probably took home more for herself. Most people in celebrity entourages are basically coffee gofers, coat holders, and door openers, anyhow.

"He's the visionary," said Oprah about Jacobs, and he moved her from her original $200,000 WLS-TV contract in 1984 to the $40 million a year she was making six years later. In fact,

Oprah credited his vision for her success nationally. "Most of what has happened is a product of Jeff's vision. Were it not for him, there's a very good chance that I would still be hosting a local show here in Chicago."

Oprah had gone from local host to national syndication and a production studio owner. Chicago people are proud of Harpo Studios because it is the most modern film and TV production studio in the Midwest and can do everything that a studio anywhere can do. The hope was that it would attract production work away from Hollywood and New York in addition to doing the 220 Oprah talk shows every year as well as her specials and films. The xenophobia of Chicago was evident with the opening of the remodeled Harpo Studios. Chicago has always resented New York and Chicago's image of "the second city." Now Middle America's metropolis resented Los Angeles, since it had passed Chicago as the second most populous city in America. So when the stunningly modern Harpo Studios opened, everyone in Chicago was proud, even competitors who might lose business to the new facility.

"She's bringing high-quality production facilities to the city. She does good work. I see this as a positive," said Carmen Trombetta, general manager of the competing Northwest Telecommunications.

Ruth Ratny, who ran *Screen* magazine, which reports on entertainment in Chicago, saw the emergence of Harpo Productions not negatively, just differently:

"The real impact is in the public relations arena. The PR benefit is incalculable, but there are no jobs there. When Oprah bought it, the idea was that there would be film stages rented out, but this isn't happening. The studio is for Oprah, the same way the M-G-M studios were for M-G-M."

Even so, the studio served an important competitive purpose for Oprah, since it gave her control over her production and its costs. Only King World's distribution did not rest totally in her hands. Even there, she controlled a piece of the action by either owning or having the option to a million or more shares of the syndication company.

Jeffrey Jacobs said, "To succeed in this business, you have to be competitive economically. By controlling your facility, you can compete with just about anybody. We have security, control of our destiny."

This is the same philosophy that has worked so well for the Disney organization, which is obsessive about controlling every aspect of its productions. So Oprah, with Jeffrey Jacobs's guidance, gained control of the *Oprah Winfrey Show* in October 1988 and moved its production from the studios of WLS-TV to the Harpo Studios that Oprah, operating as Harpo Productions, had bought primarily for the talk show and other special Oprah projects. It had been Chicago Studio City at one time and then Studio Network and Fred Niles Studio, but now it was Harpo Studios, and it boasted the very latest in broadcast technology.

Throughout all these expansions and changes, Oprah continued to exercise control. Following the advice of Bill Cosby, she signs all the checks and keeps ultimate control of her money and her empire. Every expenditure has to cross her desk and be explained to her. "I think not signing the checks and not knowing where the money is, is a sign that you are losing control," she said. "It's God's way of telling you that have too much."

Other celebrities over the years have lost millions because they allowed others to control the checkbook. Even when control passes to a member of the family, there is no assurance that the money will be properly watched and handled. Shirley Temple is just one example of a star who ended up broke because her father squandered the millions she had earned in movies.

In April, Oprah signed some checks happily when she paid for the wedding of Debra DiMaio, including flying fifty guests first-class to Florence, Italy, for the ceremony, followed by a two-week, all-expenses-paid honeymoon on the French Riviera. Oprah missed the wedding because of airplane travel connections and canceled flights.

Oprah was now syndicated to 20 million viewers internationally; 1990 was also the year that another former Nashville TV personality, Pat Sajak, didn't make it in late-night TV. Sajak, the host of the most popular of all King World features in syndication, *Wheel of Fortune*, made a stab at late-night talk TV beginning in 1989, but by 1990 it was clear he didn't have the audience appeal, and the show was canceled.

Oprah's busy schedule was starting to hurt her relationship with Stedman. He had moved to Chicago six months earlier from North Carolina—to his own apartment. While this meant they spent more time with each other at the beginning of their new geographic closeness, soon their time together diminished from several times a week to twice a month. Finally, in May, Stedman gave Oprah an ultimatum. Either they would become a real couple or not. If they were to become a real couple, that meant being together much of the time instead of Stedman being an appointment in Oprah's calendar book. If it couldn't be that way, Stedman said he would walk out of the relationship.

Oprah reacted to the crisis as she frequently does, namely, with a massive, instant "solution" that papered over the problem and gave the appearance of curing whatever was wrong without actually doing so. She suggested they abandon their long-held position of not living together until marriage and that Stedman immediately move into her twenty-four-room apartment. He agreed, but kept his own place, too.

Oprah had the place remodeled for $4 million, providing special space for Stedman as well as herself. What also was needed was a remodeling of the relationship and Oprah's time commitments. She had to make Stedman part of her regular life and cut down on the projects that were consuming all of her time. She had to be a genuine fiancée instead of an occasional date.

At the same time there was trouble in other parts of the family. Back in March, Oprah's half sister betrayed a deep family secret by selling to the *National Enquirer* the story that Oprah had given birth to an illegitimate child when she was fourteen. That might have proved of little consequence, given the public reputation of the *National Enquirer*. But the story was picked up in the May 6 issue of the widest-circulating, most respectable Sunday newspaper supplement, *Parade* magazine.

The story appeared in family newspapers all over the country. She told *Parade*, "The experience was the most emotional, confusing and traumatic of my young life."

Beyond that, she had hoped to keep this episode of her life private until she was ready to cope with it and perhaps share it with young girls to help them confront and deal with unwed pregnancy. The story made her so sick when Stedman called it to her attention just after she had done a scene for *Brewster Place* that Oprah had to go to bed. She would not speak to her half sister, Patricia Lee, for another two years.

As June arrived, Oprah got ready to host the seventeenth Daytime Emmy Awards in New York, which turned out to be a disappointment for her in two ways. One, her weight of 160 pounds made it almost impossible for her to squeeze into her size 14 wardrobe and two Sally Jessy Raphael won the Out-standing Talk/Service Program Award and Joan Rivers the Outstanding Host Emmy, which some thought was a sympathy award for her having been dumped so unceremoniously by FOX and for having to endure her husband's suicide. Oprah didn't get Outstanding Director, either. That went to Russell Morash of *This Old House*. The Emmys were a clean lockout for Oprah. Following the Emmy show, Oprah secretly went on a strict diet to rid herself of thirty pounds and blamed the liquid diet for her previous problem. She had stopped exercising, grabbed any kind of food she could, and ballooned up.

On June 20, ABC aired an Oprah special, *In the Name of Self-Esteem*, focusing on what Oprah felt was the cause of most of the problems of the world. Because of lack of self-esteem, Oprah believed people abused others who were weaker; wars were fought; crimes were committed; and an endless assortment of brutality was visited by one person upon another. Oprah wanted to explain how important self-esteem is to everyone's happiness.

Maya Angelou was one of Oprah's guests on the program, and she talked about being abused by her parents and then being raped as a young girl. This experience so traumatized Angelou that she lost the power of speech for years. She felt being raped meant she was worthless. Also on the program were an inner-city teacher and a counselor from a drug rehabilitation center. They spoke about how low self-esteem made kids fail at school and how it pushed young people into using drugs.

The year 1990 was a big one for doing things with her money. She brought some notoriety to herself in the staid world of antique collection when she attended an auction of Shaker furniture in upstate New York on August 5 and spent $470,000 on a counter, two armchairs, a rocker, a box, and a basket for her Indiana farm. The auctioneer praised her choice of items. Along with everyone else, he noted that she did not participate in the arcane, silent way, as is the custom at most auctions. Instead, she talked a lot, hooting and yelling with excitement and pleasure during the bidding. While the $470,000 she spent that day along with her other expenditures during the year might seem extravagant to the average person, one should recall the pledge she made at the Miss Fire Prevention contest years before that she would be a "spending fool." Even if she spent a good deal, she also earned $50 million a year. By the end of 1990, she was worth $250 million and spent $35 million the previous two years. These expenditures included:

- $2 million to buy and redecorate the Indiana farm
- $1 million for jewelry, $500,000 for gowns, and $130,000 for shoes and purses
- $200,000 for thoroughbred horses
- $500,000 for international vacations
- $4 million for a 24-room luxury apartment
- $1 million for five fur coats

In addition, Oprah figured she needed $1 million a year for walking-around pocket money. She also had a limousine and a twenty-four-hour driver, a hairdresser, and a makeup artist who were part of her professional expenses. Beyond that, during the previous two years, she bought her mother a $158,000 condo in Milwaukee and sent her $5,000 a month for expenses plus $1,200 a month expense money to her half sister, Patricia. She bought her father and stepmother a $330,000 house and spent $200,000 furnishing it. She also would send

Tennessee State $250,000 a year to maintain the ten scholarships she had established in her father's name, along with $1 million to Morehouse College in Atlanta and bountiful contributions to the Chicago Academy of the Performing Arts. Her generosity to Stedman was very limited, for he refused to accept gifts, not wanting to feed the gossip that all he cared about was her money. But he did permit her to pay for their vacations together.

Nor did he object to the $45,000 a day she spent on their July second weeklong Mediterranean cruise aboard the yacht *Talon* with Stedman's fifteen-year old daughter, Wendy, and some friends. At ports along the way, they spent $190,000 shopping, dined in local restaurants, and had fun playing games and being lovers.

She pledged to herself once again to slim down from her near-record 205 pounds after the cruise. To help her lose weight, she hired Rosie Daley, the chef at Cal-a-Vie, in September to be her personal cook and prepare good-tasting food. Daley prepared all her meals, went with Oprah to the Indiana farm, made lunches for her to take to work, and even supervised what she ate in restaurants. During the first six weeks of the Rosie Daley regime, Oprah lost twenty pounds. Rosie's reign meant the banishment of butter, salt, and fat, along with cream sauces, and the introduction of vegetables and grains that satisfied Oprah's feelings of hunger by filling her up without adding fat and lots of liquid.

Rosie Daley helped Oprah lose weight even if she was expensive, but Oprah could afford it. She wanted to slim down for her own self-esteem and because it meant holding on to Stedman. The Stedman factor played an important part while also depressing her. Stedman's enthusiasm for a thinner Oprah again made Oprah realize that fat mattered to him. Deep down she knew that her value to him as a woman depended on how she looked and not entirely on what kind of human being she was.

She found herself in that woman's trap she had repeatedly vowed she would never get caught in again. Namely, she needed to certify her human worth in terms of having a man, and she couldn't have a man on the basis of being an intelligent, decent, wonderful human being. She had to have him on the basis of her body. It was now late 1991. She and Stedman had been dating, and the romance had been blowing hot and cold since 1986. The rumor mill began to churn out the report that Oprah and her boyfriend planned to marry in June 1992 at Harpo Studios. Before that could happen another Oprah show became controversial.

Oprah's July 6 show allegedly drove Michael La Calamita of Northlake, Illinois, to suicide. He appeared on a segment called "Bad Influence Friends" and became a target of ridicule and humiliation. When he returned to his hometown, he had become too well known from the *Oprah* show and was unmercifully harassed by people. In despair, he finally hung himself from a ceiling fan in his home on July 18. Nothing further came from this tragedy, and Oprah again was wrestling with her weight problem.

By November, the July diet had proved a failure. She had gained sixty-nine pounds, and at five feet seven she weighed 199 pounds. Stedman refused to move into the $4 million apartment and called off the romance. He was a fitness nut and couldn't understand her refusal to diet, exercise, and stay slim. The relationship turned platonic, and everybody warned her she would lose Stedman if she didn't lose weight. She became defiant, said to hell with men, and told her November 5 audience that she would never diet again. Secretly, on November 10, she was back on a diet with Stedman. Their romance blossomed, and she became energized by a new project.

At the beginning of November, ABC and Oprah announced her association with a new version of after-school specials, to be aired the next season and to deal with the problems of young people. Oprah would produce and host these specials, to be created by Harpo Productions. The announcement for ABC was made by its president of sports, daytime, and children's programming, Dennis Swanson, the same executive who originally hired Oprah at WLS-TV. ABC's after-school specials had been on the air for twenty years, during which they won sixty-four Emmys. Most of them aired in the afternoon opposite the *Oprah Winfrey Show*. The purpose of tying in with Oprah and Harpo Productions was to enhance the ratings of the specials because Oprah was so popular with viewers of the same age who normally watched the after-school specials.

Ame Simon, director of the specials, explained: "The audience is obviously there for Oprah at that time [of the day], and I would think that the affiliates will be pleased that, in one way or another, they'll get Oprah. [From ABC's viewpoint] we wanted to do a deal with Oprah and we wanted to do something new with the specials to bolster the audience levels. We think that the new shows will provide a new way of dealing with issues."

Interestingly, the after-school specials were designed to appeal to high school teens, but over the years the audience has been predominantly eighteen- to thirty-four-year-old women, since the lead-in for the after-school specials has been the popular soap opera *General Hospital*. In the past, after-school specials consisted of fictional dramas, but the new version under Oprah's management would focus on issue-oriented nonfiction programs about self-esteem, drugs, sex, makeup, and dress, not unlike what she produced for the adult market on the *Oprah Winfrey Show*. Peggy Charren, head of Action for Children's Programming, expressed concern that by moving from dramas to nonfiction the programs would become dated sooner and not provide the longevity of dramas conveying a simple message.

The contrast could be seen in one of the after-school specials on January 28, 1993, when the program turned out to be teens talking about the deteriorated state of race relations in America, with Oprah appearing in the middle of sound-bites of hate, despair, and frustration. Neo-Nazis spoke of genetic controls and compared the high birthrates of nonwhites with those of whites, with one Neo-Nazi teen predicting that within ten years he would either be in jail, dead, or in an all-white America. That brought the venom from a young black man, who declared that the only satisfactory payback for all the years of subjugation of his people was the total destruction of the white race. For the most part, the participants felt that the media overgeneralized about them and about race relations. It was a stimulating and fiery session, in contrast to the more orderly and traditional presentation of a dramatic story that had been the format of the specials before Oprah took over.

Along with Christmas came Oprah's legendary generosity. Each producer received two round-trip tickets to anywhere in the world for two weeks plus $10,000 and free hotel accommodations. Two months later, Oprah took this same group with her for a vacation to the British Virgin Islands.

As delighted as the participants were, at least one former employee apparently did not like working for Oprah. She told Fred Goodman, when he was writing an Oprah/Madonna comparison article for the December 1991 *Working Woman* magazine, "She's always called a great motivator, but if I asked you to do something for me and promised you a Bulgari bracelet or a Rolex watch, you'd be pretty motivated. You could say that her management style has more to do with bribery than psychological persuasion. In basic terms, her management style is, 'If you're good, you'll get a gift, trip or cash.'"

DiMaio gave Oprah a flock of sheep for her Rolling Prairie farm.

CHAPTER

20

Trashing Trash TV

From the late 1980s to the early 1990s, as Oprah became a multi-million-dollar talk-TV star, a growing number of critics, including those who do the same thing that Oprah does, attacked what they labeled "trash TV" and specifically named Oprah, Geraldo, Sally Jessy, Donahue, and a number of lesser lights in the field.

One of the key opening assaults on trash TV was launched by the influential TV critic for the *Washington Post*, Tom Shales, who is highly respected professionally by his colleagues.

Late in 1988 he wrote in the *Post*, "Talk Rot infests the airwaves and pollutes the atmosphere. Where TV's daytime talk shows once dealt, at least on occasion, with serious social and political issues, they now concentrate mainly on the trivial and the titillating. Hours and hours are frittered away on shock, schlock and folly." He said the American public was becoming "the most over-informed uninformed people on earth—a nation of boob-tube boobs spoon-fed nothing but low-fiber fluff."

Shales blamed the Reagan administration's permissive and weak regulation of broadcasters for opening the floodgates to sleaze and the degeneration of daytime talk TV into trash TV. He cited the reaction of Phil Donahue when somebody called his show "intelligent." He said, "We are dangerously close to being referred to as an intelligent talk show. If that happens,

210

we're doomed. Call me 'outrageous.' I'd rather be called sleazy than to be identified as intelligent."

Ralph Nader entered the discussion, targeting the Oprah show in particular. "They get all their ideas from the *National Enquirer*." Shales noted that Oprah received her best ratings with her November 15, 1988, weight-loss program, "Diet Dreams Come True," when she pulled the sixty-seven pounds of fat around the stage in a little red wagon. He sarcastically commented that other recent Oprah topics included subservient women, paternity fights, man hunting, threesomes, wife beaters, and Joan Collins.

Not that Oprah was Shales' only target. He labeled *Geraldo* the barrel-bottom talk hour, starring "dauntless panderer Geraldo Rivera dealing with transsexuals and their families, teen prostitutes, swinging sexual suicide, mud-wrestling women, Charles Manson, serial killers, kids who kill, battered women who kill, and of course, male strippers." Shales expected that Geraldo will ultimately get to male strippers who kill, too.

Shales did strike a positive note on Geraldo when he answered the question Geraldo posed in another of his shows, "Has TV Gone Too Far?" Yes, yes, a thousand times yes, was the Shales reaction. Geraldo's reaction was to attack Oprah and whine about how people like Shales are always picking on him.

Geraldo started out at KABC-TV in Los Angeles under the name Jerry Rivers and then changed it back to the original, Geraldo Rivera, when being Hispanic became advantageous. Geraldo startled Oprah when he suddenly unleashed an attack on her and other colleagues in the television talk as well as on himself. It was somewhat like the infantry platoon leader in dire combat circumstances who calls down an artillery barrage on his own position because his placement has been overrun by the enemy.

Geraldo roared, "I'm sick of trash TV! Shows like *Oprah* and *Donahue* and even my own have gone over the line and we've all got to stop piping sleazy, perverted material into America's homes! I'm the first to say, 'I'm stopping it!' Now it's time for the others to follow. Oprah, enough of the sleaze! Daytime talk shows have covered such shocking topics as sex with animals, sex-change operations, lesbian marriages, incest, and worse. And it seems that with each passing week, the topics get more and more bizarre."

While everybody was trying to digest this astonishing *mea culpa* from the man whose nose was broken in a chair-swinging, on-the-air miniriot on his show, Geraldo quickly slipped into a spasm of self-pity:

"I can look back at shows I've done, and while many were excellent, I have to admit I went overboard a number of times. In November of last year [1989] alone, I did shows on sex-crazed women, battered lesbians, and a topless donut shop. But I'm judged far more harshly than the others on daytime TV. Their shows are just as outrageous as mine, at times more so. Oprah did a show on which a perverted sex practice was described, and medical experts later said two viewers died while they were trying to practice what they'd seen on *Oprah*. Despite that, almost nobody got on her case. If I had done that show, it would have been international news. My God! I probably would have been slapped in prison!"

Shales didn't spare the man who was once respected as a TV talk host. Shales now felt that Donahue had sold out for money while admitting that he still provided the most substantive shows. By comparison, in a recent week Shales watched Rivera doing ex-pimps and ex-hookers, Oprah telling women how to break out of the bad-guy cycle and dump losers, "and Sally Jessy Raphael, another tiny-minded entry in the talk show race, offering make-up tips."

Donahue admitted to Shales that he has been forced to offer stupider programming. "Yes. It gives me no pleasure to say yes. We used to be the only kid on the block, swaggering around the mountaintop, and so we could feature programs that interest me as a news junkie, things that our show was unique to present—public service and so on. We knew we could not keep the audience if we did not have variations on the theme of the male stripper.

"I have to say that we do feel the pressure. This is a nation with a seriously diminished interest in serious news. The media is reflecting this. *Time* and *Newsweek* covers look more and more like *People* magazine covers. Against that observation has to be considered the enormous competition and profit squeeze that these fewer and fewer and larger and larger media companies feel. The evidence is pretty overwhelming that as we move into the twenty-first century, Americans have more and more interest in Madonna and less and less interest in the Persian Gulf or Central America."

NBC is once again owned by a company that paid a lot of money for it and is primarily in the lightbulb and appliance business; CBS is controlled by a family of professional investors who were primarily in the hotel business; and ABC is owned by a company run by salesmen who also paid a lot of money for it. All of these network owners are very bottom line profit conscious.

Oprah's response to Tom Shales's criticism was silence. Producer Debra DiMaio would only say they weren't saying anything and then took a jab at the competition while saying "nothing." DiMaio declared, "We don't put ourselves in the same category as Geraldo and Morton Downey Jr., so we are sticking to our policy of not commenting."

The irony of Oprah's not commenting is that she has a couple of dozen people on her staff assigned to public relations and public information. Shales says that all these people do is not relate to the public and not give information to the public. He wrote, "Winfrey may have shed a wall of fat, but she is protected by a hefty squad of public relators." Ralph Nader chimed in with "It's easier to get through to Ronald Reagan than it is to get to Oprah Winfrey."

However, when Oprah appeared in mid-January at an ABC-TV press conference before seventy-five reporters to promote her ABC miniseries *The Women of Brewster Place*, she spent most of her time defending her version of trash television and talking about her celebrity life. She told the reporters that being lumped together in the same trash bag as *Geraldo* and *The Morton Downey Jr. Show* was something she wasn't very happy about but accepted as going with the territory.

Beyond that, Oprah brought an entirely new perspective to the trashing of daytime TV shows by critics like Tom Shales by contending that his views demonstrated an antiwoman prejudice. Oprah said, "I was talking to Gloria Steinem about it. Many of the shows that people like Phil [Donahue] and myself get criticized for, shows like 'Women Whose Husbands Leave Them' are female-oriented. These shows may sound sleazy, but they're not. I know, because I sit there and I look at the pain these people experience every day of their lives. I also get the letters, sometimes four thousand a week, that show me that these shows are touching people."

"And so it continues," concluded Shales, "the daily parade: wackos, loonies, stars, celebrities, freaks, geeks and gurus. Much of it is appallingly entertaining. Little of it is remotely worthwhile. On one of her few serious, outer-directed shows, Winfrey dealt with declining literacy among the young and the escalating crisis in American education. In promos she looked into the camera and asked, 'How dumb are we?' There's every possibility that talk rot is making us dumber."

After Shales wrote about the subject, other critics and intellectuals made trash TV a favorite TV topic, with the primary target, surprisingly, Donahue.

Coincidentally, around Oprah's thirty-sixth birthday, Donahue, the king of daytime talk, also nicknamed Mr. Sensitive, reflected about the whole talk-show industry and his book *Donahue: My Own Story*. In spite of occasional stories to the contrary, Donahue has remained popular and is still seen on two hundred stations around the nation. Everybody in America knows who "Donahue" is, even if many don't know that his full name is Philip John Donahue and that he has a college degree in marketing from Notre Dame.

Until 1986, he owned the daytime television talk circuit. Then came the whirlwind, Oprah, forcing Donahue to adjust his schedule in many cities so that they wouldn't face each other. They arrived at an amicable truce in which Donahue dominated the morning and Oprah the afternoon.

Geraldo Rivera appeared a year after Oprah, with Sally Jessy Raphael jumping over from radio to afternoon television in 1988 and Joan Rivers arriving in 1989. A. C. Nielsen, the program-rating pollster, ranked *Wheel of Fortune* and *Jeopardy* the top-two syndicated shows in 1990, with Oprah fifth (8.6

percent share of the audience), Geraldo ninth (6.1 percent share) and Donahue tenth (6.0 percent share).

Still, Donahue often led the way and was regarded as the grand old man in the field, having started in Dayton, Ohio, when Oprah was thirteen and still playing the Horse in her mother's Milwaukee apartment. Donahue spent twenty-three years interviewing everybody from Jimmy Hoffa to George Bush and Pete Rose. He began by trying to be serious, thoughtful, and sensitive about momentous national and international issues of politics, economics, and medicine, but times have changed for talk television and for Phil Donahue. At some point in the last four years, he realized that he either had to buy into trash TV or go under as a performer and newsman–talk-show host. The ratings were dropping, and he began discussing transvestites, dwarf tossing, and sexual dysfunction to hold his audience, which had found out about sex, fat, and love from Oprah and Geraldo.

Some of his viewing audience were stunned by this transformation of the white-haired father of TV talk, to the extent that the Public Broadcasting Service (PBS) convened a panel of television critics to discuss Donahue in particular and the sorry state of television talk shows in general. This event later appeared as a PBS special. The *Los Angeles Times* reported on January 28, 1990: "The panel was particularly hard on Donahue because he was once viewed as the sage of the talk show circuit: a beacon of intelligence in the often tawdry world of afternoon soap opera and game shows."

Author David Halberstam said that the *Donahue* show had "lost its soul," and humorist Art Buchwald said that the only way he could get on the show was to go through a sex-change operation. Donahue replied that times and tastes have changed. He pointed to Peter Jennings, who, in mid-January, 1990, presented a news broadcast on date rape, and NBC News, which offered a segment on excessively vulnerable wives. "If we did this on daytime," he said, "it would be called trash TV."

In the spring of 1989, Donahue and ten other talk-show hosts and journalists, like *Washington Post* critic Tom Shales,

Larry King, Geraldo Rivera, and Morton Downey Jr., appeared on a televised panel at Columbia University about news versus entertainment. Donahue quickly became the target of most of the jibes, starting with a film clip of him prancing around the stage of his show in November 1988 in red panty hose and a dress. Donahue defended himself and Oprah and the rest because they are getting out information the public wants and can use in their lives. He offered "no apologies—not for cutting deals to get 'hot' guests on the air before anyone else or for putting tossed dwarfs and roller-game queens and transvestites on the air during the after-school viewing hours or for airing panel discussions on such topics as 'Catching Your Mate in Bed With Someone Else."

In disgust Donahue slashed back at those who criticize Oprah, Geraldo, Sally Jessy, and himself. "Come on," he said. "Let's get rid of the pretense and understand that we've got an unholy alliance between the media, which is focused on ratings and circulation, and a community of people it serves in the marketplace who are focused on Madonna, Jim and Tammy Faye, and Zsa Zsa!"

In a dramatic example of Donahue's unholy alliance, he started fighting with state officials in North Carolina in May 1994 for the right to televise the execution of David Lawson. Lawson was sentenced to death for the 1980 murder of Wayne Shinn after he broke into Shinn's home. In North Carolina condemned prisoners are allowed to invite people to witness their executions, and usually friends and relatives are chosen, along with official witnesses and five reporters. In this case, Lawson specifically asked Donahue in April 1994 to videotape his execution and to broadcast it on his show, which Donahue was anxious to do, suing the state authorities who have refused him permission. Said Donahue back in 1993, "I would be pleased to have an execution on the *Donahue* show. What's wrong with it? Let's see future bad guys watch these people fry right here on television." The North Carolina Supreme Court turned Donahue down in May.

Donahue conceded that he had turned to so-called trash TV to attract audiences and to stay on the air. His explanation was that American audiences, more interested in being titillated than in being taught, had descended into an "MTV coma." He didn't necessarily like it, nor was he proud of some of his shows, but still, he said, "if you don't understand how we survive in TV, no argument I make is going to make a difference. We get paid to draw a crowd. When we don't draw a crowd, we don't get paid."

He is as critical of what legitimate journalists do, or rather *don't* do, as they are of what he *does* do. Donahue, a C-SPAN fan who reads widely and seriously, wants to know why most major corruption in government has never been uncovered by the "journalists" who criticize Donahue and Oprah and Rivera for the kind of subjects they deal with on the air. For example, neither Watergate, the HUD scandal, the savings-and-loan crisis, Iran-Contra, Sen. Bob Packwood's sexual harassment, nor any other memorable malfeasance in office has been uncovered by any of the media stars. Donahue wants to know, if they are so pure and perfect, why is this true?

Donahue was fifty-four in 1990 and wanted to continue broadcasting and reaching out to the several million women who view him every weekday. To do that he believed he had to do a balancing act that would match the Wallendas' high-wire act, teetering between being Walter Cronkite and Dana Carvey. "We're being asked to give them the news. We are asked to be a BBC media, and part of our job is to attract an MTV audience. I don't want to be a dead hero."

Trash TV was proliferating not just for English-speaking American audiences but also for the burgeoning Spanish-speaking viewers in the country. Witness Cristina Saralegui, the Spanish-language version of Oprah who appeals to a much more conservative audience than Oprah does but deals with the same subjects and the shock value in the Hispanic culture of an aggressive Spanish-speaking woman telling her Latino audience, "Up to a few years ago a woman was valued on the basis of one thing—whether or not she was a virgin."

With that *Cristina* was off and running, interviewing women complaining about how in their culture women are supposed to remain virgins while the men sleep around all over town. Then on came a Hispanic plastic surgeon whose speciality was hymen-reconstructive surgery for young Hispanic women who were terrified that their fathers would find out they were no longer virgins. Even a few women in the audience of mostly timid females had the courage to admit that they had lost their virginity, with the justification that "a woman should lose her virginity to the man she loves. Not necessarily to the man she marries."

Hispanic television broke new ground copying English-speaking trash-TV shows driven by Yankee greed, since the two main Spanish-language networks in the United States are mostly owned by Hallmark Greeting Cards (Univision) or financier Saul Steinberg's Reliance Capital (Telemundo).

Some of the other popular shows following the English-language pattern include knockoffs of *Entertainment Tonight* (*Desde Hollywood*) and Barbara Walters (*Portada*, featuring Teresa Rodriguez). The most popular Spanish-language show in the entire Western Hemisphere is *Sábado Gigante* (*Giant Saturday*), a three-hour combination of *Oprah-Wheel of Fortune-Tonight* and an old-fashioned Mitch Miller sing-along except that the host gets the studio audience to sing along with the sponsors' commercials. The host is the famous Don Francisco, whose real name is Mario Kreutzberger.

The full impact of trash TV hit in the early 1990s, with more tabloid shows such as *Hard Copy* and *Inside Edition* and more programs starring big-name, "legitimate" newspeople like Diane Sawyer, Connie Chung, and Dan Rather offering titillating segments pandering to the lowest common taste. Just after ABC gave Diane Sawyer a new $7 million contract and a new tabloid show, her first guest in the grab for ratings was Charles Manson, whose appearance on Geraldo Rivera a few years before was ridiculed by the legitimate news media.

On July 4, 1993, Howard Kurtz wrote in the *Washington Post* about a national survey of TV news in the 1990s under the headline "Murder! Mayhem! Ratings! Tabloid Sensationalism Is Thriving on TV News." He said, "Night after night local newscasts around the country are going tabloid. While crime news has always been a staple of local television, a new sensationalism is sweeping the airwaves as once-sedate network affiliates highlight sex and violence in search of big ratings."

Kurtz noted that the graphics at the stations surveyed in Chicago, San Diego, Los Angeles, and Miami read: "Syringe Scare," "Voyeur Murder," "Tollway Murder," "Wheelchair Murder," "Rap Music Murder," "Serial Rapist," "Caught in the Crossfire," and "Alligator Attack."

The so-called legitimate, hard-news shows had been transformed into *Oprah* and *Donahue* clones in only five years since Oprah had gone national and brought a new variation of news and information to television.

CHAPTER

21

1991

The year 1991 started off happily with a new, even more lucrative contract with King World. The King brothers, with whom Oprah allied herself, were out on the road making more and more money for Oprah by raising rates, renegotiating contracts, and squeezing every dollar they could out of stations that needed Oprah as the early lead-in show in the afternoons. In some instances, stations were actually losing money on her show, keeping it only because they made money from the shows that immediately followed hers and for which there was a ready-to-watch audience in place.

A new factor in the syndication business arose in the form of Rupert Murdock, the Australian tabloid publisher who had bought into the Twentieth Century-Fox studios and launched a fourth television network, Fox. This new network was not a major competitor of the traditional three networks at the beginning, but just the fact that Fox existed meant more competition for the advertising-agency dollars and better deals.

The downside for Oprah came in the form of the failed *Brewster Place* weekly series in which she had so much faith and had so enjoyed doing both as an actress and producer-director. The loss from *Brewster Place* would reach about $10 million.

As Oprah celebrated her thirty-seventh birthday, it did not appear that she and Stedman were moving any closer to the wedding chapel. Stedman had become increasingly concerned that Oprah didn't have the will to give up her frenetic career life and become a wife. Clearly, some compromise had to be made. Oprah certainly would never be the little woman sitting at home sewing, baking Toll-House cookies, tending to little Stedman III, and having dinner waiting on the table when her man came home. For one thing, she couldn't sew, and for another, she was a lousy cook, and the idea of babies was wonderful as an intellectual concept but repellant as a day-to-day reality filled with dirty diapers.

Stedman refused to spend his life trotting in the shadow of this powerful woman, picking up her discarded mink, and making sure the limousine was brought around to the front door on time. The very masculinity and pride that attracted Oprah to him were the traits that kept him from being the docile doormat. Moreover the dynamic enthusiasm and mind-boggling energy that attracted Stedman to Oprah kept her from being the domestic princess. Although balance was needed, it seemed beyond reach, and yet both of them wanted the relationship to work because each was drawn to the other and to the relationship. Both had invested too much time and energy to simply walk away on a whim.

Perhaps Oprah's high-octane approach was the most difficult hurdle in achieving the needed compromise and balance. Her approach to a problem was to overwhelm it, as only a person with her money could do. She had hoped, dreamed, and expected that Stedman would do something romantic in 1991—they had been dating for almost five years—like proposing to her on Valentine's Day. Valentine's Day came, but no engagement ring. Instead, Stedman and Oprah had "a talk." He told her flat out that he was very skeptical about their relationship and the future. He couldn't see her toning down her life and her schedule so that they could be a regular married couple. He was tired of being an appointment on her calendar and wouldn't settle for anything less than a full-time involvement as her husband and a full-time involvement by her as his wife.

Oprah was deeply disturbed by Stedman's feelings and panicked, fearful that he might decide that he had had enough and walk away. While it was difficult for Stedman to romance such a high-profile, powerful woman, it would be devastating to Oprah for him to publicly walk out on her after all the time they had to consolidate their relationship. Sexist as it would appear, the truth is that millions of women fans would conclude that Oprah couldn't hold on to her dream man and would think that she either wasn't sexy enough in the bedroom or couldn't keep the weight off to remain desirable to him. Certainly the money, the makeup, and a wardrobe that every woman would envy should have assured keeping any man. Her solution to the situation was the same as it was to any other crisis: Pour money on it with thoughtfulness and dramatic action—overwhelm the problem.

She rented the premier honeymoon getaway in the Caribbean, Necker Island, for $10,000 a day! Owned by the legendary Richard Bramson, English recording company and airline multimillionaire (Virgin Records and Virgin Airlines), it is a small island just northeast of Virgin Gorda in the British Virgin Islands, with only one ten-bedroom house atop Devil's Hill cliff and a staff of nineteen servants and security guards.

Along with the Balinese meeting house architecture with sliding roof panels to admit the balmy trade winds, a master bedroom opened to views of the sea. The bedroom featured a white and blue Balinese fabric cover, private sundeck, and private jacuzzi, with Haitian paintings and Mexican pottery to accent the dark, natural Brazilian Ipe wood finishes. Oprah and Stedman basked in the sun, fished, played tennis, made love in the jacuzzi, had drinks from the glass-top table supported by a statue of a nude woman lying on her back, and danced to a private band especially brought in for the night. Every morning Oprah exercised and worked on her weight. It was a glorious ten days of romance, sunsets, and the sound of the reeling ground doves, pelicans, and hummingbirds along with the crashing surf. It brought the excitement and euphoria of love back into their lives and the tacit understanding that there would be a wedding in September.

There was a weakness in this Necker Island solution,

however, in that Oprah again applied the same technique to one of her problems. When something was wrong, she flooded it with overpowering solutions that stopped working the instant they were no longer there. That is exactly what happened with the weight-reduction crash program that sliced off those sixty-seven pounds earlier. As soon as she stopped using the drastic solution, the weight started creeping back onto her hips. In the same fashion, she went on a vacation ten days to Necker Island to repair her fraying romance, and it worked wonderfully for those ten days. Oprah did the same thing when she determined that Stedman loved to ski and was very good at it. To help hold her romance together by getting away for ski trips with Stedman, in April 1991, Oprah bought eighty-five acres, with a luxurious cabin, for $4.5 million in Telluride, Colorado, so that she could ski there with him when they wished. These grand gestures were not what the romance needed. It needed Oprah to invest the one thing she has never been willing to invest for long, and that is her time. Stedman wanted them to be a couple, hanging around, being together, sharing and having their own private life. That wasn't the way Oprah was used to handling "problems," and she saw Stedman's needs as a problem to be dealt with, usually by spending money instead of spending time.

When the two lovers returned from Necker Island, Oprah felt she had solved that problem and moved on to something else, namely, running a very expensive business with two hundred employees and killer stress to produce show after show. In the process she began to ignore her weight and started to balloon up to over two hundred pounds by indulging herself on high-calorie, high-fat junk foods, desserts, and regular visits to her restaurant, the Eccentric, while totally abandoning exercise. Soon her staff became worried, and her doctor told her she had to drop at least thirty pounds or her life would be in jeopardy.

So why does she load on the pounds? Some popular psychologists would agree with what Oprah would tell Jane Pauley in a September 6 interview, that weight was a defense—a way of protecting herself. The secret truth may be that Oprah is frightened of marrying Stedman and that gaining weight is a way of putting off that day when she cannot back out of the marriage. She did, in fact, postpone the wedding again after they returned from Necker Island, and she began eating more. She said it was because she refused to be a fat bride, but it might have been the other way around: She was getting fat so she wouldn't have to be a bride. So everybody quietly witnessed the self-fulfilling prophecy at work as Oprah sabotaged the one thing she told people she wanted more than anything else.

On March 13 she did her first major show on child abuse, motivated by the story she saw on television in mid-February about four-year-old Angelica Mena of Chicago, who was raped, strangled, and dumped into Lake Michigan. Michael Howarth, thirty-one, a new tenant who had moved in next door to Angelica's mother's apartment, was arrested and confessed to the crime. Oprah said, "I vowed that night to do something, to take a stand for the children of this country."

On the show, she announced a TV special she would produce shortly, *Nine*, about being a child today. Then she brought on Andrew Vachess, a New York attorney and author, who has devoted his life to fighting crimes against children. She also hired former Illinois governor James Thompson, of the law firm of Winston and Strawn, to draft a federal law that would create a national registry of child abusers so that landlords, employers, and public officials could keep tabs on these offenders and better protect little children from them. Soon afterward, Oprah and Governor Thompson met with Sen. Joseph Biden (D-Del.) in the senator's office in Washington, and he agreed to sponsor Oprah's bill. Hearings were held on November 12 before the Senate Judiciary Committee, with Oprah as one of the star witnesses.

"I wept for Angelica," she said, "and I wept for us, a society that apparently cares so little about its children that it would allow a man with two previous convictions for kidnapping and rape of children to go free after serving only seven years of a fifteen-year sentence."

The National Child Protection bill, or the "Oprah bill," as it quickly became known, would make an FBI-administered computer database available to schools and employers to check on the child-abuse histories of applicants for positions working with or caring for children, but only with the applicants' consent. She said she would also sponsor laws requiring mandatory sentencing of child abusers. She declared, "We have to demonstrate that we value our children enough to say that when you hurt a child, this is what happens to you. It's not negotiable."

Days later, the Oprah bill was attached to the Brady bill on handgun control and was killed by lobbying from the National Rifle Association. Senator Biden comforted Oprah by telling her that they had done well for a new bill and that it had almost passed. A bitter and disappointed Oprah retorted, "Almost doesn't save a child."

Then, in May, the weight problem became so out of control that Oprah checked herself into a very expensive weight reduction center in Southern California, Cal-a-Vie, for a week of dieting, exercise, and therapy that only trimmed off five pounds from the Oprah hips before she had to return to work and on to New York for the June 27 Daytime Emmy dinner at the Marriott-Marquis hotel. It was a home-run victory for Oprah in which she scooped up the Outstanding Awards for Host, Show, and Director. She brought along many from her staff, including Mary Kay Clinton and senior producer Ray Nunn.

On September 6, two days before the fifth anniversary of going national with the *Oprah Winfrey Show*, Oprah celebrated by going on another national television show with a Chicago connection. She appeared on *It's Real Life*, with Jane Pauley. Oprah had become nationally famous by going *to* Chicago, and Jane Pauley had become nationally famous by *leaving* Chicago for the *Today* show in New York, replacing the newscaster who had been Oprah's role model for years, Barbara Walters.

Pauley was in Chicago again that day to film Oprah doing her show, and much of what Oprah told her reflected her deep feelings about important issues in Oprah's life and helped us understand the public person better. One of the first things illustrated was how Oprah maintains complete control of all the elements of the program. Oprah briefs her staff and guests beforehand. A videotape is used to brief the audience on what it is expected to do. The audience is just another actor in the play. Pauley was on her own show, interviewing Oprah, not as in control as Oprah, and the giggly schoolgirl quality of Pauley would seep through when she told Oprah, "I was telling a group of people that I was excited to interview you because, 'Well, Oprah and I have—have so much in common,' and a lady I was talking to, who happened to be black, said, 'May I ask what?' And I'm not sure I could articulate what it is, but I was being quite sincere."

The observation that Oprah made that was very significant and may reflect a problem in her own life with her boyfriend Stedman was when she told Pauley, "I'll tell you what frustrates me the most. It is these women who still live their lives for men. I want to just shake them sometimes! But I've been one of those women, so I understand. I understand that you have to come to it in your own time."

Also significant was the reemergence of an ongoing contradiction in Oprah's personal philosophy: her firm belief in predestination and God's will directing all of our lives versus the concept of free will and each of us controlling and responsible for our own lives. She said, "I'm really proud of this television show [the Oprah Winfrey Show]. Every day my intention is to empower people, and my intention is for other people to recognize by watching our show that you really are responsible for your life. I think I can be a catalyst for people beginning to think more insightfully about themselves and their lives."

Then she and Jane talked about the never-ending obsession that permeates Oprah's life, food and weight. "I was a total compulsive eater for most of my life. That's how I worked out my junk and other people work it out through alcohol or drugs or just bad relationships. So that's not my problem. You know, mine, you know, comes out in my hips. For me the weight is me trying to protect myself or feeling fearful or not being all that I really could be."

About the failure of the Brewster series, she said, "Wasn't the time, and I wasn't willing to listen to the instinct that said, 'Wait.' I should have waited. I was anxious...."

By the end of the year Oprah was happier about her weight

than she had been in a long while. With the help of chef Rosie Daley and with a return to regularly exercising, Oprah was down to 170 pounds. Not entirely where she wanted to be—150 pounds—but a lot closer than when she started—at 205 pounds. She looked and felt a lot better when Stedman told her he had to go to Nevis and St. Kitts Islands in the Caribbean on business the first week in December. He wanted her to come along. Even more important, Stedman insisted on paying for the trip and the $2,000-a-day suite where they stayed. It was important for both of them and for their relationship for Stedman to feel like a man, and Oprah knew it. They spent the six days—when Stedman wasn't tending to business—dancing, romancing, relaxing, and of course, shopping. It was a wonderful time that promised good times ahead for both of them.

CHAPTER

22

Some of Oprah's Shows

O prah's shows range from the banal to the blockbuster and from the crude to the classic. When putting on 220 programs a year, or about 1,800 from the time she went national, it is difficult to make them all consistently classics.

Some of her early show titles illustrate the point: "Shere Hite on Men," "America's Poor," "Joke a Minute," "Cured of AIDS," "TV's Leading Men," "Ramifications of Sexual Abuse," "Get-Rich-Quick Schemes," "Courtship Violence," "Ugly People," "Donald and Ivana Trump," "Dirty-Dancing Contest," "Male Bashing," "Celebrity Mothers," and "Autoerotic Asphyxia." While this last show was highly controversial, some of the others were boring.

Some of the classic shows during this period included the one with women who had borne children sired by their own fathers. Talking to one of the fathers from his prison cell, Oprah became disgusted and ended up calling him "slime." The program from all-white Forsyth County, Georgia, took courage and generated news. It was also one of the early indications to white America that black America did not universally love Oprah when she was picketed by Rev. Hosea Williams and about twenty other blacks, who were all arrested. Oprah's other classics from the late 1980s included "Casanovas and the Women Who Love Them," "Parents Whose Children

Have Been Hurt by Baby-Sitters," and "Women Who Give Up Men and Become Lesbian."

One of Oprah's most memorable shows took place in 1990. "I did a show last year with Trudy Chase," Oprah said, "who was a victim of just severe sexual and child abuse, and in the midst of her telling her story, I started crying uncontrollably. I could not stop. It was all of my own stuff coming out. It was my own stuff coming out on national television."

Other memorable moments might include when she interviewed Marla Maples on her October 28, 1992, show and startled her by suggesting that Marla was "the other woman" who had broken up a marriage. Marla responded that, actually, her affair with Donald Trump had encouraged Ivana to move on with her life and discover new horizons and that everybody involved had grown from the experience. Oprah observed that the whole sordid public affair would end up making Marla a better person and that "intention rules the world. So good intent means you'll win out in the end." On the same show Oprah explored Rod Steiger's years-long chronic clinical depression due to a chemical imbalance in his brain for which he must take medicine, and interviewed Angie Dickinson, whose father was an alcoholic and whose sister, Mary Loy, has Alzheimer's. These segments were followed by Annette Funicello, who had come down with multiple sclerosis, and syndicated columnist Glenn Plaskin, who authored a book about the turning points in the lives of celebrities and how they are just like ordinary people when faced with a crisis.

One notable couple on the show in July 1988 was Gene Simmons, retired lead singer of Kiss, and his girlfriend Shannon Tweed, thirty-one, a pregnant former Playmate. Gene, thirty-eight, boasted that he had slept with over two thousand women.

Then there was the case of a priest, Raymond Carrigan, who faked his death so he could move to California and open a stationery store. And Julie Halligan, a woman who was artificially inseminated and pregnant twice so she could still be a virgin when she married. Cher confessed to Oprah that she really wanted to marry the bagel maker she lived with for a time, Rob Camilletti, but decided he was too young. Sly

Stallone confessed to being hypersensitive to criticism, and Warren Beatty explained why he wanted to be a dad.

Oprah's shows continued in large part to focus on diet, sex, love relations, and personal concerns of women. Her November 4, 1992, show, "Women's Love Affair With Food," brought in a panel of women guests to discuss how tired they were of food controlling their lives. The theme was that food was not the problem, just the symptom of a deeper trouble. Food was the temporary solution to a permanent problem. In Oprah's case, she believed it related to her history of sexual abuse. At the end of this program she announced a follow-up program on the theme "When Food Is Love," about how women substitute the sensual feelings of eating for the missing sensual feelings of love.

On October 4, 1993, Oprah interviewed girls between ten and fifteen years of age who wanted to become pregnant because they thought it would be neat or fun to have a baby. Ofelia deliberately got pregnant at eleven and said she was prepared to be a mother because she loved babies and knew how to change diapers and give them baths. Natasha, fifteen, said her generation was a lot more mature than Oprah's.

"Desperate Moms, Desperate Measures" was about the 10 million young latchkey children left alone at home every day. Because of the growing number of single mothers who have to work to support their families, children are being left alone at younger ages, with disastrous results. The show featured taped calls of frightened youngsters calling hotlines and police seeking someone who would talk to them and comfort them while they waited for their mothers to come home. On a related theme, two weeks later, on November 3, 1993, Oprah focused on how states are tracking down deadbeat dads to force them to pay for raising their estranged children.

Other shows during 1993 included interviews with retiring basketball star Michael Jordan, Dr. Deepak Chopra, Maya Angelou, Polly Klaas's parents, and Diana Ross. Topics included "Hilarious TV Moments," "Stranger Danger for Adults," "Sorry I Stood by My Man," "Family Dinner Experiments," "Teen Dating Violence," "Real Slaves to the Middle Class," and "I Killed Somebody and Can't Live With Myself."

Of these programs, one of the most controversial was the conversation with Dr. Deepak Chopra, which brought complaints from some medical professionals who think he is a quack because he has a celebrity clientele, including Michael Jackson, and because he preaches the new mind-body medicine. In his bestselling book *Ageless Body, Timeless Mind*, he claims we can defy the aging process and illness through mental discipline. "Whenever you have a thought," he says, "you make a chemical that goes along with the thought and there are receptors to these chemicals in all cells in your body and they help you fight against cancer and infection."

Chopra went on to espouse a concept of personal responsibility, which is also half of Oprah's contradictory life philosophy, that is, that we are responsible for everything that happens to us. Chopra told Oprah's sixteen million viewers:

"We are participants in everything that happens in our life. To that extent, we have to take responsibility. If you come to me and you say, 'I have this problem,' I can tell you what are the things in your life that you can change, whether it's in your diet, your lifestyle, your sleep patterns, your relationships. Basically, it amounts to the toxic things in your life, toxic environments, toxic food, toxic drink, toxic relationships, toxic emotions."

The idea of toxic environments, toxic relationships, and toxic emotions all appealed mightily to Oprah; she has been evangelizing about that concept for years. Then, at the end of the program, she wrapped it up by delivering the biggest secret of all—of course, only after the next commercial. It went like this:

WINFREY: Okay. We're going to come back with the absolute secret to the most perfect healthful life. We'll be right back with that. This is the answer. We have it. I got it for you in a moment.

(Theme Music. Announcements. Theme Music)

WINFREY: Okay, this is a secret to a perfect, healthful, happy life. We come to the planet to really do one thing, and that is to learn how to love. Love is it. Love is really it. Isn't it true?

DR. CHOPRA: Yes. Think about love. Talk about love. Seek it and encourage it in everyone. And then that gets rid of everything, because love is the ultimate truth. And it's not a mere sentiment. It's not a mere emotion. It's the ultimate truth at the heart of creation. It's the experiential knowledge of who you really are."

Certainly the ultimate closing to the ultimate secret to happiness on an Oprah show.

CHAPTER

23

Oprah in England

In England, Oprah's selected reruns are called *Oprah Gold* and are very popular, much to the surprise of Americans. Not all of her shows are telecast in the United Kingdom, because some of them are incomprehensible outside of American, or at least North American, culture. Still, most of them have a big audience overseas, particularly in Great Britain.

Americans who view *Masterpiece Theater* and the *BBC World News* think of the British as being too sophisticated and formal when, in fact, they are the sires of the purple tabloid. In fact, many American tabloids, such as the *National Enquirer*, the *Star*, and the *Globe*, are run by either the British or Aussies. The British are apparently repressed sexually and enjoy scandal in their newspapers and on TV. So even though they don't quite understand what's going on with the *Oprah Winfrey Show*, they gobble it up. Marcus Berkman of the *Daily Mail* says that Oprah makes much more than any comparable English TV-talk-show host, but she is worth it.

Berkman writes, "For anyone who relishes the freakier side of human endeavor, these reheated shows have been an absolute treat. You might sneer, but just try turning over to watch something else. It's physiologically impossible. For in Oprah's show all the techniques of 'tabloid television' have been refined and distilled and perfected so that even the most skeptical viewer will find his curiosity is swiftly engaged."

One of the simplest techniques about which Berkman raves is known to writers and showmen the world over. It is called "the hook." You only have a few seconds to hook your audience. In broadcasting, the show directors know they have about five seconds to do so. In literature, you must grab the reader in the first sentence or two by making it one the reader *must* read—it is not a voluntary decision. The same thing is true in sales pitches. You must appeal to what is important to the prospect and grab him or her with it instantly.

Thus, Berkman notes with amazement that Oprah does not open her show the way British hosts do. In England, the host starts talking as the introduction music fades and says something like "Hello, hello, welcome to the Charlie Jones Show [wait for applause]. Today our guests will include..." Instead, Oprah steps right up to the microphone and says, "What kind of woman would hire a hit man to murder someone in her own family?"

Bang! You *must* know what comes next. You are hooked into the beginning of the show. Moreover, with this breathless, rushed opening, Oprah also conveys that there is so much outrageous, fascinating, juicy stuff to jam into the show that we have to get right with it. Then she cuts away to a commercial.

The rerun that Berkman was commenting on concerned a woman who hired a hit man to kill her son-in-law. Wow! That's bad! That's evil! But wait, says Oprah after you say hello to the depraved woman. It doesn't turn out the way you think it will. There is a twist in this story that you will never believe! Well, of course you'll believe it. You can hardly wait a second longer. You have to know what comes next!

We'll be back after this word.

Well, Oprah is indeed back after the commercial, and her audience is on edge to learn what new revelations await. Here it is. This despicable woman didn't actually hire a hit man; she just thought he was a hit man. In reality, he was an undercover cop!

And there you are with the woman and her husband, live

by satellite from Florida, along with her lawyer and the police tapes showing her making the murder deal.

The marvel for Berkman is that something bigger and stranger is always coming up right after the next commercial. We Americans know that, of course, and we go to the john during the commercial. The British, not as exposed to commercials for as long as we have been, sit through them fascinated, with their legs crossed.

Berkman continues: "But, of course, everything on Oprah reveals the strange and mysterious ways in which America functions. Still, I can't believe that every [talk] show can be anywhere near as entertaining or grotesque as Oprah's is day after day. This particular show rounded off with a psychotherapist who suggested we all want to kill our closest relatives. Solutions? None. Conclusions? Only that the world's mad. But I wouldn't have missed a minute of it."

Another foreign assessment of *Oprah Gold* came from the September 18 issue of the *London Independent*, which ran an interesting evaluation of Oprah that gives us still another viewpoint of the number-one daytime talk-show host in America. "[Oprah] is America's bright-smiled, look-you-in-the-eye Public Shrink Number One. She is a Redeemer: of her people and her sex.

"Oprah's answer to any human problem is talk and talk is what drives the Box in America. Out of their corners they come, the poor and downtrodden, the raped and abused, to tell their tales." The *Independent* then described how the two thousand letters Oprah receives every week are computerized and culled looking for possible show topics and guests.

While Oprah is neither the only talk-show host in America nor the oldest, the *Independent*'s appraisal contends she is the smartest, toughest, and the best because she works at what she does starting every morning when she arises at five-thirty and prepares herself. For a public speaker, she has two qualities that she began learning and using under the tutelage of Hattie Mae back in Mississippi, when she could barely walk. These qualities were subsequently reinforced by her father and stepmother during her late teens: knowing how to listen and speaking eloquently.

As for other people's evaluations of Oprah, Oprah's life as reported in her biographies is a bit unreal, according to the *Independent*. It says there are three biographies (actually five, not counting this one), all short on pages and big in print, written for kids.

Interestingly, the *Independent* perceived something explored in this biography of Oprah, namely, that the Oprah we see and know from television and public appearances is not the private Oprah. There is another Oprah who only occasionally surfaces in public, and then in a guarded manner. The *Independent* commented on Oprah's condemnation of her four-year affair with an unnamed married man while she was working in Baltimore and over whom she contemplated suicide, and her decision that she was never going to give up her power over her life to another person.

To repeat what she said: "I thought I was worthless without him. The more he rejected me, the more I wanted him. I felt depleted, powerless. I had given this man power over my life, and I will never, never—as long as I'm black—I will never give up my power to another person."

About that decision, the *Independent* wrote: "A lot of the real Oprah, intensely private...comes out in that statement. Those who know her well describe her as a private person acting out in public.

The *Independent* went on to observe the control factor of which we have spoken in other parts of this story and that while Oprah is sincere in her feelings about some of the people who appear on her show, her "package" is carefully organized and controlled. The newspaper declared, "Her Chicago operation is replete with young black producers on the make ('a sort of Moonie collective,' one Chicagoan said) who are ruled ferociously by the Oprah ego." In its concluding judgment of Oprah, the English newspaper said, "It is amazing to think how unthinkable she was a mere 20 years ago."

Actually, a mere seven years before, when the King brothers were having trouble selling television-station managers on the concept of a fat black woman on TV.

Getting Ready to Fly

CHAPTER

24

1992—Year of the Engagement

As 1992 opened, Oprah was earning an estimated $30 million a year, and Harpo Studios had begun to attract outside business, including some running shoe commercials and some interior scenes for a Tom Selleck movie. The studio was Oprah's workaday world, beginning with her usual arrival at 6:30 A.M. and continuing all through the day shooting programs, holding meetings on finances and projects and legal matters, and ending late at night. So late that Oprah had an apartment built on the premises so she could crash there instead of returning to her Water Tower condo.

The beginning of the year saw Stedman Graham fly to Washington, D.C., to attend a reception of 250 supporters of Clarence Thomas, the conservative black Supreme Court associate justice, and his wife, Virginia, at the luxurious residence of Paul Hersh. The reception was given by Armstrong Williams, Stedman's ultraconservative business partner and local Washington, D.C., radio-talk-show host. As usual, the Graham-Williams connection attracted no particular attention in spite of the anomaly of Stedman Graham's ultra-right-wing associations, the Anita Hill–Clarence Thomas controversy, and

Oprah's publicly espoused views on women's equality and other liberal issues.

January also started as usual with the National Association of Television Programming Executives (NATPE) convention in New Orleans, where syndicators and producers wooed station programmers from around the country to try out new television shows or keep old ones and extend their contracts. It is the important marketplace for Oprah and Donahue and all the others in the television-talk-show business and their syndicators, such as the King brothers.

The trend in the 1992 NATPE show focused on late-night programs. As King World chairman Roger King succinctly put it, "Johnny Carson is retiring." Many people in the business saw late night as up for grabs and providing a golden—in both senses of that word—chance for new talent or proven old talent.

Roger King, for one, wanted to put reruns of Oprah on in late night; the reruns cost virtually nothing, and the late-night audience does not get to see her during the afternoon. There were scheduling and profit problems with the idea, but Roger would never admit that the idea wouldn't work. It just had to be done differently.

Other syndicators, like Multimedia, tried to sell Rush Limbaugh for late night; Tribune broadcasting pushed Dennis Miller, and someone else had Whoopi Goldberg available. MCA-TV had the feisty Kitty Kelley but wanted her on in the daytime because they thought she would prove more appealing to a daytime audience, with her insider stories of celebrities.

One interesting announcement at NATPE indirectly involving Oprah came from Alvin D. James, chairman of the Minority Broadcasting Corporation (MBC), made up of Dallas businessmen. Their plan was to create a network catering to black viewers only and they claimed to have ten stations lined up at the outset and would start with six hours of programming daily. That would include *Good Morning, Black America, Fame and Fortune,* and *Sports Lifestyles,* starring Oprah's Stedman Graham. Unfortunately, the idea didn't attract enough cable systems to make it workable.

Roger King experienced his biannual scrape with the law when he pled no contest again on January 15 in Las Vegas for assaulting Robert Rothstein of Woodland Hills, California, outside Caesars Palace the previous October 25. According to witnesses, a drunken Roger followed Rothstein and Rothstein's father-in-law, Moses Levy, of Bellevue, Washington, out of Caesars Palace, yelling and cursing the two men. Rothstein and Levy tried to keep walking, but King jumped Rothstein and began beating him up. Three hotel employees came to Rothstein's rescue and held King until the police arrived. He was fined $1,000.

If Roger continued to behave in this fashion, he would probably have to leave the business as the result of a jail term or something more serious. This Las Vegas incident was the third in four years, the previous one occurring in Atlantic City, when Roger again assaulted a man, Jeffrey Silverman, and was fined $6,000.

Since he is acknowledged as a brilliant salesman on whom the success of the company depended, his removal for whatever reason could hurt the profits of King World. Under Roger and his brother, Michael, King World's profits rose 11 percent in 1991, for a net of $93 million on gross sales of $476 million. and since Oprah is a major stockholder of King World, his removal could sharply affect her personal fortune. The only weak spot in King World profits for 1991 involved the Buffalo TV station WIVB-TV, owned by the syndicator in conjunction with Oprah. The Buffalo TV station lost $7.8 million, a larger sum than the station had lost in 1990.

As had been the case for the last six years, the beginning of the year was also a happy time, for Oprah's birthday falls on January 29. This year, Oprah's devoted and mostly female Harpo staff gave her a surprise present for her thirty-eighth birthday: a male stripper who gyrated seductively and shed everything except for the briefest red bikini. It was fun but didn't match Stedman's surprise when she got home that evening. He bundled her into a horse-drawn carriage, and the two trundled down along picturesque Lake Shore Drive and around to the River North district, finally arriving at the Eccentric and the 150 guests waiting to serenade her. The entrée of the evening was especially prepared by chef Michael Kornick, meat loaf and potatoes Oprah.

The sumptuous birthday party was symbolic of how Oprah was surrounded by the trappings of success and intellectually aware that she was a special phenomenon who had achieved beyond most people's fantasies. Still, Oprah claimed she suffered from insecurities and feelings of low self-esteem. She said she couldn't relax. She had been on several vacations with Stedman and was unable to let go. She had to be going, doing, reading, talking, shopping, walking, all the time.

She said, "I discovered I didn't feel worth a damn, and certainly not worthy of love unless I was accomplishing something. I suddenly realized I have never felt I could be loved just for being."

Even with the boys and men who abused her sexually as a teenager in Milwaukee, Oprah felt she invited the mistreatment and it was her fault. She now believes workshops with John Bradshaw helped her face up to the reality of her feelings and that she had regained control of her life. John Bradshaw is a portly fifty-nine-year-old recovering alcoholic who spent nine and one-half years in a monastery and left the day before he was to be ordained a Catholic priest. His PBS specials have been extremely popular, as have his books about getting in touch with the inner child. He is described as "a charismatic family therapist and irresistible and inexhaustible public speaker who is always jetting off to speak to a conference hall full of broken people hoping for a quick fix." He conducts weekend workshops called "Healing Your Inner Child," to which participants show up with a teddy bear, symbolizing the connection with their inner child. Bradshaw's third book, *Homecoming: Reclaiming and Championing Your Inner Child*, was a number-one bestseller and brought him to the *Oprah Winfrey Show* in 1991, where he and Oprah became acquainted.

The core of his thesis about our lives is that when a parent abuses a child physically or emotionally, the child takes the blame, believes he or she is at fault, and becomes bad to keep the parent's love. From that point on, the child grows up confusing abuse with love and constantly gravitates toward abusive relationships in adult life. "The child is still trying to win that abusing parent's love," says Bradshaw. "The feeling is: 'This time I'm going to get it right.'" This, he says, is Freud's theory of the "repetition compulsion," which leads abused children into being abusing parents generation after generation. It is the basis of a whole movement among alcohol and substance abusers and their adult children.

Oprah related to the Bradshaw theories because she saw her defilement by others during her childhood as the root cause of two other problems in her adult life: her need for control over situations and people around her and her obsession with food. Her need for control constituted a form of emotional armor that prevented others from assaulting or molesting her. Her obsession with food physically gave her gratification that soothed her in troubled times; psychologically, it made her fat and unattractive to men; if she were slim and sexy, they would try to seduce her and hurt her. Being fat protected her from exploitation.

"Food for me is comforting," she explained. "It also calms me." Unfortunately, she discovered to her disappointment, it also turned off the one man she wanted to attract, Stedman Graham, who backed away from sexual and romantic involvement with the fat Oprah.

On the air the previous year, she emphatically declared that she would never go on a diet again, and as she has thought more about it, she has reaffirmed that vow while changing around the definition of what "dieting" involved. She came to the view in early 1992 that the overeating and the excessive weight were symptoms of a much deeper problem. So while she may never diet again, she will work toward the solution of that deeper problem, and that will free her from her fixation with control and weight. She knew she loved being thin and with a great figure. That was all part of communicating with her inner self and learning how to make her life more fulfilling through mind-body medicine, New Age healing, and self-actualization, which Dr. Deepak Chopra and John Bradshaw taught. Thus, it was natural that Oprah would be drawn to Marianne Williamson.

In keeping with her admiration of New Age and self-actualization, Oprah had the Hollywood–New York celebrity guru Marianne Williamson on her show to tout Williamson's newest book: *A Return to Love: Reflections on the Principles of a Course in Miracles*. This book sells for considerably less than the two main *Course in Miracles* books, which retail for $110 each.

"I have never been as moved by a book as I have by Marianne Williamson's book," Oprah said as she distributed a thousand copies that she had brought for the studio audience, and reported that she had personally experienced 175 miracles. Since Oprah was so taken by the message in *A Return to Love*, and Marianne Williamson, we might look at what the book and Williamson advocate for some clues to understanding Oprah.

The book is supposedly a modern-age biblical tract, or New Age gospel, mysteriously dictated by an unidentified miracle voice that has mesmerized New Age followers since 1975. It claims that the material world is a dream, an illusion, and that all our unhappiness stems from the separateness we have from others, whom we mistakenly think are different entities living in illusionary material bodies. This makes us afraid, angry, and hateful of others when we should be loving and forgiving. This same concept applies to being overweight. We must concentrate on love and ignore our physical bodies, Williamson says.

David Gelman, writing for *Newsweek*, saw Williamson's appearance on *Oprah* and its impact on book sales as another demonstration of Oprah's influence on her audience. Beyond that, Gelman believes America longs for psychic support. He said, "In a spiritually famished time, pop preachers from Robert Bly to John Bradshaw to Williamson are garnering huge audiences from inspirational books and lectures that urge people to get in touch with their inner man, their inner child or, in Williamson's case apparently, their inner ectoplasm." He further notes that the book reads "like a Christian religious tract—although the author herself is resolutely Jewish."

Originally launched by a $100,000 donation from Hollywood's first billionaire, David Geffen, Williamson, an ex--nightclub singer, created a spiritual following in her two nonprofit Centers for Living, one in New York and one in Los

Angeles, to transform people's lives. The centers prepare and deliver meals to 330 homebound AIDS patients and give charismatic lectures to powerful and rich people. The "Course in Miracles" lectures are about how to become better human beings by loving and forgiving. *People* magazine characterized Williamson as "Hollywood's most compelling—and perplexing—spiritual guide since Werner Erhard swept through Tinseltown with his est movement in the 1970s."

Some call Williamson's philosophy a blend of religion and self-help, which is consistent with Oprah's contradictory mix of predestination and personal responsibility. Off camera and beyond the tape recorders of reporters, she is reportedly a coarse-talking tyrant and control freak. Some say that she's more like Leona Helmsley than Mother Teresa. She often refers to herself as "the bitch for God." Her book sales soared to the top of the *New York Times* bestseller list for four weeks as a result of her appearance on the *Oprah Winfrey Show* that day.

In March 1992, another book touched Oprah's life when she was included in a new reference work by Dr. Jessie Smith, *Notable Black American Women*, placing her among those black women she had revered over the years, such as Sojourner Truth and Harriet Tubman. Dr. Smith, a librarian at Fisk University, worked on the volume for twenty years and included the biographies of five hundred black women in American history, beginning with the poet Luch Terry Prince in 1730 and concluding with astronaut Mae Jamison today. The common threads she discovered about American black women included the endurance, the persistence, and the strength to hold their families together.

These common threads were Oprah's shared legacy, and they served her well as she continued to launch new projects. Oprah created a set of four specials dealing with the entertainment business. These specials would examine celebrities— how they thought and lived and why; how celebrities dealt with their loss of privacy; how fame restricted their lives so that they could not be like ordinary people. What were the unusual pressures and dangers of becoming a public person that the rest of us do not have to endure? Oprah's first show would be aired in May, with interviews of Meryl Streep, Goldie

Hawn, Dustin Hoffman, and Michael Bolton in a format that seemed remarkably like the one used by Barbara Walters, Oprah's early idol.

Before she could do those interviews, Oprah became an interviewee herself when she allowed St. Petersburg, Florida's WTVT-TV anchorwoman, Kathy Fountain, to visit the studios of Harpo Productions. Fountain called Oprah "the Disney World of talk shows." Fountain and crew toured the studios, looked into Oprah's office, and reported that it was decorated in beiges, peach, and aqua, with display art. Fountain concluded that Oprah was too busy to become a wife and believed that instead of having children, she would adopt them. Also, Oprah was tiring of her talk show, and she hates her nose. A more intensely personal encounter than Fountain's interview came with a chill in April.

The newspapers of mid-April carried a disturbing story as Oprah and Stedman filed a $300 million lawsuit through attorney Dan Webb and Steven F. Moloover over a story in the Toronto-based tabloid *News Extra* headlined: "New Oprah Shocker! Fiancé Stedman Had Gay Sex With Cousin." Filed in Chicago in U.S. District Court for the Northern District of Illinois, the suit charged that the newspaper was guilty of "defamation, invasion of privacy and intentional infliction of emotional distress." The previous year, another tabloid had planned to print this story but decided not to do so after investigating it. The tabloid claimed its source was Carlton Jones, a cousin of Graham's, but Jones denied it ever happened and also denied that *News Extra* ever contacted him. The case ended anticlimactically when *News Extra* didn't show up in court and soon after went out of business.

The transition from personal difficulties to society's troubles came three weeks later, in May, when Los Angeles erupted in rioting after the first Rodney King verdict. Both Donahue and Oprah rushed to broadcast programs on the riots in Southern California from Los Angeles. On Monday, May 4, Oprah taped two shows from KABC-TV's studios on Prospect Avenue in Hollywood. The first show almost turned into a riot itself when looters and victims confronted each other in the studio. Oprah said, "I wasn't frightened of physical harm because I recognized that people just wanted to be heard. Martin Luther King said that rioting is the voice of the unheard."

Still, even though Oprah was quite proud of those two programs, her regular staff said that the shows severely drained her as she witnessed face-to-face the raw emotions of fear and hatred openly expressed by both sides. Oprah declared, "It was stirring. It was what television should do. It was utilizing the power of media for the good. You can't do better than that, I think."

She found most moving the black owner of a family firm whose business and life savings were destroyed overnight by his own people and an antagonistic young rioter who opened the show belligerently insisting it was his right—no, his duty—to loot and burn after the Rodney King verdicts. This young man came on at the end of the same program filled with remorse, face in his hands, crying. The most lasting impression on Oprah was made by the black teenager who said the Rodney King verdict meant black lives were worthless. "That's really what it all boils down to on our show. People want their lives to mean something."

On May 8, Oprah was again interviewed, this time by *USA Today*, to whom she confided her fantasy of eating anything in the world that she wanted without thinking about calories or fat and to "take great pleasure from all the grease on the potatoes." When asked about marriage, she answered, "Marriage to me means offering—sacrificing—yourself to the relationship. To become one with the relationship. I'm not capable of doing that right now."

The marriage question rose again as *USA Today* interviewed Oprah on May 19 about the first of her evening specials, *Oprah: Behind the Scenes*. As we noted before, she would talk to Meryl Streep, Goldie Hawn, Michael Bolton, and Dustin Hoffman. It was an interview about her interviews.

"It's so sexist!" she thundered at Christopher John Farley, the interviewer, about the marriage question. Sexist or not, she answered the question again: "I probably will. I'd say we are closer to it now than we've ever been. We really are. And that's the best answer I can give." It was a different Oprah who, on her twenty-eighth birthday in 1982, woke up crying for fear she would never get married.

That *USA Today* interview, however, was supposed to be about her first network prime-time special that night. Oprah said she would interview celebrities where they shine as contrasted with Barbara Walters, who interviewed them where they live. She also mentioned her new movie project based on Toni Morrison's Pulitzer Prize novel *Beloved*. Oprah would once again play an abused black woman, Sethe, an escaped slave haunted by the memory of her murdered daughter. Another project in the works at Harpo Studios was an ABC movie set for 1992–93 season: *Overexposed*, the true story of a woman who appeared on Oprah's show to reveal how her ex-lover harassed her with videotapes he had taken of their sexual times together and how he threatened to make them public and humiliate her.

Oprah shared two important facts with interviewer Farley: (1) She refuses to go on any more fad diets. Instead, she now has her own chef. "I've probably gained and lost hundreds of pounds. Now I know the only sensible thing is to eat less food and to work out and to get to the real heart of why you eat...you don't overeat because you're hungry." And (2) she hates the tabloid press: "Oprah Has Elvis's Baby, Moves To Mars." For Oprah, tabloids are the potholes on the road to success. "The only thing I hate about the press is the tabloids," she said. "I think they're verbal pornography."

Oprah's first special didn't do all that well, coming in third in the ratings behind NBC's *Cruel Doubt* and CBS's *Intruders* miniseries. However, the ratings of the *Oprah Winfrey Show* in the May Nielsen rating sweeps continued the good news that the Oprah show was, once again, number one in its time period throughout America, as it had been for twenty-two consecutive rating periods.

Her success with good ratings for her show was not matched with good ratings for keeping to her secret diet. She had puffed up to over 180 pounds and was growing. Oprah stopped exercising and returned to munching fat-filled snacks and shoveling in the chips, macaroni, and rich desserts while ignoring the guidance that Chef Rosie Daley tried to give her on diet and nutrition.

Beyond that, everybody, including Stedman, had tired of coaxing or bullying her to keep her weight down, and those who no longer wanted to play fat patrol were afraid to speak out and anger her. A month later, Oprah, weighing 200 pounds, flew west to Las Vegas for an awards banquet and had considerable trouble walking any distance without gasping for air.

She may have been weak on keeping her diet, but she continued strong in influencing her viewers. The pulling power of Oprah was demonstrated once more on her June 1 show when she asked viewers to send in $1–$100 to support Elizabeth Taylor's AIDS campaign and received a munificent $400,000.

But unbeknownst to Oprah, something not so wonderful was happening inside Harpo Productions. During much of May and June, one of her trusted senior producers was stalking his ex-girlfriend. Ray Nunn met his girlfriend in 1985, when he was an ABC bureau chief, and in 1990, when Oprah hired him, he came to Chicago. His girlfriend joined him, and they moved in together.

For two years, all seemed to be fine. Then, in the spring of 1992, they broke up, and Nunn went crazy. He started to stalk his former girlfriend, threatening her and her friends, calling twenty to thirty times a day until she went to court and obtained a restraining order, which Nunn promptly violated, forcing her to phone Oprah directly. When Oprah checked the woman's story and decided it was true, she went ballistic. "I will not stand for this!" she declared. "I will not allow that to be done from my very own company headquarters!" Instantly, Nunn was gone from the staff.

On a pleasanter note, on June 23, Oprah collected her second straight Daytime Emmy for the Outstanding Talk/Service Show and her third Emmy as Outstanding Talk Show Host. In her acceptance speech she mentioned her boyfriend: "Thank you, too, Stedman, for putting up with all the long hours—it's our sixth anniversary!" And there still was no ring.

It was also the year-and-one-half anniversary of the child-abuse tragedy in Chicago, but Oprah had not forgotten the calamity of Angelica Mena, four, the little girl who was abused, murdered, and thrown into Lake Michigan, and her bitter disappointment when Congress—the representatives of the people—wouldn't pass her modest bill to help prevent child abuse and child murder. Having failed in the political arena, Oprah turned to a more powerful medium and the one she knew best, television, to perform a remarkable feat on behalf of endangered children throughout America. One of the dramatic demonstrations of Oprah's media clout came with a program in which she had a strong personal interest, *Scared Silent: Exposing and Ending Child Abuse*.

In 1979, Arnold Shapiro produced a successful TV program featuring hardened criminals in New Jersey's Rahway State Prison who talked to teens about the horrors of prison. The TV special was called *Scared Straight*. He created a second program in 1992 about child abuse, *Scared Silent: Exposing and Ending Child Abuse*, based on the findings of the U.S. Advisory Board on Child Abuse and Neglect. He brought it to Oprah to get her backing and involvement as narrator. Oprah signed on because it was the kind of project she believed in; as a result, they got PBS and three of the major networks to agree to show the program.

PBS, NBC, and CBS all broadcast it at the same time, and ABC did so two nights later so that it would not conflict with *20/20*. The same program had never appeared before on all four networks.

Oprah introduced the documentary with "I'm Oprah Winfrey, and like millions of other Americans, I'm a survivor of child abuse. I was only nine years old when I was raped by my nineteen-year-old cousin. He was the first of three family members to sexually molest me."

In addition to the television exposure, there was wide print media coverage in all the major news magazines and newspapers reflecting the conclusions about child abuse from the U.S. Advisory Board on Child Abuse and Neglect, which reported that cases of child abuse had skyrocketed from 60,000 in 1974 to 2.7 million in 1991.

The reviewers generally lauded the program, its objective, and particularly Oprah's support and participation, with *USA Today* saying she hosted the program with "low-key compassion." *Newsweek* called it "unsparing" in tone and applauded the overall nature of the show. "'Scared Silent' does an admirable job of exploring the pathology of child abusers, exposing the horrific costs to its victims and explaining why it can remain a secret even to members of the immediate family." The *Chicago Tribune* wrote: "We hear memories of molestation; witness a wrenching confrontation between an abusive father and his grown daughter; sit in on a group therapy session and hear from a 15-year-old sex offender."

The *Tribune* said the program succeeded in spite of "some minor oddities," such as the psychological jargon laced through some of the conversations, which made the traumas seem ordinary and bureaucratic. *Newsweek* thought some of the theatrical effects were sappy but that it humanized the victims and the abusers and demonstrated "the inspirational example of a few tortured individuals willing to bring their darkest secrets to light."

On September 14, 1992, *U.S. News & World Report* took issue with some of the conclusions made by *Scared Silent* and Oprah. The magazine said that contrary to the point made in the program, abused children did not necessarily become abusive parents, that only 30 percent of abused children became abusive parents. Beyond that, it challenged the notion that incest is widely reported and that reconciliation is generally possible. The magazine said that, to the contrary, incest is not frequently reported or prosecuted and that families in which it occurs can rarely live in harmony afterward. Finally, while the show focused on incestuous fathers, *U.S. News & World Report* contended that children are at least six times more likely to be abused by family adults other than the natural parents. Certainly that was true in Oprah's case; she was abused by cousins and an uncle, not by her father.

A different emotional aspect of Oprah's life came into play in October when another diet book came to her attention, *When Food Is Love* by Geneen Roth. Oprah was so impressed with the thesis of connecting our emotional state with food obsessions that she read a second book by Roth, *Feeding the Hungry Heart*. Oprah kept seeing herself described as the woman who lacks self-esteem, who was emotionally unfulfilled and found completion in food. Oprah called Ms. Roth several times and invited her to appear on a November *Oprah* show along with seven women who were obsessive eaters because of deep emotional problems they couldn't solve or confront. Roth helped Oprah realize that emotional problems and not physical hunger drove Oprah to being a binge eater. It meant confronting and dealing one more time with her deep-seated emotional problems so that she could love herself and accept herself and begin a sensible, gradual weight-loss program that would bring her down from her all-time high of 210 pounds, which she weighed when Geneen came into her life.

In October and November, Oprah did more shows on relationship problems, including the new diet theme that fat comes from emotional problems. The topic was women's love affair with food, or how women allow food to control their lives.

One of those women, she admitted, was Oprah herself. "It is a very personal and a very painful subject for me because my weight...has been exploited by more tabloid articles than I care to count. For me, weight is still an issue. I'd like to say it's not, but it is."

She then rolled a tape of her triumphant November 15, 1988, show and the sixty-seven pounds she had shed. "But there was also an aftermath, all too familiar to those who struggle with weight." Then she introduced her seven women guests, ranging from twenty-eight to forty-six years old. Mostly professionals, they suffered the same food obsessions that have dominated Oprah's life since she was a teenager.

All the women agreed that controlling their weight was a constant problem and that food had become the central problem in their lives. Yet whenever they saw themselves in the mirror or in a dress for some occasion, they were reminded that they weighed too much and were repulsed by the way they looked. Oprah said that she weighed 148 pounds when she lived at home in Nashville, which was an ideal weight for her, but after moving to Baltimore she put on eight pounds the first two weeks. After moving to Chicago, she put on another twenty pounds in the first month. She believed that loneliness drove her to seek gratification through food.

Tammy Briton, from Los Angeles, sounded as if her life story leading to binge eating were identical to Oprah's. "I was molested as a child...and I knew I could never tell anybody about that because they wouldn't believe it. It felt good...but it made me feel bad, and I ate and I stuffed it down because that was the only way I could protect myself."

Oprah recalled when she was on her fasting diet back in 1988: "I remember walking in the house once, and Stedman was playing Pac-Man, and I wanted him to pay attention to me. But he wasn't. I remember going to the refrigerator and standing there, staring and thinking, I got to eat. I got to eat. I got to eat. That's when I first started to connect the thing about food and emotions."

Then the panelists talked about how they were all actually members of a secret society of binge eaters; they all recognized, but didn't acknowledge, each other. Ellen Shuman, an on-air reporter for WCPO in Cincinnati, said, "The last time I was very much into binges there was a day at work I just needed to leave. I never ate in front of anyone when I was in that mode, and I drove to a Burger King, got a normal lunch, and drove around and parked somewhere I wouldn't be seen. While I'm sitting there, I saw a woman drive in who also appeared to be rather large, and she disappeared around the building. I finished my lunch and went to find a dumpster, because you never take the evidence back to work. [The other woman] was parked on the other side of the dumpster doing the same thing."

When Oprah asked her guests their greatest fear, Shuman said, "Not ever getting at whatever is going on underneath that keeps me from being able to be emotionally intimate with people." In the end, Oprah concluded that many women reach for food when they are really groping for something else and then made the connection between her history of sexual abuse and her eating habits as an adult.

The relationship between emotional and physical needs is part of a growing trend in alternative medicine, known as body-mind medicine. Some of the leading practitioners of this new alternative medicine, such as Dr. Deepak Chopra, would appear on her shows. What Marianne Williamson preached about the mind and the spirit healing the body was a variation. This "new kind" of medicine sweeping the country was also very old. Its principles have recently been recognized by the National Institutes of Health, the largest federally sponsored research institute in the United States, which has established an Office of Alternative Medicine.

Medicine has primarily focused on treating the body as separate from the mind and the emotions, even though we know that the mind and the body work together, are part of the same system, and are intimately connected. Every thought and emotion in our brain becomes an electrical signal in our nerve communication network. When your eyes or ears sense danger, they send the signal to your brain, which in turn sends a signal to specific organs and tissues of the body, such as the adrenal glands, which can release adrenaline and other powerful substances that give you a temporary surge of extra energy and power. As your body gears itself up for movement, your muscles tighten in response to these signals so that you can either fight or flee.

We know that tension-related physical problems are very rare among the rural people of India, China, Japan, and the Philippines, which is due in part to people living a more relaxed, accepting lifestyle, at a slower pace, with strong ties to extended families that provide emotional support and help reduce tensions. Beyond that, people in these cultures have traditions which incorporate meditation and rituals designed to soothe the mind and the emotions, which, in turn, relax body tensions. In general, Orientals are more calm and serene than Westerners. So Oprah's focus on the impact of emotions on her physical condition is supported by many medical researchers and practitioners. Physical problems, moreover, are not usually due to a single incident. One's lifestyle, attitude, emotional and mental state, posture, diet—all play a role, with each of these factors adding a little more burden until the load is so great that something has to be done to relieve it. In Oprah's case, along with many other women, that means eating.

As with many details about Oprah, the specifics of the

biggest event in her personal life in 1992 are garbled. The event was her formal engagement to Stedman, which was made public, according to *Jet* magazine, when Oprah told her best friend, Gayle King Bumpas, during a November 6 interview on WFSB-TV in Hartford, Connecticut. According to this story, Stedman popped the question, in a manner of speaking, during a mid-October weekend at the Indiana farm, and Oprah instantly accepted. In that version, Stedman gave the servants the night off, cooked a dinner of chicken, and as the two sat eating at the kitchen table, gave Oprah a note. The pent-up emotions of the six years of their courting overflowed into tears as she read Stedman's words saying that he loved her and wanted her to be his wife. Exploding with happiness, she came around the table to him, and they embraced as she repeated, "Yes, yes!"

Stedman later said that he didn't expect such an instant and positive response, for she had stalled the response several times in the past. When she made him promise not to publicly announce anything, he suspected that she was building up to another delay about the marriage, but he agreed.

Another version of the proposal story was reported on November 23 in *People* magazine by Elizabeth Sporkin. According to this account, on the afternoon of October 10 Gayle King Bumpas and Oprah were hanging out in the kitchen at the Indiana farm, waiting for Stedman to show up from Chicago with a tape of a future *Oprah Winfrey Show*. As he pulled in to the parking space next to the baronial house, Oprah ran outside to meet him, only to return breathlessly happy a few moments later, gushing to Gayle, "You are not going to believe this. Stedman just proposed." The actual words, as reported by Oprah, were, "I want you to marry me. I think it's time." And Oprah answered, "Ah, that's really great."

Whichever story is true, Stedman was pleasantly surprised when she spilled the story over the airwaves on her friend's TV show when Gayle asked Oprah, "Shall we talk about husbands and marriage?" Oprah's father found out about the proposal from a customer at his barbershop who, in turn, had heard it on the national news. Some friends said Oprah was finally comfortable with being Mrs. Graham because of the counseling of her latest adviser, Geneen Roth, who has been trying to get Oprah to accept Oprah for what she is and not what she thinks everybody else feels she ought to be.

Stedman was half-sure that Oprah would not say yes as quickly as she did, and while he had selected the diamond ring for her, he hadn't actually bought it. Why spend $17,000 for a diamond that the lady won't wear?

Oprah told Gayle about her apprehensions. "It does scare me a little bit, the whole idea of being married to somebody for the rest of your life. You don't want to wake up ten years from now and say, 'My God, who is this I've married?' So it scares me a little bit, but I think it's the right thing to do."

Although bothered by the constant media attention to everything they do, Stedman says, "I love her, and she's worth it."

Friends and fans have been conjecturing about Oprah and Stedman for the last six years that they have been dating. At different times, each has said he or she wasn't sure, wasn't ready, or wasn't asked. Some friends think Oprah was pushing because she wanted to have children and had set her thirty-eighth year as the time for her first pregnancy. Hollywood casting director Reuben Cannon, who came to know Oprah well during the casting and shooting of *The Color Purple*, has a different view. He says, "She doesn't do anything under pressure. She trusts her spiritually guided instincts. She knows exactly what she needs at a certain time." When Oprah's friend Patti LaBelle heard the news, she said, "It's about time, because the man is too good to let go."

Looking back on 1992, it was another good year for the relatively inexpensive television-talk-show format with high ratings such as *Oprah*. In fact, many in television wanted to copy King World's and Oprah's success. The year 1992 was the sixth season that King World had syndicated Oprah, and during those six years they grossed $705 million. The *Oprah Winfrey Show* reached the point where it netted $100 million a year. Besides Oprah, the current crop of mainline television talk shows at the end of 1992 included Joan Rivers, Jenny Jones, Jane Whitney, Sally, Montel, Jerry, Maury, Rush, Whoopi, Arsenio, Byron, Geraldo, Vicki, and Regis and Kathie Lee.

Others, of course, were in the wings warming up even as television programmers met in industry seminars and conventions and asked when TV talk shows would reach the point of saturation.

Just how many talk shows can America handle? Nobody actually knows, and since the profits can be astronomical if such a show hits, everybody keeps making them and trying to sell them.

Karen Miller, vice president of programming and development for the CBS station group, has what many believe is a salient explanation for why so many shows are being created and touted. "One has to believe that as talk shows age, the audiences age with them." In other words, different age groups of women—the overwhelmingly predominant gender watching talk shows—watch different hosts with whom they relate.

Thus, says Miller, "my mother may still prefer to watch Donahue, but I may have more of a tendency to watch Oprah or Geraldo. It all comes down to viewer loyalty to a certain host, and each one has a certain demographic profile. However, for me, as a programmer, the key is to find fresh blood and new faces to lure in the younger demographics, the core of eighteen to thirty-four demographics that drive the ratings for any talk show."

For advertisers, the eighteen- to thirty-four-year-olds are key because that age group is in its family-formation years, building sponsor loyalties and buying the "big ticket" items—the expensive purchases, such as furniture, major appliances, cars, food, and clothing. The implication for Oprah is that her audience of contemporaries is aging and moving out of the core eighteen–thirty-four age bracket soon and will become less and less attractive in the next few years to advertisers.

One analyst who specializes in the television syndication business said, "These shows really are huge profit centers, and you don't have to be Oprah to make money." He estimates that Sally Jessy Raphael probably grosses $40 million a year and Geraldo $10 million. Overall, talk shows are estimated to generate about $500 million a year in gross income in barter and in license fees. Jessica Reif, a financial analyst who follows television programming and syndication stocks for Oppenheimer & Company, upgraded her evaluation of King World at the end of November on the grounds of its perform- ance in 1992 because of the popularity of *Oprah* and *Wheel of Fortune*. She said that in 1992 no new show compared to King World's performance, and she predicted that the stock would reach $36 a share by 1994, from its current price of $28.75 a share.

Who are the advertisers that support talk shows such as *Oprah* and *Donahue*? Locally they could be anybody, but the national advertisers are mostly food or home-care-products firms and drug companies. The top-ten national advertisers for Oprah in 1992, who paid out a total of $42 million to be on her show, were:

Philip Morris	$ 7.1 million
Kellogg	3.5 million
Procter & Gamble	3.1
Campbell Soup	1.9
Sara Lee	1.8
General Mills	1.6
Sandoz Ltd.	1.6
Nutri-System	1.4
Eastman Kodak	1.4
Nestlē USA	1.3

The top-ten national advertisers on the *Donahue* show during 1992, for a total of $20.4 million, were:

Philip Morris	$ 4.9 million
Unilever	3.8
SmithKline	1.5
Warner-Lambert	1.4
Schering-Plough	1.4
Nutri-System	1.2
Royal Appliance	1.1
Procter & Gamble	1.0
Block Drug	1.0
Grand Metropolitan	0.7

In brief, television talk shows are crafted around topics of interest to women primarily in the eighteen- to thirty-four-year-old age bracket, are mostly produced and run by women in that age category, and are mostly paid for by advertisers selling products that appeal to women in that age group.

Television talk shows are trashed as being stupid, inconsequential, or just plain weird by critics, all of whom are men. There is no record of any woman critic trashing television talk shows, but it is a regular sport for male critics to do so. Conversely, it is rare to find a male critic trashing NFL football or NBA basketball or golf tournaments or prizefights. Those kinds of programs are mostly targeted at males, mostly run by males, and mostly paid for by advertisers trying to reach males. People groping for the meaning of love, Oprah's kind of program, are in direct contrast to people hurtling at one another in contact sports. Each is an engaging and attractive form of entertainment and on occasion serves to educate the audience for which it is designed.

CHAPTER

25

1993—More Talk Shows but No Wedding

On New Year's Eve, 1992, Stedman and Oprah attended the wedding of Ellen Rakietan and Peter Kupferber. Ellen was one of the *Oprah Winfrey Show* producers and a member of Oprah's inner circle. Ellen's new husband was a financial consultant.

The day after the wedding, Oprah and Stedman attended a bull-riding rodeo in Phoenix that Stedman had promoted. Along the way the two talked over their relationship and agreed that each would have to give a little more and make sacrifices so they could be together more and make their romance work better. One source said that as part of the deal Oprah insisted on their having a baby the first year of their marriage, which is something Stedman had previously resisted. From the warmth of Arizona, they flew a few weeks later to Washington, D.C., to attend the inauguration of Bill Clinton.

As they talked about the possibility of a wedding, Oprah and Stedman began planning to hold the event in the second week in June. Stevie Wonder would sing. However, friends were saying that the two were in such a romantic state that they might not wait that long and could get married as soon as April or May. Then, suddenly, another turnabout occurred as Oprah told *People* magazine on February 11, the day after her smashingly successful interview of Michael Jackson, that the tabloids had reported that she and Stedman were marrying in April and that it wasn't true. Not June, either.

Part of the problem may have been that Oprah was distracted by the annual convention of the National Association of Television Programming Executives (NATPE) in San Francisco, where participants believed syndicated talk shows in 1993 could be grouped into three categories: gold—Oprah; silver—Donahue, Sally Jessy Raphael, Geraldo, and Regis and Kathie; and, finally, bronze—Maury Povich, Montel Williams, and the rest.

The biggest rumor floating around the convention this year was that Oprah, who owned every aspect of her show except the distribution mechanism, wanted to control that part, too. Not that Oprah wanted to buy King World, of which she was already a major stockholder, but that she would do her own syndication after her contract with King World expired in August 1995. As soon as that word got back to Jeffrey Jacobs, Oprah's lawyer and money man at Harpo Productions, he tried to kill it. "That's the last business I want to be in." Then he got on the phone and called everybody who might have been affected by the rumor and told them to ignore it.

Also circulating at the NATPE was the new book by former Paramount Pictures and NBC Entertainment chairman Brandon Tartikoff, in which he assessed Oprah's success, namely, that she wasn't an academic and didn't come across like one. Therefore, said Tartikoff, she asked the questions most of us would ask and made it more interesting for the average viewer. He said he didn't think the work required a Ph.D. in sociology and that, in fact, to have one could prove a hindrance.

The hottest thing at the 1993 NATPE convention was the conservative talk-show host who bridged radio and television and whom everybody called by one name, just as they did with Oprah. His name was Rush—Rush Limbaugh. Rush had been introduced to station representatives at the previous year's NATPE convention, where pundits predicted he didn't have a chance at succeeding while Bill Cosby's knockoff of the old

Groucho Marx show *You Bet Your Life* and Whoopi Goldberg were sure winners. Now Cosby's show was dead, Whoopi was dying, and Rush was skyrocketing. NATPE delegates were lined up to have their pictures taken with Rush, who said he had been convinced he would succeed from the first because his show is the only place you can get what he offers: the conservative point of view.

Exuding total confidence everywhere he went, just as he does on the air, where he referred to himself as "talent on loan from God," Rush assured participants that there was little chance of any competition to his program. He offered this logic as evidence: "Name me one existing entertainer in New York or Los Angeles who would be willing to lose all his friends and be ostracized by everyone he knows once he announces that he's a conservative on the air." As a mark of his national status, his book *The Way Things Ought to Be* was number one on the *New York Times* bestseller list.

Limbaugh's ratings of his radio talk show, syndicated to 560 stations, went through the roof as the most popular radio talk show in the country, with 10 million listeners, and his first-year ratings on his television talk show were very good for late-night talk, where he often beat Arsenio Hall and David Letterman. Dick Kurlander, programming vice president for Petry Television, a marketing consultant who advises 115 televisions on what programs to buy in syndication, said that in spite of the negative views about Rush by the media pundits at the last NATPE, "we recommended him this time last year to our stations solely on the strength of Rush. We always believed it was an easy call. To us it was a no-brainer that he was going to succeed. Just look at his track record and the pure ratings he receives in radio."

Of the sixteen television talk shows on the air at the time of the 1993 NATPE convention, Oprah was the top talk program by far, with a rating of 10.6 points, each point equaling roughly a million households. Oprah was not the top syndicated program of the 114 syndicated shows in the country. She was number four, behind her brother King World programs *Wheel of Fortune* and *Jeopardy*. The next closest television talk show to Oprah was Donahue, with a 7.4 point rating, and he was eleventh ranked among all syndicated programs. Following Donahue was Sally Jessy Raphael, with a 6.2 rating; Geraldo, with a 5.0 rating; Maury Povich, with a 4.3; Regis and Kathy Lee, with a 4.0; and, finally, Rush Limbaugh with a 3.6. So in one year Rush had become the eighth-ranked television talk program.

Sally Jessy Raphael thought that the sixteen television talk shows which would be on the air by September did not overcrowd the spectrum. She said, "I'm surprised there weren't sixteen talk shows on ten years ago. There's not too many talk shows any more than there are too many pubs in London. Americans like to share stories and that's what talk shows do."

Probably the happiest woman at the NATPE in 1993 was Jenny Jones, whose talk show started strong two years before but floundered because she concentrated on soft subjects and the ratings began to slip. Then she went for more sensational topics, such as wading into her female audience and demanding, "Are you happy with the size and shape of your breasts?" Now her ratings were up, and her show was more secure, although she only pulled 2.2 rating points and was still curious why people would come on her show to discuss intimate problems about sex and relationships. "These stories are so personal and private," she offered. "I think these people must delude themselves into thinking that if they can just tell their side of the story, people will think they're not so bad."

Oprah's February 10 special interview of Michael Jackson at his Neverland ranch north of Los Angeles turned out to be the ratings smash of the decade. Oprah probed his lifestyle, his childhood, family lifestyle, his fears and quirks, his virginity, and the blotchiness of his skin. The reviews were mixed and mostly critical, but the ratings were stellar and made Oprah and the ABC network happy.

March came, again the wedding plans were postponed, and Stedman took off for a fourteen-day Amazon cruise without Oprah to celebrate his forty-first birthday on March 6. Later, the two spent eight hours watching videotaped marriage counseling by therapist Harville Hendrix, a University of Chicago professor who wrote two books on improving relationships and who appeared on the *Oprah Winfrey Show* eight times. Meanwhile, always with a full agenda of projects, Oprah began planning a sixty-fifth birthday party for her good friend Maya Angelou, dieting and losing weight (down to 180 pounds), and working on the autobiography that Oprah called the best diet she has ever been on.

On April 3, Oprah threw what one guest called "the mother of all birthday parties" for her close friend Maya Angelou at Wake Forest University in Winston-Salem, North Carolina. The two-day event transformed the quiet southern academic campus, where the guest of honor is a professor of American studies, into a celebrity-filled, flower-covered gala. More than two hundred guests flew in from Africa, France, England, and parts of the United States to attend the festivities, held in a gigantic transparent tent on the grounds of the Graylyn Conference Center at the university. Oprah said it was a celebration of life, Angelou, and ourselves, referring to the predominantly black guest list for which Oprah transported flowers from all over the world and chefs from New York and Chicago, along with fifty-two waiters from New York. Sylvia Weinstock baked the special birthday cake and topped it with delicious, edible sugar flowers. Guests included actor Roscoe Lee Browne; singer Gladys Knight and her fiancé; talk-show host Les Brown; Barbara Henricks; actress Nastassja Kinski; musician Quincy Jones; Pamela Poitier, Sidney's wife; actress Cicely Tyson; basketball star Julius "Dr. J." Erving; Roland Watts; and actor Robert Guillaume.

President Clinton had selected Angelou as the first poet laureate of the United States since Robert Frost. She had delivered her eloquent commemorative poem "On the Pulse of the Morning" at his inauguration. The president joined the birthday party by satellite. In her response to Oprah's birthday greeting, Angelou thanked Oprah for "this birthday party of unutterable beauty and elegance" and said that if she could have chosen a daughter, she would have picked Oprah, adding, "Oprah, beautiful, tough, and bodacious, is the kind of daughter I would have wanted to have." Then, pointing to Stedman, she said, "Oprah loves me and I love her, but I know this is a dry run for an event scheduled later this year," an obvious reference to the on-again-off-again wedding.

Angelou's popularity soared after the nation heard her inauguration poem, and not only did the sixteen-page reprint of "On the Pulse of the Morning" become a bestseller; so did the rerelease of her autobiography, *I Know Why the Caged Bird Sings*, originally published twenty-three years before and through which Oprah first learned about Maya Angelou and related to her because their two lives had several parallels.

After having honored Maya, Oprah was, in turn, honored by the same magazine that had insulted her months before when it ran a composite cover photo with her head and Ann-Margret's body. *TV Guide* announced its selection of the best daytime-television talk-show hosts of the last four decades. It named Arthur Godfrey as the best of the 1950s, Merv Griffin for the 1960s, Phil Donahue for the 1970s, and Oprah Winfrey for the 1980s and best all-time host. It may have soothed some of the animosity over the faked cover photo.

With all that attention given to Oprah, it was a relief to her when Stedman Graham received a little attention of his own on the *Life Choices* show, hosted by Eric Chapman, out of Columbus, Ohio, where Stedman talked about his founding of Athletes Against Drugs. The former professional basketball player in the European League said that athletes were a major influence on his life, and he felt that they could encourage young people to stay away from drugs. "I knew how much athletes affected me. They were my role models." His organization, which now has ninety-two athletes, including Michael Jordan, Olympic athletes, and high school athletes, works with fourth-, fifth-, and sixth-graders to help them get into sports clinics and away from drugs.

At the end of April the *Washington Post* television critic decided to immerse himself in television talk. Predictably, the idea was picked up a few weeks later by the *New York Times* television critic and, even more predictably, a few weeks after that, in June, by the *Los Angeles Times* television critic. The *Washington Post's* Peter Carlson locked himself in a room and watched television for twenty-four hours, which brought him to the conclusion that talk shows had become a major cultural phenomenon and growth industry for celebrities down on their luck, unemployed political hacks, and ink-stained wretches called journalists. To Carlson it was a cacophony of strange people and stranger subjects and so affected him that he wrote a poem about talk shows and their hosts, concluding: "It's beautiful! It's awful! It's America in all its goofy glory, sounding its barbaric yawp over the roofs of the world!"

Walter Goodman of the *New York Times* didn't expose himself to the torment of twenty-four hours of talk shows, only a comparison among Oprah, Donahue, and Geraldo. His conclusion was less poetic and more direct: "Believe it or not, sex was on everybody's tongue." Donahue had men convicted of rape who had been released from jail after DNA tests proved them innocent. Oprah had couples for whom sex had gone out of their marriages after the arrival of a baby. Geraldo had two sisters who enjoyed sex with each other's man.

Goodman wrote in the *Times*, "Experts were at the ready on all the programs, like first-aid workers, kits packed with jargon and prepared for anything. But no doubt I'm the one who is missing the point. Truth is the wrong word for shows that offer viewers information, speculation, titillation and even a touch of edification, not to mention an opportunity to join in the game."

Howard Rosenberg of the *Los Angeles Times* did the same as Peter Carlson by covering a twenty-four-hour stint but didn't write a poem about his experience. He had several conclusions about the state of talk in America in 1993. For one, there is more talk than things to talk about, and second, anybody who can dress himself is deemed qualified to be a talk-show host.

Critic Rosenberg also brought up what he considered a disturbing trend in television programs, namely, phony talk shows. These programs pretend to be legitimate talk shows but are actually half-hour or hour-long commercials with the misleading genre name of "infomercials." Examples that he encountered in his twenty-four-hour-long vigil included Cher doing an infomercial on Lori Davis's hair products, concluding with "Well, we're just about out of time for this edition of 'Focus on Beauty,' but before we go, I just want to tell you...Lori has made this one-month free trial offer that I just can't believe." Others included Ron Popeil selling his electric food dehydrator and Sarah Purcell with the "Hamilton Beach Showcase."

At the end of May, *Jet* magazine reported that the word "Oprah" had entered the lexicon of teenagers as a verb meaning "to engage in persistent, intimate questioning with the intention of obtaining a confession; usually used by men of women, as in 'I wasn't going to tell her, but after a few drinks, she oprah'd it out of me."

On May 31, 1993, *Business Week* reported on the rankings of the three network newscasts, noting that ABC was number one and CBS was number two, with NBC trailing in the number three spot. It did not attribute ABC's success entirely to anchor Peter Jennings or his stellar news crew, but pointed out that the *Oprah Winfrey Show* is on most ABC stations earlier in the afternoon and that Oprah captures the audience, which then sticks around to watch the local news afterward, which in turn helps retain viewers for the ABC network news with Peter Jennings. That sequence underscored the value of Oprah to both local stations and the ABC network.

In fact, the local stations do more than simply follow Oprah Winfrey's time slot. More and more, they piggyback stories on whatever was featured on *Oprah* so that there is the anomaly of a talk-show host deciding what "news" is used by the professional journalists. Perhaps the most egregious example of how that was being done came when KABC-TV, the ABC-owned-and-operated station in Los Angeles, turned most of its eleven o'clock evening newscast that immediately followed the Oprah special on Michael Jackson to stories about Michael Jackson. Only sports and the weather were retained from the normal news format.

While many news directors of local TV stations agreed that KABC went too far, their criticism was only about the degree to which it was done. Bruno Cohen, the news director of KNBC-TV in New York, and others believe that "tie-ins" are all right. "It's a question of balance," according to Cohen, who believes that a good tie-in is fine if it's not overused and the rest of the newscast delivers the important hard news. However, in the real world, justifications for tie-ins are getting flimsier and have nothing to do with journalism. For example, that particular broadcast of the KABC-TV evening news had ratings *four times higher than normal*. That's the real story of tie-ins.

Before one jumps too quickly to the condemnation of those outsiders who would exploit the *Oprah Winfrey Show*, it is appropriate to consider something much more serious that no one on the inside of the Oprah organization wants to talk about willingly. A segment of the *Oprah Winfrey Show* in May serves as an illustration.

Sandra Moss, one of the featured guests on a show about depression during May, told Oprah and the audience about her fifteen years in hell when she was overwhelmed by a fatalistic pessimism that repeatedly made her consider suicide. This perky redheaded New York waitress became consumed by these suicidal obsessions until she sought out medical help and a doctor put her on medication, which ended her chronic depression and literally saved her life.

Sandra became so enthusiastic about her personal emotional turnaround that she began to campaign for others who are enduring what she went through to get medical help. "People don't have to get as ill as I got before I got help," she said.

Sandra's story was supplemented by others in the audience who experienced the same deep depressions and had also found a medication that proved, in their lives, a miracle drug. Called Prozac, it permitted them to reclaim their lives.

Was it a coincidence that all these people were in Chicago that day and just happened to be in the audience and on Oprah's show? No. It was a carefully executed public relations ploy by the drug firm that makes the antidepressant drug endorsed by Sandra and others on the show. The public relations firm, Burston-Marsteller, representing Eli Lilly, the makers of the controversial antidepressant Prozac, essentially had transformed the *Oprah Winfrey Show* into a free infomercial for their client's product.

According to one version of how the show originated, Nicole Riley, a media-relations specialist at Burston-Marsteller's Chicago office, called a producer at the *Oprah Winfrey*

Show to promote the idea of a show on depression and offered to provide interviewees and experts. Another version came from Rudy Guido, a producer of the *Oprah* show, who claimed he suggested the idea independently, but when he learned about the Burston-Marsteller contact, he used them to find people with "depression experiences" to appear on the show.

This is all part of an advertising and "awareness" campaign that public relations firms put on for a wide variety of clients ranging from African dictators to professional associations. Sheila Raviv, an executive vice president of Burston-Marsteller in Washington, defends these kinds of programs: "We believe it was a good cause. There is very little money available to do public education."

Sandra Moss defended her participation for the same reason. She said, "Eli Lilly has only one drug on the market. The reality is, they're making a lot of money from it. They should invest back in community awareness. A lot of people will be helped."

Critics, on the other hand, make the point that whether the cause is a good one or not is irrelevant because often the worthiness of causes is in the eye of the beholder. The issue is whether it is right or wrong to air a program that promotes a commercial product without the public's being aware of it. It is not the same as celebrities and experts who appear to promote their latest book or movie; that is right out front, and the audience knows it. In the case in point, Sandra Moss and others were flown into Chicago by the commercial firm to appear on the show so they could describe their dreadful experiences and how their lives were saved by the medicine made by the manufacturer who was secretly underwriting their appearance. Beyond that, professional mental health workers criticize this particular kind of endorsement because not everyone with depression should take Prozac. It is an ethical question, and as with such questions in the past, such as the satanic Jewish cult program, the Oprah people remain mute.

As the *Chicago Tribune* would later report, "The underlying business interest [here] illustrates how any issue—from the treatment of a debilitating illness to the advocacy of the policies of a foreign government—is routinely promoted in public discussion, often without the public's knowledge."

What makes this incident even more significant is that (1) it happens all the time, (2) it was done with the full cooperation of the show's producer, and (3) Oprah didn't tell her audience the truth about Sandra and other shills who appeared on her program under the guise of random audience members.

Americans can expect to see this kind of manipulation of television shows in the future. For example, NBC will run a two-hour program probing health-care reform anchored by Tom Brokaw without commercials. NBC news president Andrew Lack was pleased to announce on May 3, 1994, that the entire program will be underwritten by a $3.5 million grant from the Robert Wood Johnson Foundation, a nonprofit, philanthropic institution. Sounds wonderful and noble. Since it will be paid for by a "nonprofit, philanthropic institution" it must be objective, benevolent, and meritorious. Correct? No. This is another example of drug companies buying "awareness" programming to advertise their viewpoints while keeping their direct connection confidential. The Robert Wood Johnson Foundation is the creation of the drug and medical supply giant Johnson & Johnson. It is doubtful Johnson & Johnson would pay $3.5 million to get publicity for a cause or political position it opposed.

Another instance of talk-show manipulation on the *Oprah Winfrey Show* and others may well be the new drug Luvox. This will begin as a publicity surge to popularize a disorder called obsessive compulsive disorder (OCD), which is an embarrassing malady afflicting about 4 million Americans and for which the drug Luvox is supposed to offer relief. OCD victims have compulsions that they understand are nutty, but they can't get rid of them. Some will check and recheck door locks or irons or stoves for hours to make sure they are locked or off; they will wash their hands over and over again until the skin is raw; or they will fixate on some terrible thought that they can't get out of their mind.

With the FDA approval of Luvox expected soon, we shortly will see doctors' offices flooded with brochures about it, magazines and newspapers will be sprouting articles about

OCD, many of them planted, 800 information numbers will be established, and experts will start popping up on television talk shows like mushrooms in the forest after a rain.

The reason for the sudden popularity of OCD is that two drug companies, Upjohn and the Belgian firm Solvay SA, have developed Luvox to control OCD. These companies are only awaiting the approval of the Food and Drug Administration (FDA) before they unleash a multi-million-dollar promotion and "awareness" campaign—of which Oprah and other talk-show hosts may be a part.

As reported in the *Wall Street Journal*, "The selling of OCD offers a vivid example of how diseases have come to be packaged and marketed. The strategy solves a vexing business problem for drug companies which increasingly want to market directly to patients but face Food and Drug Administration curbs on advertising. Publicizing a disease sidesteps the FDA, creating a warm aura of public-spiritedness along the way. If all goes well, it also stirs a demand for the drugs."

The *Wall Street Journal* story described how the drug companies have selected typical OCD sufferers and sent them to their public relations firms for media coaching so they will be articulate guests on talk shows. Moreover, the drug companies keep their connection with the promotion campaign secret as much as possible.

The *Journal* noted, "Most consumers have no idea the studies and public-service messages actually are part of a plan to sell drugs. The drug companies typically leave few fingerprints, running their disease campaigns through public relations firms, patient groups, 'institutes' and other third parties."

The big hunt in the spring of 1994 was for a "celebrity sufferer," such as a major entertainment or sports figure who could be trotted around to all the talk shows as a spokesperson for OCD and help generate the buzz about the disease and the drug company's cure. One possibility was Donald Trump, who was thought to have the ailment, but that didn't pan out. Either he doesn't have it or won't admit to having it. A second choice could be a hockey goalie named Clint Malarchuk, who openly admits to OCD and how it makes him drive over his car routes incessantly to reassure himself that he hasn't killed anyone. He may be a future guest on the *Oprah* show as well as *Donahue, Geraldo,* and the rest.

In fairness, let's note that this kind of self-serving promotion, often funded in secret, is pervasive throughout the business and the media community. In Hollywood and New York, for example, there are companies that specialize in "product placement" in motion pictures. They are hired by manufacturers to place the products of their clients into movie scenes so that the public will see their movie heroes using a certain brand of TV set or razor or computer or washing machine or car. These manufacturers also pay to have actors in films wearing caps and clothing with the manufacturer's logo or name on them. It is the same with race-car drivers and sports figures wearing items with a "sponsor's" identification on it. The way the payoff chain works in movies is that the manufacturer pays the product-placement specialist, who, in turn, pays the producer of the movie.

In a comparable way testimony at congressional hearings in May 1994 revealed that tobacco companies have been paying over $1 million a year to get movie actors to smoke cigarettes in their films so as to perpetuate the image of adventure, glamour, and excitement connected with cigarette smoking. All of these secret payments to promote a product were also common in the record business, where record promoters, working for various recording companies, were notorious for providing radio-station disc jockeys with women, drugs, and money in exchange for the disc jockeys playing certain records, frequently to build up a consumer demand for those recordings. Called "payola," it was ruled illegal, and several people prominent in the music business lost their jobs and went to jail over this form of bribery.

Tom Shales, respected TV critic for the *Washington Post,* wrote in late May 1994 about how the unrevealed interests of corporations are slanting the news we get from television, which is the sole source of information for almost 80 percent of the American public. He commented that Cap Cities/ABC's program *20/20* aired an extremely favorable ten-minute review of the Stephen Sondheim–James Lapin Broadway musical

Passion. Hugh Downes, the coanchor on *20/20*, said Sondheim was considered by many to be America's greatest composer of popular music, and another reporter, Bob Brown, declared that Sondheim was one of the best-known composers this country has ever produced. Oprah's idol, coanchor Barbara Walters, chimed in with "I am passionate about Stephen Sondheim and looking forward to seeing *Passion*." Amid all this gushing, no one mentioned that Cap Cities/ABC is an investor in *Passion* and has a strong financial interest in it doing well at the box office. The same thing happened when *Entertainment Tonight* promoted the new *Star Trek* movie without mentioning that both *Entertainment Tonight* and *Star Trek* are owned by Paramount. Shales wrote, "Viewers deserve to know if self-serving interests are involved when they see a story they assume to be objective."

So what is happening in the secret promotion of drugs on the television talk shows, like Oprah's, is a common form of self-serving promotion in business.

Meanwhile, Oprah went again to New York for the Daytime Emmy Awards, where she won the Outstanding Talk Show Host Emmy for the third year in a row and paid tribute to Donahue for creating the form. "He's the master at what he does. He made it possible for there to be an Oprah." Also of interest to Oprah because they belong to the King World pantheon of syndication moneymakers was *Jeopardy*, which won the top award for best game show for the fourth time in a row, and Pat Sajak, Oprah's former Nashville colleague, who won best game host for *Wheel of Fortune*.

A few weeks after the kudos from her colleagues, Oprah was blasted by the medical establishment over her July 12 show, when she had New Age guru Dr. Deepak Chopra on with his new book, *Ageless Body, Timeless Mind*. Many traditional doctors objected to her promoting the New Age medicine, but Oprah was very much into New Age and self-actualization and ignored the critics.

The one critic Oprah couldn't ignore was Stedman. The October wedding was called off in August, and Stedman laid down another ultimatum: He would not marry Oprah until he became the first priority in her life. The two didn't take their usual summer vacation together, and when he returned after a two-week business trip in Europe, she was "too busy" with her movie *Ain't No Children Here* to see him. By August, she had lost sixty pounds and was jogging regularly. She even entered a 13.1-mile race in San Diego on August 15 under the name Bobbi Jo Jenkins. While she didn't finish first, she completed the run in a respectable two hours and sixteen minutes.

"People told me running would be fun," she said at the finish line as she was signing autographs. "When I first started training, I said, 'What's fun about this?' But today was a lot of fun."

For Oprah, 1993 would also turn out to be a big interview year, with three major national magazines and an important regional journal publishing profiles about her. In August, *People* magazine would publish a cover story about the "Richest Women in Showbiz," of whom Oprah is the wealthiest. October *Ebony* would print a cover story on her, as would November *McCall's*, and also in November, *Chicago* magazine would do a feature profile breathlessly entitled "Oprah Talks! About the Wedding, the Book, Her Trim New Figure and the Changes in Her Life."

At the end of August, *People* magazine published a comparison of rich women entertainers: Madonna Ciccone, Oprah, Mary Tyler Moore, Liz Taylor, Jane Fonda, Goldie Hawn, Barbra Streisand, and Dolly Parton. All of these stars have earned their fortunes, and most of them are hands-on managers of their money. Parton parlayed her singing earnings into Dollywood, a theme amusement park near her Locust Ridge, Tennessee, home. While Parton has money men around her, she doesn't seek advice from them, only information so she can make her own decisions. Madonna is much the same way and is notorious for going over expenses with a fine-tooth comb, demanding justification for even the most minute item. Streisand likes to invest in real estate and does it through front people. She knows her name will make sellers jack up the price, and besides, she insists on preserving her own privacy. In contrast, Mary Tyler Moore left it all to her husband, Grant Tinker, during the eighteen years they were married.

While Oprah relies heavily on attorney–financial adviser

Jeffrey Jacobs, she is also obsessed with tight personal control. As *People* described it, "Oprah Winfrey is frankly into control. The 39-year-old talk-show host relies on only one advisor: her longtime lawyer and partner, Jeffrey Jacobs."

The article then listed some of her major expenditures, for which she needs approval of no one—no committees, no boards, no stockholders. In 1991 she spent $3 million for an eighty-five-acre ranch and ski getaway in Telluride, Colorado, plus $1.3 million for a log-and-stone cabin, adding to her real estate holdings of an $800,000 Chicago condo and a 160-acre farm near Michigan City, Indiana. She also paid for the entire wedding in Italy and honeymoon of her executive producer, Debra DiMaio.

People wrote, "Winfrey's whims may sound extravagant, but they actually add up to money well spent.... The producer whose wedding she paid for is a prized member of the staff she considers part of her extended family and on whom she relies to put on her syndicated talk shows which pays her company more than $45 million a year." In fact, Debra DiMiao is the key person who got Oprah the job that moved her from Baltimore to Chicago and ultimately into national syndication.

People concluded that Oprah may spend a lot of money, usually on investments that appreciate in value, and that she is not a frivolous spender. "Not long ago, Oprah stood in the aisle of a K-Mart [*sic*] near her Indiana farm agonizing over whether to buy a $7.95 doormat decorated with cats or one festooned with cows...." Jacobs says, "'She still has both feet on the ground; she just wears better shoes.'"

Oprah says that her business ability is emotion-based. "I don't do anything unless it feels good," she told *Crain's Chicago Business*. "I don't move on logic. I move on my gut. And, I have a good gut."

In September 1986, Oprah went national for the first time, and seven years later, in September 1993, she made the cover of *Forbes* magazine as the number-one richest entertainer in America, and by natural extension, the world. She was referred to in Wall Street terms by *Forbes* as "a vertically integrated entertainment powerhouse." The *Oprah Winfrey Show* is seen in over 99 percent of U.S. TV markets and in sixty-four countries, generating over $170 million in revenue. Winfrey's two-year take—$98 million ($46 million in 1992 and $52 million in 1993).

A close second behind Oprah on the *Forbes* list of wealthy entertainers was Steven Spielberg, with Bill Cosby as number three. These figures suggest why talk shows are so popular with producers and talk-show stars. Much of Steven Spielberg's 1993 income came from the biggest-grossing film of all time, *Jurassic Park*, which took in some $600 million in that year and from which Spielberg received $72 million, or 12 percent of the gross. In contrast, out of the gross income the *Oprah Winfrey Show* made, Oprah received on the order of 25 percent. This windfall occurs because a television talk show is vastly cheaper to produce than a big movie directed by Spielberg. One television financial analyst summed it up with "Nobody gets a deal like Oprah. Nobody."

In October, Oprah's friend and inspiration Maya Angelou issued her new book of spiritual and personal-style essays: *Wouldn't Take Nothing for My Journey Now*. It began as a few short pieces in *Essence* magazine when Oprah called Angelou and said, "We need more of this."

One can understand Oprah by understanding those people who are her guidance and inspiration, like Maya Angelou. *Wouldn't Take Nothing for My Journey Now* includes Maya's thoughts about a woman's tenderness: "A woman will need to prize her tenderness and be able to display it at appropriate times in order to prevent toughness from gaining total authority and to avoid becoming a mirror image of those men who value power above life and control over love."

Or about integrity and faith: "If a promise is not kept, or if a secret is betrayed, or if I experience long-lasting pain, I begin to doubt God and God's love. I fall so miserable into the chasm of disbelief that I cry out in despair. Then, the Spirit lifts me up again and once more I am secured in faith."

Other material published in October that provides an insight into Oprah included another profile, written by Laura Randolph for *Ebony* magazine, which once again repeated details of her life: her deep pain when a Canadian tabloid charged Stedman with being gay and the agony of her own half sister, Patricia, betraying Oprah by telling the world she had suffered a pregnancy and miscarriage at fourteen. Also repeated: her ambivalence regarding her parents; how her mother never really seemed to care much about Oprah until she became rich, and how Oprah has publicly expressed doubts that Vernon Winfrey, the man who saved her from becoming an unwed teenage mother and delinquent, is her biological father. The article's implied theme is that Oprah doesn't really feel a strong tie to anyone in life and that she has been afraid to admit that truth until now—even to herself.

Toward the end of October, on the twenty-seventh, Stedman launched something new for him, too, at George Washington University in Washington, D.C., the Forum for Sports and Special Event Management and Marketing, an institute to train people in the business of sports. Stedman had worked with the university to develop a curriculum and would also teach in the summer.

"I want to try to get more minorities and women involved in the industry behind the scenes," he said. "In order to get more minorities and women into management positions, we need to create a program that studies the industry. I believe if we provide diversity in the front offices and management, we'll be able to create more opportunity and empower people—and get people off the streets. A lot of blacks and Hispanics want to work in sports, but they don't know how to get involved."

He cited the giant imbalance between the number of minorities who are on sports teams versus the number of minorities in sports management as a major inspiration for the creation of the institute.

In October, the Federal Trade Commission and the *Washington Post* finally came to a conclusion that Oprah had arrived at four years earlier, namely, that liquid diets don't work for long and that much of the weight you take off using them creeps back. The results of a one-year-long study revealed that the liquid diet programs, such as the one used by Oprah, Optifast Core, made by the Swiss firm Sandoz, Ltd., took off weight but didn't keep it off. The study said that on the average those individuals using these programs lost forty-seven pounds but regained two-thirds of it back within two and a half years. At the time of Oprah's Optifast Core diet, the public attention on Oprah launched a great diet-product war. Optifast was a liquid diet given to obese dieters at hospitals instead of solid food, and the dramatic success of Oprah's use of it brought a boom for these kinds of hospital diets, with Graduate Hospital in Philadelphia reporting five hundred calls a day after Oprah talked about her diet. Following Oprah's praise for her liquid diet, for which she did not get paid, the diet industry's sales skyrocketed to $3 billion, an increase of 15 percent from the previous year.

However, the news leaked out that Oprah had regained eighteen pounds, and horror stories began to surface of people's health being adversely affected by these diets. By March 1990, Rep. Ron Wyden (D-Ore.) was holding congressional hearings about the diet business. Testimony was heard from people like Sherri Steinberg, who lost weight so fast on a Nutri/System diet that she developed serious gallbladder disease. The hearings also delved into celebrity tie-ins in the aggressive advertising programs that many of the diet companies used in which entertainment and sports figures such as Tommy Lasorda, manager of the Los Angeles Dodgers, were used. While Oprah was not used in Sandoz's Optifast commercials, the tie-in with her was clearly there, given the estimated 40 million people who saw or heard about the "little red wagon" show.

There was another kind of tie-in linked directly to Oprah that sought to exploit her popularity to boost news shows on the stations on which she appeared. One blatant example originally occurred in February, when the ABC-owned station in Los Angeles, KABC-TV, turned over practically all of its eleven o'clock evening news to Michael Jackson stories immediately following Oprah's special on Jackson.

Now, nine months later in November, came an even more audacious tie-in that went beyond what KABC-TV did. In Los Angeles, as in many cities, Oprah appeared on the local ABC-owned or affiliated station, and it was logical that these ABC stations used Oprah tie-ins when they could, but the week of November 8—Sweeps Week, when the national Nielsen ratings were taken for each station—saw what the television industry would call the first "tie-in hijacking." Oprah was featured all week long on the news broadcast of another network-owned station, KNBC, in direct competition with the ABC station that carried the *Oprah Winfrey Show*.

For five days, the NBC-owned station in Los Angeles featured a series of Oprah stories: "Her Secret Past," "Oprah Mania," "People Whose Lives She's Changed," "The Oprah Empire: Spending $80 Million A Year," and "Her Very Private Life." Naturally, it turned out that there was less than met the eye; the programs were rehashes of old stories about Oprah, with some inaccuracies. Station executives stood at the ready with vague and innocent explanations of what they were doing—all in the name of a better America and pristine journalism.

News director Mark Hoffman of KNBC admitted that what he was doing was unorthodox in promoting a program that appeared on a competitive station but that it was the right thing to do. In fact, the constraints of being a professional journalist almost forced him to do it. "I think she is a force in popular culture," he said. "She's one of the highest-paid performers in the industry, and she has a huge impact on society almost every day. That's news."

Hoffman did admit that it would be fair to say he was trying to get the audience from the very highly rated Oprah show to watch to NBC local news afterward instead of staying stuck on the ABC local news channel, but he hedged. "I do hope that the series pulls some of their viewers over to us," he declared. "But that isn't the motivation. You always want to do impact pieces that people find interesting and thereby compel them to watch. And Oprah is interesting. She speaks to millions and millions every day on a wide range of topics that clearly have an effect on her audience."

To understand the value of using, even indirectly, the drawing power of another station's star, one only has to examine the lead-in show ratings. The *Oprah Winfrey Show*, which leads into the local KABC news, draws a 27 percent share of the Los Angeles audience, while *Sally Jessy Raphael*, which leads into the local KNBC news, only draws a 10 percent share of the audience, and that has only been true since September 1993, when Sally Jessy replaced *Donahue*, who was doing even worse against Oprah.

Sally Jessy, born Sally Lowenthal to a well-to-do family in Scarsdale, New York, grew up in Puerto Rico because her father was in the rum business, and knocked around the broadcasting business for years before she won a solid position on NBC's syndicated radio program *Talknet* giving advice to the lovelorn. Finally, she appeared on national syndicated television in October 1983, two and one-half months before Oprah started on WLS-TV in Chicago. Now she generally ranks third or fourth in markets across the country, behind Oprah, Donahue, and sometimes Geraldo, but ahead of the rest of the talk-show pack.

As she tells her own story, "I am the longest unsung overnight sensation in the history of show business! For twenty-six years I couldn't pay the credit-card bills. We moved twenty-five times looking for work. I've been fired eighteen times. At times we lived on food stamps and slept in our car. It was twenty-six years before I made $22,000 a year." In January 1992, the worst month of her life, she almost lost her adopted son, J.J., in a car accident, and three weeks later, she lost a daughter, Allison, to respiratory failure.

Jeff Wald, the news director at an independent Los Angeles TV station, KCOP, summarized what was really happening in this tie-in hijacking. "It just shows how competitive local news has become. You have stations grasping at anything they can think of to grab an audience that is becoming more and more split between all the competing programming. We are all so desperate to get as much of that audience as we can, all bets are off."

The announcement of A. C. Nielsen's ratings of syndicated programs just before Thanksgiving made Oprah happy and the King brothers at King World even happier.

Nielsen ranked Oprah again as the highest-rated talk show, with a 10.1 percent share of the audience on 232 stations around the country. Oprah was ranked number four of all syndicated programs nationally. Even better for King World, *Wheel of Fortune* was ranked number one overall with a 14.7 percent share of the audience, and *Jeopardy* ranked number two, with a 12.2 percent share. The shares mean the number of households with television sets on and tuned to that show at that time. Each 1 percent is equal to a little less than a million households, and experts can only estimate how many people in each household are watching. So of the top four syndicated programs ranked by Nielsen for the week ending October 31, 1993, King World, in which Oprah is a major stockholder, had three programs. Others in the top ten included two different versions of *Star Trek* (number three and number five), *Roseanne*, *Entertainment Tonight*, a weekend version of *Wheel of Fortune*, *Inside Edition*, and *Married...with Children* as numbers six through ten.

The general public probably doesn't pay much attention to such reports, but Oprah and her business partners do because they involve millions of dollars and Oprah's ability to maintain her luxurious lifestyle and indulge her legendary generosity.

These figures are largely responsible for the King family fortune having reached a net worth of at least $465 million. The corporate result was that King World had a 7.4 percent increase in profit for fiscal year 1993.

Chief financial officer Jeff Epstein said King World was ready for the opening of the much-touted and much-hyped information superhighway. "Our key focus is coming up with programming to ride on the information superhighway when it's built. *Wheel of Fortune* and *Jeopardy* are two of the most widely used shows in the interactive game area and are used on the Interactive Network. Wouldn't it be fun to play *Wheel* and *Jeopardy* at home and win prizes?" It certainly would be fun for King World, which at that point sat on a third of a billion dollars in cash and no long-term debt.

Around this time Oprah used some of her earnings to option another bestselling book written by National Book Award–winner Toni Morrison, whose literary works have become some of the hottest properties in Hollywood. This time, Oprah optioned the movie rights to Ms. Morrision's 1987 novel *Beloved*, a film Harpo Productions would produce. Oprah would play the lead.

In 1993 there were two stars named Michael on Oprah

shows, beginning with her record-breaking special interview of the boy-child megastar Michael Jackson that aired February 10 and, nine months later, in November, having the other Michael, retiring basketball star Michael Jordan, on her regular *Oprah Winfrey Show*. The Michael Jordan interview did not prove nearly as dramatic as the Michael Jackson program, even though Oprah raised questions about Jordan's gambling and the murder of his father.

David Hiltbrand of *People* found Oprah's questioning of Jordan weak but not unusual. He wrote, "The diva of deep dish is having quite a year. Of course, celebrities know they're assured of a friendly reception on Oprah. Winfrey broaches sensitive topics but accepts vague responses without an aggressive follow-up. For instance, Jordan, when asked about the charges of compulsive gambling that have dogged him this year, said, 'I don't think I did anything that was totally illegal.' That kind of evasion may pass muster with Oprah, Mike, but don't try it with Mike Wallace."

Michael Jordan's sister Angela was in the audience for the taping, but no media people were allowed in the studio for fear that they might interfere or upstage Oprah. It was a question of control. Orpah probed Michael's feeling about the murder of his father, which was committed by some marauding youths looking for someone to rob and/or kill when they found the older Jordan asleep in his car along the interstate in the Carolinas.

Oprah asked if Michael wanted to say anything to those young men accused of murdering his father, and he said that there was nothing he could say that would matter. He didn't want to know them or their reasons for murdering his father. He only wanted to remember the positive things about his father, like the fact that he was at Michael's last basketball game.

Of course, part of the motivation for Michael's appearance was to promote his book *Rare Air*, which he wrote with help from former *Chicago Sun-Times* sportswriter Mark Vancil and former *Sports Illustrated* photographer Walter Iooss. The first printing of 300,000 was already sold out, with another 90,000 in press.

Just before Thanksgiving, Oprah did two dramatic shows about her weight again in which she joyfully talked about her long struggle to keep off the pounds and how she had shed 72 pounds in eight months down to her present 150. Beginning at 222 pounds in March, she chronicled, with readings from her diary, how she had bicycled, run, and hiked over twenty-three hundred miles with the help of her personal trainer, Bob Greene, and ate tasty but low-fat meals prepared for her by her personal chef, Rosie Daley.

At the end of her story, Stedman came onstage as Oprah announced to all, "I just wanted America to know that Stedman has loved me no matter what size I was." She spoke on camera to Stedman directly: "You stood by me and loved me no matter what—and I thank you for it." It was a nice moment, but there was no hint of a new schedule for a wedding date, which is what everyone really wanted to hear.

Oprah and Stedman decided to spend Thanksgiving with her close friend Maya Angelou at her home in North Carolina, where they gathered to watch Oprah's latest movie for television, *There Are No Children Here*, on ABC-TV, another true-life drama based on Alex Kotlowitz's book about black families living in a Chicago public housing project.

The program received generally good reviews for both its subject matter—the grim life of young blacks trying to survive and make it out of the public housing "projects" to a better life—and the cast. It is the story of how a caring black mother, LaJoe Rivers, played by Oprah, tries to hold her family together, even though she has a useless husband who drinks too much and works too little but who can sweet-talk her into loving him and taking care of him no matter how badly he betrays her.

Her oldest son is already doing time in prison, leaving her two young sons she is trying to save. With her eleven-year-old, Lafeyette, it may already be too late, because he seems headed toward following his older brother into prison, but with the nine-year-old there is an inbred will to escape from the projects and the life.

Maya Angelou played LaJoe's mother, a paragon of patience and faith that all will turn out right. LaJoe's dream is to get her family out of the project and away from the drug dealers and the gangs and the teen murderers. She saves every penny she can to buy a home away from the urban war zone. When the time comes to buy the modest dream home that will be the salvation of her life and the life of her family, she loses the money to a con artist who tricks her and steals her money.

The two child actors, Mark Lane as Lafeyette and Norman Golden II as Pharoah, received rave reviews. "It is in their pained and confused faces, their complex and crushing daily dilemmas that 'There Are No Children Here' finds its power," said James Endest of the *Hartford Courant*. For some reviewers Oprah in person was too overpowering, and viewers couldn't forget she was Oprah, but she did a good job nevertheless.

Oprah wanted to make this film because she drove by the Henry Horner public housing project every day on her way to work and admitted she was a little uneasy about the kind of young people she saw there. When she started shooting the location shots during the summer in that same public housing project, those previously threatening young people became her friends.

"After spending time with them this summer, I look at the group to see if there's somebody there that I know," she said. "You find people in the projects who have as much desire for fulfillment and enrichment—to be somebody—as anywhere else in the world. The lesson is that we really are all the same and it doesn't matter how you're packaged; the heart is always the same."

To show the people and children of Henry Horner Homes where her heart is, Oprah took the half million dollar fee she received for the film and set up a scholarship fund for the children of Henry Horner to help them get out of the project. The other contribution Oprah made may be more important, if less tangible, and that was the movie itself, for without her push and without the money from Harpo Productions, the film might never have been produced.

In November, *McCall's* magazine profiled Oprah, as *Ebony* and *People* had done previously. The *McCall's* piece was written by Jill Brooke Coiner, who writes on TV and entertainment for the *New York Post* and *CNN*. She dealt with what now have become the usual questions: the wedding, the book, and the weight, and Oprah gave what, for the end of 1993, were the usual answers. She maintained that she never set a date for the Big Wedding to Stedman and that they will get married when they are ready, which is not now but could be in 1994. The book had turned into something she didn't want to release, but she was glad that she had done it. Controlling her weight actually related to controlling her deep-seated feelings and coming to terms with her internal demons, not calories.

At the end of November, Oprah saw another tiny step forward taken in her commitment to Angelica Mena to do something about child abuse when a new set of crime bills that parents, angry women, and Oprah had testified for and pushed passed the House of Representatives. The bills made it tougher for those who commit domestic violence and violence in schools and in the workplace and harder for schoolchildren to get guns. It was now illegal to evade child custody laws by taking a child out of the country. A comparable anticrime bill had passed the Senate earlier, and the two bills had to be reconciled in a conference committee. Neither was all that advocates of more protection for spouses and children wanted, but it was a step forward. Observers said a reconciled conference bill had a good chance of being passed and signed into law in 1994.

The various bills included the Violence Against Women Act, which requires all states to enforce protection orders issued by other states and other shields for women and children who are victims of domestic violence; the Young Handgun Safety Act, which limited the accessibility of handguns to young people under the age of eighteen; and the two bills of particular interest to Oprah: the Jacob Wetterling National Child Protection Act and the Crimes Against Children Registration Act.

The first requires those convicted of crimes against children to register with the state for ten years after their release from prison so as to provide a list of suspects when searching for kidnapped children. The second was the one that Oprah had campaigned for the previous year. It set up a national registry of people convicted of crimes against children so that police, child-care centers, and youth groups can screen job applicants and avoid hiring those with a criminal record of abusing and assaulting children.

The end of 1993 proved kinder to Oprah. The previous year, she had fired her financial guru's wife, Jennifer Jacobs, as her dresser after a scathing assessment by Mr. Blackwell, the flamboyant fashion gadfly, but the November 22, 1993, version of Mr. Blackwell's list was easier to take when he dubbed Oprah "absolutely incredible. The best she's ever looked."

Others, of course, did not fare so well. He called actress Demi Moore "totally an enigma. Can't figure out who she was to begin with and why she's ended up the way she has. Now she's looking like Bruce Willis's boyfriend rather than his wife." Of Roseanne Arnold, "Beautiful, if only she'd keep her mouth shut." Oprah's friend and costar in *The Color Purple*, Whoopi Goldberg: "Whoops! Terrible, but she goes out of her way to look so bad." Finally, the most tongue in check assessment of all, Mr. Blackwell's assessment of Mr. Blackwell: "A bitch, but a brilliant image, the jewels, the hair, every-thing."

Of particular financial interest to Oprah was the news revealed on November 29 by financial columnist Dan Dorfman about the possibility of Cap Cities/ABC buying out the King brothers and taking control of King World. Cap Cities/ABC, Dorfman wrote, "already has said it's on the acquisition prowl [and] may be in talks to take it [King World] over or is weighing an offer. Whether the rumors are the usual Wall Street hog-wash is unclear. But they may have been sparked by a recent King World report by stock analyst Jessica Reif of Op-penheimer & Co. 'I have no idea whether they're talking or not, but it's a natural deal,' she told me."

Jessica Reif's reason goes along these lines: Up until re-cently, federal regulations prohibited networks from owning interests in syndicated programs, which is why, in the early days of the *Oprah Winfrey Show* being syndicated nationally out of ABC's WLS-TV, the station and network had to bring in a third party to do the syndicating, namely, King World.

That situation changed in late 1993 when the federal courts modified the so-called financial interest/syndication rule known in the broadcasting industry as the "fin/syn rule." So now, for the first time, ABC could become involved in the enormous income generated from syndicating *Wheel of Fortune, Jeopardy*, and the *Oprah Winfrey Show*.

Since ABC-owned-and-affiliated stations are King World's largest customer and if King World were sold to another network, such as NBC or CBS, ABC would be in the unhappy situation of paying millions of dollars in license fees for the *Oprah Winfrey Show* to a rival network, it is understood that Cap Cities/ABC would want to buy King World.

The King brothers, who own 25 percent of King World, know the current price of King World shares is around $47 a share, which should move to about $50 a share in 1994, because that's when many of the station contracts for *Wheel of Fortune* and *Jeopardy* expire and the renewal fees will be bumped higher. Reif calculated that Cap Cities/ABC would probably be willing to pay $60 a share or a total of $2.2 billion for King World; at that price, a deal would be very appealing to the King brothers and most of the other stockholders, including Oprah.

This is of more than passing interest to Oprah and Jeffrey Jacobs because of Oprah's status with King World as the number-one moneymaker and a major stockholder in the syndicator. Beyond that, Oprah's contract with King World was due to expire in September 1995. She wanted a better deal, even though she already has the best deal in television, because she knows that neither Cap Cities/ABC nor any other major buyer will want to acquire King World without the *Oprah Winfrey Show*.

Ironically, the King brothers had a problem with the *Oprah* show for a long time in that it was too successful. Ideally, the brothers would rather have had several more shows that were successful beyond *Oprah, Wheel*, and *Jeopardy*. Diversification would make King World less dependent on the whims of Oprah and Merv Griffin. Unfortunately, the brothers had proven over and over again that they were great syndicators and lousy producers. The new shows they developed continued to fail. In December 1993 that pattern of failure was demonstrated again with the Les Brown talk show they had launched months before with such high hopes. The ratings proved so bad they had to cancel it. The last Les Brown show aired on January 14, 1994.

Unwilling to face reality, the Kings came forth immediately with another talk-show host. Oprah understood what they were doing and was confident about the uniqueness of the *Oprah Winfrey Show*. It had a special niche in the talk-show market, so she wasn't all that worried about new King brothers talk shows cutting into her audience. Then King World announced in December that it was launching still another talk show on January 17, but this one was very close to Oprah's show, an outspoken black woman with an unusual name, *Rolonda*, starring former *Inside Edition* and WABC-TV personality Rolonda Watts. Oprah didn't like that idea one bit.

26

Michael, Michael, Michael

No single show Oprah has ever done has commanded the audience and the critical comment to equal her special prime-time interview with Michael Jackson—the ratings left television executives panting.

The February 10, 1993, Oprah special interview with Michael Jackson earned one of the highest ratings of any television show in history (39.3 percent of all U.S. homes and a 56 percent share of all the sets turned on at the time), with an average of 62 million viewers at any given moment. Ninety million people watched at least part of the show.

Beyond that, King World, which handled the syndication, had sold the Michael Jackson special to fifty countries worldwide. Fred Cohen, who is president of King World, said Germany's RTL Plus channel and France's Canal Plus ran the program live in spite of the fact that the time difference had it coming on in the early morning in those countries. It was Jackson's first public interview in fourteen years, during which he answered a variety of intimate questions, including his crotch grabbing on camera, the early child abuse he endured, rumors of his plastic surgery, and talk about his virginity. One of the many revelations made for the first time by Jackson was that he didn't bleach his skin so as to appear white. "I am proud to be a black American." Instead, he suffers from a hereditary skin disease called vitiligo, which had turned 80 percent of his skin white. This was later confirmed by his dermatologist. He does use makeup to even out the color and hide the blotches.

He talked about his childhood and hating rehearsals forced upon him while other children were playing. He saw other children having a good time, and it made him cry. He also didn't want to go on a tour of South America so much that he hid and wept. His father abused him with taunts and insults about how he looked. That also made Michael cry as a child. When Oprah asked if his father had ever beaten him, Michael said, "Yes," and then, in an apparent aside to his father, said, "I'm sorry. Please don't be mad at me." Ironically, his latest record album, *Dangerous*, is dedicated "to my dearest parents, Katerine and Joseph Jackson."

He denied some of the nutty things that are rumored about him, such as that he sleeps in a hyperbaric chamber and the photo suggesting that he actually tested the equipment at the burn center he established after he had accidentally been burned severely in a 1984 television commercial for Pepsi Cola. He did admit to some minor plastic surgery, including having his nose remodeled and a chin cleft created.

George Varga, the pop music critic of the *San Diego Union-Tribune*, summarized his feeling about the revelations made by Jackson to Oprah when he headlined his story "Jackson Is a Victim of the Life He Has Created for Himself." Varga, writing for an admittedly conservative newspaper but in a town that has many Jackson fans, didn't think Oprah did a particularly good job of interviewing Jackson; to him, she was too obsequious and asked too many softball questions. The interview, which took place in what Varga called Jackson's "lavishly furnished prison of a heavily guarded California estate," didn't probe deep enough into the psyche of the rock star for Varga's tastes.

He wrote, "Not once did the gushing Winfrey ask him if he was happy or if he had sought the professional help that now is the only thing purportedly keeping him from a drug-fueled death. Not once was he asked if he might bear a great deal of the responsibility for his tormented life."

Actually, Jackson answered Varga's question himself when he summarized his own life. "I am one of the loneliest people on this earth. I cry sometimes because it hurts. It does. To be honest, I guess you could say that it hurts to be me."

On the other side of the continent, the reaction was similar from Patricia Smith of the *Boston Globe*. "By agreeing to be interviewed by a gushing Oprah Winfrey, Michael made a final attempt to pull himself up from the abyss. He whispered his confusion and giggled on cue, while his droopy eyes begged for absolution. He pointed a wary finger at his father and introduced the world to the disease that had wasted his skin. The guided tour of his well-appointed prison yielded no new clues. 'Here I am,' it all seemed to say. But in the end, Michael Joseph Jackson was nowhere to be found."

Six months after the Oprah interview, at the beginning of September 1993, Michael's world transformed from the fantasy of his Neverland ranch in the idyllic San Ynez Valley north of Santa Barbara to a level of Dante's Inferno when a thirteen-year-old boy accused him of sexual abuse. The charges and countercharges, clarifications, confusions, and contradictions filled the tabloids, the news broadcasts, and the public's mind. Op-Ed pieces argued pro and con; former servants and employees came forward to confirm or refute the charges; tapes were produced and lost; bewildered and bewildering spokesmen for both sides made news, generating more heat, but little light, on the issue.

Talk of bribes, blackmail, and hush money entered the fray, and few people raised the question of where the accusing thirteen-year-old's parents had been during all the months of alleged abuse by Michael. Michael's public relations–crisis control apparatus wobbled, made much worse by Michael's publicly toting a diminutive thirteen-year-old Emmanuel Lewis around for the cameras.

Initially, the defense was wobbly and confused and began with Jackson's attorney, Howard Weitzman, denying everything on behalf of Michael and countercharging that the thirteen-year-old boy's father was trying to blackmail Jackson over a failed $20 million movie deal. Meanwhile, Jackson was in the midst of his Pepsi-sponsored world tour, which began to disintegrate when Jackson canceled two concerts in Bangkok, claiming dehydration and illness. The Los Angeles police searched Neverland for pornographic tapes, and his sister Janet and friend Elizabeth Taylor jetted to Singapore to be with Jackson. His other sister, La Toya, broke with the family and said she had warned Michael he would be caught someday. The tabloids, both television and print, went into ecstasy over the story, with the so-called legitimate press panting close behind.

London's *Daily Star* labeled Michael "Sicko Jacko," while the the *Sun* more euphoniously called him "Wacko Jacko." Howard Stern observed to his millions of listeners, "Suddenly, Pee-Wee Herman is an upright citizen," while *Tonight* show's Jay Leno observed, "Someone said when you hear the name Michael Jackson it epitomizes all that's kind and good. So did the name Heidi until a month ago."

The sweetness of Jackson's words about young children written in his 1988 autobiography *Moonwalk* now echoed back with an ominous twist. "I love being around them. There always seem to be a bunch of kids over at the house and they're always welcome. They energize me—just being around them."

During the Oprah interview Jackson talked about his mislaid childhood and how he particularly missed slumber parties in his youth; it was slumber parties that he had with the thirteen-year-old who was now accusing him of molestation. The young boy, accompanied by his half sister and mother, had traveled overseas with Jackson to Monte Carlo as well as to Florida and Disney World. The charges alleged that the boy slept with Jackson, was lured into the bathtub with Jackson, and that Jackson had performed oral sex on the boy, who Jackson warned would go to jail if he told.

The charges against Jackson were apparently pushed forward by the father, not the mother, and the father apparently coauthored a movie script that Jackson was supposed to have agreed to underwrite. As part of the convoluted nature of the affair, at about the same time that the charges were filed against Jackson by the father on behalf of his minor son, a judge ordered the father to pay the mother $68,804 in overdue child support.

Commenting on the public's revulsion and fascination with the child-abuse charges, University of Michigan professor Melvin Guyer, who is both a psychologist and an attorney, observed, "There's a social hysteria about child abuse. It began with the McMartin Pre-School case and continued with Woody Allen. There has been a feeding frenzy in which the ordinary presumptions of innocence are not applied. The allegations are treated as evidence. The public gets to be puritanical and voyeuristic at the same time. Their attitude is basically, 'This food is terrible, and there's not enough of it.'"

Other experts express skepticism over the charges. Lynne Gold-Bikin, chairman of the family-law section of the American Bar Association, noted that the child in question was in the center of a messy custody battle between mother and father. She cautioned that such children are notoriously unreliable witnesses, because they are trying to protect themselves by pleasing both parents, which cannot be done. J. Randy Tarborrelli, who has written biographies on several celebrities, including Jackson, said that everybody he talked with about Jackson wanted huge sums of money to tell anything. That was not Tarborrelli's experience when doing books about Diana Ross, Cher, Carol Burnett, and Roseanne Arnold.

Attorney Guyer says that the very allegations against Jackson have turned him into a Humpty Dumpty in that he can never put his reputation back together again, just as happened with Pee-Wee Herman and Woody Allen. Professor Richard Epstein of the University of Chicago Law School made the point about the irony of the power of the weak in society. "The strong are subject to the depredations of the weak, but they cannot effectively retaliate in kind. That's one of the problems of being rich and famous." He also cites a corollary rule: "Another problem is that many celebrities start to think that ordinary rules don't apply to them. A likelihood of serious misconduct may arise."

Elizabeth Taylor flew to Michael's side overseas and finally bundled Michael off to a London clinic for treatment of what was claimed to be his long-standing addiction to painkillers.

This got him out of sight for a time and postponed examination of his genitals by the Los Angeles authorities to see if they matched the description given by his thirteen-year-old accuser. Patricia Smith, a reporter for the *Boston Globe*, said that should cause Michael no trauma, since he has always been naked.

The fall of Michael Jackson has been a tragedy to many of his fans, but especially so to those who are black and who hold Michael, Oprah, and Bill Cosby in special reverence because of what they symbolize to their fellow African Americans. Donu Kogbara, writing for the *Manchester Guardian*, gave voice to the confusion and hurt of Michael's black fans. "Since the news of Michael Jackson's alleged paedophilia burst upon a world hungry for juicy scandals, I and many other black people have been even more depressed than we were when Mike Tyson was jailed for rape. He is our Michael—just as Oprah Winfrey and Bill Cosby belong to us in a way that they will never belong to their non-black devotees. I have only encountered two types of reaction from blacks [about Michael's situation]. Some have muttered about racist conspiracies and offered unconditional support. . . . Others have gone in for the clucking exasperation one reserves for self-destructive naive [friends]. Even if he wins, he'll never recover from the mud slinging. Nor will we, his loyal and long-suffering black fans who have watched with mounting dismay his narrowing nose, his whitening skin, his bizarre hermit tendencies and his refusal to get himself a grown-up lifestyle."

USA Today reviewer Edna Gundersen was dazzled by the program, saying she was fairly sure Michael was a carbon-based life-form with a Y chromosome and exceptional vocal cords, but didn't know much more before the Oprah interview.

Of course, if she could only repeat the interview today, with the controversy swirling around Michael, Oprah would be in heaven. She would probably want to know where the parents were during all of Michael's alleged child abusing. It's the question everyone wants the answer to and nobody is asking out loud. Oprah would.

Ex-employees were flipping in different directions, some with questionable motivation. Two Filipino employees claimed to have direct knowledge of his abuse of little children and were willing to talk about it on TV for money and in the courtroom if they returned to the United States from the Philippines. Some ex-drivers and bodyguards also claimed to have direct information they were willing to sell to the tabloids or whoever wanted it. By November 1993, things got too hot in the United States for Norma Staikos, who was manager of Jackson's estate, Neverland, so she and her husband left the country and returned to their native Greece.

As things grew worse, Michael finally returned to the United States and Neverland under heavy guard and weeks later made a four-minute impassioned plea for understanding on nationwide television that probably raised as many questions as it was supposed to answer.

Of course, an even bigger interview is probably in the making now that Michael, one rock king, has married Lisa Marie Presley, the daughter of another rock king. The programmers at every talk show including Oprah's are scrambling to interview the newlyweds. May 26, 1994, in a quickie ceremony in the Dominican Republic Lisa became Mrs. Lisa Marie Presley-Jackson and announced, "I'll dedicate my life to being his wife." There was disbelief until it was officially confirmed by the *New York Times* and blessed by *Daily Variety* with one of it's trademarked headlines, "It's official: Glove at first sight; now wedlock."

The couple honeymooned at Donald Trump's Mar-A-Lago estate in Palm Beach while everybody was asking why? Some speculated the match was fostered by the Church of Scientology of which both are members. A media psychologist at California State University, Stuart Fischoff, expressed a common view that, "She's marrying a cultural Mount Rushmore. For him, the cynical view is this could dissuade people that he's been fooling around with boys."

In January 1994, Jackson made an out-of-court multi-million-dollar settlement with the boy's family and hoped that it would all go away. The thirteen-year-old boy's father, a Beverly Hills dentist, decided on taking a leave of absence from his practice and sent a letter to his patients: "As you may know, we are going through some trying times right now." Michael Jackson could say the same thing.

27

Noprah: The Book

During the week of May 22, 1992, Oprah announced that she was writing her autobiography for Alfred A. Knopf as a reflection on her life as she approached her fortieth birthday in 1994. She stipulated at the outset that it was not to be an all-white project—she would need a ghostwriter and an editor—and that race was a factor. Knopf accommodated and gave Oprah a white ghostwriter, Joan Barthel, and a black editor, Errol MacDonald.

Her motivation to write her autobiography came from her thinking about her life "as I near my fortieth birthday in January 1994." The publication of the book itself would excite the publishing world.

After years of wooing by the publishers, who rightly saw her life story as one to inspire, entertain, and educate millions, she agreed to be published by Alfred Knopf, America's most prestigious book-publishing imprint. So the process began.

When the word got out to booksellers around the nation, it was as if the White Sox had actually won the pennant; as if Elvis had shown up at the Memphis airport; as if John F. Kennedy were restored to the White House; or, even closer, as if they had finally found that pot of gold at the end of the publishing rainbow. Millions of people dote on her daytime show, and every one of them was going to rush into the nearest bookstore and buy three copies of her autobiography: one to be left to the purchaser's children, one to read for herself, and one to give to a best friend. It was going to be the publishing and bookselling bonanza of the age.

On Memorial Day weekend, 1993, Oprah's attendance at the annual American Booksellers Association (ABA) Miami convention was a triumphal procession. Feted everywhere she went, she spoke to eighteen hundred mesmerized booksellers in the huge luncheon room. She told them that her book was about her life and, more importantly, about people and how they can "empower" (a favorite word) themselves. More important to booksellers, she told them that her book would bring people into their bookstores who had never entered one in their lives. She brought the booksellers to their feet.

When she walked off the stage in Miami to thunderous applause, the booksellers, moved by visions of enormous sales, were also genuinely touched by Oprah and what she said.

Oprah should have felt inspired; in truth, she was very depressed. She would later explain what she was actually thinking to herself behind the smiles and the waves and the bubbly portrait she projected of herself. "Oh, God, what have I done? I've said I've written this great book, but I don't think what I've promised is what I have." Soon after, she announced to the publishing world that she was indefinitely postponing release of her book in spite of the fact that it had essentially been completed by Oprah's ghostwriter. The stunned silence, bewildered head shaking, and lame explanations left everybody searching for a breath of fresh air to clear their heads. The bottom line for booksellers was that there was going to be no Oprah blockbuster pyramided in the store windows in the peak fall buying season of 1993.

Whatever the book world anticipated Oprah's autobiography would be, it was something entirely different to Oprah. The process of reviewing her life, evaluating what she was and had done, and explaining—less to the reader than herself—had a cathartic effect and made Oprah reexamine where she had been and what had happened along the way. A central revelation formed during this process. It became clear to Oprah that throughout her life, as hard as she struggled at everything she did to please other people, she never felt she was doing enough well enough. Some of the things she had to confront in her autobiography included her continual weight problem, her promiscuous teen years, as reflected in her later relationships with men, and her connections with the people important in her life.

Her ghostwriter, Joan Barthel, had done a craftswoman's job in laying out the apparent milestones of her life with details about the what, when, where, who, and how. It was a workmanlike autobiography that followed the traditional pattern of celebrity autobiographies: hello—born, went to school, got a job, got that award, hobbies, and lists of likes and dislikes. Perfectly normal and routine and not Oprah.

Oprah, in one of her myriad explanations about why she didn't go ahead with the book, said that she wanted a work that would provide insight into, and critical evaluation of, her life. Oprah needed to answer the question "why" so that she could understand the why of her life herself and then impart the answer to her readers and fans so that it would empower them to be who and what they wished to be in their lives. Oprah hoped her autobiography would serve as a therapeutic experience for her and for her followers—not just the road map of some celebrity's life.

Oprah needed to draw out the energy of companions and colleagues to recharge herself and jump-start Oprah in the right direction. Therefore, soon after the American Booksellers Association convention, she called on seven intimate friends and asked for their assessment of her book in the form it then existed. The results were depressing and reassuring. They were depressing because they were largely negative. Stedman is quoted by one source as saying, "Well, we have all the details of your life, but who is this going to help? I thought you wanted to write a book that would empower people." Oprah didn't like what he said but saw his viewpoint as a valid criticism.

Some people think that Stedman was shocked at the revelations of Oprah as "a sexually active adolescent." That is, she was having sex with every boy who wanted it because she knew that was what the boy desired and she didn't want to make them angry or disappointed with her. She had sex to be popular, and it worked for a time, until she got pregnant.

The book revealed that the pattern continued into adulthood, when Oprah became infatuated with one man after another, always choosing the guy who would mistreat her the most. She felt that was what she deserved and probably got pleasure from the punishment. Such an attitude could hardly inspire a man who is in love with a woman and wants to spend the rest of his life with her enjoying affectionate sleep-in Sunday mornings and long walks in the brisk Indiana twilight with their five golden retrievers. Perverse as it is, the old saw that mommy told us a long time ago has always been true and continues as a verity between men and women: Every man wants to be a woman's first, and every woman wants to be a man's last.

The meeting proved reassuring because it confirmed Oprah's personal sense that this version of the manuscript was not the story she wanted friends, fans, and family to read about on a midsummer day at the beach. Not that writing the manuscript was a loss; it allowed Oprah to open the psychic cupboard and release all the demons that had been screeching and scratching inside. She was forced to endure that same introspection she demands of her TV show guests.

For example, her weight demon. Food obviously gives us all nourishment, but we also connect it to all sorts of sexual, religious, and economic rituals. We shower the bride and groom with rice as a symbol of fertility; we kill living animals as a sacrifice to please our gods; we follow strict dietary laws about dairy products in order to appeal to the deities we worship; we know that food has a delightful effect when we eat caviar or chocolate; and food can affect sexual appeal.

In the age of the French court of Louis XIV, well-endowed, rounded women were popular, and in the Jazz Age of F. Scott Fitzgerald, flat-chested, anorexic women became the desired partners. Today the cult of anorexic women competes with the cult of big-busted women. All desperately use food as a tool to gain acceptance from friends, family, a man, or or an audience. The American College of Sports Medicine estimates 62 percent of the female athletes in gymnastics, ballet, figure skating, and long distance running are anorexic or bulimic to please their coaches, judges, and fans. That includes gymnastic stars such as Cathy Rigby and Christy Henrich. Henrich dieted, starved, and vomited herself down to fifty-two pounds when all the vital organs in her body gave up and she died on July 26, 1994 at the age of twenty-two. Being sexually desirable is the weapon women have always had to control men and extract from those obtuse creatures what women want for themselves. Food plays a critical role in making oneself sexually desirable just as it does when a woman wants to keep men away. One defense is to use food to become sexually undesirable.

For Oprah, food has been a bridge over bad times that could make her spirits rise when her fortunes were crashing down. The use of food—or abstinence—would allow her to become sexually desirable to a man when she wanted to be seductive. In food, Oprah has had a metaphor for her life. It is a measure of her happiness and a mark of her success. She is notorious for ballooning up and down the scale.

But the book made her look behind the fact of food to the why of food in her life. Oprah says the eating was her way of apologizing to the world and announcing that while she was rich, with a great life and boyfriend, she was still fat, so, see, she didn't have everything. Given her history of eating to cope with depression, that sounds more anecdotal than accurate.

Dr. Kathryn Zerbe, an eating disorder expert and author of *The Body Betrayed* says there is an increasing incidence of eating disorders.

Laura Randolph interviewed Oprah for *Ebony* magazine after Oprah canceled publication. Randolph characterized the book incident this way: "[She drew] from the well of rage of someone who was desperate—desperate to be liked. . . . The possibility of living for herself without caring who thought what about her did not take root for Oprah until she did this book."

Finally, the publisher's spokesman, William T. Loverd, revealed that the book wasn't juicy enough, that Oprah felt there wasn't enough of herself in it, and that it had not been written as best it could be, which contradicts what Oprah said. Loverd's boss, Knopf president Sonny Mehta, added to the confusion by saying, "Oprah has written an extremely strong and honest book."

Oprah insists that writing the book was a great act of self-discovery for her, adding it "opened my mind in ways that I would not have unless I had the time devoted to years of therapy. I'm just trying to step back from that and assess what does that all really mean."

Meanwhile, Zebra Books rushed into print a biography of Oprah in 1993 under the byline Nellie Bly. A real Nellie Bly existed at one time. Decades ago she had been an intrepid reporter for the Hearst newspapers in New York. This Nellie Bly is actually Sarah Ballick, the executive editor at Kensington Books, which is a publishing sister to Zebra. Meanwhile, Oprah's collaborator, Joan Barthel, believes that Oprah is still going to do her book but isn't sure when, according to Ms. Barthel's agent, Joy Harris.

One of the ironies of all the uproar over Oprah's book is that she has been a wonderful promoter of other people's books. As previously mentioned, many authors have had only modest success with the sales of their books until they have appeared on the *Oprah Winfrey Show*. An appearance can make the sales of an author's book skyrocket. Examples are rampant of Oprah's ability to promote books, and for that matter, record albums. Sales of Marianne Williamson's book and Michael Bolton's record album, for example, were energized after Oprah's endorsement.

An unusual example was the cookbook that was spawned on Oprah's November 23, 1993, show with her personal chef, Rosie Daley, as they talked and demonstrated preparation of tasty, low-fat meals. From this program there evolved an extraordinary cookbook, *In the Kitchen With Rosie: Oprah's Favorite Recipes*, published by Alfred Knopf on May 8, 1994. *In the Kitchen With Rosie* may take some of the pain away for Knopf from the 1993 cancellation of Oprah's autobiography, because the cookbook became the fastest-selling hardcover book in the history of American publishing. Before it was officially released on May 8, 1.4 million advance copies were sold by bookstores all over the country, and everybody was scrambling to reorder.

The national bookstore chain Barnes & Noble reported that it sold twenty thousand copies the first day it put Rosie's cookbook on display, sending Barnes & Noble executive Maureen Golden into the high sierras of happiness. "It's bigger than *Scarlett*, bigger than Madonna, bigger than Rush and Howard," she exclaimed. Oprah has helped make all this possible by appearing on the dust jacket with Rosie, writing the introduction to the book, and sprinkling her comments throughout. When the book was launched and obviously a runaway bestseller and sure to bring Ms. Daley enormous profits for a long time, Oprah smiled at Rosie and said, "Merry Christmas—for life."

The *New York Times* reported in it's "Eating Well" column by Marian Burros that the cookbook was selling so fast it was breaking best-seller list records all over the country and Rosie's publicity agent didn't care whether or not anybody interviewed Rosie. Who needed it, after all, with the endorsement of Oprah? Robert Wietrak, a director of merchandising at Barnes and Nobel, raved, "This is the biggest, I mean the biggest. No one on the planet could have predicted this." The yogurt chicken is his favorite.

Although it is not promoted as a low-fat cookbook everybody understands that it contains the magic secret, the elixir of happiness sought after by women everywhere, of how to lose weight without starving or eating blah food. Rosie's approach is to substitute ingredients without substituting the two Ts: texture and taste. The central secret is heavy spices that makes bland food blast the taste buds.

Meanwhile, there are two printing crews working 24-hours a day to generate 200,000 of Rosie's cookbooks every day in order to keep up with the demand. So far, more than four million copies have been sold.

The power of Oprah in the world of books is such that everyone wants to appear on her program to tout their works. Conversely, most publishers are afraid of offending Oprah for fear she might ban their authors from touting their books on her show. One estimate is that an appearance on the *Oprah Winfrey Show* is worth at least 100,000 copies in book sales. That is awesome and intimating clout for someone reluctant to release her own book.

CHAPTER

28

The Weight-Struggle Diary

$\mathcal{A}$bout her weight struggle, Oprah told Jane Pauley in 1991, "I was a total compulsive eater for most of my life. That's how I worked out my junk. Other people work it out through alcohol or drugs or—or just bad relationships. . . . You know, mine, you know, comes out in my hips. The whole weight thing has been a burden to me, but not a burden the way other people assume it to be. For me, the weight is me trying to protect myself or feeling fearful or not being all that I really could be."

Even for those who were accustomed to Oprah's constant references to her weight, her November 22 and 23, 1993, shows were remarkable. The key parts of the programs revolved around excerpts from Oprah's private dairy, which chronicled her journal through her private dieting hell, starting back on the night of November 15, 1988, after she did the "little red wagon" show.

That night, Oprah wrote in her diary that she had experienced a moment of ebullience unlike any she had ever known during her ten-year-long battle with fat. She ended her diary entry with "It's finally over." Sadly, it was only beginning again, like the struggle of the mythological Sisyphus damned by the gods to roll a huge rock to the top of a mountain, only to have it roll back down.

The frustration about weight surfaced in her diary again on November 29, just two weeks after the day of exhilaration, when she could get into a pair of size 10 jeans. She lamented to her diary that she had gained five pounds in those two weeks and was up to 150 because she was out of control with her eating. "I've got to bring it to an end," she pleaded with herself.

On December 13, she wrote that she was back eating junk food and that she couldn't figure out how to stay thin and didn't really know the right food to eat. She wistfully asked her diary how she was ever going to make it through the holidays without putting on weight. The answer came in her entry for the day after Christmas. She had gained five more pounds and didn't want to a attend a party to which she was invited in Aspen because of it.

The year 1989 began, and Oprah told her diary she was going to start dieting again on January 2. Instead, she confessed that she made pork chops and ate them. She was asking the diary what she could do; the idea of fasting again repelled her. It was something she didn't think she could manage.

By January 7 she was reciting to her diary, "I'm out of control," because she started the day fasting, then broke down and had three bowls of raisin bran, later followed by caramel and cheese corn. She came back to her house and stood staring at the food in the cabinets and dreaming about french fries with tons of salt on them.

By January 19, she weighed 158 pounds and panicked, for she felt on the verge of the abyss again, compulsively eating everything she could lay her hands on and dismally concluding that she had to get professional counseling, which she promised her diary she would do the following Monday. When Monday the twenty-first came, she shamefacedly admitted to her diary, "I lied to myself about professional counseling. I'm not ready to submit to it."

Six weeks later, on March 9, 1989, she confided to her diary a prayer over her frustration, saying that what she wished for was to get rid of weight as a factor in her life. She told the diary that she desperately wanted not to eat or drink anything that would keep her from her goal of losing weight.

The next weight entry jumped ahead to the one-year anniversary of her famous "little red wagon" show, written November 14 on the day of her anniversary show, when she weighed 168 pounds. "I'm thoroughly disgusted with myself. I couldn't even get thin for the anniversary show. Where is my resolve? Every day I awaken with good intentions, and then I fail."

Nine days later it was Thanksgiving, 1989, and Oprah had gained another seven pounds. "I've lost my resolve trying to find a way to carry on the battle." Another week and Oprah again expressed the depth of her frustration. She cooked a dinner of chicken and rice for the thin Stedman, and she was only supposed to have salad but downed a generous helping of the chicken and rice instead. "I'm still battling what has been for me a lifetime struggle. I'm going to lick this, I just don't know how right now." Two weeks passed, and the new Harpo Productions studio remodeling was coming along well. She had much going for her, and yet she wondered to her diary, "Everything's going so well, so why do I still feel compelled to eat?"

Two months passed, and she was up to 180 pounds. "I'm in dire need of help with my weight, almost on the verge of being overcome." She had a specialist come in and analyze her hair to see what vitamins she needed and admitted that she was still looking for the miracle cure to her weight problem. "I'm not inching, but galloping toward the 200-pound mark." By April 28, 1990, she was exhausted from working on the *Brewster Place* project, and her long hours forced her to eat from the snack table in the studio—fatty, high-calorie foods. By June 12, she writes, "I'm carrying fat around. It's overcoming me, 191 pounds overcome." Six days later she chastises herself: "I woke up the past four days hating myself because I hadn't fasted or at least stuck to some kind of plan."

From 168 pounds in mid-November, 1989, she had gone to 180 in mid-February and 191 at the beginning of June. She was looking fatter and dumpier with each passing week, until her key executive producer talked with her privately in the middle of August about her weight and her badly fitting clothes. On August 15 she wrote in her diary, "I cried in my office with Debra.... I cried for my poor miserable self having gotten to this state. Scale said 203 this morning. Controlled—just controlled by it....By the end of the day...feeling diminished, less of a person, guilty, ugly...."

Three weeks after her thirty-seventh birthday, she went on vacation and returned weighing a record 226 pounds.

Since her life is on public parade at all times, Oprah had the honesty to do a show in December 1990, about the collapse of her Optifast success diet, entitled "The Pain of Regain." The point she made then was that "if you lose weight on a diet, sooner or later you'll gain it back."

"I've been dieting since 1977," she woefully admits, "and the reason I failed is that diets don't work. I tell people, if you are underweight, go on a diet and you'll gain everything you lost plus more. Now I'm trying to end a way to life in a world with food without being controlled by it, without being a compulsive eater. That's why I say I will never diet again."

One study by the National Center for Health Statistics says that 27 percent of American women are overweight, and according to Dr. Keith Berndtson, a weight-management doctor at Rush-Presbyterian-St. Luke's Medical Center in Chicago, 95 percent of the weight lost from dieting is regained unless the patient exercises, which most of them don't do.

A colleague of Dr. Berndtson's, Dr. Theodore B. Van Itallie, says, "If patients simply lose weight and then don't make permanent changes in eating and exercise, regain is inevitable. Oprah's experience shouldn't be used to discourage people from legitimate weight loss, but simply to point out the problem of maintenance and to stress the long-term nature of the commitment. People must exercise, monitor their eating, and recognize early that they're regaining weight, but often they deny it until they get so fat that they can't hide anymore."

That's what Oprah did. For one thing, she dropped out of her diet group and thus gave up her support group. The reason had to do with her celebrity. She was afraid somebody in her group would be feeding information on her to the tabloids, and she was probably right.

Certainly the tabloids monitor her every move—part of the price of being a multimillionaire star—because her fans savor every tidbit about her life and use her as an adored role model. So everybody knew when she stopped shopping at Chicago's chichi Oak Street boutique for slender women, Ultimo, and started shopping again at the Forgotten Woman, Chicago's store for large, full-figured women.

Also, she dumped her exercise program and stopped working out regularly. "I thought I was cured, and that's just not true," she said. "You have to live in a world with food." The resulting regain was predictable and inevitable.

It's a problem she also shares with many big—in both senses—stars, such as Delta Burke, Susan Ruttan, Jennifer Holliday, Elizabeth Taylor, Dom DeLuise, and Roseanne Barr. Many of these stars, including Oprah, are saying what she said about diets. Essentially, to hell with it. I am who I am and take it or leave it. They want to show the public that they can be just as sassy, sexy, and with it as skinny stars.

Roseanne says there's a sexist double standard. "A fat man's called a big guy, but a fat woman is always just a sexless pig." At one taping of her TV show in 1991, Roseanne, at 240 pounds, and her husband, at 320 pounds, got into a physical confrontation over a single chocolate chip cookie.

Embarrassed afterward, they decided to put a fancy gym into their home and hire personal trainer Ray Sommers to get their weight down, and it worked for a time. Still, Roseanne, who has tried every diet known to man plus three yet to be invented, calls them all "big ripoffs that exploit people in pain. Being fat is a symptom of a deeper psychological problem." Oprah says the same thing, and this plays well with many women in the audience, because they, too, have endured the frustration of dieting without lasting success. Also, it is part of the new culture of the victim, where no one is responsible for his or her actions anymore.

In Oprah's case, she is the victim. She reasons that she was not fat as a child, so something happened along the way to victimize her and turn her into a fat adult. She claims she was a wounded and abused child, molested over and over again from the age of nine, when she was raped, until she became a tough and savvy fourteen-year-old able to defend herself. She endured all of that without getting fat, and then she became a television personality at nineteen in Nashville. "I was first put in a really stressful situation," she said, and she turned to food for solace and serenity. Roseanne Arnold blames her weight on her being an incest victim, and her husband blames it on his past drug and booze problems. In any case, Oprah loves all the attention the public gives her and hates the attention it gives her weight.

"I'm just sick of it," she exclaims. "Sick sick sick sick sick sick sick sick sick sick. We all make it an issue. I'm as guilty of that as anybody. I would like to reach a point where it is not an issue with me. I wish that I'd kept my weight off, but I do not feel like a failure. I feel like someone who has a weight problem. I feel like, oh, another forty million Americans who are dealing with this in their lives."

Still, Oprah refused to give up the dream of a diet that would bring happiness. She is particularly anxious about her love affair with Stedman Graham, who is tall, slender, and drop-dead handsome to the point that, as we have seen, many of her close friends can't believe this movie-star male could love chubby Oprah unless it was for her money.

After years of waiting, they finally got engaged, and while they were set to marry in 1993, it didn't happen. Oprah, who wanted children, was now facing an unhappy fortieth birthday, with the genetic clock ticking and the secret belief that her weight is keeping Stedman from marrying her. "Who wants to get it on with a fat woman in bed?" she sadly asks herself.

Stedman says they will marry when they will marry— hardly the answer a woman wants to hear. He asked Oprah during a weekend at their getaway farm in Indiana, "Do you think I could only view you, with all you have to offer, as a person with a weight problem? Look, if you're happy, I'm happy." Still, Oprah isn't happy and goes back to dieting.

She said, "My greatest failure was believing that the weight issue was just about weight. Dieting is not about weight. It's about everything else that's not going right in your life."

The moment of decision for Oprah came in June 1992, when she had ballooned to the highest weight in her life, 235 pounds, and decided she knew why her attempts at dieting weren't working.

"Three-quarters of my life has been spent in a state of constant diet," she declared. "I came to believe that if the food tasted good, it was loaded with calories. If something was good for you and low in calories, it tasted that way. But now I realize that good-for-you food can taste good, too."

She still thinks she had to be ready emotionally before she could whip the fat cells, and she shares this belief with her army of fans along with a new "Stay Slim Forever Diet" and a list of dos and don'ts. Part of her being ready emotionally had, as with most everything she does, a spiritual element to it.

"What I've learned through my thirteen-year ordeal with weight is that you really can't begin to work on the physical until you first get at what's holding you back emotionally. The reason we don't move forward in our lives is because of the fears that hold us back, the things that keep us from being all that we were meant to be.

"I believe we were all brought to the planet for a purpose. It took me fifteen years to face my deepest fears, which I couldn't admit to anybody, including myself. My biggest fear was not being able to confront. I had a fear of not being liked. Plus, I had a fear of saying no. I ruled my life by what other people wanted me to do. It was an emotional problem that manifested itself physically. I never really allowed myself to feel anything, because I covered it up with food."

Since she started running regularly in August, Oprah has clocked twenty-three hundred miles jogging and has turned on to a low-fat, good-tasting, nutritious diet. The result is that she is now down to 150 pounds, with only 20 percent of that body fat. Her bra size dropped from 44DD to 36C.

"I hated myself because of my weight, but I want America to know that my fiancé, Stedman Graham, has loved my heart and loved me no matter what size I was. He stood by me."

In spite of that inspirational thought, you have to wonder if Oprah herself believes her weight didn't matter in her love life.

What may finally be the answer to Oprah's weight problem came when she met and hired a chef who could cook diet foods in a delicious way. In constrast to Oprah, Rosie Daley is a petite white Irish-American woman from a big New Jersey family. Rosie and Oprah met during Oprah's stay at the Cal-a-Vie spa in California in the spring of 1991. Oprah was so taken by the delicious low-fat food that she took Rosie aside and tried to hire her. Rosie politely turned Oprah down, just as she had Paula Abdul and others before her. She loved her job and enjoyed California as a place to raise her twelve-year-old son. Oprah persisted, calling, cajoling, pleading, promising, and demanding, and finally Rosie gave in and moved to Chicago, where she is still trying to make the transition from California.

At the beginning, when Rosie started working for Oprah, in September 1991, Oprah was filled with good intentions, but she had also had a lifetime of bad eating habits, developed in the South, where food is deep-fried, swimming in gravy, loaded with butter, and scarce on vegetables. So Rosie tried to give Oprah the kind of food experience she liked—textured, crunchy, spicy food, without the calories and the fat, such as she had been used to in her childhood. Oprah understood that it was an emotional problem, as she has said repeatedly. In her introduction to Rosie's bestselling cookbook, Oprah said she knew the role food has played in her life beyond the basic nourishment. "Food meant security and comfort. Food meant love. It didn't matter what you ate, just that you had enough. I've paid a heavy price for believing that."

Rosie won't talk about what she's paid but admits that it is quite generous, given that she is virtually at Oprah's constant call and has to be where Oprah is most of the time, whether in Chicago or the Indiana farm or in Hollywood or New York.

Rosie began cooking as the ninth of thirteen children when she discovered at age six that if you cooked you didn't have to wash dishes. She wanted to be an artist and moved from her home state of New Jersey to Encinitas, California, to be close to one of her older sisters, and sustained herself working in seafood and health-food restaurants. She married a carpenter, Billy St. John, and had her son before they divorced, then took a job as a cook's helper at the Cal-a-Vie in 1989. Her twelve-year-old son continues to live with Rosie's sister in Encinitas.

Her approach was to combine her artistic inclination with the knowledge she had gained about health-food cooking; she thinks of food as an artistic creation that is eaten—sort of consumable art. Her normal schedule is to walk four blocks each workday morning to Oprah's luxurious condo, where she prepares lunch and snacks for Oprah and delivers them to Harpo Studios. Then Rosie goes back to the condo to prepare dinner for Oprah and Stedman. Following that, she sets up fresh juice and muffins for breakfast and then goes home. She is a lucky chef in that a full-time maid takes care of all the cleanup afterward. Spare time is spent with her boyfriend, who, not surprisingly, works in a restaurant. Rosie and Oprah are a good combination together, with the tasteful method to weight loss a blessing for Oprah and the lifelong security the association with Oprah has brought to Rosie. They are both enriched, and Oprah has come up with several cooking tips:

- Always go for good taste—don't punish yourself.
- Steam veggies—Don't fry them in oil.
- Check food labels—watch out for high fat content.
- Have more variety than just fruit and veggies.
- Avoid salt—use stimulating spices in its place.
- Use nonfat items (nonfat yogurt) for cream sauces.

With her personal chef, Rosie Daley, playing fat cop for Oprah, a great change slowly started taking place, and Oprah has lost 72 pounds in eight months, leading up to her November 23, 1993, show entitled "Welcome to Oprah and Rosie's Cooking School." Oprah and Rosie talked while Rosie demonstrated ways to cook tasty, low-fat dishes for the audience. Oprah has come up with three rules for successful weight control out of her association with Rosie:

OPRAH'S THREE-STEP SYSTEM
1. *Food Is Not The Enemy*
   You have to rethink your attitudes toward food. It is not your enemy. Instead, it is here to make you feel good and keep you strong.

2. *Eat Only What's Right*

The big secret is that *food can taste good and also be good for you!* If you pay attention, you can find plenty of foods that are low-calorie and low-fat that also are fun to eat, taste good, and are nutritious. Oprah cut down her fat intake dramatically by shunning fried foods, cooking with nonstick sprays, and carefully checking labels for fat content. Your mouth can't tell the difference, but your hips can. Also, the introduction of nonfat salad dressings, cream cheese, and even cinnamon rolls is making it a lot easier.

3. *Have A Fun Exercise*

People are driven away from exercise by the silly macho slogan No Pain, No Gain. Who on earth except a sicko goes out *seeking* pain?

It is possible to find an exercise that you really enjoy so that you welcome the chance to do it. In Oprah's case it's jogging, skiing, and working out with her personal trainer, Bob Greene. However, walking is the simplest, least stressful, and easiest exercise. Greene says walking is the number-one exercise for weight loss because it's free and puts little strain on the joints. Dr. Dean Ornish, author of the bestselling book *Eat More and Weigh Less*, is a strong advocate of walking twenty to thirty minutes every day as the preferred form of exercise.

This is the weight regime that Oprah is following and it seems to be working.

29

1994—Gateway to More Millions

The new year opened with the fulfillment of a promise that Oprah had made to the dead Angelica Mena. She stood over President Clinton's shoulder in the Roosevelt Room of the White House and watched him sign into law a bill that had become known as "the Oprah bill" (It was officially called the National Child Protection Act.) It establishes a national database of all indictments and convictions for child abuse, sex offenses, violent crimes, arson, and felony drug charges. Joining the president and Oprah for the occasion was Health and Human Services secretary Donna Shalala; author Andrew Bachss, who has written about child abuse; former Illinois governor Jim Thompson, whom Oprah had hired to shepherd the bill through Congress; Rep. Pat Schroeder of Colorado; Sen. Joseph Biden of Delaware; Children's Legal Defense Fund president Marian Wright Edelman; and former football great Lynn Swann. The bill created national data that anyone providing child-care services can check to see if a prospective employee can be trusted with children.

As 1994 began, the ratings came in spelling happiness and sadness for various talk-show hosts. Oprah, still the number-one talk show in America, went up another 12 percent in the ratings to a 11.5 point share of the viewing audience. Geraldo did well, with a 10 percent gain, but that only brought him up to a 4.3 point share. Les Brown, King World's hopeful talk-show entry of last year, dropped to a 2.3 point share and was canceled. Other talk shows dropped in the ratings but were still profitable. Donahue dived 9 percent to a 6.1 point rating, and Sally Jessy Raphael plunged 10 percent to a 5.6 point rating, but both of them were ahead of Geraldo.

Oprah's 11.5 point share meant that 11.5 percent of all the television sets on at the time she was on the air were tuned to her show. One point, or 1 percent share, is about 942,000 households in which there may be one or more viewers.

The number-one syndicated show continued to be King World's *Wheel of Fortune*, with a point rating of 16.8, up 14 percent. So it promised another good year for King World, with the three top-rated syndicated programs in the country still *Wheel*, *Jeopardy*, and *Oprah*. As one executive at competitor Multimedia assessed the talk shows, "There's Oprah, and then everybody else drops way off after her."

In his assessment of the competition, the feisty, plainspoken Roger King is mean and direct. "Geraldo is the worst television ever produced," he says. "They ought to go back and look at what they are putting on the air. When you talk about good talk, you talk about Oprah Winfrey. She has respect for her viewers. She doesn't overexploit every possible minority in the country. (Geraldo) has neo-Nazis and the KKK on there, who don't like Jews, don't like blacks, and don't like Irish. That eliminates my whole company. Why should we give these people forums? Just to exploit it and pump up the numbers?" Roger King apparently was unaware that Oprah also has had Ku Klux Klan members and neo-Nazis on her show.

The beginning of 1994, as with the start of every year since she went national in 1986, brought the annual convention of the National Association of Television Programming Executives in Miami. Everywhere there were booths, hawkers, displays, and hostesses in ball gowns and bikinis and the omnipresent three-inch heels. Lyle Waggoner and his wife hustled a new show idea of theirs, *Here Comes the Bride*, by shaking hands with all comers under a big, pink sequined heart, while Jake Steinfeld, in the USA Direct infomercial booth, demonstrated a Firmflex bodybuilding machine. At the Home Shopping Network booth, Ivana Trump was autographing her book, and visitors to Disney's Buena Vista TV booth could be photographed with Aladdin and the Genie or with Siskel and Ebert, the well-known TV critics based in Chicago.

Also, a variety of celebrities greeted the station program executives to convince them to purchase reruns or new shows which would invariably boost ratings and commercial sales. Among them were Hulk Hogan, Jerry Seinfeld, the Laker Girls, Wink Martindale, Regis and Kathie Lee, Burt Reynolds, Ed McMahon, Susan Powter, Xuxa, the Pink Panther, World Wrestling Federation's Doink the Clown, and Samantha Martin from Zany Animal Stunts.

The Miami Beach High School Marching Band periodically paraded through the convention center, and inside the Paramount booth visitors were given an open bar and buffet. There are, in fact, so many booths serving snacks, food, drinks, and even meals that it is possible to spend the entire day wandering the convention center drinking and eating. Many of the visitors, however, preferred meals in quieter nearby restaurants, where business cards could be exchanged and deals made. In 1994 the most popular symbol of being a "with it person" was walking around the place with a cellular phone glued to your ear, as if Universal or Disney or ABC couldn't function without talking to you every five minutes.

Everybody was in the happy sales mood no matter what was going on inside his or her head, hustling, hyping, and hoping. Of the sixty-five new shows being offered at the NATPE convention, about a dozen would actually get on the air, and even the shows already on the air were nervous and selling because it's a fickle business and station programmers are always looking for something new and exciting.

Meanwhile, away from the exhibit floor seminar panelists earnestly discussed fin/syn, retransmission consent, and the effects of TV violence on our children. However, the most intense discussions on panels, in corridors, and over meals and drinks focused on one overriding issue: What makes a talk show succeed? Everybody knew that, if a talk show caught on with the viewing audience, it was a gold mine for the syndicators and the producers, which is why there was a terrible glut of shows on the air and a bigger glut of shows trying to get on the air.

The same question has plagued the producers and directors of creative performances since the beginning of time. What makes a successful movie or book or play or board game? William Goodman, well-known Hollywood writer, summarized the truth quite simply when he said that no one has the slightest idea. The best minds in filmmaking, book publishing, play production, television-talk-show creation, have researched, analyzed, and pondered, but no one knows the answer. For example, would the movie *Casablanca* have been a success if the lead stars had been Ronald Reagan and Rita Hayworth? Probably not, but they were the first choices, and the producers couldn't get them and were forced to settle for Humphrey Bogart and Ingrid Bergman. The same story can be told about scores of other movies and plays.

What makes Oprah a runaway success? January 21, 1994, *Variety* said: "the often overweight, sometimes svelte, black woman from Chicago is the undisputed queen of the medium and one of the most successful personalities of all time." What is her secret that can be applied universally?

Why does one woman comedienne, Jenny Jones, work and another woman comedienne, Joan Rivers, get canceled? Why does one black male motivation speaker, Montel Williams, succeed and another black male motivational speaker, Les Brown, fail?

Derk Zimmerman, president of Group W Productions, has researched the question carefully and concluded, "What we found, especially in daytime, is a real thirst for information, but information that is relevant to the individual viewer. That makes them feel they haven't wasted their time. They've learned something about what's going on around them. They've gotten something they can take away from the show and either use in a conversational sense or how to make yourself look better. Self-improvement. How to keep yourself fit. But I think you have to start with a compelling personality. I don't think daytime talk shows are format-driven as much as they are personality-driven."

Roger King's contribution to the debate was to disagree. He believes it is vital that the host is an entertainer, and after that "a talk show is topics, topics, topics."

This time the NATPE met in Miami, just as the American Booksellers Association convention had seven months earlier, when Oprah had been the star. In fact, that was the buzz about this convention."Where's Oprah?" Oprah usually showed up for the NATPE convention because as the main trade convention it was important, but at the 1994 meeting Oprah was nowhere to be found, and as with all such trade organizations, variations from the norm immediately brought rumors. When Oprah didn't appear, speculation instantly mounted about shaky relations with her syndicator, King World.

King World's bosses, Roger and Michael, dismissed the rumors with the wave of a hand, saying Oprah simply wanted to spend her fortieth birthday at home. In fact, she wasn't doing anything of the sort. She was spending her fortieth birthday at a lush Hollywood party. A spokesperson for Harpo Productions said simply that Oprah's schedule was too tight for her to attend the NATPE convention. "She was taping shows this week for the February ratings books, and she wants to celebrate her birthday this Saturday at a small dinner party given by friends."

None of these pronouncements calmed the rumor factory that said Oprah was seriously thinking about not renewing her contract with King World when it expired in 1995. On January 25, financial analysts attending the annual King World luncheon expected Stephen Palley, chief operating officer, to announce that Oprah had signed a new contract with the syndicator. Instead, he simply said they were in negotiations and the final contract had not been signed yet.

That statement fueled the rumor mill even more with talk that she was angry at all the Oprah imitators (Bertice Berry, et al.) who were trying to steal her niche, and she felt particularly betrayed by the King brothers for their rolling out a competitive show, *Rolonda*, featuring an outspoken black woman, Rolonda Watts.

According to *Daily Variety*, *Rolonda* features "a young, highly personable black woman with a background in broadcast journalism (which) hits a little too close to home." Moreover, King World was marketing *Rolonda* with the slogan Your Next Favorite Talk Show, as if Oprah were over the hill. Some people claimed that the King brothers were in fact selling *Rolonda* as the next Oprah.

The *Oprah Winfrey Show*, whose contract expired in 1995, was the centerpiece of King World's profits, accounting for gross revenues of $180 million a year, of which King World takes 43 percent, or about $77 million. That's why many observers thought the King brothers were stupid to annoy Oprah. They may have thought Oprah would be forced to renew with them in 1995 because her current contract forbade her from taking her show to another syndicator for two years after her contract with King World expires.

However, a woman with all of Oprah's millions could just sit out the two years and spend the time doing other high-profile things, such as movies. It seems like a classic cat-and-mouse game, with both sides thinking he or she was the cat. The additional twist, of course, was that earlier talk about a Cap Cities/ABC buyout of King World for $2.2 billion, which would be severely affected if Oprah were to announce she would not renew when her contract expired in September 1995. The value of King World shares would drop sharply, which, in turn, would hurt Oprah, since she was a major stockholder.

King World and Oprah continued to talk about renewing her contract, and by the middle of February negotiations had reached an impasse. The renewal of Oprah's contract, if it happened, would extend her relationship with King World until September 1997 and would make the possibility of selling King World for a major profit more likely. However, as of February 16, the Oprah renewal talks hit a snag, with Oprah refusing to agree to a renewal of the noncompetition clause that kept her from going to another syndicator for two years after she terminated her agreement with King World. This was not a minor issue; in Hollywood it was a "deal killer." It was reported that in the midst of negotiations, Oprah stood up, politely excused herself, walked out of the meeting, and never came back.

The suspension of negotiations brought immediate expressions of concern from many stations that carried Oprah, and this put additional pressure on King World to settle. "Every day that passes from now on makes it more questionable whether she is going to continue. There is no question that something is amiss," said Dick Kurlander, the director of programming at the station-representation firm Petry Television.

At the same time these negotiations were in progress, the results of the February sweeps weeks came out showing the *Oprah Winfrey Show* and *Maury Povich* as the big winners, with Oprah's ratings up 18 percent to a 10.6 percent share of the audience. Meanwhile, the new *Rolonda* show did badly, with a 17 percent drop to a 1.9 percent share, for last place among the talk shows and another demonstration that the King brothers could syndicate but couldn't produce.

Finally, on March 21 a deal was struck between Oprah and King World that extended her contract, giving King the exclusive right to distribute the *Oprah Winfrey Show* until the year 2000, which made King World a much more attractive takeover buy. In exchange, Oprah obtained an option on a million and a half shares of King World stock to add to the 1 million shares she already had. It gave her the outright option to buy another half-million shares plus additional options to buy another 250,000 shares a year each year she renews the show with King World from 1997 through 2000. Wall Street immediately reacted favorably to the deal and hiked King World stock 3³/4 to $39 a share. Oprah agreed to a five-year anticompetition clause, meaning she cannot go to another syndicator for five years if she leaves King World. On the other hand, if King World is sold or merged with another company, about which there is much speculation, the anticompetition clause is canceled.

Oprah received a large slice of the fees for first-run syndication. Before this contract, King World received 43 percent of the operating profit from the *Oprah Winfrey Show*; under the new contract, that will continue for two more years, after which the percentage drops to 35 percent and ultimately to 25 percent.

To pay for this very rich new contract, Roger and Michael King were on the road instantly, renegotiating their *Oprah Winfrey Show* agreements with stations to take them to the year 2000 at much higher prices. They are also renegotiating the contracts for *Wheel of Fortune* and *Jeopardy*, and while block booking and leveraging will be denied by King World, it is pretty much a given in this kind of situation.

Sure enough, April 11, 1994 *Variety* told the story with the headline "King World Ups Oprah's Price," going on to say that television stations wanting to keep Oprah on their schedule would have to be prepared to pay from 10 percent to 25 percent more than the $100,000–125,000 per week they were now paying, and in many major markets, over $160,000. The battle began in major cities such as Boston and Pittsburgh, where competing stations began bidding against each other for the show. King World, in addition to more money, also wanted a third commercial minute out of the twelve minutes that are in the show available for sale to advertisers. Up until now, King World had two minutes. It would take this third minute and sell it to national advertisers for more money.

All the stations paying that big money were surprised when the May ratings for the *Oprah Winfrey Show* dived. The two leading women talk-show hosts both dropped significantly in the April 18–24, 1994, Sweeps Week ratings. Oprah dropped 20 percent in the ratings to a 7.0 point share of the audience, which is the lowest she has been in five years! She is still way ahead of Sally Jessy Raphael, who also lost 14 percent of her audience, dropping to one of her lowest ratings, a 3.8 point share. Geraldo gained a little, to get a 3.3 point share of the audience, and Jenny Jones had a 2.7 point rating.

Overall, Oprah dropped from the fourth most popular syndicated program to a tie for seventh with *Roseanne*. Previously, she was bested only by King World's *Wheel of Fortune* and *Jeopardy*, with *Star Trek: The Next Generation* in third place. Dropping to seventh, Oprah is now surpassed by the same three as before plus *Entertainment Tonight*, and variations of *Star Trek* and *Wheel*: *Star Trek: Deep Space Nine* and *Weekend Wheel of Fortune*. Oprah is the only talk show in the top fifteen rankings for April 18–24. While none of this news was heartening, it also did not represent something to seriously worry about, since it was only one Sweeps Week rating. The only sweet thing about the ratings report for Oprah was that the look- and sound-alike the King brothers had been touting as "the next Oprah," Ms. Rolonda Watts, was in the cellar, with only 1.9 rating points. Once again it looks as if the King brothers have picked a loser.

For Oprah, the future is platinum. The exact figures fluctuate as the market changes, but today Oprah is worth around a third of a billion dollars. With her earnings between now and the turn of the century, she should add another $300 million. Add to that the reasonable increase in the value of her 2 million or more shares of King World, her real estate and movie income all adjusted for inflation, and she should be hovering around the $1 billion mark as we enter the new century.

CHAPTER

30

Is Oprah Dangerous to America's Health?

Few nations are as caught up in self-actualization and self-improvement as are Americans. Self-betterment books, courses, seminars, retreats, weekends, programs, videotapes, and audios are a multi-billion-dollar stock-in-trade of the American marketplace and communications system. We pay billions of dollars a year into the pockets of gurus, experts, motivators, expediters, seers, mediums, and preachers of doctrines, plans, and systems. We do it to become prettier, smarter, nicer, richer, more successful, and not so fat.

Critics of shows like Oprah's say they aren't serious, but some people take them to be and are misguided. Psychologists, sociologists, and some viewers see the *Oprah* show, for example, as trivializing important personal and social issues. They say that Oprah's shows exploit the troubled, disenchanted, and dysfunctional and that they do it to titillate and make a buck. They abuse people's natural curiosity about other people's private lives to humiliate, sensationalize, and profit from people's confusion and misery.

The *Oprah Winfrey Show* and the other talk shows have enormous impact. Dr. Harry Croft, San Antonio psychiatrist with his own talk show in Texas, says, "These shows have tremendous power to do a lot of potential good, but I worry that potential isn't used in the right way. If it were, they probably wouldn't get the good ratings they get."

Croft is one of a large number of behavioral health experts who feel that Oprah and the other talk-show hosts not only don't help people but actually hurt them. There were, of course, the cases of suicide or death caused by some shows, including two deaths attributed to Oprah's autoerotic mastur- bation show. While admitting that the shows have given publicity to previously little known social problems, such as incest, child abuse, and lesbian discrimination, and have allowed people to realize that their problems are common to many others, they also do injure people's lives.

For one thing, they lump human problems together and equalize them, which, in fact, trivializes them because "Wo- men Who Used to Be Men Marrying Men Who Used to Be Women" gets thrown in with "Child Abuse." Dr. Joyce Brothers notes that the sensational topic brings in the viewers like spectators to a freeway accident. "It tends to lessen the impact of these shows on more important topics." Conversely, these programs sensationalize exotic issues and make them seem more important than they are. For example, on one day in 1993, Oprah, Donahue, and Sally Jessy each had programs on the terrible and widespread threat to the American home, infidelity. That same day, the results of a national study were released revealing that only 15 percent of Americans were unfaithful to their spouses.

Also questionable are the people who volunteer to appear on these programs and look for some weird angle that will interest the program booker. Steve Wiegan, writing in the *Sacramento Bee*, said, "Upward of 10,000 people reportedly call Geraldo Rivera's 900 telephone number each week, hoping their claim to be part of some group like 'Trans-sexual Nazis Who Voted for Perot' will catch a producer's fancy."

Patricia Priest wrote her doctoral dissertation at the Univer- sity of Georgia and studied the motivations of people wanting to be on television talk shows. Some do it for personal ego, the chance to be famous for a few minutes, while many do it because they are promoting something—a viewpoint, a book, a product, a cause, or revenge against someone they feel has done them wrong. Some examples are Sherrol Miller, forty-five, a registered nurse from Louisville, Kentucky, who toured the talk shows as "the 10th Wife of a Gay Bigamist Con Man Who Died of Gangrene"; the High Priestess Sabrina Aset of the Church of the Most High Goddess, who wore a red-spangled minidress so she could perform her religious duty of having sex with every male in her congregation—a total of 2,686 men by her count; and the husband who discovered years later that his wife was a lesbian.

Interestingly, talk-show hosts such as Oprah, Donahue, and Sally Jessy refused to help Ms. Priest in her studies of talk-show-guest motivation. They wanted complete control over what she did and the material she developed. So she did her study independently, tracking down and interviewing talk-show guests directly or through their therapists.

She found that few of the guests needed to be remunerated to appear. They were willing to pay their own way to get on *Oprah* or *Donahue* to spread their message, talk about their lifestyle, or get their few minutes of fame. Many of them did not care for television talk shows and used them simply as a way to gain publicity. One of the main benefits for these guests was that they felt a validation of themselves or their lifestyle by having been on television. Many thought it was a way of opening up dialogue on controversial subjects in which they had an interest. Kate Bornstein, a forty-four-year-old transsexual lesbian; Joy Schulenbourg, a thirty-five-year-old gay parent; and Susan Henningson, a forty-five-year-old woman who married her sister's former husband, all felt they promoted better understanding of people in similar situations. They also felt empowered by appearing on television and that they had become some kind of social elite. Carol Austin, a forty-eight-year-old who had been through ten plastic-surgery operations, summarized the point of view: "If you're on the *Donahue* show, you've made it. There's nothing else other than maybe we could be invited to the White House for dinner."

Contrary to the view that *Oprah* and other talk shows are beneficial, studies by the American Psychological Association, reported by Frederick Thorne in the *Journal of Community*

Psychology, disagree. Studying the audience, the researchers noted "considerable frustration, conflict and maladjustment," and assessing the professional validity of the "expert" advice given the show was damning. The study said, "Evaluation of the advice provided by the guest 'experts' suggests that some advice is invalid, unrealistic and not always suited to particular groups of women. Actualization neuroses may arise from acquiring unrealistic personal goals and being made discontented with the status quo and that considerable harm might be done by widely disseminating unproven or inapplicable concepts which may have sensational appeal but are not solidly grounded in scientific fact." In other words, according to Frederick Thorne, the *Oprah Winfrey Show* could be dangerous to some people's health.

Another study done by Beatrice Robinson concluded that "neither professional nor lay experts [on these shows] use generally accepted standards of scholarship when communicating family knowledge to the TV audience."

The underlying point appears to be that many of those appearing on television talk shows are promoting their own agenda without regard to its value or relevancy for the audience and that the producers are permitting this to happen provided it is sensational enough to draw the needy or the curious viewer, regardless of its effect on the audience. Beyond that, the "experts," brought on the shows to give them verity, are often giving poor or wrong advice.

Sonya Friedman thinks most talk shows are damaging to people's lives, and she not only is a licensed psychologist in New York City but had her own daily talk show on CNN for several years. Her opinion of shows like *Oprah* is that they "deal with disillusion and destruction. They are the freak shows of American television." Defenders of these shows generally fall back on three lines of defense: (1) The guests know what's going to happen; (2) the audience understands what's happening; and (3) we work hard to make it all fair and helpful.

Many of the producers of such shows as *Oprah* and *Sally Jessy* defensively claim that the guests know what they are getting into when they come on a nationally broadcast TV show. Beyond that, they are treated "sensitively" and are often given help after they have appeared. Burt Dubrow, Sally Jessy Raphael's executive producer, claims, "We never leave these people. We will send them on our time to therapists to help them out, to keep in touch with them."

They also defend what they do on the grounds that in order to be successful, they have to do a lot of shows—250 a year—and they have to be stimulating, interesting, and lively to attract and hold their audience. What they don't mention is that a lot of money is at stake and if they don't attract a big enough audience, they won't attract sponsors, who will pay outrageous sums of money. They also don't say that because of the enormous amounts of money at stake—millions and millions of dollars every month—they can't leave things to chance; they can't hope that things will turn out to be stimulating, interesting, and lively. They have to be sure they will. This means more setups, more control of guests and audience, more manipulation to make the shows more dramatic, more outrageous, more showbiz.

To do this the producer must carefully control the guests as well as the audience. The audience has waited months to get tickets and is coached beforehand, given signals to clap, scream, yell, and emote on cue while the star is on camera. This is not an audience. It is a cast of supporting players. Guests are pushed to say what the host wants said to make the predetermined point the host has in mind. And while Geraldo brags that he never pays guests, Donahue is open about paying them, having paid two of the cops accused in the Rodney King beating $25,000 for showing up onstage.

Donahue declares, "Why should multinational corporations like Time Warner and General Electric get their software [he means their guests] for free when the money they make on the ratings generated by these interviews certainly benefits their stockholders? I don't see the great moral agony here."

What Donahue also doesn't see is that having paid a guest a lot of money to appear gives the show control over the guest and what the guest says and does. That wouldn't be the case if he or she were not being paid. Having the ability to pay for something doesn't make it right. In other circles, doing so is sometimes called a bribe.

"In my darkest moments, I think people are going to start indulging in bad behavior simply to get on television. There is no longer a sense that there is a public interest that may not be the same as our own personal interest, and I think talk shows contribute to this. They encourage us to view interests and movements in terms of what's good for me, not what's good for the U.S.A."

That's the fear of Wendy Kaminer, a fellow at the Radcliffe Public Policy Center in Cambridge, Massachusetts. That fear is more than just speculation. It is the attempt of people in an impersonal and harsh world to get certification that he or she exists and is somebody of value. That validation occurs by being on TV. Most of us are aware of our helplessness and meaninglessness in the totality of the universe, but for some, such unimportance is intolerable, and they seek to be known and remembered and to be somebody. In centuries past, becoming significant meant building the pyramids, conquering vast empires, discovering radium, trekking to the North Pole, or writing the history of Rome. Today it's being on television—being on *Oprah*—since that is the most common universal communication and medium of recognition.

National Public Radio (NPR) commentator Daniel Shorr said some years ago that politicians and public figures spend a lot of time jumping up and down, waving their hands, to be recognized by the television camera. They know that unless they are on national television, they don't, in fact, actually exist.

In addition, alliance with someone who already is recognized as "somebody" certifies us as "somebody, too." That is why people want their pictures taken beside political leaders, entertainment stars, and famous people or want to be seen talking to Oprah on television. It certifies that they are "somebody." Ancient warriors used to drink the blood of their fallen enemies who fought bravely and died nobly because they thought that would infuse them with the courage and nobility of these intrepid men. Fans seek to bond with heroes, heroines, glamorous celebrities, and public figures so that they, too, can be glamorous and famous. That's what being on *Oprah* or *Sally Jessy* or *Donahue* can mean.

Arthur Bremer was a twenty-one-year-old naive klutz who fell in love with a young girl, Joan Pembrick, age fifteen, and began to act so goofy around her that she got disgusted and broke up with him. He told her with great alarm on one date that he had a penis so large that if he didn't take medication for it, it would literally explode.

In any case, he vainly tried to get Joan back and decided that what he needed to do was get on TV; the best way to do that was to kill President Richard Nixon. So he stalked Nixon for a while here and in Canada but couldn't get close enough to fire a shot. In disgust, he switched his target to a governor who was also a candidate for president, George Wallace of Alabama. He stalked Wallace for a long time and kept a diary explaining he was doing it to get on television. That would certify that he was an important person and make his ex-girlfriend come running back to him. His diary entry for May 4, 1972, under-scored his concern about getting on TV (Text as written by Arthur Bremer without editing).

"It seems I would of done better for myself to kill the old G-man Hoover, In death, he lays with Presidents. Who the hell ever got buried in 'Bama' for being great? He certainly won't be buryed with the snobs in Washington. SHIT! I won't even rate a T.V. enterobption in Russia or Europe when the news breaks—they never heard of Wallace. If something big in Name flares up I'll end up at the bottom of the 1st page in America. the editors will say—'Wallace dead? Who cares?' He won't get more than 3 minutes on network T.V. news. I don't expect anybody to get a big thobbing erection from the news. You know, a storm in some country we never heard of kills 10,000 people—big deal—pass the beer and what's on T.V. tonight."

A few days later, at a shopping center in Laurel, Maryland, Arthur Bremer shot and crippled for life the governor of Alabama.

When John Hinckley Jr. decided that if he were Jodie Foster's lover his life would be happy and fulfilled and he would be "somebody," he decided he had to do something to impress her and win her love. What he wrote to her was lost in the avalanche of three thousand cards and letters she received every month. He was a lost soul searching for some way to be "somebody" while drifting through life as an unanchored, bewildered nobody—part of the flotsam of a society filled with debris of failed families, schools, and economic systems. In the theater of his mind, however, there was the gleaming scenario of being with Jodie Foster—being her lover, her companion, her protector—being "somebody" because she anointed him as worthy of being her man.

Days later, after Hinckley shot President Reagan, along with his press secretary, Jim Brady, the police found another letter addressed to Jodie Foster in John Hinckley's hotel room. He explained what he was doing. "Jodie," he was saying, "let me be somebody."

Five hours after he shot President Reagan, he was being questioned by Secret Service agents. Hinckley's question for those agents was: "Is it on TV?" Of them, he was asking, "Am I somebody?" Hinckley believed he could turn himself into "somebody" just by being on television.

In August 1975, Lynette "Squeaky" Fromme began a correspondence with Chuck Rossi at NBC. She was a worshipful follower of the man she thought of as Jesus Christ resurrected—Charles Manson. She knew that if Manson could get on television to tell the world his philosophy, it would immediately trigger a public outcry for a new trial and vindication of her God, Manson.

Squeaky wrote Rossi, "The media *can* be used to unwind the tangles of a world running in circles toward what it fears most. Manson can explain the self-destructive thought. He can explain the Christ thought. But he must have the opportunity to bring this message of salvation to the world otherwise our lives will terminate in the drug store, booze bottles and morgues of a decadent and polluted Tate-La Bianca society. If Manson is not allowed to explain, there will be many more young murderers, beginning with the person typing this letter."

Rossi couldn't convince NBC to turn itself over to Charles

Manson, so Lynette Fromme found another way to get herself and Charlie on television: She would stalk and kill the president of the United States, Gerald Ford. That would please Charlie.

Fromme learned that President Ford was going to visit Sacramento, and that morning, September 5, 1975, she staked out the Senator Hotel and watched Ford and his entourage emerge at 9:45. The group began walking across the street and the forestlike capitol grounds toward the gilt-domed structure. As the group moved, spectators and fans eddied around the edges, waving and shouting greetings to the president. The genial Ford returned the waves and the greetings and quickly noticed a petite young woman in a red gown and red turban moving along with them at the edge of his escort group. She shifted closer and closer and moved slightly ahead of where the president was walking in the center of his escort.

Then the childlike young woman turned and stepped boldly into the path of the president until she was just two feet from him and they were literally face-to-face. As she faced Ford, she fished into her robe and produced a pistol, which she aimed right at Gerry Ford's genitals. Stunned, Ford stopped, bewildered as to what to do. He couldn't flee, since his retinue of aides and Secret Service bodyguards had hemmed him in and literally held him entrapped, confronting his assassin.

The nature of her pistol was that the hammer was pulled back in cocked position in order to fire with the least delay. Seeing the danger and the pistol cocked back and everybody practically on top of each other, a Secret Service man instantly wrapped his hand around the back of the pistol in such a way that the web between his thumb and forefinger would keep the hammer from driving home and exploding the cartridge in the chamber. His colleagues grabbed Fromme and threw her to the ground in less time than it takes to talk about it.

Fromme was right. It got her on television, but it didn't do much to get Charlie Manson on TV. However, nineteen years later, ABC-TV's $7-million woman, Diane Sawyer, launched a new magazine show on TV of the type that is getting more and more like Oprah's every day. Her main guest? Charlie Manson. It got a 30-share rating, the highest in that time slot that night.

These are only a few examples of what concerns Wendy Kaminer about programs like Oprah and the rest. About what evil people are willing to do to get on TV. The critics of Oprah's show and her competitors' programs say that:

• They exploit people who have serious psychological problems that cannot be solved between commercials for floor wax and feminine hygiene products. Gerald Goodman, a psychology professor at UCLA whose speciality is intimate communication, refuses to appear on *Oprah* and other shows because instant diagnosis is called for by the host; this is not helpful and is sometimes harmful to the guest.

• They glorify victims without helping them reconstruct their lives and move beyond the pain. Two television critics, Brian Lowry, writing in *Variety*, and Virginia Postrel, of the *Los Angeles Times*, speak about the glorification of victims and what it means to society as a whole. For example, prospective jurors sit around the holding room watching *Oprah* and other talk shows; they see how people are victimized and how they are not responsible for what they do no matter how horrible, and then the jurors are called in to hear a case where the Menedez brothers, Ellie Nessler, the Bobbitts, or Michael Jackson's accusers are playing the victim in real life. Postrel noted that being a victim has become a possible alibi for virtually any abhorrent behavior. As Lowry casts it, "You're overweight? It's because you were abused as a child. Your marriage ended unhappily? It's because you witnessed a bad marriage growing up. You abuse your kids? It's because your parents abused you. The appeal of shows like Oprah hinges largely on their ability to tap into this culture of victimization."

• They encourage confrontations among people without seeking reconciliation. They want conflict on camera because antagonism is more dramatic.

In response to this criticism, Oprah, her producers, and those on comparable shows say that they have shined the light into a lot of dark corners of our lives and our society and made it easier for people to talk about what used to be taboo subjects. They say that this makes people stronger and more tolerant.

Some psychologists agree. Frank Farley, president of the American Psychological Association, says, "Focusing on personal stories can be a wonderful thing in that people can learn more about themselves by learning about others. Self-knowledge is a form of power."

Of course, the question about the self-knowledge learned from the *Oprah* or *Sally Jessy* show is whether it is accurate or applies to everybody. Ben Saunders of the Crime Victims Research and Treatment Center at the Medical University of South Carolina says, "These shows tend to feature the most extreme, titillating cases, as opposed to the regular, everyday cases. The result is that it sets up a situation where these rare experiences become the norm in the popular culture."

Yet talk shows seem to be part of an inevitable historical progression. Decades before the talk-show mania and the self-actualization books began to flood the market, America was embracing the concept that we could cure ourselves of whatever ailed us through self-analysis and self-improvement. In some ways, it marked an abandonment of relying on outside forces, such as religion or God or acceptance of fate. Some believe it was launched by the visit of Sigmund Freud to the United States in 1909, when his school of psychoanalysis swept the nation, with substantial help from advocates such as Karl Menninger and Theodor Reik. The result is an abiding faith in the belief of self-analysis and self-cure, with some guidance from gurus such as Oprah, Donahue, Sally Jessy, John Bradshaw, Leo Buscaglia, or M. Scott Peck, whose book *The Road Less Traveled* has been on the bestseller list for over *ten years*.

Speaking to a jammed meeting of the American Psychological Association in Toronto in August 1993, psychologist Sonya Friedman said, "You think we're voyeurs? We're nothing compared to the American public. The demand for these shows is enormous." Then she and other psychologists at the meeting critiqued what they felt dangerous about most talk shows, including the *Oprah Winfrey Show:*

"One reality of the television talk show that is rarely discussed in public is that there are an enormous amount of hours to be filled by shows in order for them to stay on the air and to make money for their producers. Of the type of group-therapy, titillating, shock talk shows being discussed here, there used to be in 1986 basically two national shows: *Oprah* and *Donahue.* By the end of 1993, there were seventeen, with each show doing five hours every week. The producers have to deliver to their audiences. That means finding 4,420 groups of guests and topics every year that are stimulating and unusual enough to draw an audience. It makes for interesting and profitable television, but should that be the only criterion for the use of the public airwaves?"

31

The Big Four-O Birthday

Oprah's fortieth birthday held a lot of surprises for her, starting with her show of January 27 (which aired on February 4), when she thought she would be doing a program on juries and out popped Aretha Franklin, Gladys Knight, Cheryl Tiegs, Phylicia Rashad, and Beverly Johnson to serenade her, along with the staff and audience. She was so flabbergasted that for one of the rare times in her life, Oprah didn't know what to say.

She did know what to say to Miriam Kanner, who wrote a fortieth birthday story on Oprah for the *Ladies' Home Journal*. Looking back on the four decades of her life, Oprah, of course, has something to say. She thinks that she has learned several rules that are important for living, and of those she would share with Ms. Kanner, the first was "Don't Let a Bad Childhood Stand in Your Way." On this, Oprah should know what she is talking about, since she had both a bad and a good childhood. Fortunately, the good childhood for Oprah came second and undid a lot of the bad childhood, but not every child is that lucky.

Her second lesson, which is something she has learned the hard way, is to "Eat Reasonably, Diet Privately." Her failure to do either during most of her forty years—particularly the last ten—has caused Oprah a lot of grief. She has been under the microscope of millions of women during the many futile tries she had made at losing weight and keeping it off.

Her third lesson is: "Don't Be Satisfied with Just One Success—and Don't Give Up After Failure." Here again, she has known both: her failure as an anchorwoman in Baltimore; her success as a talk-show host in Baltimore, Chicago, and nationally; her nomination for an Oscar and her disappointment at not getting it; her less than successful show *The Women of Brewster Place*, her successes with the Michael Jackson interview and *There Are No Children Here*; and, of course, her endless cycle of success and failure with diets.

Her fourth lesson is: "Do What You Want to Do, When You Want to Do It...and Not a Moment Sooner." In case anyone has been living in a dark, isolated cave for the last nine years, Oprah is talking about the marriage and the book. The marriage that is on, off, on, off, on, off, and who knows. In this February 1994 interview, Oprah's latest view on the marriage is: "There was a time in my life when I needed marriage to validate myself, but now I'm very content with what my relationship gives me. I'm very sorry I ever mentioned Stedman's name to the press. This whole wedding thing might not be such a big issue if I had never mentioned it. But if I hadn't, then everybody would be asking, 'Who's the mystery man?' 'Is she a lesbian?'"

As to the book, Ms. Kanner believed from her interview that the stunning cancellation of the publication of the autobiography was due, as Oprah said at the time, to her feeling that it failed to tell the story she wanted to share with the world. A spokesman said that she had wanted to include a part about the wedding and the marriage, but that seems farfetched, since the wedding and the marriage are continuously vague and ephemeral. Ms. Kanner's conclusion is probably close to the mark when she says, "Some things are just too personal to share with the world."

Finally, the fifth revelation at age forty is one that has long-term significance to Oprah's future, her show, and her relationship with Stedman and others who are closely involved in her life but may not continue to be so. It is, "You Can't Do It All Yourself." To illustrate what this point means, Ms. Kanner quotes Betty Friedan. "You're going to become more and more yourself; you're going to care less what other people think. You're going to be free to take new risks."

At forty, Oprah calls herself "a woman in progress." That is a feeling fraught with change and new arrangements.

For her birthday, she and Stedman flew to Los Angeles, where her longtime producer, Debra DiMaio, hosted a birthday party for her as part of an expensive and delightful weekend for the forty-year-old Oprah. The tab included $80,000 to jet friends in to Los Angeles and put them up in luxury suites at the sylvan and hidden retreat of the Bel-Air Hotel, with its lush foliage and tame swans, and provide adequate security for everybody; $15,000 for the dinner party, with fifty guests on Friday, January 28, the day before Oprah's actual birthday; and $35,000 on a Beverly Hills shopping spree for dresses, jewelry, a purse, and some gifts for her two nieces in Milwaukee.

The festivities began at 7:00 P.M. Friday, when Stedman and Oprah arrived at the posh French restaurant L'Orangerie, with Oprah sporting a svelte new figure in a $4,000 designer silk gown, with a sheer stole and cross-strap white heels. The guests included director Steven Spielberg, Maria Shriver, composer Quincy Jones, with his girlfriend, actress Nastassja Kinski, Sidney and Joanna Poitier, Marianne Williamson, and best friend Gayle King Bumpas, who read a moving tribute to Oprah followed by the traditional "Happy Birthday" serenade from the group.

The animated group dined on rack of lamb, artichoke mousseline, along with soft-boiled eggs stuffed with caviar, and concluded with the conventional birthday cake: a tiered chocolate mousse. The guests enjoyed the wine and cuisine until the late evening, when the men were sent on their way and the women adjourned to the Bel-Air Hotel and Oprah's private bungalow. Everyone slipped into pajamas, and they had an old-fashioned slumber party, talking, laughing, and carrying on like teenagers until 3:00 A.M., during which Williamson and Oprah decided to plan a worldwide weekend convocation of love, understanding, and God, which they planned to have in conjunction with the pope.

On Saturday, Oprah and Stedman breakfasted in bed on

strawberries, grapes, melon slices, and rolls. Stedman gave Oprah his own private birthday gift of intimate lingerie, which the exuberant Oprah immediately used in their own private boudoir fashion show. Then each went off on separate ways to pursue their favorite public activities: golf for Stedman and shopping for Oprah. The shopping was preceded by lunch with Gayle King Bumpas and several other women at the Beverly Hills special celebrity hangout, the Ivy, until two in the afternoon. Then everyone rushed off to go shopping with Oprah.

Stedman and Oprah returned to their suite at the Bel-Air for a candlelight dinner on the patio, where he presented her with the best birthday gift she received that weekend: a four-page letter telling her how much he loved her.

CHAPTER

32

A Look to the Future

The immediate future for Oprah and Harpo Productions will involve a refocusing on the *Oprah Winfrey Show*, which is the foundation of Oprah's empire, and on the movies. Her friend and executive producer Debra DiMaio said, "Oprah and I both have a renewed appreciation for the show. The power of this vehicle and the opportunity to touch people's lives is really quite amazing." The number of outside projects and distractions, which occupied too much time in 1993 and part of 1994, will be put aside, since it is stretching Oprah too much; even if she can get along on five hours' sleep, she does need at least that much time.

The movies now in the mill are Toni Morrison's *Beloved*, about the tragedies and problems endured by an escaped slave woman. The film will star Oprah and is slated to begin shooting in the summer of 1995. The second movie Oprah contemplates is *Their Eyes Were Watching God*, by Zora Neale Hurston. It deals with a woman going through three marriages.

On the *Oprah Winfrey Show* in the future, DiMaio says that Oprah wants to concentrate on programs that actually help people's lives, with such topics as creating and sustaining better relationships, battered women, alcoholism, and making people feel better about themselves.

The reason for this re-thinking of the show is an ice-cold reality check that hit when Oprah's ratings dropped to the lowest point they had been in three years. It wasn't panic time because Oprah was still number one in daytime TV talk, but certainly it was a time for a serious look at the texture and content of the program. Oprah, stung by criticism from her rich, tony friends and the media critics, wanted to do uplifting programs about spiritually, the meaning of life, world peace and building self-esteem. DiMaio wanted Oprah to return to talk show basics, namely, tough, hard-edged topics for which the format is infamous such as women who want sex with their stepsons, incest among lesbians, and the sin that terrorizes mothers. She knew that the soft topics will win the praise of the critics and have people changing channels away from Oprah in droves.

In the May sweeps ratings, the Oprah showed dropped 7 percent overall and 11 percent among the critical 18-49 year-old female category which is the mainstay of the program. Observers thought that some of the newer, hotter shows were moving up on Oprah, particularly for that key 18-49 year-old female audience. These newcomers included Jenny Jones, Montel Williams and Ricki! hosted by Ricki Lake and coming on as the fastest growing talk show in TV history. Along with Oprah, Donahue suffered a drop that was the worse it had experienced in the last ten years.

Oprah's first forty years have been a remarkable journey, and while no one can predict the future for the world's richest black woman, there are some informed and carefully calculated observations that appear evident about her future.

Her enormous popularity as a television-talk-show host will fade in the next several years for a number of reasons. The tabloid format is running out of variations on the same subjects, which are sex, fat, and children, and the audience is overwhelmed with Oprah and Donahue clones, each more shrill than the other. The audiences will eventually tire of them, just as they have tired of other fads in the past. Beyond that the most important production person on the show has left. Debra DiMaio, who is the key production person in

Oprah's entire TV show success and who helped make Oprah the star she is, stunned the Harpo organization and the talk-show universe by suddenly announcing on June 22, 1994, that she was history, gone south, out of there and absolutely 100 percent leaving, effective *the next day*! The parting of Oprah and Debra, two of the world's most infamous control freaks even in an industry polka dotted with control freaks, was not a totally amicable split. Debra had been with Oprah since Baltimore days and it was Debra who got Oprah the job hosting *A.M. Chicago* that led to Oprah's huge international success. Debra is one of the four people who are responsible for giving Oprah the opportunity to use her talents to become the richest and most powerful black woman in the world (the other three people who are responsible are her father, Vernon Winfrey, and the King Brothers).

Everybody connected with the operation thought of Debra and Oprah as twin sisters even if one was white and the other was black. One former *Oprah* producer, no longer with the company but still afraid to identify himself publicly because of Oprah's awesome power in the industry, told *TV Guide* writer Gretchen Reynolds, "Oprah and Debbie were practically joined at the hip. There aren't many people Oprah really trusts, but Debbie was one. I'm sure of that."

Another resentful former producer labeled DiMaio as, "very, very tough to work for—the worst." This observer claimed Debra had a lot of able people on staff and she enjoyed making them feel like half-witted bumblers. The Oprah operation was like working in a dynamite factory where the slightest spark produced chaos. She was a mercurial tyrant, former employees charged, who reveled in abusive language and in destroying people's self-esteem which is an interesting situation with a program that publicly preaches the importance of self-esteem to millions every weekday.

As time demands from outside interests grew, Oprah would spend less and less energy on her talk show and, conversely, DiMaio spent more and more energy finally controlling the program, the scripts, and the guests. The number one rating that the show has consistently garnered and industry praise most recently expressed with two more Emmys for Best Show and Best Host in May of 1994 is testimony that she was good at it.

Still, the internal tension reached a combustion point, with a revolt by Oprah's top producers, ironically, shortly after the show won those two Emmys in late May. They met secretly with Oprah, reeled off their litany of Debra's sins and announced they were quitting. Faced with this ultimatum and personal crisis, Oprah did what she always has done since becoming an international star, she seized upon the bury-it-in-money solution. She gave Debra several million dollars and asked her to seek her life elsewhere. It is a decision that many predict will have a profoundly negative effect on the show. Happily, this happened after the King Brothers had renewed key new syndication contracts for the show during which they were already encountering resistance.

Oprah issued a press release saying, "Debra was a guiding force behind the scenes and I will be forever grateful to her for lending me and our production staff her talent and creativity." Debra issued a vague press release about searching for new challenges elsewhere and July 7, Tim Bennett, who had been program director at WLS-TV when Oprah first came to Chicago to host *A.M. Chicago*, was hired away from being general manager of WTVD-TV in Raleigh/Durham, North Carolina to take over.

The station reactions to King World's renegotiating the *Oprah Winfrey Show* contracts and extending them to the year 2000 indicate this is so. There is more resistance to signing Oprah to the year-2000, which means that station programmers are not convinced that her popularity will hold up for another six years.

For example, in Oprah's old stomping territory of Baltimore, WMAR-TV let Oprah go to rival WBAL-TV. WMAR-TV's general manager, Joe Lewin, said, "Good business sense has prevailed, and we will use the opportunity to reposition this station as the most comprehensive provider of local news and information programming." Translation: Joe Lewin doesn't think Oprah will be that hot for that long. Though Lewin expressed the same reluctance about *Wheel of Fortune* and *Jeopardy*, he changed his mind in May 1994 and signed renewal contracts for those two game shows through 1999.

The price range for a station's buying *Oprah* hovered between $100,000 and $125,000 a week, although in the biggest markets, such as New York and Los Angeles, it's over $160,000; the King brothers want from 10 percent to 25 percent more under the new year-2000 contract with Oprah. Joe Lewin said, "There are a lot of other options for a lot less money."

And it is possible that Oprah is tiring of the format herself. She has proven herself, and she doesn't have to do the talk show anymore. She has all the success and all the money she will ever need. Will it make any difference if Oprah is worth a billion dollars instead of a half a billion? She is chary of the way talk shows have become sleazy, and she is now part of that sleaziness and doesn't enjoy the association.

From a business viewpoint, it is possible Oprah will phase out of her last contract with King World by using guest hosts more and releasing her time for more exciting new projects. King World, as such, will be gobbled up by a large television operation both because the King brothers also have plenty of money and because Roger King is a disaster looking for a place to happen, which would severely hurt the company. His inability to restrain his drinking and aggressive behavior will probably, unfortunately, end in tragedy.

The bright future for Oprah involves gradually withdrawing from the incredible public pressure of her talk show and devoting her time to making motion pictures, which is the one thing that to her has class and is fulfilling. However, she would be wise if she understood what the King brothers have never understood, and that is that no one is good at everything. The King brothers, for example, are excellent at syndicating programs and lousy at producing them. In the same vein, Oprah is excellent at acting in movies and not as good at directing them. She should let other people do the directing and stick to the acting; it makes her a better actress and the film a better movie. It is also something she needs to do to prove herself as an actress; if she always acts in movies she owns, it will take away from the public recognition of her as an actress.

Oprah's private life will continue to become more private as she becomes the queen of the rich black class, which is almost a secret tier of people in American society. As the socioeconomic divide between Oprah and the majority of blacks in America grows wider, she may be accepted less by black Americans as one of them. In fact, at this point Oprah is in some important ways more rich than she is black. She is, ironically, about as far removed in real life from the black women she plays on the screen as one can imagine.

Oprah is also much more spiritual in private life than she reveals in her public life. She says, "As corny as this sounds, my faith in God got me through." She tries to read from the Bible every morning while listening to gospel music. This is something she does not like to talk about too much for fear it will be misunderstood, but it is an important part of focusing herself for the day ahead. "I call it my morning ritual, 'centering up.' At night I get on my knees and pray. I feel incomplete without it."

Whenever she is feeling down, Oprah reaches for her Bible and cues up Aretha Franklin's "Amazing Grace" on the stereo and talks to herself: "Oprah, are you going to be a victim, or are you going to take charge of your life?" Her view that we are in charge of our own lives is repeated in what she does and says on and off camera. "I'm truly blessed. But I also believe that you tend to *create* your own blessings. You have to prepare yourself so that when opportunity comes, you're ready. I think that the path of our spiritual involvement is the greatest journey we all take. And I think that is part of the reason why I am as successful as I have been, because success wasn't the goal. The process was. I wanted to do good work. I wanted to do well in my life."

Oprah believes she is what the universe meant her to be right now, just as a hooker who stands on Sunset Boulevard and La Brea is what the universe meant her to be at that moment. She says, "I am helping people be all that they can be. I am all that I can be, but I am not God...I'm not God. I keep telling Shirley MacLaine, 'You can't go around telling people you are God.' It's a difficult concept to accept."

In Oprah's eyes, the pain of human misery and the astonishing success she has had are all part of the same meta-physical scheme of the universe. They are one with her, and she is one with them.

Even so, Oprah does not exactly feel about her family that way, and she will continue to distance herself from them. The only blood relative still alive who really might have mattered to her is Vernon Winfrey, and she wouldn't even embrace him without reservation. She thanks him for what he and her stepmother, Zelma, did to make her present life possible but still refuses to accept him unequivocally as her biological father and bond with him. Part of that rejection is the lingering fear and hatred of her uncle, whom she believes raped her and probably impregnated her, which Vernon would not acknowledge or do anything about afterward. She would feel guilty if she didn't provide support for her mother and her half sister, but she looks upon them as people who were never there when she needed them and who only showed up at her doorstep when the money started flooding in.

Oprah has three major goals she would like to achieve in 1995:

She would like to do another major movie role for another major Hollywood producer like Spielberg instead of one financed by her own production company, although she has two movies in development for Harpo Productions. She has wanted to be a star actress since she was in East Nashville High and won a trip to Hollywood in a speaking contest. She still wants to be acknowledged as a movie actress and to prove that her performance in *The Color Purple* was not an anomaly.

She wants to coordinate a worldwide prayer convocation involving herself, Marianne Williamson, and the pope. This is in concert with her spiritual and New Age feelings and ever broadening search for bigger projects. The pope has not been consulted on this project yet, but Oprah and Marianne have worked out the plan.

Finally, although Barbara Walters was Oprah's idol and role model from the time Oprah got her first television job at WTVF-TV in Nashville, Oprah wants to beat Barbara out and have the first live interview with Princess Di. She says, "Getting the princess would be the highlight of my career. I have a great deal of respect for her because she has shown that she no longer wants to be a princess on a pedestal." English press sources say that Princess Di has said *Oprah* is the one show she wants to appear on and is trying to get the cooperation of the royal family to permit her to do it. For Oprah, getting Princess Di to dish up the secrets of a royal marriage gone sour would be the high point of her career as a talk-show host.

Three things Oprah is highly unlikely to do: write a book soon, have a baby, or get married to Stedman Graham.

Oprah is a very private person, with an agenda she rarely lets anyone see, and writing her autobiography is meaningless if it is simply a recitation of the "official Oprah" story about where she went, whom she saw, and what they said. In order for her autobiography to be special and powerful—which is the only way she would want it to be—she will have to reveal to the world things that she has probably never before revealed to anyone, and that's something she is not prepared to do.

The idea of having a baby is lovely in theory, but the reality of the pregnancy, the pain of childbirth, and the limitations on her life do not make the process of having a child appealing to Oprah. As she says, "Having a child come from my body isn't as important to me as being able to change the life of a child. There are so many little black children out there I would adopt in a second." The idea of adopting a child is a pleasanter alternative to giving birth, and when one is worth half a billion dollars, one opts for the pleasanter alternatives in life. Adopting a child carries with it another important aspect that attracts Oprah: She doesn't have to be married to have an adopted child. Moreover, adopting one also means that the man in her relationship does not have an important control over the relationship and over Oprah as the natural father of their jointly conceived child. The child is *her* child, not *theirs*.

Which brings us to the much overasked question about when she and Stedman will get married. At this point, the indications are strong that the answer is never. In the nine years they have dated, several wedding dates have been set and canceled, and when she was asked in early 1994 when the new date will be, she snapped, "There is no date! In spite of all the worldly pressure for me to have a wedding, I no longer feel what I felt many years ago—that I had to have a man in order to make myself whole." That doesn't sound like a woman anxious to marry, and the chances are she will not marry—at least not Stedman.

On September 6, 1991, Jane Pauley interviewed Oprah and asked her how many times she is asked about the marriage between her and Stedman Graham, and she answered at least ten times a day. "No matter where I am, what I'm doing. In bathrooms, in—you know."

The frustration came out in Oprah's reactions to the endless curiosity about her and Stedman. "Everybody's, like, in my business. They're, like, 'Well, when are you going to get married?' and, 'Why aren't you married?' and, 'So what are you waiting on?'"

Also, her frustration about being judged by him on her physical appearance: "If Stedman looked differently—he's really quite a handsome guy. And I think if he looked differently, if he were, you know, squatty, or, you know, if he were as overweight as I am, people wouldn't say that [that he's going to break Oprah's heart]. It's really—it's really, really, very sexist."

Consistently, Oprah has answered the questions about Stedman and marriage over the last few years in one of three ways, and none of them sound like a woman who is determined to get married, or at least married to Stedman Graham.

One of her answers to the question of whether she will marry Stedman is, "I probably will. I'd say we are closer to it now than we've ever been. We really are. And that's the best answer I can give." That's the answer she gave in 1992 to Christopher John Farley of *USA Today*, and she is still not married or apparently close to it yet. The answer is an equivocal one and sounds like the kind of answer a waffling politician would give.

Another of her stock answers to the question runs along the lines that Stedman wants to be his own person and not known as Oprah's boyfriend or Mr. Oprah. The implication there being that the problem is with him and his reluctance to give up his identity entirely. If they marry, it is inevitable that his identification will come from his famous wife. Secretly, this probably riles Oprah and some of her close feminist colleagues, who know that if the situation were reversed and Stedman were the famous one, he would have no problem with it and would expect that Oprah wouldn't, either.

Finally, Oprah rhapsodizes about how wonderful it is for them to be together and *not* be married. She says, "I'm allowed great freedom in this relationship right now, and I think that if I'm married, as good as Stedman is, I think that his expectation of what I should be would change. I really do.' Cause I think he's pretty old-fashioned in that respect, you know, that a 'wife' ought to be home sometimes, and I'm not ready for that right now."

That definitely is not the view of a woman eager to get married. Couple that oft-stated view of Oprah's with her repeated talk about the joys of adopting children and it doesn't make for the sound of wedding bells. Then, in May 1994 the stories began circulating over a big fight between the two because Stedman wants a wife and a son and Oprah is not ready to be a wife or a mother.

Beyond that, Oprah will probably not marry Stedman for at least three reasons. He has failed Oprah in the relationship at critical times. He has repeatedly rejected her when she has gained weight, her most vulnerable time. He has withdrawn from sexual relations with her during her fat periods and has said cutting things that he shouldn't have said publicly; he has also not said supportive things that he should have said publicly. While Oprah has covered for him by explaining to the world "what he really meant," she hasn't fooled herself.

Stedman did not strike at the propitious moment. There is a season for all things, the Bible says, and in relationships there is a time for the wooing and a time for the bedding and a time for the wedding. Stedman waited seven years to propose, during which time Oprah became richer and more famous and realized more and more that she needed Stedman less and less. Not that she doesn't want to have a significant man in her life, but it doesn't have to be Stedman Graham. Had Stedman understood his woman, he would have married her five years ago, when she was still eager for it and while she was still overweight. There is the possibility she has passed him by and people were thinking that was so when Oprah attended on June 13, 1994, the first White House state dinner held for the Emperor and Empress of Japan. She came without Stedman. Instead Oprah arrived with one of her favorite men, Quincy Jones. Stedman purportedly had another social engagement!

Finally, Stedman is handsome, but he has not achieved all that much on his own; in fact, he probably would not have achieved what he has without his Oprah connection. Oprah has moved beyond Stedman in who she is, and she doesn't need him anymore. Oprah is adored and embraced by the glamorous, the rich, and the powerful. She can go anywhere, with anybody, and do anything in the world she wants to do; without her, Stedman is a conservative cipher trying to make a small public relations company and a couple of sports-related enterprises take hold, with the possible hope of some television connection. However, much of his present success, modest as it is, relates to his being Oprah's man.

Whatever her missteps and stumbling along the way, the journey of Oprah Gail Winfrey from Hattie Mae's pig farm in Mississippi to the pinnacle of wealth, power, and success in American television is a journey we must all admire. In looking for the secret to her achievement, too many observers focus on her poise or brashness or honesty. The secret is much more complex, as is Oprah herself. There is an inner strength of spirit and a belief in self that is as astonishing as the outer trappings of her success. Oprah is more akin to Maya Angelou, Dr. Deepak Chopra, and Marianne Williamson than she is to Donahue or Sally Jessy Raphael.

She is the ultimate American success story. That a tiny, illegitimate black girl from dirt-poor Mississippi can transform herself into the richest and most powerful black woman in the world is a triumph of the human spirit and the American dream. It is a message of hope that uplifts us all.

As always, Oprah says it best herself. "I'm finally ready to own my own power, to say, 'All right, this is who I am. If you like it, you like it. And if you don't, you don't. So watch out. I'm gonna fly.'"

PARTIAL LIST OF SOURCES

NEWSPAPERS AND MAGAZINES

Ad Day
"Nobody I Know Watches Me Says Donahue," by Sherrie Shamoon, May 20, 1988, p. 4.
"Oprah Broadcaster of Year," by Sherrie Shamoon, June 2, 1988, p. 4.

Adweek
"Therapy TV: Counseling Is Taking to the Tube," by Kathy Brown, May 4, 1987.

Amsterdam News (New York)
"Is Wall Street Trying," by Carl Bloice, January 23, 1993, p. 5.

Arizona Republic
"TV Talk Shows Accused of Trivializing Trouble," by Alison Bass, October 16, 1993, p. A10.

Atlanta Journal and Constitution
September 16, 1993, p. A1.

Boston Globe
"Living Dangerously: Michael Jackson's Descent Into Fairy-Tale Hell," by Patricia Smith, November 17, 1993, p. 81.

Brandweek
"Hello, Self-Actualization," by Judith Schwartz, August 26, 1991.

Broadcasting
"Late Night Plans for Oprah Shelved," December 21, 1987.
"Reality Explosion—TV Talk Shows," by George Mannes, August 29, 1988, p. 37.
"Oprah Show," March 27, 1989.
"Oprah Doing Well," February 5, 1990.
"Supply Side of Talk Shows," by Dick Robertson, January 14, 1991, p. 62.
"King World Still King of Cassandras," by Mike Freeman, July 5, 1991, p. 49.
"Talk, Talk, Talk: Syndicators Crowd Field," by Mike Freeman, September 30, 1991.
"Getting the Picture," December 9, 1991.
"From Dayton to the World," by Kathy Haley, November 2, 1992, p. S7 ff. (photo of Donahue).

"High Ratings at Low Cost Attract New Talk Show," by Steve McClellan, December 14, 1992.

"Can We Talk?" by Mike Freeman, December 14, 1992, p. 26.

"Oprah to Self-Syndicate?" by Mike Freeman, January 18, 1993.

"Talk Shows Fighting for Key Time Slots," by Mike Freeman, August 30, 1993, p. 15.

Business Journal of New Jersey

"The Business Journal 50," by George Peaff Jr., December, 1989, p. 31.

Business Week

"The Diet Business Takes It on the Chins," by Joseph Weber in Philadelphia, April 16, 1990, p. 86.

"All This and Candid Camera, Too," by Susan Duffy in New York, January 21, 1991, p. 64 (photo of Michael and Roger King).

"Move Over, Jane Fonda, Here Comes Pudgeball Nation," by Sandra D. Atchison in Denver, April 19, 1993, p. 29.

Calgary Herald

"Oprah Winfrey Show On Guns," by Alexander Stuart, September 18, 1993, p. A5.

Chicago Daily Law Bulletin

"Winfrey, Boyfriend Win Libel Suit by Default," by Mary Holden, May 1, 1992, p. 3.

Chicago Magazine

"Doyenne of Dish," by Marcia Froeklke Coburn, March 1992, p. 82.

"Oprah Unbound," by Gretchen Reynolds, November 1993, p. 86.

Chicago Tribune

"Oprah Conquers Tonight Show Challenge," by Jon Anderson, January 31, 1985, p. 11 (photo).

"Talk About a Hoax!," by Steve Johnson, September 2, 1988, p. 1 of *Tempo*.

"The Mogul Shows Off Her Studio, Her Control," by Mark Caro, March 18, 1990, p. 1 of *Tempo* (photo: Phil Greer).

"New Overseas Audience for Oprah," August 5, 1990, p. 3 of *Tempo*.

"Salhany on Difficulty of Selling Oprah," April 12, 1992, p. 3.

"Celebs Gather For Chicago Academy," May 28, 1992, p. 18.

"Oprah Not Marrying Stedman in April," February 11, 1993, p. 30.

"Chicago Is No. 1 When It Comes to Talk Show Audiences," by Marla Hart (freelance writer who covers TV industry), April 18, 1993 (photo: Jenny Jones, Bertice Berry, Oprah, Jerry Springer).

"The Unseen Guest: How Talk Shows Are Turned Into PR Vehicles," by Nancy Millman, May 26, 1993, p. 1 (photo: Sandra Moss, PR guest by Ari Mintz).

"Oprah Watch," June 9, 1993, p. 3.

"Oprah Lights Up Chicago Housing Authority," by Frank James, July 15, 1993, p. 1 (photo: by Val Mazzenga).

Chicago Tribune, September 10, 1993. p. 24.

Columbus Call and Post

"Telling People How to Achieve Success," December 31, 1992.

"Talk Show Host's Future Hubby Gets Spotlight," May 20, 1993.

Computer Graphics World

"Photo-Retouching," by Barbara Robertson, November 1990.

Crain's Chicago Business

"Will Oprah Play in L.A.?," September 15, 1986, p. 3.

"Oprah Buys West Side Studio," by Steven R. Strahler, September 19, 1988, p. 2.

"Oprah and Harpo Productions," by Jeff Borden, October 9, 1989 (picture by Mary Herlehy).

"Can Chicago Become L.A. on the Lake?," by Jeff Borden, March 26, 1990, p. 19.

Daily Mail (London)

"Grotesque World of Grand Oprah," by Marcus Berkmann, August 28, 1993, p. 37.

"The Pain That Made Oprah Scrap Book," by George Gordon, September 22, 1993.

Essence

"An Intimate Talk With Oprah," by Susan Taylor, August 1987, p. 57.

"The Sixth *Essence* Awards," May 1993, p. 110.

Ebony

"10 Hottest Couples," by Laura Randolph, February 1993, p. 106.

"Women at the Top in Entertainment Industry," by Lynn Norment, March 1993, p. 106.

"Prime-Time Poet," by Karima A. Haynes, April 1993, p. 68.

"100 Most Influential Black Americans," May 1993.

"Oprah's Party for Maya Angelou," June 1993 (photos by Roland Watts), p. 118.

"Getaway Places of the Famous and the Powerful," September 1993, p. 138.

"Oprah Opens Up . . . ," by Laura B. Randolph, October 1993, p. 130 ff. (photo: Paula Elledge, Ron Galella, Ltd. AP; Jim Smeal/Galella, Ltd.; Jean Krettler/ABC).

"New, Back and Black," November 1993, p. 68.

Facts on File

"Forsyth Country Oprah Show," February 13, 1987, p. 96E1.

"Satanic Jew Oprah Show," May 12, 1989, item 198901418.

"Mass Murder Rumor," October 31, 1991, p. 822B2.

"Liquid Diet Makers Cited," October 31, 1991.

Forbes

"Highest Paid Performers," October 1, 1990 (photo backstage at Harpo Studios by David Carter).

"King World," by "K.H.," January 6, 1992 (photo by Mojgan B. Azimi).

"The Top 40," by Peter Newcomb and Lisa Gubernick, September 27, 1993, p. 97.

"Oprah's Got All the Money," by Steven Zausner, October 18, 1993, p. 22 (photo: Richard Pasley/LGI).

The Globe

Ken Harrell Interview With Anthony Otey, October 12, 1993, p. 6.

The Guardian (Manchester, England)

"Jacko's Not Wacko and We Love Him," by Donu Kogbara, November 16, 1993, p. 22.

Hartford Courant

"Gayle King and Oprah," February 11, 1992, p. A1.

Hollywood Reporter

"New Oprah Deal Changes Channels in Baltimore," by Steven Brennan, April 11, 1994, p. 4.

"Oprah Veteran Hudson Named Exec Producer," by Stephen Galloway, August 4, 1994, p. 6.

The Independent

"Turning Traumas Into Gold: Oprah Winfrey, World's Highest Paid Entertainer," September 18, 1993, p. 14.

Journal of Applied Family and Child Studies

"Family Experts on Television Talk Shows," by Beatrice Robinson, July 1982, pp. 369–78.

Jet

"Stedman Attends Clarence Thomas Party," December 30, 1991, p. 30.

"Oprah to Marry Stedman," November 23, 1992, p. 61.

"Oprah and Stedman File Suit," April 13, 1992, p. 12.

"Oprah Raises Money for Elizabeth Taylor Project," June 1, 1992, p. 64.

"Oprah Is Truth Seeker," June 8, 1992.

"Oprah Nation's Favorite Talk Show Host," June 22, 1992, p. 34.

"Oprah Wins Two Daytime Emmys," July 13, 1992, p. 54.

"Oprah Receives Horatio Alger Award," February 1, 1993.

"Michael Jackson Gives Interview to Oprah," March 1, 1993, p. 56 (photo).

"Oprah at Spelman College Graduation," June 14, 1993, p. 28 (photo: Oprah overcome with emotion).

"Oprah Talks Candidly About Weight and Wedding," October 11, 1993. p. 35.

"Jordan Crowd Pleaser on Oprah," November 15, 1993, p. 50 (photo: Jordan chats with Oprah).

Ladies' Home Journal

"Oprah at 40," by Miriam Kanner, February, 1994. p. 96 ff.

Los Angeles Times

"Ecclesia Children Saw Fatal Beating," by Ethan Rarick, October 20, 1988, part 2, p. 3.

"Once Upon a Time There Was a Man Who Had a Great Idea for an Afternoon Talk Show on Television... Donahue's Dilemma: Balancing Truth, Trash," by Dennis McDougal in New York, January 28, 1990, p. 8 of calendar section (photo: Ray Stubblebine and Elena Seibert).

"Record Fees Paid Oprah," June 8, 1991, p. D2.

"Oprah and After School Specials," by Jane Hall, November 7, 1991, p. F10.

"King World Chairman in Hot Water Again," by John Lippman, January 10, 1992, p. D1 (photo).

"King World Chief Pleads No Contest to Battery," by John Lippman, January 15, 1992, p. D3.

"The Power, the Glory, the Glitz," by Terry Pristin, February 16, 1992, p. 6 of calendar section.

"Scenes with Oprah," by Bruce Ingram in Chicago, May 17, 1992, p. 4 of *TV Times*.

"Talk Shows: The Good and the Bad," December 23, 1992.

"The Rush Is On," by Daniel Cerone, January 28, 1993, p. F1.

"All Ears, All Day in TV Hell," by Howard Rosenberg, June 27, 1993, p. 4 of calendar section (photo: Paul Natkin).

"KNBC moves Donahue Aims Sally at Oprah," by Steve Weinstein, September 4, 1993.

"KNBC Climbs Aboard the Oprah Bandwagon," by Steve Weinstein, November 8, 1993, p. F2.

"No Children Role Takes Oprah to Projects," November 27, 1993, p. F15.

"Donahue Dropped in Dallas," January 22, 1994, p. F2.

"*Oprah Winfrey Show* deal," February 18, 1994, p. C-2.

"704 Hauser Braces for Race Issue," by Greg Braxton, April 7, 1994, p. F1.

"Oprah," May 3, 1994. p. C-2.

Los Angeles Sentinel

"Blacks Offended by Oprah," June 10, 1993, p. A3.

Louisville Courier-Journal
"All In The Family," by Richard Des Ruisseaux, May 31, 1989, p. 2A.
"Just Between Friends," by Tom Dorsey, June 11, 1989, p. 1T.

McCall's
"Oprah, Setting the Record Straight," by Jill Brooke Coiner, November 1993, p. 146 ff. (photo: Timothey Greenfield-Sanders).

Macleans
"Packaging the News," by Rae Corelli with William Lowther in Washington, October 30, 1989, p. 82.
"Michael Jackson Opens Up," February 22, 1993, p. 36. (photo: Bauer-Rex/ PONOPRESSE).

Marketing and Media Decisions
"Is Oprah Winning The Show?," by Marianne Paskowski, November 1986, p. 28 (photo).

Montreal Gazette
"The Trouble With Talk TV," by Alison Bass, October 17, 1993, p. B7.

National Enquirer
"Oprah's Amazing Roots," by Jim Nelson, David Wright, and Donna Barr, March 8, 1994, p. 28.
"Oprah Fights Back With Big Changes to Stop Show's Plunging Ratings," by Diane Albright and Reginald Fitz, August 16, 1994, p. 20.

National Review
"Talk of the Town," July 29, 1991, p. 37.

Nation's Business
"Should You Go on Diet?" by Phyllis Barrier, July 1989, p. 61.

New Republic
"I Hear America Chatting," by TRB, October 3, 1988.

New York Times Magazine
"The Importance of Being Oprah," by Barbara Grizzuti Harrison, June 11, 1989, p. 28.

New York Times
"Donahue vs. Winfrey: Clash of Talk Titans," by Nan Robertson, February 1, 1988, Section C, p. 30 (AP photos).
"Talk Show Hoaxers Face One of Their Victims," by Jeremy Gerard, September 8, 1988, p. C17 (photo: Tani Freiwald and Wes Bailey; NYT/Jack Manning).
"Oprah's Oddyssey," by Pat Colander, editor of *Naperville City Star*, a Chicago suburban weekly, March 12, 1989, section 2, p. 31, photos of Oprah with Jeffrey Jacobs (Paul Natkin).
"Big Bucks, Touch Tactics," by Tom Dunkel, senior editor of *New Jersey*

Monthly, September 17, 1989, p. 56.

"Popular Entertainers," by Michael Norman, October 1, 1989, section 6, p. 29.

"King World," July 26, 1992 (photo Roger and Michael King, by Bill Bernstein/ Outline).

"On the Talkies," by Walter Goodman, January 24, 1993.

"Watching Oprah, Geraldo and Phil," by Walter Goodman, May 17, 1993.

"Book Notes: Oprah Winfrey, Writing," by Sarah Lyall, June 9, 1993.

"The Best, or Maybe Worst, of the Talk Show World," by Karen Schoemer, June 27, 1993.

"Oprah," March 21, 1994, p. C7.

"Eating Well," by Marian Burros, May 25, 1994, p. C3.

"Book Notes," by Sarah Lyall, June 8, 1994.

Newsday

"Oprah: Power for a Price," by David Friedman, January 17, 1989, Part II, p. 9.

"Oh, The Wonder of Oprah," by Richard C. Firstman, November 1, 1989, Part II, p. 4 (photo by Paul Natkin b/w and color cover photo).

"Oprah," by Al Cohn, April 10, 1990, p. 8.

"Premature Oprah Baby Died," by Al Cohn, May 2, 1990, p. 8.

Newsweek

"Let the Talk Wars Begin!" by Harry Waters, with Janet Huck in Los Angeles, October 6, 1986, p. 62 (photo by Paul Natkin—Photo Reserve).

"Untrue Confession of a Devious Duo," September 12, 1988 (photo: Bailey, Friewald; John Swart), p. 80.

"Transition Confirmed," May 14, 1990, p. 79.

"Big Women, Big Profits," by Nina Darnton, February 25, 1991.

"Michael Jackson and Rainbow Express," by Sylvester Monroe, July 25, 1988.

"Arsenio Hall's Late Arrival," by Harry F. Waters, April 10, 1989, p. 68.

"The Power of Talk," by Howard Fineman, February 8, 1993, Cover story, p. 24 ff.

Orlando Sentinel-Tribune

"Oprah's Competition," November 14, 1991.

"Uncle Might Have Fathered My Baby at 14, Oprah Says," September 23, 1993, p. A2.

"In No Hurry to Get Married," October 12, 1993.

People Magazine

"Sexual Perversity in Chicago: Two Actors Gain Indecent Exposure on Oprah, Sally and Geraldo," by Barbara Kleban Mills in Chicago and Jilly Pearlman in New York, September 19, 1988 (photo: Peter Serling), p. 61.

"Daytime Talk Program Ratings Jump," by Elizabeth Sporkin, February 3, 1992, p. 58.

"Oprah Wins Emmy," July 6, 1992, p. 39 (photo).

"The Divine Miss W," by Susan Schindehette and Robin Micheli in Los Angeles, March 9, 1992, p. 34 ff. story, February 14, 1994.

"Oprah," November 23, 1992, p. 132.

"Oprah and Cher," January 21, 1991.

"Oprah's Crusade," by Mary H. J. Farrell with Katy Kelly in Washington, D.C., and Barbara Kleban Mills in Chicago, December 2, 1991, p. 68 ff. (photos grimacing, with Vernon, and at 16).

"Michael's Malady," by James J. Nordlund, March 1, 1993 (photo: Michael Jackson with Oprah; Neal Preston/Outline Press), p. 46.

"Never, Never Land?" by Kim Cunningham, March 1, 1993, p. 92.

"Flush Femmes," Shelley Levitt, Joyces Wagner, and Laura Meyers, L.A.; Lucina Fisher, Chicago, August 30, 1993, p. 64 (photo: Angela Restagno/Ron Galella; Harrison Jones/Outline Press).

"Cookin' for Oprah," by Cynthia Sanz, May 16, 1994, p. 85.

Philadelphia Tribune

"New Reference Book Lists Achievements of Black Women," by Jessie Smith, March 31, 1992.

Playboy Magazine

Playboy Interview of Dave Barry, by Fred Bernstein, May 1990, p. 61.

Playboy interview of Siskel and Ebert, by Lawrence Grobel, February 1991, p. 51.

Public Relations Journal

"1992 Education Report Card," by Judith T. Phair, February 1992, p. 22.

Publisher's Weekly

"Behind the Bestsellers," by Daisy Maryles, May 30, 1994, p. 18.

St. Louis Business Journal

"Diet Dollars Fatten Hospitals," by Patricia Miller, November 21, 1988, p. 1A.

St. Louis Post-Dispatch

"Oprah Testifies Before Senate," November 18, 1993.

St. Petersburg Times

"Oprah Up Close," by Janis D. Froelich, September 12, 1987, p. 1D.

"Behind the Scence of Oprah," May 11, 1992, p. 7D.

"Teen Oprah Dream Turns Dark," by Nancy Weil, October 2, 1993, p. 6.

Sacramento Bee

"A Slim Winfrey," by Milt Whalev, August 17, 1993, p. A2.

"Listen Here, People!," by Steve Wiegan, November 19, 1993, p. SC1.

Sacramento Observer

"Oprah's Charms Crowd," by Debra Lewis, November 18, 1992, p. A6.

San Diego Union-Tribune
"Jackson Is a Victim," by George Varga, November 21, 1993, p. E-8.

The Straits Times
"I Knew Oprah," by Irene Hoe, September 17, 1993.

Stamford Sun Reporter
"Network with Black Business," September 23, 1992.

Saturday Evening Post
"TV's New Daytime Darling," by Charles Whitaker, July 1987, p. 42.

TV Guide
"Best Daytime Talk Show Hosts," April 17, 1993, p. 54.
"The Oprah Myth," by Gretchen Reynolds, July 23, 1994, p. 9.

Time **Magazine**
"A Hyannis Hitching," by Dierdre Donahue and Susan Reed, with additional reporting by Katy Kelly, May 12, 1986, p. 53.
"People Sense the Realness," by Richard Zoglin with Cathy Booth in New York and Jack E. White in Chicago, September 15, 1986, p. 99 (photo by Harrison Jones).
"Oprah," by Alan Richman, January 12, 1987, p. 48.
"Does She Have a Sister Named Ohcuorg?" by Tim Allis, March 2, 1987, p. 108.
"Lady with a Calling," by Richard Zoglin, August 8, 1988, p. 62.
"Photo Hoax," December 25, 1989, p. 8. (photo).
"Big Pain, No Pain," Cover Story, Ron Slenzak, January 14, 1991, p. 82.
"Take a Viking to Lunch," by Paul Gray, June 10, 1991, p. 70.
"Forget About Losing Those Last Ten Pounds," by Anastasia Toufexis, July 8, 1991, p. 50.
"Running Off at the Mouth," by Richard Zoglin, October 14, 1991, p. 79 ff.
"Her Man Stedman," by Elizabeth Sporkin, Barbara Kleban, and Luchina Fisher in Chicago, Bob Langford in Raleigh, and Sabrina McFarland in New York, November 23, 1992, p. 132.
"Hollywood Takes It Off," January 13, 1992, p. 72.
"Peter Pan Speaks," by Richard Corless with Daniel S. Levy in New York, February 22, 1993, p. 66.
"Stay Tuned for the Hype!" by Richard Zoglin, May 24, 1993, p. 74.
"Oprah Springs Eternal," by Christopher John Farley in Chicago, August 30, 1993, p. 15 (photo: Michael Abramson for *Time*).

Toronto Star
"Oprah's Greatest Shame," September 26, 1993, p. D2.

U.S. News & World Report

"Liquid Diets," by Lisa Moore, Steven Findlay, John Glass, and Nancy Linnon, December 5, 1988, p. 92.

USA Today

"Oprah Show with Beau," January 26, 1989, p. 2D (photo).

"Oprah's Dearest," June 4, 1989, p. 5, USA Weekend (photo: color of Oprah and Gayle King Bumpus and color of Oprah and Stedman).

"The Other Oprah," by Julia Lawlor, June 4, 1989, p. 4, USA Weekend (photo: Ron Slenzak color).

"Kings of TV Syndication," by Dennis Cauchon in Los Angeles, January 18, 1990, p. 1B (photo: color of King brothers from King World; graphic from Neilsen Syndication Service; color photo by Steve Crise Photo).

"Return to Brewster," by Matt Roush, Chicago, May 1, 1990 (photo: EAR Photo, color, ABC).

"Oprah's Brother Dies," January 4, 1990, p. 2D.

"Talk Shows Aren't Just Hot Air—They're Hot," by Brian Donlon, January 24, 1992, p. 3D (photo Robert Hanashiro).

"Black TV Network Planned," January 23, 1992, p. 3D.

"Oprah's Fantasy," May 8, 1992, p. 2D.

"Oprah in Her Prime," by Christopher John Farley, May 19, 1992, p. 1D (photo: EAR Photo, color).

"Read About Oprah," May 21, 1992, p. 1D.

"Oprah Wins 2nd Emmy," June 24, 1992.

"He's Got Everybody Talking," by James Cox, August 18, 1992, cover story, p. A1.

"Talk Is Cheap—and a Syndication Hit," by Jefferson Graham, January 28, 1993.

"Oprah's Book Delay Leaves World Guessing," by Deirdre Donahue and Ann Trebbe, June 17, 1993, p. 1D.

"Oprah Winfrey: Autobiography," June 21, 1993, p. 2D (photo: EAR Photo, color).

Oprah Story, September 14, 1993, p. 1D.

"Is Cap Cities Eyeing King World?" by Dan Dorfman, November 29, 1993, p. 3B (photo: of King Brothers by Steve Crise).

Jeannie Williams's column, January 28, 1994, p. 2D.

"What Stokes the Fires That Burn Within Black Men?," March 22, 1994, by DeWayne Wickham.

"Ailes Takes to New CNBC Stump," by David Lieberman, April 28, 1994, p. A1.

Vanity Fair

"Bull Rush," by Peter J. Boyer, May 1992, p. 156 ff.

Variety

"Oprah to Become Winfrey Property," August 4, 1988.

"Oprah Acquires Chicago Complex," September 19, 1988.

"Vet Yakkers Lengthen Lead," by Elizabeth Guider, December 2, 1991, p. 36.

"Riot Weary L.A. Viewers," May 4, 1992.

"Oprah Talks Her Way to Syndie Win," August 13, 1992.

"King World Greenlights Journal," October 19, 1992.

"Brown Talker Sold in 3 Major Markets," October 21, 1992.

"Donahue Loses," November 12, 1992.

"King World Upgraded," November 17, 1992.

"Sweeps Spell Trouble for Donahue," December 7, 1992.

"News Is Bad for King World's Oprah," December 23, 1993.

"Syndies Suffer Thanksgiving Blahs," December 10, 1993.

"Oprah Pic Shows Ratings Clout," November 30, 1993.

"There Are No Children Here," November 24, 1993.

"King World Reigns in Syndie Ratings," September 23, 1993.

"Sally Bumps Phil/L.A. TV Skeds Firmed," August 24, 1993.

"Oprah/Jeopardy Are Syndie Winners," August 4, 1993.

"Donahue Adds Year to Contract," July 27, 1993.

"Oprah Autobio Off Indefinitely," June 17, 1993.

"A Gain Again for King World," April 15, 1993.

"Jackson-Oprah Special Set Worldwide," February 19, 1993.

Oprah story, February 7, 1994.

Oprah story, February 17, 1994.

Army Archerd column, February 1, 1994.

"TV Hall of Fame Adds 7," June 20, 1994, p. 6.

Wall Street Journal

"Creating A Buzz: With Remedy in Hand, Drug Firms Get Ready to Popularize an Illness," by Michael W. Miller, April 25, 1994, p. 1.

"Hope for Tomorrow: P & G Aims to Salvage Soap Operas," by Gabriella Stern, April 25, 1994, p. B1.

Warfield's Business Record

"Oprah and the Diet Drink Industry," by Terrence O'Hara, July 9, 1993, p. 4.

Washington Post

"And Now, HEEEEEEEER'S Oprah!," by Stephanie Mansfield, *Washington Post*, October 21, 1986, p. D1.

"Oprah Winningly," by Barbara Feinman, *Washington Post*, December 4, 1989.

"A Kiss Between Pals," by Michael E. Hill, June 11, 1989, p. Y8 (photo).

"Friendly Persuasion: Oprah and Joys of Buddyhood," by Tom Shales, June 13, 1989, p. C1.

"In Praise of Malcolm X," by Desson Howe, November 20, 1992, p. N44.

"Gawk Shows," by Patricia J. Priest, January 10, 1993, p. C1.

"How To Live Without Answers," by Dotson Rader, April 25, 1993, *Parade*.

"The Heart of Talkness," by Peter Carlson, April 25, 1993, *Post* magazine, p. 19.

Oprah story, September 14, 1993.

"High Cost of Shedding Pounds," by Cristine Russell, October 12, 1993. p. Z7.

Working Woman

"The Companies They Keep," by Fred Goodman, December 1991, p. 53 ff. (Photos by Paul Natkin).

"The *Working Woman* 50," by Janet Bamford, May 1993, p. 49 ff.

TELEVISION-SHOW TRANSCRIPTS

Oprah Show Transcripts

"Step Problems," March 29, 1988.
"Shere Hite on Men," March 30, 1988.
"America's Poor," March 31, 1988.
"Sportstars," April 4, 1988.
"Cured of AIDS," April 5, 1988.
"Drunk Drivers Who Have Killed," April 6, 1988.
"Adult Children Who Move Home," April 7, 1988.
"Fatal Attraction," April 12, 1988.
"Ramifications of Sexual Abuse," April 14, 1988.
"Adoption Rejection," April 19, 1988.
"Courtship Violence," April 21, 1988.
"Donald and Ivana Trump," April 25, 1988.
"Dirty Dancing Contest," May 2, 1988.
"Male Bashing," May 4, 1988.
"Autoerotic Asphyxia," May 11, 1988.
"Day Before Thanksgiving," November 24, 1993.
"Priestly Sins," October 7, 1992.
"Barry Manilow," September 4, 1992.
"Celebrities Who Changed Their Lives," October 28, 1992.
"Conversations With Oprah: Deepak Chopra," December 7, 1993.
"I Love You to Death," April 17, 1990.
"What Your Husband Says Behind Your Back," February 28, 1994.
"People Who Have Led Miserable Lives," March 17, 1994.
"New Prime-Time Stars," May 1, 1989.
"When Your Mother Rules Your Life," April 4, 1990.
"Women's Love Affair With Food," November 4, 1992.
"Good Taste," October 19, 1993.
"Guns: The Problem or the Solution," October 22, 1993.
"Polly Klaas's Parents," December 20, 1993.
"Conversations with Oprah: Maya Angelou," December 6, 1993.

"Desperate Moms, Desperate Measures," October 21, 1993.
"Diana Ross," October 25, 1993.
"Who Does Baby Michael Belong To?" October 26, 1993.
"Divorcing Your Best Friend," October 27, 1993.
"Encounters With Departed Loved Ones," October 18, 1993.
"Girls Having Babies," October 4, 1993.
"I Killed Somebody and Can't Live With Myself," March 9, 1993.
"Love Lies and Spies," November 9, 1993.
"Take a Trip to Dream School," November 2, 1993.
"My Child Is Too Expensive," November 1, 1993.
"Michael Jordan," October 29, 1993.
"Michael Jordan," November 25, 1993.
"Should You Lose Your Child If You Smoke?" October 28, 1993.
"Make-Over Follow-Ups: How Do They Look Now?" November 12, 1993.
"12 Steps to Happiness," October 14, 1993.
"Oprah's ½ Price Bargains," November 16, 1993.
"What Are You Doing With the Rest of Your Life?" October 5, 1993.
"Follow-Up: What Happened to Woman With Amnesia?" October 7, 1993.
"America's Most Wanted Custody Payment Runaways," November 3, 1993.
"Living Near Your Murderer," October 6, 1993.
"Am I Normal?" October 1, 1993.
"They Don't Know Who They Are," September 30, 1993.
"Only Good News," November 5, 1993.
"True Love Reunited," November 4, 1993.
"Real Slaves to the Middle Class," August 27, 1993.
"Can Sex Offenders Be Rehabilitated?" October 20, 1993.
"Teen Dating Violence," November 8, 1993.
"Sleepless in Seattle: Match-Ups," November 18, 1993.
"Family Dinner Experiments," November 19, 1993.
"Sorry I Stood by My Man," October 15, 1993.
"Hilarious TV Moments," November 17, 1993.
"Viewer Mail," November 15, 1993.
"Can You Solve This Murder," October 13, 1993.
"Welcome to Oprah and Rosie's Cooking School," November 23, 1993.
"Real Life Fugitives," October 11, 1993.
"Oprah's 40th Birthday Party," February 1, 1994.

20/20 Show Transcripts
"You Have to Be Perfect," April 9, 1993.

Real Life With Jane Pauley
"Oprah Interview," September 6, 1991, NBC-TV.

BOOKS

Everybody Loves Oprah, by Norman King, William Morrow, New York, 1987.
Oprah Winfrey: Media Success Story, by Anne Saidman, Lerner Publications, Minneapolis, 1990.
Oprah: Up Close and Down Home, by Nellie Bly, Zebra Books, New York, 1993.
Oprah Winfrey: TV Talk Show Host, by Margaret Beaton, Children's Press, Chicago, 1990.
Current Biography Yearbook, H.W. Wilson Company, New York, 1984, pp. 430 ff.
Magill's Literary Annual, Salem Press, Pasadena, California, 1983, "The Color Purple"/Walter, p. 139.

PERSONAL SOURCES, INTERVIEWS, AND CONTACTS

Sarah Gallick, executive editor of Kensington Books and author of *Oprah: Up Close and Down Home*
Judy Mann, columnist, *Washington Post*
Joe Mullen, private detective
Kitty Kelley, author
Karen Feld, celebrity columnist
Ray Healy, vice president, *Forbes*
Chuck Conconi, *Washington Post* and *Washingtonian*
Arlene La Point, manager, Burrell's transcripts
Bill Carter, general manager, WJZ-TV, Baltimore
Jerry Turner, anchor, WJZ-TV, Baltimore
Chris Clark, WTVF-TV, Nashville
Sherry Burns, WPLG-TV, Miami
Geoffrey Morris, editor, *National Review*
Mike Hoyt, *Columbia Journalism Review*
Steve Edwards, former *A.M. Chicago* host
Dennis Swanson, ABC-TV
Miriam Kanner, *Ladies' Home Journal*, Chicago
Gretchen Reynolds, *Chicago* magazine
Howard Rosenberg, TV columnist, *L.A. Times*
Tom Shales, TV columnist, *Washington Post*
Lloyd Sachs, reporter, *Chicago Sun-Times*
Willis Edward, president, Beverly Hills NAACP
Stuart Fischoff, professor of media psychology at California State University at Los Angeles

INDEX